Alice Munro *Everlasting*

ESSAYS ON HER WORKS II

ESSENTIAL WRITERS SERIES 52

ONTARIO ARTS COUNCIL
CONSEIL DES ARTS DE L'ONTARIO

an Ontario government agency
un organisme du gouvernement de l'Ontario

Canada Council   Conseil des arts
for the Arts   du Canada

Guernica Editions Inc. acknowledges the support
of the Canada Council for the Arts and the Ontario Arts Council.
The Ontario Arts Council is an agency of the Government of Ontario.
We acknowledge the financial support of the Government of Canada.

Alice Munro *Everlasting*
ESSAYS on HER WORKS II

Edited by J.R. (Tim) Struthers

GUERNICA
EDITIONS
TORONTO • CHICAGO • BUFFALO • LANCASTER (U.K.)
2020

J.R. (Tim) Struthers, editor
Michael Mirolla, general editor
Joseph Pivato, series editor
Cover and Interior Design: Rafael Chimicatti
Cover Art: Derived from a painting,
Glimpse (2017), by Ron Shuebrook

Guernica Editions Inc.
287 Templemead Drive, Hamilton (ON), Canada L8W 2W4
2250 Military Road, Tonawanda, N.Y. 14150-6000 U.S.A.
www.guernicaeditions.com

Distributors:
Independent Publishers Group (IPG)
600 North Pulaski Road, Chicago IL 60624
University of Toronto Press Distribution,
5201 Dufferin Street, Toronto (ON), Canada M3H 5T8
Gazelle Book Services, White Cross Mills
High Town, Lancaster LA1 4XS U.K.

First edition.
Printed in Canada.

Legal Deposit – First Quarter
Library of Congress Catalog Card Number: 2019946792
Library and Archives Canada Cataloguing in Publication
Title: Alice Munro everlasting : essays on her works II / edited by J.R. (Tim) Struthers
Names: Struthers, J.R. Tim, 1950-
Series: Essential writers series ; 52.
Description: Series statement: Essential writers series ; 52
Identifiers: Canadiana (print) 20190164956 | Canadiana (ebook) 20190164964
ISBN 9781771834384 (softcover) | ISBN 9781771834391 (EPUB)
ISBN 9781771834407 (Kindle)
Subjects: LCSH: Munro, Alice, 1931-—Criticism and interpretation.
Classification: LCC PS8576.U57 Z516 2020 | DDC C813/.54—dc23

Alice Munro Country: Essays on Her Works I
and
Alice Munro Everlasting: Essays on Her Works II
are dedicated to Alice Munro
with admiration, with gratitude, and with love
for a lifetime spent working so ardently
in devotion to the form of the short story.

Contents

Returning to the Source:
Alice Munro, Flannery O'Connor, and Eudora Welty

Charles E. May

*The material never saves a work of art, the gold it is made of
does not hallow a statue. A work of art lives on its form, not on its
material; the essential grace it emanates springs from its structure,
... [which] forms the properly artistic part of the work, and on it
aesthetic and literary criticism should concentrate.*
— José Ortega y Gasset, *The Dehumanization of Art* (69)

*I believe that the artist's fundamental loyalty must be to form,
and his energy employed in the activity of making. Every other diddly
desire can find expression; every crackpot idea or local obsession,
every bias and graciousness and mark of malice, may have
an hour; but it must never be allowed to carry the day.*
— William H. Gass, *Finding a Form* (35)

*The critic is one who glimpses destiny in forms: whose most profound
experience ... is that moment at which things become forms
– the moment when all feelings and experiences on the near
or the far side of form receive form, are melted down
and condensed into form. It is the mystical moment of union
between the outer and the inner, between soul and form.*
— Georg Lukács, *Soul and Form* (8)

At first glance, one might not think that the stories of Eudora Welty, Flannery O'Connor, and Alice Munro share the same narrative world and perspective: Welty's mythic, poetic "season of dreams" ("First Love" 3), O'Connor's gothic characters and theological complexity, and Munro's unique form of lyrical realism. However, what they have in common outweighs their surface differences: early in their careers, all three writers discovered that the genre best suited to their obsessions and their talents was the short story. The demanding qualities of the short story that set it apart from the more diffuse characteristics of the novel are so closely bound up with the vision of these three writers that it is impossible to understand the significance of their work without understanding how they use the genre.

Since the beginning of the short story as an historically-recognized genre in the mid-nineteenth century, short-story writers and critics have agreed that the form depends more on a unified structure and consequently a formalized ending than the novel does. "It is only with the *dénouement* constantly in view," Edgar Allan Poe insisted in "The Philosophy of Composition," "that we can give a plot its indispensable air of consequence, or causation, by making the incidents, and especially the tone at all points, tend to the development of the intention" (127). More recently, Clark Blaise has noted that although "Stories begin mysteriously," they "end deliberately": "The opening anticipates the conflict. The ending immortalizes the resolution" (32).

The main tradition of American criticism has found this characteristic of the short story abhorrent, believing that it sounds cold-blooded and mechanical. However, those few critics in the United States and elsewhere who have taken the short story seriously have made some helpful suggestions about the significance of the formality of the genre, especially its emphasis on endings. For example, the relationship between the importance of endings and the short story's dependence on tone has been noted by critics as diverse as H.S. Canby and Georg Lukács. Canby suggested that the climax is emphasized in a story because it creates for the reader "a vivid realization of [what] moved the author to write"; hence "the art of the short story becomes as much an art of tone as of incident" (303). Lukács notes that since the short story focusses on a fragment of life lifted out of life's totality, it is "stamped with its origin in the [author's] will" (*The Theory of the Novel* 51). The form thus is inevitably "lyrical in nature," says Lukács, because of the author's "form-giving, structuring, delimiting act" (*The Theory of the Novel* 51).

Eudora Welty has linked the short story's lyricism to an underlying originating impulse within the writer that compels him or her to return to it obsessively. "It seems likely," Welty has said, "that all of one writer's stories do tend to spring from the same source within him. ... all of one writer's stories carry their signature because of the one impulse most characteristic of his own gift" ("Writing and Analyzing a Story" 108). Welty suggests that although each story has a life of its own, "it may become clear to a writer in retrospect ... that his stories have repeated themselves in shadowy ways, that they have returned and may return in future too – in variations – to certain themes. They may be following, in their own development, some pattern that's been very early laid down" ("Writing and Analyzing a Story" 108).

Welty says, for example, that when writing her first story, "Death of a Traveling Salesman," she discovered by instinct that the story approach most natural to her was the journey or search for "some form of the secret of life" ("Looking Back at the First Story" 98). Several years later, she seems to confirm this when she discusses the writing of a late story, "No Place for You, My Love," that describes the journey of two people in which relationship is "a pervading and changing mystery" – not made so by words in life, she says, but "words have to make it so in a story" ("Writing and Analyzing a Story" 114). Writing "Death of a Traveling Salesman," she says, taught her very early in her career that "procedure is an essence of what [the] writer knows to be truth of feeling," and that the writer simply invents the characters and their actions to carry this truth out ("Looking Back at the First Story" 99). What Welty means by "procedure" is that process of the writer's mind, wherein the stuff of the world is continually becoming something more than what Munro has called "only life" ("Dear Life" 307) – "the moral, the passionate, the poetic, hence the *shaping* idea" ("Writing and Analyzing a Story" 109). "It's the form it takes when it comes out the other side," says Welty, "that gives a story something unique – its life" ("Writing and Analyzing a Story" 109).

Of the many Welty stories that focus on form as life, one of the most important is "A Memory," from *A Curtain of Green*, which recalls a point when the artist began to look at reality through the frame of art. Since she started taking painting lessons, the young unnamed girl in the story has made small frames of her fingers to look out at everything. Reality for the future artist must be in keeping with the frames she establishes, or else she feels terrified by a vision of wildness and disorder. Her perspective on the world is aesthetic and thus spiritual rather than physical, for she is constantly hovering on the brink of seeing what is not quite there in actuality. Her sense of exaltation stems from the sense that every observation "almost" reveals to her "a secret of life" and that even "the smallest gesture of a stranger" is "a communication or a presentiment" ("A Memory" 148-49). The experience of the young girl marks the point at which the dreamer stops to look at the world formally and becomes the artist.

Reading Welty's collection *The Golden Apples*, Alice Munro says, filled her with "[g]ratitude and amazed delight" ("Golden Apples" 23) – it was the kind of writing she most wanted to do, the kind of writing that did not simply and realistically duplicate the world outside, but that created a world infused with significance. Welty's ability to create a world, says Munro, does not just mean setting out "the right furniture" or putting "the right concerns in people's heads – so true, as we say, to life" ("Golden Apples" 23). "[M]ore than a sharp eye and a quick ear" ("Golden Apples" 23-24) is involved. "The story must be imagined so deeply and devoutly," says Munro, "that everything in it seems to bloom of its own accord and to be connected, then, to our own lives which suddenly, as we read, take on a hard beauty, a familiar strangeness, the importance of a dream which can't be disputed or explained" ("Golden Apples" 24).

Munro's awareness of this "hard beauty" in Welty's work, as well as Welty's early realization that "procedure is an essence of what [the] writer knows to be truth of feeling" ("Looking Back at the First Story" 99), suggests a seeming paradox about the writer's signature impulse that readers often do not recognize: that the "life" of the art work the writer tries to create is not a replication of what Munro has called "only life" ("Dear Life" 307), but rather a radical transformation wherein, as Georg Lukács argues, "things become forms – the moment when all feelings and experiences on the near or the far side of form receive form, are melted down and condensed into form" (*Soul and Form* 8). Seamus Heaney once remarked on this seemingly paradoxical truth that it is artifice that creates "life" in the art work, noting that, for example, "when a form generates itself, when a metre provokes consciousness into new postures, it is already on the side of life" (158). Heaney's remark recalls Anton Chekhov's insistence that it is *"compactness* that makes short things alive" (82). Life in the short story, in other words, is the life of artifice shimmering with significance – not the "one damned thing after another" of sequential, everyday reality.

As Hayden White argues, and short-story writers such as Welty, O'Connor, and Munro agree, the wish to narrativize is based on the "demand that sequences of real events be assessed as to their significance as elements of a *moral* drama" (24). Our "desire to have real events display the coherence, integrity, fullness, and closure of [fiction]" is based on our desire that events have meaning, significance, moral justness, says White (27, 24-27). Frank Kermode reminds us, "We always underestimate the power of rhetorical and narrative gestures" (146). Endings, for example, says Kermode, are always "faked, as are all other parts of a narrative structure that impose metaphor on the metonymic sequence" (147). In other words, any time we arrange a narrative sequence to achieve a meaningful end, we inevitably "fake," by inventing, the ending. For this faking of an ending is the very act that makes meaning out of the "one damned thing after another" that meaningless events (as opposed to end-directed and meaningful discourse) always are; such fakery thus constitutes the essence of short narrative art.

It seems hardly necessary to say that the only narrative which the reader ever gets is that which is already discourse, already ended as an event, so that there is nothing left for it but to move toward its end in an aesthetic, eventless way, that is, via tone, metaphor, and all the other purely artificial conventions of fictional discourse. Consequently, it is inevitable that events in the narrative will be motivated or determined by demands of the discourse – demands that do not necessarily have anything to do with psychological or phenomenological motivation of the narrated events in the actual world. Moreover, the fact that a good short story works by a delicate and tightly organized pattern of language – not by argument, direct statement, temporal plot, or character complication – means that what the short story strives to discover and create is too subtle, too ambiguous, too complex, too inchoate, to be communicated by those rhetorical means by which nonfiction and long fiction often communicate. A good short story cannot be skimmed, read quickly, or adequately summarized. Consequently, when one reads a short story once through, one is often apt to be vaguely dissatisfied or unfulfilled. As Poe suggested in "The Philosophy of Composition," it is only by getting to the end of the story that we can begin again at the beginning to experience it as the non-sequential patterned form that it is (127).

Those who accuse the short story of being too formal, with too much artifice, forget that the royal road to art, as José Ortega y Gasset delineates it in *The Dehumanization of Art*, is the "'will to style'" (23). And "to stylize," he says, "means to deform reality, to derealize; style involves dehumanization" (23). The short story writer realizes that the artist must not confuse reality with ideas, that he must inevitably turn his back on supposed reality and "take the ideas for what they are – mere subjective patterns – and make them live as such, lean and angular, but pure and transparent" (35). The lyricism of the short stories of such writers as Eudora Welty, Flannery O'Connor, and Alice Munro lies in this "'will to style'" in which reality is derealized. Their stories are more "poetic," that is, more "artistic," than we usually expect fiction to be; they help define the difference between the loose and baggy monstrous novel and the taut, gemlike short story.

In his biography of Alice Munro, Robert Thacker quotes *New Yorker* fiction editor Deborah Treisman on her discovery of the intricacy of Munro's stories when she came to the magazine in 1997. Reading a Munro story, Treisman says, "something from page three will come and hit you on page thirty, but you had not registered the matter when you first read page three" (qtd. in Thacker 498). This is, of course, an important characteristic of the short story established by Poe almost two hundred years ago when he defined the word "plot" as "pattern" and "design," not simply the temporal progression of events. Poe insists that only when the reader has an awareness of the "end" of the work and perceives its overall pattern will seemingly trivial elements become relevant and therefore meaningful. Reflecting on Munro's method after an interview, Lisa Awano suggested that the structure of her interview reflects the structure of Munro's stories, for when she re-read Munro's closing remarks, she unexpectedly found connections that led her "back to the beginning of the interview – to listen again and hear it anew, in a more textured way" (Awano, "An Interview with Alice Munro" [2013] 181).

Unfortunately, it is just the author's attention to pattern and design, this fully integrated sense of interrelated wholeness in which "something from page three will come and hit you on page thirty," that makes good, literary short stories read so infrequently and usually not so well. Not many readers have the time, patience, attention, and dedication to read a story the way an editor such as Treisman reads a story, or as Francine Prose urged in her book *Reading Like a Writer*. Prose's central point is that to be a good reader, one must be knowledgeable of, and sensitive to, those elements of writing that constitute the craft: words, sentences, narration, characterization, dialogue, and details. Prose reminds us of something that beginning students, as well as experienced critics, of literature often find hard to accept – that subject matter is not all that important, that what the writer most often wants to do is write really great sentences.

Alice Munro has never been one to care about commenting on her work, saying "Writing or talking about writing makes [her] superstitiously uncomfortable" because her explanations tend to become "treacherous, half-untrue" ("The Colonel's Hash Resettled" 183). It is significant that one of the few times she did write about her fiction, she talked about the problem of "What Is Real?." Munro says the questions she gets asked quite often – "'Do you write about real people?'" and "'Did those things really happen?'" – are usually "asked by people who really don't understand the difference between autobiography and fiction," people who "don't know what fiction is" (223) and read fiction only as a series of connected events, one thing after another. Like Welty, Munro also talks about a "truth of feeling" that only the "procedure" of form can embody. Munro says she writes a story the way she reads a story – not processing it one thing after another, but entering it at various different points. She says when she writes a story, she does not think of it as a temporal series of events. Instead, she says she wants to build a structure, "like a house," and she knows "the feeling" she wants to get from being inside that house ("What Is Real?" 224). She does not have a pre-planned "blueprint" of a house she wants to build to get a desired "effect," but wants to build a house or story "to fit around the indescribable 'feeling' that is like the soul of the story" ("What Is Real?" 224).

Munro says such terms as "feeling," "effect," and "soul" embarrass her for their indefiniteness, but she just has nothing else to use. She doesn't know where this "feeling" comes from, but she starts gathering material – memory, observation, invention, anecdotes, bits of overheard speech – and then tries to fit these together, for they seem to have something to do with each other, to make "the shape" she needs to embody "the feeling" she has ("What Is Real?" 224). She never feels she has completely got it right, thinking that "Every final draft, every published story, is still only an attempt, an approach, to the story" ("What Is Real?" 225). Trying to get it right, she says, "is more important than anything" ("What is Real?" 225). Getting it right is, of course, finding the connection between soul and form that Georg Lukács talks about (*Soul and Form* 8). It is this moment when form embodies soul, or enables soul to shine forth, that constitutes the mysterious union the artist recognizes as central to his or her art – when form makes life possible – not "only life," but life infused with meaning and significance. Munro says she uses "bits of what is real, ... in the world, as most people see it," but then transforms those bits into "something that is really there and really happening, in my story" ("What Is Real?" 226).

Like Welty and Munro, Flannery O'Connor, keenly aware of the formal demands of the short story, also makes the distinction between what many readers, hungry for context and content, fail to make between "only life" and the "life" that form makes possible, and for which the short-story writer is constantly in search. Recently, Penguin published a new iPad app on Jack Kerouac's *On the Road* that quickly became a big seller. Although the app indeed features the full text of the iconic book, what has made it so popular is not the text, but the "enrichments" that accompany it – commentary, maps, audio recordings, photos. Whereas general readers are always Googling everything, looking for context, and academics publish background articles that explore historical, political, social, and cultural frameworks, writers still hold to the importance of form and universal significance. Flannery O'Connor reminds us, for example, that the concept of a writer's "country" goes beyond the actual geographical or social region in which a writer's characters seem to live, arguing that a writer's "true country" lies in the realm of the "eternal and absolute" (*Mystery and Manners* 27). O'Connor says "the peculiar burden of the fiction writer [is] that he has to make one country do for all and that he has to evoke that one country through the concrete particulars of a life that he can make believable" (*Mystery and Manners* 27).

Critics who like to talk about "Alice Munro Country" are perhaps underestimating Munro's fiction when they think her "true country" is the landscape of rural Ontario, or even the working-class people who live there. In her *Guardian* review of *Dear Life*, Irish writer Anne Enright challenges what she calls "a kind of deliberate smallness" about what readers think writers do when they assume that Alice Munro writes about what it is like to be a woman in rural Ontario, when it is pretty clear that Munro just uses those women to write about the human condition. "Her work is, in this regard," Enright says, "steadfast. Her characters are bare and true," possessing that kind of "hard beauty" that Munro attributes to the characters of Eudora Welty ("Golden Apples" 24).

In her best-selling collection of lectures, *One Writer's Beginnings*, Eudora Welty tries to answer the questions "What is it that makes a writer become a writer?" and "What is it that sets a writer apart from others?" by describing the actual events and details of her life that she transforms into the stuff of story and by her own meditating on the meaning of these sources of her fiction-making. The central key to the secret of the writer, Welty suggests, is his or her ability to determine the difference between mere events and significant events. A relation of mere events may be simply a chronological retelling; however, significant events follow what Welty calls a "thread of revelation" (*One Writer's Beginnings* 69). Although many experiences are too indefinite to be recognized alone, Welty says, in a story they come together and become identifiable when they take on a larger shape. Writing develops a sense of where to look for these connections, how to follow the thread, for nothing is ever lost to memory. Memory is a living thing, urges Welty, and all that is remembered joins and unites the young and the old, the present and the past, the living and the dead.

Welty once said, "the first thing we see about a story is its mystery. And in the best stories, we return at the last to see mystery again. Every good story has mystery – not the puzzle kind, but the mystery of allurement. As we understand the story better, it is likely that the mystery does not necessarily decrease; rather it simply grows more beautiful" ("The Reading and Writing of Short Stories" 164). More so than in the novel, the short story most often deals with experience for which there is no clearly discernible logical, sociological, or psychological cause. As Welty says, "The first thing we notice about our story is that we can't really see the solid outlines of it – it seems bathed in something of its own. It is wrapped in an atmosphere. This is what makes it shine, perhaps, as well as what initially obscures its plain, real shape" ("The Reading and Writing of Short Stories" 163). To Conrad's Marlow, sitting Buddha-like on the deck telling the story of Kurtz in *Heart of Darkness*, "the meaning of an episode was not inside like a kernel but outside, enveloping the tale which brought it out only as a glow brings out a haze, in the likeness of one of these misty halos that, sometimes, are made visible by the spectral illumination of moonshine" (9). Many short-story writers describe the form in terms of secrecy and mystery, for it seems there is something about the primal urge of storytelling that tends toward the obsessive, the mysterious, and the objectification of desire and fear. The writer who has commented most extensively on the short story's embodiment of mystery is Flannery O'Connor.

O'Connor always claimed that "The peculiar problem of the short-story writer is how to make the action he describes reveal as much of the mystery of existence as possible," since the short-story writer "has only a short space to do it in and he can't do it by statement" but must do it "by showing the concrete"; consequently, "his problem is really how to make the concrete work double time for him" (*Mystery and Manners* 98). O'Connor adds that for this kind of writer, the meaning of a story does not begin except at a depth where adequate motivation and psychology have been exhausted. Such a writer, she says, will be interested in what we don't understand rather than in what we do. O'Connor relates an anecdote about lending some stories to a woman who lived down the road from her. When the woman returned them, she said, "'Well, them stories just gone and shown you how some folks *would* do'" (*Mystery and Manners* 90). O'Connor reports that she thought to herself that "that was right; when you write stories, you have to be content to start exactly there – showing how some specific folks *will* do, *will* do in spite of everything" (*Mystery and Manners* 90).

The short story's focus on mysteriously motivated behaviour is at least as old as Poe's exploration of the perverse in "The Black Cat" (*Selected* 280-88), "The Tell-Tale Heart" (*Selected* 244-48) and "The Imp of the Perverse" (*Selected* 309-14). Whereas the novel may focus on cause and effect in time, the short story accepts the fact that what makes characters behave the way they do is not so simple. For example, critic

Peter M. Bitsilli says the complexity of Chekhov's characters leads us to feel there is something about them we do not understand, something "hidden from us," something that is part of Chekhov's appeal (125). According to Ambrose Bierce, the problem with realistic novelists is that they do not know "all men and women sometimes ... act from impenetrable motives and in a way that is consonant with nothing in their lives, characters and conditions" (243-44). And more recently, short-story writer Edith Pearlman says she has "a taste for the inexplicable and the semisurreal" (418) and likes "endings, not wrappings-up" that dispense with "that sine qua non of realism, motivation" (419). Pearlman quotes the poet Amy Clampitt who wrote, "who knows what makes any of us do what we do?" (qtd. in Pearlman 419), an insight Pearlman says writing workshops should keep in mind.

When Geoff Hancock told Alice Munro that he saw her "as a lyricist" who "give[s] voice to our secret selves" (Hancock 76), Munro replied, "That's absolutely what I think a short story can do" (Munro in Hancock 76). "Mostly in my stories I like to look at what people don't understand. What we don't understand" (Munro in Hancock 90). Daniel Menaker, who was once Munro's *New Yorker* editor, says that "You get the feeling she's trying to help you get at some true emotional psychological insight, but that often takes the form of a kind of philosophical surrender to the unknowability of people's motives and characters, a dark existential uncertainty about what makes people tick" (qtd. in Edemariam).

Many critics have examined what might be called Flannery O'Connor's "signature," or what she herself terms her "true country" – her unrealistic symbolic narrative style, her characters' confrontation with complex religious trials beyond their understanding, and her themes dependent on paradoxical concepts of Christian theology. Her own writing career provides a clear example of Welty's conviction that in retrospect a writer might recognize something obsessive in his or her work. Near the end of her brief and tragic life, O'Connor felt compelled to return to her first published short story, "The Geranium," and rewrite it with a different focus, retitling it "Judgement Day."

Consequently "Judgement Day," her final story, occupies the crucial position as the final story in her final collection, *Everything That Rises Must Converge*. Anglo-Irish writer Elizabeth Bowen even coined a term for this obsessiveness in short fiction: "The first necessity for the short story," she says, "is *necessariness*. The story ... must spring from an impression or perception pressing enough, acute enough, to have made the writer write" (156-57). Sherwood Anderson uses a metaphor to describe this engagement: "Having, from a conversation overheard..., got the tone of a tale, I was like a woman who has just become impregnated. Something was growing inside me. At night when I lay in my bed I could feel the heels of the tale kicking against the walls of my body" (358). And Lorrie Moore suggests that short stories "are perhaps more attached [than novels] to the author's emotional life and come more out of inspiration than slogging" (Moore in Gaffney 80). For Moore, "To write a short story, you have to be able to stay up all night. ... There's urgency and wholeness in stories" (Moore in Gaffney 79).

Critic Michael O'Connell argues that "Judgement Day" emphasizes the ways Flannery O'Connor translates personal experience into universal drama, quoting O'Connor, who said that when rewriting "it is possible to exhaust your material ... what you have to do is try to deepen your penetration" (qtd. in O'Connell 352). And indeed, most critics argue that the difference between the first and the final version of the story shows O'Connor making a deeper penetration of what she calls her "true country." O'Connell claims that "Judgement Day" "serves as an affirmation of one of the most fundamental tenets of [O'Connor's] faith: that death is not a desolation but rather a homecoming that can be approached with joy" (362-63). And several critics have pointed out how this story is different from other O'Connor stories in that it ends with a kind of redemptive peace when the old man, Tanner, actually does go back to his source and return to his true country.

A basic difference between the first and the last version of Flannery O'Connor's "beginning and end" story is that "The Geranium" is a plot-based story with a transparent metaphor – the geranium. The story does not explore, penetrate, struggle. I suggest that O'Connor knew this and was determined, if it was the last thing she ever did (which, sad to say, it was), to correct this error and penetrate deeper into the story that was her signature – the attempt to return to her "true country." The same can be said of Eudora Welty's return in "No Place for You, My Love," in her final collection, *The Bride of the Innisfallen*, to the approach that seemed most natural to her in her first story, "Death of a Traveling Salesman." In her essay "Writing and Analyzing a Story," Welty says she did not want "to sound mystical," but that, although "No Place for You, My Love" was "a circumstantial, realistic story," in it "the reality *was* mystery" (114). And Alice Munro is even more emphatic about returning to the source of her writing with what she calls the "Finale" of presumably her final book, *Dear Life* – those four "*not quite stories*" that mark both "*the first and last*" things she has to say about her own life (*Dear Life* 255).

***

Eudora Welty's and Alice Munro's affirmation of the central importance of form for the short-story writer can be seen in their discussion of the form-based beginnings of two of their stories: Welty's "A Worn Path" in her first collection, *A Curtain of Green*, and Munro's "Images" in her first collection, *Dance of the Happy Shades*. Welty once said that the question she got most often in the mail from students and teachers was whether Phoenix Jackson's grandson in "A Worn Path" was really dead ("'Is Phoenix Jackson's Grandson Really Dead?'" 219). The question, like the question that Munro says she often gets about whether what she writes about is "real," suggests a faulty understanding of the source and the significance of stories. Welty says, "A fiction writer's responsibility covers not only what he presents as the facts of a given story but what he chooses to stir up as their implications. In the end, these implications too become facts, in the larger, fictional sense" ("'Is Phoenix Jackson's Grandson Really Dead?'" 220).

Suggesting that the "origin of a story" can sometimes be "a trustworthy clue ... to its key image," Welty says one day she "saw a solitary old woman ... walking ... in a winter country landscape" and it was this sight that made her write the story ("'Is Phoenix Jackson's Grandson Really Dead?'" 220). Welty says the old woman's "persisting in her landscape was the real thing, and the first and the real were what I wanted and worked to keep" ("'Is Phoenix Jackson's Grandson Really Dead?'" 220). This description of the image of the old woman in the landscape as "the real thing" is reminiscent of Henry James's famous story of that title (James 117-44); it reminds us that for the artist, "the artistic thing" is more real than the merely real thing. Welty says that although she imagined some details about the old woman's appearance, it was her "full-length figure moving across the winter fields [that] was the indelible one and the image to keep, and the perspective extending into the vanishing distance the true one to hold in mind" ("'Is Phoenix Jackson's Grandson Really Dead?'" 220-21).

Welty says she invented some passing adventures for old Phoenix, for these things are parts of life's uncertainty, but reminds us, "A narrative line is in its deeper sense, of course, the tracing out of a meaning, and the real continuity of a story lies in this probing forward. ... What gives any such content to 'A Worn Path' is not its circumstances but its *subject*: the deep-grained habit of love" ("'Is Phoenix Jackson's Grandson Really Dead?'" 221). Welty says what she hoped to make clear was that "the only certain thing ... is the worn path," which is the habit of love that "cuts through confusion and stumbles or contrives its way out of difficulty" ("'Is Phoenix Jackson's Grandson Really Dead?'" 221). "The path is the thing that matters" ("'Is Phoenix Jackson's Grandson Really Dead?'" 221). Welty adds that old Phoenix's way might be a parallel to the way of the writer of stories, for "The way to get there is the all-important, all-absorbing problem, and this problem is your reason for undertaking the story" ("'Is Phoenix Jackson's Grandson Really Dead?'" 221). You try to reach a meaning, Welty says, and you will "make the trip ... just on hope" ("'Is Phoenix Jackson's Grandson Really Dead?'" 221). As Welty says in her essay on her first story, "Death of a Traveling Salesman," what she knew she was going to learn was that "procedure" – that is, all the elements of pattern and form, rhythm and tone, language and syntax – "is an essence of what [the] writer knows to be truth of feeling" ("Looking Back at the First Story" 99).

Alice Munro has also talked about the source of one of her stories in a single formal image and its development as a search for some emotional truth ("The Colonel's Hash Resettled" 182-83) – what Welty calls the real "subject" of the story, and what O'Connor calls the writer's "true country." Munro says that her story "Images," in *Dance of the Happy Shades*, began with a picture in her mind of meeting a man in the woods who was coming down the river-bank carrying a hatchet, and a child watching him, while her father, unaware, bent over his traps. "From this picture," she says, "the story moved outward," with her remembering things that were not really memories at all ("The Colonel's Hash Resettled" 182). She remembers going with her father along the river to look at traps, although she never had gone; she remembers her "mother's bed set up in the dining-room, although it was never there" ("The Colonel's Hash Resettled" 182). Munro says it is "difficult to sort out the real memories ... used in this story from those that are not 'real' at all," for she says she did not invent those but rather "found them" ("The Colonel's Hash Resettled" 182). "And it is all deeply, perfectly true to me, as a dream might be true, and all I can say, finally, about the making of a story like this is that it must be made in the same way our dreams are made.... This is the given story" ("The Colonel's Hash Resettled" 182-83).

The basic paradox of the short story understood by Welty, O'Connor, and Munro – that "story life" is what matters, not "only life" – is echoed by the seeming contradiction expressed here by Munro: that the dream-like reality of "the given story" is more "real" than "only life." American poet Randall Jarrell once suggested, "Reading stories, we cannot help remembering Groddeck's [view that] 'We have to reckon with what exists, and dreams, daydreams too, are also facts; if anyone really wants to investigate realities, he cannot do better than to start with such as these. If he neglects them, he will learn little or nothing of the world of life'" (32).

In a discussion of narrative time, Paul Ricoeur says that "every narrative combines two dimensions": "the episodic dimension, which characterizes the story as made out of events," and "the configurational dimension, according to which ... significant wholes [develop] out of scattered events" eliciting a pattern from a succession. Consequently, following the story in time is not as important as apprehending the end as implied in the beginning and the episodes leading to this end. "By reading the end in the beginning and the beginning in the end," says Ricoeur, "we learn also to read time itself backward, as the reca-pitulating of the initial conditions of a course of action in its terminal consequences" (180). Jayne Anne Phillips describes this counterpart of time as a kind of eternal return: "I think that stories in reality are often circular; past and present and future are mixed up in terms of the way we think; and the closer a story can get to that – the more completely it can represent that – the more timeless the story becomes" (Phillips in Stanton 43). And in a remark that Poe would have loved, Russell Banks says that the short story and the novel "bear greatly different relations to time. The novel ... has a mimetic relation to time ... so once you get very far into a novel, you forget where you began – just as you do in real time.

Whereas with a short story the point is not to forget the beginning. The ending only makes sense if you can remember the beginning" (Banks in Faggen 62).

One of America's finest short-story writers, Joy Williams, claims that short-story writers love the dark and are always fumbling around in it. "The writer," says Williams, "doesn't want to disclose or instruct or advocate, he wants to transmute and disturb. He cherishes the mystery.... He wants to escape his time, the obligations of his time, and, by writing, transcend them" (7). And Alice Munro says, "I write because I want to get a feeling of mystery or surprise. Not a mystery that finishes you off, but something that makes the character or reader wonder. I don't really like interpretations. I don't want to make definite explanations" (Munro in Awano, "An Interview with Alice Munro" [2006]). Short-story writer Amy Hempel agrees that she doesn't like having anything spelled out, but insists that mystery is *not* mere vagueness. "Mystery is controlled. It involves information meted out only as *needed*. ... I not only *don't* want the explanation, I want the mystery" (Hempel in Winner 45).

Because of historical tradition and the aesthetic conventions that adhere to short narrative, short stories are less apt to focus on characters defined by their stereotypical social roles than on characters defined by their archetypal metaphysical roles. As Frank O'Connor famously argued in *The Lonely Voice*, the short story deals with situations that compel characters to confront their essential isolation as individual human beings, not as social masks within a particular cultural context. Characters in the short stories of Welty, O'Connor, and Munro do not confront their social roles; they reveal what their authors see as their essential roles as isolated human beings.

For example, in Welty's "A Piece of News" in *A Curtain of Green*, although Ruby Fisher is caught in a marriage in which she is most likely abused and which allows her no sense of herself as an independent social entity, this is not Welty's real "subject." When Ruby sees a story in a newspaper describing how a woman named Ruby Fisher was shot in the leg by her husband, her recognition, "'That's me'" ("A Piece of News" 23), followed by her elaborate, self-pitying fantasy of her death and burial, is an effort to find a sense of identity in a basic and primal way. When her husband comes home and points out that the newspaper is from another state and swats her fondly across the backside with it, both Ruby and the reader feel a puzzling sense of loss. It is not social isolation that Welty's women suffer from, but rather a more basic sense of separateness; and it is not social validation that they hunger for, but, as Robert Penn Warren noted in a famous essay, "Love and Separateness in Eudora Welty," love that will heal the separateness and magically give them a sense of order and meaning.

What links O'Connor's "Judgement Day," the final story in her final collection, *Everything That Rises Must Converge*, and Munro's "Dear Life," the titular final story in presumably her final collection, is the two authors' attempts to transform a biographical event into a fictional story by going deeper into the event to discover what universal meaning it has. Welty's "A Worn Path" is a fable of that same process, for it is about a journey that ends with its beginning and must be traversed continuously. Munro has been most emphatically concerned with this process by which "only life" becomes fiction in two of her late collections – *The View from Castle Rock* and *Dear Life*.

The View from Castle Rock is made up of two separate sets – five family chronicles that Munro says are "something like stories" ([ix]) and six pieces drawn from her own life that she emphatically declares are "*stories*" ([x]). In the foreword to the collection, Munro describes them as "two streams" that flow into "one channel" ([x]), explaining that after doing research and reading in the history of her Scottish family, she put the material together over the years "and almost without [her] noticing what was happening, it began to shape itself, here and there, into something like stories" ([ix]). Not stories, Munro stresses, but "something like stories." Munro also says that during these years she was writing "a special set of stories" ([x]), which she did not include in the books of short stories she was publishing because she felt they did not belong. "They were not memoirs but they were closer to my own life than the other stories I had written, even in the first person" ([x]). By contrast, Munro explains, "In other first-person stories [in which] I had drawn on personal material ... I did anything I wanted to with this material. Because the chief thing I was doing was making a story" ([x]).

Munro says that in the "special set of stories" included in the second half of *Castle Rock*, "I was doing something closer to what a memoir does – exploring a life, my own life, but not in an austere or rigorously factual way. I put myself in the center and wrote about that self, as searchingly as I could. But the figures around this self took on their own life and color and did things they had not done in reality" ([x]). Munro says that so many of these characters moved so far beyond their beginnings in real life that she could not remember who they were to start with. She concludes, "You could say that such stories pay more attention to the truth of a life than fiction usually does. But not enough to swear on" ([x]).

One of the many differences between writers and most readers, of course, is that writers are generally more interested in "story" than in so-called "real life." At author readings, one of the most common questions that readers ask is whether the event in the story "really happened." This, of course, is one of the reasons why biographies and autobiographies are more popular than fiction; if the work is just a "story," it seems less important, less interesting, less "real" to many readers. Writers don't feel that way; like Munro, they are more apt to refer to life as "only life" ("Dear Life" 307), whereas most readers are more apt to refer to a story as "just a story."

Although this issue is most often raised with long fictions, it does occasionally crop up with short stories. For example, when Rick Moody's short piece "Demonology" was first published in the journal *Conjunctions*, it was listed as a memoir. However, the following year it was included in *Prize Stories 1997: The O. Henry Awards* and identified as a story. In an interview for *The New York Times on the Web*, Moody told editor Bill Goldstein that he is always "trying to muddy the surface" of the nonfictional "with fictional techniques" by paying particular "attention to form and structure" (Moody in Goldstein). What makes "Demonology" so affecting are Moody's efforts to transform a powerful personal experience into something that has universal significance. The title of the piece stems from the fact that the sister's death from arrhythmia takes place within the context of Halloween, her children dressed as demons and monsters, beating back the restless souls of the dead in search of sweets. This narrative demon motif is repeated throughout the story until ultimately the sister is transformed into a "revenant" that compels Moody to find a way to use language to communicate his grief. The story ends with Moody considering how he should have constructed it, telling himself he probably should have fictionalized it more. He says he should have "let artifice create an elegant surface" for the story, thus making his sister's death "shapely and persuasive" rather than "blunt and disjunctive" ("Demonology" 435).

It is in the four pieces that make up what Munro in *Dear Life* calls her "Finale" that we understand Munro's urge to return to what Welty would call the "signature" source of her work. We might ask why Alice Munro gives us "The Eye" as a memoir rather than a story. Was it because she felt the event that she recalls from when she was five years old – her first encounter with death – would not have yielded a complex story, but only a cliché? Of course, it is unlikely that Munro can recall in such detail the events of something that happened when she was five; it is more likely that she recalls some of the events from what her mother told her over the years, whereas other aspects of the recollection may have actually been invented. Munro might very well have made the event recounted in "The Eye" into a story, for the child's fascination with the romantic life of the hired girl, Sadie, and her own ambiguous relationship with her mother can be seen in a number of Munro's stories. The central thematic implication of the story centres on the scene of the child looking down into the coffin and seeing the eyelid of the dead girl lifting a tiny bit. This does not frighten the child, but rather it falls "into everything" that she knows about Sadie and also "into whatever special experience was owing to myself" ("The Eye" 269). There is a sense of recognition here, a sense of identity, not the sense that a five-year-old would feel, but rather a sense that a woman would later remember as a mutual understanding, or a sense in which a writer might see thematic implications.

"Night," which is about the mystery of motivation, is a much more discursive account, based largely on someone thinking about something rather than seeing or doing something. We do not know the age of the child in this piece, but she is old enough, or young enough, to have some fantasies about strangling her younger sister during the night, and she loses sleep over it. Her brief talk with her father one night when she walks out of the house is enough to make her identify with him and to appreciate his wisdom. For when she tells him about her fantasies of strangling her sister, he says not to worry, for "'People have those kinds of thoughts sometimes'" ("Night" 283). Sensing that there are simply some human desires and fears which cannot be understood, she knows that he has given her just what she needed to hear.

In "Voices," the protagonist, presumably Munro, is ten years old and accompanies her mother to a dance in a home to which a prostitute has brought one of her girls. But it is not the young woman that so fascinates the child. Rather it is the talk she overhears by some of the Air Force men stationed nearby who try to comfort the young woman; the child marvels at how they bow down and declare themselves in front of the woman. Later, she thinks of those men, and hears their voices directed to her: "Their hands blessed my own skinny thighs and their voices assured me that I, too, was worthy of love" ("Voices" 298). This fascination with mysterious sexuality and the ambiguous discovery by a woman that she may be desirable to men is a common theme in many of Munro's stories. Because of this thematic possibility, "Voices" is the closest of these three memoir pieces to merging into the realm of fiction.

But it is the title piece, "Dear Life," that offers the clearest insight into how Munro sees the relationship between "memoir" and "fiction." Although "Dear Life" seems to fit into the category of memoir – "exploring a life" in a factual way, with the self at the centre – given Munro's irresistible compulsion to write stories, this "personal history" (as *The New Yorker* termed the piece) often merges into the thematically rhetorical stuff of fiction. The title piece is certainly the most self-reflexive, or at least the most self-conscious, of the "Finale" pieces, for Munro provides a running commentary on the relationship between reality as remembered and as invented throughout.

We are introduced in the first paragraph to the individuality of this little girl at the centre of the story, for one of the bridges she must cross on the way to school is "a wooden walkway which occasionally had a plank missing, so that you could look right down into the bright, hurrying water. I liked that, but somebody always came and replaced the plank eventually" ("Dear Life" 299). It is thematically important that the little girl likes the gap made by the missing plank, for it does not frighten her as it might some children, but suggests a threatening, yet fascinating, view of her own vulnerability.

Readers of Munro's fiction will recognize the source of some of her stories in this piece of "personal history," the most familiar being the whippings by her father for "talking back," which she converted to fiction in "Royal Beatings" in *Who Do You Think You Are? / The Beggar Maid*. However, at certain points in "Dear Life," Munro reminds us that what we are reading here is not fiction. For example, when she describes the house of a man named Roly Grain, which was "like a dwarf's house in a story," she suggests that although he could be the stimulus for a story here, he is not, for the man "does not have any further part in what I'm writing now, in spite of his troll's name, because this is not a story, only life" ("Dear Life" 307).

In "Dear Life," Munro finally gives into the compulsion to convert events that occurred in "only life" into meaningful fiction when she recounts a story her mother told her about "a crazy old woman named Mrs. Netterfield" ("Dear Life" 310). The first story the mother tells focusses on a day when the grocer forgot to put butter into the old woman's order. When the delivery boy is opening the back of the truck, the old woman notices the butter is missing and goes after the boy with a hatchet, which makes him drive away without closing the truck's door. Munro says that some things about the story puzzle her, though she did not think about them at the time, for example how the old woman knew the butter was missing and why she happened to have a hatchet with her. However, when Munro thinks about the event as a writer, she considers the issue of plausibility that governs fiction, but may have nothing to do with "only life."

It is with the second incident involving old Mrs. Netterfield (which takes up roughly a third of "Dear Life") that Munro begins to transmute "only life" into a story. She begins it in her writerly voice recalling not the experience (for she was too young to remember), but her mother's telling of it. "It was a beautiful day in the fall. I had been set out to sleep in my baby carriage on the little patch of new lawn" ("Dear Life" 311). The mother is in the house washing baby clothes by hand. Since there is no window in the front, she has to cross the room to look out a window to check on baby Alice, a view which lets her see the driveway. At this point, Munro as writer steps in with her inevitable questions: "Why did my mother decide to leave her washing and wringing out in order to look at the driveway?" ("Dear Life" 311). After considering possible reasons, including watching for her husband to come home with groceries for something she was making for supper, Munro returns to what her mother saw – old Mrs. Netterfield coming down the lane. Then, again thinking like a writer, she considers the possibilities – that is, not what she knows, but what she thinks may be the case: "My mother must have seen Mrs. Netterfield at various times before she saw her walking down our lane. Maybe they had never spoken. It's possible, though, that they had. My mother might have made a point of it, even if my father had told her that it was not necessary. It might even lead to trouble was what he probably would have said" ("Dear Life" 313).

The mother runs out and grabs baby Alice from the carriage and carries her into the house, locking the door behind her. "But there was a problem with the kitchen door. As far as I know, it never had a proper lock. There was just a custom, at night, of pushing one of the kitchen chairs against that door, and tilting it with the chair back under the doorknob in such a way that anybody pushing it to get in would have made a dreadful clatter" ("Dear Life" 313). Then, writer that she is, Munro asks further questions about motivation, inner thoughts, background information that she does not know from "only life," but would have to invent if she were to write a story: "Did my mother think of any weapon, once she had got the doorknob wedged in place? Had she ever picked up a gun, or loaded one, in her life? // Did it cross her mind that the old woman might just be paying a neighborly visit? I don't think so. There must have been a difference in the walk, a determination in the approach of a woman who was not a visitor coming down the lane, not making a friendly approach down our road. // It is possible that my mother prayed, but never mentioned it" ("Dear Life" 313-14).

The mother sees the old woman investigate the blanket in the carriage and fling it to the ground; she hides in the dumbwaiter, listening to the old woman walking around the house and stopping at every down-stairs window. Then Munro poses another question as writer. After noting that the old woman did not have to stretch to see inside even though she was not very tall, Munro asks: "How did my mother know this? It was not as if she were running around with me in her arms, hiding behind one piece of furniture after another, peering out, distraught with terror, to meet with the staring eyes and maybe a wild grin" ("Dear Life" 314). Munro says her mother "stayed by the dumbwaiter" because "What else could she do?" ("Dear Life" 314). She thinks her mother would not have gone into the cellar because it would have been more horrible to be trapped down there in the dark, and she could not have gone upstairs because she would have had to cross the room "where the beatings would take place in the future, but which lost its malevolence after the stairs were closed in" ("Dear Life" 315). Munro says the earlier versions of her mother's story of old Mrs. Netterfield end here with the old woman peering in the windows, but that in later versions the old woman gets impatient and goes away. What the mother calls "The visitation of old Mrs. Netterfield" ("Dear Life" 315) actually seems to end for Munro the protagonist when she asks her mother at some point what became of the old woman. Her mother's stark reply: "'They took her away.... She wasn't left to die alone'" ("Dear Life" 316).

But it is not the end of the story for Munro the writer. She tells about when she was married and living in Vancouver, but still getting the weekly paper from home; she sees the name Netterfield as that of the maiden name of a woman living in Portland, Oregon who has written a simple and sentimental poem about living in Munro's home town. Munro realizes from reading the poem and the letter that she had lived in the same house Munro lived in. Munro the writer considers this: "Is it possible that my mother never knew this, never knew that our house was where the Netterfield family had lived and that the old woman was looking in the windows of what had been her own home?" ("Dear Life" 318). Munro then considers some of the perhapses that can convert a mere event into a story, thinking that the woman who wrote the poem was the daughter of the old Mrs. Netterfield who "perhaps" came to take her away. "Perhaps that daughter, grown and distant, was the one she was looking for in the baby carriage. Just after my mother had grabbed me up, as she said, for dear life" ("Dear Life" 318). And this, of course, is when Munro the writer discovers just the right multi-layered title for her memoir.

In the version of "Dear Life" that appeared in *The New Yorker*, Munro ends this "childhood visitation" by describing an event in her mother's life that she later converted into a fiction: "When my mother was dying, she got out of the hospital somehow, at night, and wandered around town until someone who didn't know her at all spotted her and took her in. If this were fiction, as I said, it would be too much, but it is true" (47). But, of course, those who know Munro's fiction will know that this last event did become fiction; it concludes the story "The Peace of Utrecht" in her first collection, *Dance of the Happy Shades*. When the narrator of the story hears of her mother getting out of bed and putting on her gown and slippers in order to go out into the January snow to make her flight from the hospital, she thinks this: "*The snow, the dressing gown and slippers, the board across the bed.* It was a picture I was much inclined to resist. Yet I had no doubt that this was true, all this was true and exactly as it happened. It was what she would do; all her life as long as I had known her led up to that flight" ("The Peace of Utrecht" 208).

"The Peace of Utrecht" is an important story in Munro's "writing her lives," as Robert Thacker subtitles his biography of Munro. Thacker points out that it is the first of her stories to deal with the facts and the memory of her mother. The story first appeared in *The Tamarack Review* in 1960, a year after her mother's death; Munro told John Metcalf that it was her "first really painful autobiographical story ... the first time I wrote a story that tore me up" (qtd. in Thacker 150). It is a story she says she did not want to write; but as she told J.R. (Tim) Struthers, "It was the first story I absolutely had to write" (qtd. in Thacker 150). Thacker says the story "represents Munro's imaginative homecoming to Wingham after her years away in Vancouver, home to the personal material that would subsequently become her hallmark" (150). And it is this obsessive theme, what Eudora Welty calls a writer's "signature," that marks the end of Munro's "Finale" when it first appeared in *The New Yorker*. That obsessive reference to the mother's flight from the hospital was subsequently dropped in the version of the story published at the end of her collection *Dear Life*. As Robert Thacker has explained, Munro and her editor at Knopf, Ann Close, "decided that it was too late to introduce this harrowing piece of information" (Thacker in Morra 230).

***

One of the primary characteristics of the modern short story is the expression of a complex inner state by the presentation of selected concrete details rather than by the depiction of the contents of the mind of the character or by the creation of a projective parable form. Significant reality for short-story writers beginning with Chekhov is inner rather than outer, but the problem they have tried to solve is how to create an illusion of inner reality by focussing on external details only. The result is not simple realism, but rather a story that even as it seems a purely surface account of everyday reality takes on the artificial aura of a dream.

Ever since Boccaccio secularized the old spiritual forms of allegory and romance to create a human rather than a divine comedy and thus introduced something new into the nature of narrative, short fiction has remained a hybrid form combining both the metaphoric nature of the old romance and the metonymic nature of the new realism. One might say that conflict in short narrative can only be resolved aesthetically since indeed it is only in the aesthetic world that short-story characters exist. The illusion that conflict is realistically resolved in the real world is more often maintained in the novel, where verisimilitude conceals the aesthetic manipulations of the narrative.

The short story's most basic assumption is that everyday experience reveals the self as a mask of habits, expectations, duties, and conventions. But the short story insists that the self must be challenged by crisis and confrontation. This is the basic tension in the form; in primitive story the conflict can be seen as the confrontation between the profane, that is, the events of the everyday, and the sacred, that is, those strange eruptions that primitive man took to be the genuinely real. The short story, however, can never reconcile this tension either existentially or morally, for the tension between the necessity of the everyday metonymic world and the sacred metaphoric world is one of those basic tensions which can only be held in suspension. The only resolution possible is an aesthetic one.

Eudora Welty, Flannery O'Connor, and Alice Munro know that there are two basic modes of experience in prose fiction: one that involves the development and the acceptance of the everyday world of phenomena and logical relation – a realm that the novel has always taken for its own – and the other that involves an experience that challenges the acceptance of the real world as simply sensate and reasonable – an experience that has dominated the short story since its beginnings. The novel involves an active quest for reality, a search for identity that is actually a reconciliation of the self with the social and experiential world – a reconciliation that is finally conceptually accepted, based on the experience one has undergone. The short story more often focusses on a character who is confronted with the world of spirit, which then challenges his or her conceptual framework of reason and social experience.

Wayne Booth reminds us that fiction "is so obviously built of impurities that some artists have simply repudiated it as a faulty enterprise" engaged in by "mere storytellers who are stuck with the task of providing a 'good read'" (142). Booth points out, "Since to tell a *story* is in itself to confess a betrayal of *pure* form," writers are always trying "to frustrate story in some way" (143). However, the problem for formalists is that "Sooner or later every formal critic must ... struggle with the problem of how to deal with the scandal of what is often called 'content'" (142). A primary way that critics have dealt with the scandal of content is to downgrade formal interests and identify a work's art with its ideology. Georg Lukács once argued that "The short story is the most purely artistic form" (*The Theory of the Novel* 51), suggesting that the novel gives us the totality of life by its content, whereas the short story does this only formally, by giving form to an episode in such a way that all the rest of life is superfluous (*The Theory of the Novel* 50-52).

The problem the short story must always deal with is the basic paradox or incompatibility between the inevitable subject matter of the short story and its inescapable form, for the basic subject matter of fiction, as it is of life itself, is time – which is, after all, one damned thing after another, that is, unless human beings impose some purpose, intention, significance, closure on it. The problem for the writer's relationship to the stuff of his or her story is, of course, how to convert mere events coming one after another into significance. The problem for the writer's relationship to the reader, once he or she has the reader willing to keep turning pages to find out what happens next, is to find a way to make the reader see that what happens next is not what is important. This basic incompatibility is much more compelling in the short form, which seems so atemporal, than the long form, which seems just a matter of time after all. When a reader of short stories, such as those by Eudora Welty, Flannery O'Connor, and Alice Munro, understands this paradox about the form's relationship to "only life," he or she achieves an understanding of what Georg Lukács says is the critic's "most profound experience": "that moment at which things become forms – the moment when all feelings and experiences on the near or the far side of form receive form, are melted down and condensed into form. It is the mystical moment of union between the outer and the inner, between soul and form" (*Soul and Form* 8).

Works Cited

Anderson, Sherwood. *A Story Teller's Story*. 1924. Introd. Thomas Lynch. Ann Arbor, MI: U of Michigan P, 2005.

Awano, Lisa Dickler. "An Interview with Alice Munro." *The Virginia Quarterly Review* 89.2 (2013): 180-84. *VQR Online* (2013). Web.

---. "An Interview with Alice Munro." *VQR Online* (2006). Web.

Bierce, Ambrose. "The Short Story." In "The Controversialist." *The Opinionator*. 1911. Vol. 10 of *The Collected Works of Ambrose Bierce*. New York: Gordian, 1966. 12 vols. 234-48.

Bitsilli, Peter M. *Chekhov's Art: A Stylistic Analysis*. Trans. Toby W. Clyman and Edwina Jannie Cruise. Ann Arbor, MI: Ardis, 1983.

Blaise, Clark. "On Ending Stories." *Making It New: Contemporary Canadian Stories*. Ed. John Metcalf. Toronto: Methuen, 1982. 32-35. Rpt. in *How Stories Mean*. Ed. John Metcalf and J.R. (Tim) Struthers. Erin, ON: The Porcupine's Quill, 1993. 166-69. Critical Directions 3.

Booth, Wayne. "How Bakhtin Woke Me Up." *The Essential Wayne Booth*. Ed. and introd. Walter Jost. Chicago: U of Chicago P, 2006. 140-53.

Bowen, Elizabeth. "The Faber Book of Modern Short Stories." *Short Story Theories*. Ed. Charles E. May. Athens, OH: Ohio UP, 1976. 152-58.

Canby, Henry Seidel. *The Short Story in English*. New York: Henry Holt, 1909.

Chekhov, Anton. *Letters on the Short Story the Drama and Other Literary Topics*. Ed. Louis S. Friedland. 1924. New York: Dover, 1966.

Conrad, Joseph. *Heart of Darkness: An Authoritative Text; Backgrounds and Sources; Criticism*. Ed. Robert Kimbrough. 3rd ed. New York: W.W. Norton, 1988. A Norton Critical Edition.

Edemariam, Aida. "Alice Munro: Riches of a Double Life." *The Guardian* 4 Oct. 2003. Web.

Enright, Anne. Rev. of *Dear Life*, by Alice Munro. *The Guardian* 8 Nov. 2012. Web.

Faggen, Robert. "Russell Banks: The Art of Fiction CLII." *The Paris Review* 147 (1998): 50-88. Web.

Gaffney, Elizabeth. "Lorrie Moore: The Art of Fiction CLXVII." *The Paris Review* 158 (2001): 56-84. Web.

Gass, William H. *Finding a Form*. New York: Alfred A. Knopf, 1996.

Goldstein, Bill. "Audio Interview: Rick Moody." *The New York Times on the Web.* 1 Feb. 2001. Web.

Hancock, Geoff. "An Interview with Alice Munro." *Canadian Fiction Magazine* 43 (1982): 74-114.

Heaney, Seamus. "Joy or Night: Last Things in the Poetry of W.B. Yeats and Philip Larkin." *The Redress of Poetry.* New York: Farrar, Straus and Giroux, 1995. 146-63.

James, Henry. "The Real Thing." *Selected Short Stories.* Ed. and introd. Quentin Anderson. Rev. ed. New York: Holt, Rinehart and Winston, 1957. 117-44.

Jarrell, Randall. "Stories." *Short Story Theories.* Ed. Charles E. May. Athens, OH: Ohio UP, 1976. 32-44.

Kermode, Frank. "Sensing Endings." *Nineteenth-Century Fiction* 33 (1978): 144-58.

Lukács, Georg. *Soul and Form.* Trans. Anna Bostock. London: Merlin, 1974.

---. *The Theory of the Novel.* Trans. Anna Bostock. Cambridge, MA: MIT, 1971.

Moody, Rick. "Demonology." *Prize Stories 1997: The O. Henry Awards.* Ed. and introd. Larry Dark. New York: Anchor, 1997. 424-35.

Morra, Linda M. "'It Was[n't] All Inward': The Dynamics of Intimacy in the 'Finale' of *Dear Life.*" *Alice Munro:* Hateship, Friendship, Courtship, Loveship, Marriage; Runaway; Dear Life. Ed. Robert Thacker. London: Bloomsbury, 2016. 203-16, 229-30, 231-44 passim.

Munro, Alice. "The Colonel's Hash Resettled." *The Narrative Voice: Short Stories and Reflections by Canadian Authors.* Ed. and introd. John Metcalf. Toronto: McGraw-Hill Ryerson, 1972. 181-83. Rpt. in *How Stories Mean.* Ed. John Metcalf and J.R. (Tim) Struthers. Erin, ON: The Porcupine's Quill, 1993. 188-91. Critical Directions 3.

---. "Dear Life." *Dear Life.* New York: Alfred A. Knopf, 2012. 299-319.

---. "Dear Life: A Childhood Visitation." *The New Yorker* 19 Sept. 2011: 40-42, 44-47. Web.

---. "The Eye." *Dear Life.* New York: Alfred A. Knopf, 2012. 257-70.

---. "Finale." *Dear Life.* New York: Alfred A. Knopf, 2012. 255-319.

---. "Golden Apples." *The Georgia Review* 53 (1999): 22-24.

---. "Images." *Dance of the Happy Shades.* 1968. New York: Vintage, 1998. 1-18.

---. "Night." *Dear Life*. New York: Alfred A. Knopf, 2012. 271-85.

---. "The Peace of Utrecht." *The Tamarack Review* 15 (1960): 5-21. Rpt. in *Dance of the Happy Shades*. 1968. New York: Vintage, 1998. 190-210.

---. *The View from Castle Rock*. New York: Alfred A. Knopf, 2006.

---. "Voices." *Dear Life*. New York: Alfred A. Knopf, 2012. 286-98.

---. "What Is Real?" *Making It New: Contemporary Canadian Stories*. Ed. John Metcalf. Toronto: Methuen, 1982. 223-26. Rpt. in *How Stories Mean*. Ed. John Metcalf and J.R. (Tim) Struthers. Erin, ON: The Porcupine's Quill, 1993. 331-34. Critical Directions 3.

O'Connell, Michael. "Getting to 'Judgement Day': Flannery O'Connor's Representation of Personal Dislocation." *Renascence: Essays on Values in Literature* 65 (2012-13): 351-64.

O'Connor, Flannery. "The Geranium." *The Complete Stories*. New York: Farrar, Straus and Giroux, 1971. 3-14.

---. "Judgement Day." *Everything That Rises Must Converge*. New York: Farrar, Straus and Giroux, 1965. 245-69.

---. *Mystery and Manners: Occasional Prose*. Ed. Sally and Robert Fitzgerald. New York: Farrar, Straus and Giroux, 1969.

O'Connor, Frank. *The Lonely Voice: A Study of the Short Story*. Cleveland, OH: World, 1963.

Ortega y Gasset, José. *The Dehumanization of Art*. Garden City, NY: Doubleday Anchor, 1956.

Pearlman, Edith. "Reading *The O. Henry Prize Stories 2013*: The Jurors on Their Favorites." *The O. Henry Prize Stories 2013*. Ed. and introd. Laura Furman. New York: Anchor, 2013. 418-20.

Poe, Edgar Allan. "The Philosophy of Composition." *Edgar Allan Poe: A Study of the Short Fiction*. By Charles E. May. Boston: Twayne-G.K. Hall, 1991. 127-29. Twayne's Studies in Short Fiction Ser. 28.

---. *The Selected Poetry and Prose of Edgar Allan Poe*. Ed. and introd. T.O. Mabbott. New York: The Modern Library, 1951.

---. "Unity of Plot." *Edgar Allan Poe: A Study of the Short Fiction*. By Charles E. May. Boston: Twayne-G.K. Hall, 1991. 120. Twayne's Studies in Short Fiction Ser. 28.

Prose, Francine. *Reading Like a Writer*. New York: HarperCollins, 2006.

Ricoeur, Paul. "Narrative Time." *Critical Inquiry* 7 (1980-81): 169-90.

Stanton, David M. "An Interview with Jayne Anne Phillips." *Croton Review* 9 (1986): 41-44.

Thacker, Robert. *Alice Munro: Writing Her Lives: A Biography.* 2005. Updated ed. Toronto: Emblem-McClelland & Stewart, 2011.

Warren, Robert Penn. "Love and Separateness in Eudora Welty." *Selected Essays.* New York: Random House, 1958. 156-69.

Welty, Eudora. "Death of a Traveling Salesman." *A Curtain of Green and Other Stories.* 1941. New York: Harcourt, Brace, 1946. 231-53.

---. "First Love." *The Wide Net and Other Stories.* New York: Harcourt, Brace, 1943. 3-33.

---. "'Is Phoenix Jackson's Grandson Really Dead?'" *Critical Inquiry* 1 (1974-75): 219-21. Rpt. in *The Eye of the Story: Selected Essays and Reviews.* New York: Random House, 1977. 159-62.

---. "Looking Back at the First Story." *The Georgia Review* 55.4-56.1 (2001-02): 97-101.

---. "A Memory." *A Curtain of Green and Other Stories.* 1941. New York: Harcourt, Brace, 1946. 147-57.

---. "No Place for You, My Love." *The Bride of the Innisfallen and Other Stories.* New York: Harcourt, Brace, 1955. 3-27.

---. *One Writer's Beginnings.* Cambridge, MA: Harvard UP, 1984. The William E. Massey Sr. Lectures in the History of American Civilization 1983.

---. "A Piece of News." *A Curtain of Green and Other Stories.* 1941. New York: Harcourt, Brace, 1946. 21-31.

---. "The Reading and Writing of Short Stories." *The Atlantic Monthly* Feb. 1949: 54-58 and Mar. 1949: 46-49. Rpt. in *Short Story Theories.* Ed. Charles E. May. Athens, OH: Ohio UP, 1976. 159-77.

---. "A Worn Path." *A Curtain of Green and Other Stories.* 1941. New York: Harcourt, Brace, 1946. 275-89.

---. "Writing and Analyzing a Story." *The Eye of the Story: Selected Essays and Reviews.* New York: Random House, 1977. 107-15.

White, Hayden. "The Value of Narrativity in the Representation of Reality." *Critical Inquiry* 7 (1980-81): 5-27.

Williams, Joy. "Uncanny the Singing That Comes from Certain Husks." *Why I Write: Thoughts on the Craft of Fiction.* Ed. Will Blythe. Boston: Little, Brown, 1998. 5-12.

Winner, Paul. "Amy Hempel: The Art of Fiction CLXXVI." *The Paris Review* 166 (2003): 30-63. Web.

"At the End of a Long Road": Alice Munro's "Dear Life"

Catherine Sheldrick Ross

In "Dear Life," Alice Munro returns to personal material that has engaged her throughout her writing career. Munro's biographer Robert Thacker highlighted her lifelong practice of "returning again and again to subjects of autobiographical obsession" (Thacker 1998, 14). This final time, she goes deeper – asking questions, going back over personal material and family relationships, and trying to understand. "Dear Life" is the last and capstone story of the "Finale" about which Munro has famously declared: "*The final four works in this book are not quite stories. They form a separate unit, one that is autobiographical in feeling, though not, sometimes, entirely so in fact. I believe they are the first and last – and the closest – things I have to say about my own life*" (*Dear*, 255).

What are these personal materials that Munro revisits?

> We can start, as does "Dear Life" itself, with the brick farmhouse on an elevation of land "at the end of a long road" (*Dear*, 299). This was the house on the twelve-acre plot of land in Huron County, bought by Robert Laidlaw and Anne Clarke Chamney in 1927, a month before their wedding (Thacker 2005, 40-41).

Zoom out from the house to take in the outbuildings that include the barn for the horses and the fox farm with its fences and sturdy wooden pens, first described in "Boys and Girls," a story that begins, "My father was a fox farmer" (*Dance*, 111). With its structure of matched opposites, "Boys and Girls" establishes the physiography of the house in a series of contrasts that Munro returns to in "Dear Life": boys and girls; outside and inside; male work and female work. The male space of the barn and

31

fox pens, with its "ritualistically important" outdoor work of violence and death, pelting foxes, and turning horses into pails of cut-up meat for the foxes is set against the female, domestic space of the house and its "endless, dreary and peculiarly depressing" housework of washing and putting down preserves (*Dance*, 117).

In "Night," the second of the four stories of the "Finale," the narrator says that the two faces of the brick house "looked on two different worlds, or so it seemed to me. The east side was the town side.... // To the west, the long curve of the river and the fields and the trees and the sunsets had nothing to interrupt them. Nothing to do with people, in my mind, or to do with ordinary life, ever" (*Dear*, 278). The brick house sits at the centre of this landscape, between the compass points of east and west; dawn and sunset; town side associated with ordinary life and the curve-of-the-river side associated with something mysterious and unknowable. The narrator's mother fills the interior of the house with her presence, even after her death. By the end of "Dear Life," it turns out that the house is also haunted by the ghost of another mother, who had lived there years before.

> The river that floods each spring is the Maitland River, dividing the town of Wingham, Ontario from Lower Town and flowing westward to empty into Lake Huron at Goderich. The river took on a legendary status in "The Flats Road" chapter of *Lives of Girls and Women* and it has reappeared in various guises as the Wawanash River, the Peregrine River, and the Meneseteung, this last being the river's Indigenous name. In the story "Meneseteung" in *Friend of My Youth*, the river is linked in the heightened perception of the central character Almeda with the flow of words within the shaping and channelling forms of poetry: the poem she wants to write "is the river, the Meneseteung, that is the poem – with its deep holes and rapids and blissful pools under the summer trees and its grinding blocks of ice thrown up at the end of winter and its desolating spring floods" (*Friend*, 70). In an often-quoted description in a magazine article, Munro said of the river, "this little stretch of it ... will provide whatever myths you want, whatever adventures. ... This ordinary place is sufficient, everything here touchable and mysterious" ("Everything," [33]).

> The view eastward from the house, when the leaves are off the trees, includes the town with its church spires and the square brick tower of the Wingham Town Hall. This was "the real town with its activity and its sidewalks and its streetlights for after dark" (*Dear*, 299). In contrast, the Laidlaw family lived across the bridge on the west side of the river in Lower Town (pronounced Loretown). As Munro told Alan Twigg (1981, 18), "We lived outside the whole social structure.... We lived in this kind of little ghetto where all the bootleggers and prostitutes and hangers-on lived. Those were the people I knew. It was a community of outcasts. I had that feeling about myself." When Munro revised the *New Yorker* version of "Dear Life" for publication in the collected volume, she added the word "Back," to the story's second sentence so that it reads, "Back behind me, as I walked home from primary school, and then from high school, was the real town" (299). This small edit makes more concrete the contrast of back behind me / in front of me and at the same time introduces the theme, in miniature, of the outward journey to town and the return home to the brick house.

In "Home," first published in 1974 in a very different form and collected much later in *The View from Castle Rock*, the narrator remarks that the town hadn't changed much since her childhood: "Nevertheless it has changed for me. I have written about it and used it up. Here are more or less the same banks and hardware and grocery stores and the barbershop and the Town Hall tower, but all their secret, plentiful messages for me have drained away" (*View*, 300). But in fact this contrasting geography of "real town" and Lower Town was far from being used up. Munro told Eleanor Wachtel (2015, 97), "When I moved back, I started seeing things entirely differently. ... I saw a lot of things that had to do with social class, and the way people behave to each other, that a child doesn't see. So I wanted to go into it again." "Dear Life" goes into it one last time, using the contrast of "real town" and Lower Town as a site for exploring class differences, social hierarchies, and the theme of insiders and outsiders.

> Dominating the house as she dominates so many of the stories, including "Dear Life," is the narrator's mother. As Elizabeth Hay (2016, 178) has observed, "The problem of 'the mother' for a daughter who

writes about her is fundamental to Munro's work." The mother is an outsider. She sets herself apart from rural Huron County neighbours, and deliberately so, by her "overly grammatical" speech (*Dear*, 287) and ladylike voice, by her choice of noticeable clothing for herself and her older daughter, and by her progressive ideas. In an unpublished interview with me (Ross 1991), Munro said that her mother used to "come to the school and make her presence felt. I just died – even hearing her voice in the corridor, I died. I got the message that she was so at variance with the community. I must have got this message partly through my father's mother – my grandmother – and my aunt. And maybe my father in some very subliminal way, I don't know. We were *all* embarrassed by my mother, *before* she got sick. When she got sick, that put the cap on it. ... She saw herself as different and she didn't care. We thought it was due to stupidity that she didn't care."

The mother is brave, hopeful, ambitious, self-dramatizing, and filled with self-assertion. Never doubting that her way of seeing the world is important, the mother embraces change and possibility and tries to propel her family toward a life of gentility. In "Walker Brothers Cowboy," which is about a journey into the country taken with the father, the narrator contrasts the experience of an outing with her mother with the "entirely different" experience of heading out with her father (*Dance*, 5). Her mother walks to the grocery store "serenely like a lady shopping, like a *lady* shopping," and the narrator, accompanying her, hasn't "walked past two houses before I feel we have become objects of universal ridicule" (*Dance*, 5). In "Boys and Girls," the narrator describes her sense, at age eleven, that her mother "was not to be trusted" – though kind and loving, "she was also my enemy. She was always plotting" (*Dance*, 117-18). As the narrator experienced it, the goal of the mother's "plotting" was to change the daughter's identity, her very self.

In story after story, from "Red Dress – 1946" in *Dance of the Happy Shades* through to "The Eye," "Voices," and "Dear Life" in the last collection, the narrator resists her mother's efforts to reshape her into another – more conventional and more socially successful – type of girl. As Munro said in an interview with Lisa Dickler Awano (2013), her mother "wanted a really nice little daughter who conformed, who was clever but conformed and gave recitations and didn't question anything." As the daughter grows older, the gulf widens. Munro's daughter Sheila said in her memoir about growing up with Alice Munro that her mother wanted to be "the opposite kind of mother from her own mother" (Sheila Munro 2001, 61).

The narrator rejects, in particular, her mother's puritanical view of sex, which was extreme, even for her time and place. As described in "Friend of My Youth," the mother knew that "sex was a dark undertaking for women. She knew that you could die of it" (*Friend*, 22). On topics connected to sexuality, the mother's voice took on "a solemn thrill" that "grated" on the narrator and "alerted [her] to what seemed a personal danger" (*Friend*, 20). A motif, repeated in many stories, is the special tone of voice that warns the narrator to expect an unwelcome intervention. In "Dear Life," the narrator recalled "hating a good many things she said, and particularly when she used that voice of shuddering, even thrilled, conviction" (302).

The narrator holds out against her mother to protect what is described in "Fathers" as that "self-important disputatious part" of herself (*View*, 194), which is necessary for becoming a writer. The narrator's strategies of resistance evolve from argumentative talking back at age eleven or twelve to silence and withholding of attention, and eventually to moving away – but not without her feeling ungrateful, traitorous, and guilty. Critical assessments of Munro's work have tended to see the troubled and complex relationship with the mother as what Munro has called "the real material" (Munro in Struthers 1983, 23) of her most compelling and unsparing stories (see, for example, Redekop 1992, Heller 2009, Hay 2016).

When early-onset Parkinson's disease overtakes the mother in her forties, she becomes an even more acute source of shame and guilt. The strategies of withholding and withdrawal, though necessary for the narrator's self-preservation as herself, feel increasingly unkind. The illness comes on gradually, with years before symptoms become disabling. In "The Ottawa Valley," a story about a visit to the mother's "old home in the Ottawa Valley" (*Something*, 227), the mother is forty-one or forty-two and the narrator is about ten when she notes, "Just her left forearm trembled" (237). The increasingly bizarre symptoms of the progressive disease make the narrator and her sister in "The Peace of Utrecht" feel apologetic, "as if we were accompanying a particularly tasteless sideshow" (*Dance*, 195).

All along, the watchful daughter has been aware of dangers lying in wait for her mother – she who was so lacking in a sense of precaution and so innocently unaware of how her differences set her apart. Then this person, who all her life has wanted to break out and assert herself, becomes paralyzed and is unable to talk intelligibly. Her daughter has to act as translator. It seemed, said the narrator of "Home," like "just the sort of thing she might have contrived, out of perversity and her true need for attention, for bigger dimensions in her life. Attention that her family came to give her out of necessity, not quite grudgingly, but so routinely that it seemed – it sometimes was – cold, impatient, untender. Never enough for her, never enough" (*View*, 291).

> In contrast, the father is easy-going, "a *wonderful* fitter-inner" (Munro in Ross 1991), comfortable in both his work overalls and his town clothes, who takes what comes in life and makes the best of it. In "Home," the narrator describes her father as "usually a man of great diplomacy, of kind evasions. He has always spoken to me, almost warningly, about the need to *fit in*, not to rile people" (*View*, 298). In "Voices," the third story in the "Finale," the narrator describes her father as "always sounding perfectly right for the occasion ... he understood that the thing to do was never to say anything special. My mother was just the opposite. With her everything was clear and ringing and served to call attention" (*Dear*, 290). The father comes from a family that is diligent, self-controlled, self-denying, shy, and reticent, with a horror of doing anything that could attract ridicule.

Munro told Deborah Treisman (2012), in an interview following the publication of *Dear Life*: "I was brought up to believe that the worst thing you could do was 'call attention to yourself,' or 'think you were smart.' My mother was an exception to this rule and was punished by the early onset of Parkinson's disease." As the mother becomes increasingly imprisoned in her illness, the father carries the burden of family responsibilities. Like Rose's father in "Royal Beatings," who is the "king of the royal beatings" (*Who*, 1), the narrator's father in "Dear Life" is kind, thoughtful, and patient. But he is also the one who used his belt to curb the talking back – punishments that left the daughter shamed and declaring that she wanted to die. In these punishments, which figure centrally in "Dear Life," the mother is the instigator and the father the agent, called in from the barn to deal with "some falling-out with my mother, some back talk or smart talk or intransigence" ("Fathers," *View*, 194).

> And finally there is the daughter, a beloved only child for her first five years until her brother and, a year later, her sister are born. In the "Finale" stories, we see her resistance to becoming the kind of girl her mother wants her to be. These stories featuring the daughter can be read as a *Künstlerroman* about the education and growing up of the writer. The first-person narrator of "Dear Life" and of so many other Munro stories is possessed of a prodigious memory, enormous perceptiveness, and a drive to go back repeatedly over the past, trying to get things straight. As Munro told Kevin Connolly and colleagues (1986, 8), "I remember things in great detail, sounds and smells – things having to do with the senses. And these seem to get woven together. [...] They're almost what [the scene is] about. [...] I want to have a ... I can't even say a *picture*, let's say a *texture*. And I don't make it by researching, or picking out details, I make it by going into my mind. It's really probably the thing that made me want to write the story in the first place – it's this *painful*, almost painful need to recreate – and again it's texture more than just seeing, it's everything that makes up your sensory impressions of a time and place." In an interview with Stephen Smith (1994, 24), Munro said, "I think it's also necessary for me, if I'm going to write about what is very complex and mysterious, to set it in a very definite framework of time and place."

Munro returns again and again to the relationship of the perceptive daughter to her parents, painful topics that she was able to write about only after her own parents' deaths. In the interview with Kevin Connolly and colleagues (1986, 8), Munro said that, until she wrote "The Peace of Utrecht," "I didn't really understand what writing was all about.... It turned me around. It gave me some idea of what writing could do, approaching that kind of material." Similarly, in an unpublished interview with Thomas Tausky (1984) Munro singled out "The Peace of Utrecht" and "Royal Beatings" as two breakthrough stories that were personally risky, tapping into intense emotional experiences from her own life: "Until my mother died – though the relationship with her was a very painful, deep one – I wasn't able to look at it or think about it. And the same thing happened when my father died and I wrote

'Royal Beatings.' These are stories that come out of life. You can't rush them.'" "Dear Life" returns to the core experiences captured in these two breakthrough stories: the enormous sense of embarrassment, pain, and guilt that the narrator feels about her mother and the sense of rage and humiliation associated with beatings by her father that seemed to threaten her very identity.

But how to find a shape, a story, expansive enough to capture all these elements? At the core of "Dear Life," is a brick house "at the end of a long road" (299). This house is both Munro's childhood house and also her go-to metaphor for stories themselves. When asked to reflect on the process of writing her stories, Munro has more than once invoked the image of the house. In the frequently-quoted essay "What Is Real?" Munro said that when she reads a story she can start anywhere, reading "from beginning to end, from end to beginning, from any point in between in either direction" ("What," 224). She thinks of a story not as a straight road that you follow but more like a house that you enter, move back and forth inside, and stay in for a while: "Everybody knows what a house does, how it encloses space and makes connections between one enclosed space and another and presents what is outside in a new way. ... // So when I write a story I want to make a certain kind of structure, and I know the feeling I want to get from being inside that structure. ... // ... I've got to make, I've got to build up, a house, a story, to fit around the indescribable 'feeling' that is like the soul of the story.... Then I start accumulating the material and putting it together" ("What," 224).

Turning to the example of "Royal Beatings" from *Who Do You Think You Are?*, Munro said that she used a newspaper story about a butcher and the young men who may have been egged on to give him a beating: "I put this story at the heart of my story because I need it there and it belongs there. It is the black room at the centre of the house with all other rooms leading to and away from it" ("What," 226). Some fifteen years later, in her introduction to the first paperback reissues of her *Selected Stories* (1997, xx–xxi; 1998, xvii) subsequently republished as *A Wilderness Station* (2015, xx-xxi), Munro returned to the image of the short story as a house with its enclosed spaces:

And you, the visitor, the reader, are altered as well by being in this enclosed space, whether it is ample and easy or full of crooked turns, or sparsely or opulently furnished. You can go back again and again, and the house, the story, always contains more than you saw the last time. It has also a sturdy sense of itself, of being built out of its own necessity, not just to shelter or beguile you. To deliver a story like that, durable and freestanding, is what I'm always hoping for.

The "black room" at the heart of "Dear Life" is an account of an event involving the narrator as a baby, grabbed up from her baby carriage by her mother "for dear life" (318) and carried inside the house for protection against an apparently threatening intruder. The centrality of this incident was highlighted in its initial *New Yorker* publication, where the story's title was "Dear Life: A Childhood Visitation." As is typical with Munro, you don't know what the story is really about until almost the very end. And, when you reread it, it "always contains more than you saw the last time." Through a long apprenticeship, Munro has what Robert Thacker (1983, 37) has described as "a distinctive, retrospective narrative approach" that is "the means by which past and present commingle." "Dear Life" centres on childhood events as remembered by the narrator in "old age" (318). Hence we are presented with the narrator both as a baby and in old age – in fact, both ends of the "long road" with which the story begins: "I lived when I was young at the end of a long road, or a road that seemed long to me" (299). And it has been a long road – J.R. (Tim) Struthers (2016, 165) notes that Munro has pulled off her magic trick of storytelling 148 times, and that's counting only the collected stories published in the fourteen volumes from *Dance of the Happy Shades* (1968) to *Dear Life* (2012). "Dear Life" stands on its own as a dazzling story. But when considered in context, it's like throwing a stone into a still lake and watching the expanding circles extend out and out.

Contexts: "Finale"

And what are the relevant contexts for thinking about "Dear Life"? There is the four-story "Finale," which the author herself marked off as a separate unit; then more expansively there are the fourteen volumes of collected stories, which include versions and variants of the personal material used in "Dear Life"; and beyond that there is the context of Alice Munro's own life, which has provided her with what she has called "the real material" (Munro in Struthers 1983, 23). Longtime Munro readers will find themselves making connections between "Dear Life" and previous stories in which these familiar elements – the house, the town, the river, the mother, the father, the perceptive daughter who writes – have been given an earlier treatment. Here I focus mostly on the narrower context of the "not quite stories" of the "Finale," although the temptation is almost irresistible to trace the threads back and back to earlier stories – for example, to see the scene of the encounter of Del and Mary Agnes with the dead cow ("'Day-ud cow'") in the "Heirs of the Living Body" chapter of *Lives* as a forerunner of "The Eye": "I was shy about looking at its eye. // The eye was wide open, dark, a smooth sightless bulge" (*Lives*, 44). Those expanding circles could eventually go out to contain everything in Munro's 148 collected stories.

The first story in the "Finale," "The Eye," begins, "When I was five years old ..." (257). Initially the story unfolds slowly, in a careful layering of remembered detail and current reflection. In her perceptive book, *Alice Munro's Narrative Art*, Isla Duncan (2011, 17) provides an apt description of the way in which many stories by Munro, including this one, unfold, especially at the beginning, through a "steady accumulation of retardatory and digressive devices." The set-up for "The Eye" is the narrator's statement that, after the birth of her siblings, she began to recognize a difference – a separation – between her mother's way of seeing and evaluating things and her own. We are therefore led to expect this story will be about the child's growing differentiation from the mother and her discovery of her own separate identity; and further, as the title suggests, that the story will be about perception. And so it is, but through an unexpected turn that transforms the commonly occurring rite-of-passage toward independence into a revelation of different levels of reality existing side by side.

The differences between mother and daughter are brought into sharp focus with the coming of Sadie, the hired girl, who represents a challenge to the mother's values and to her ambitions for her daughter. Sadie resembles those sly, scornful, knowing, sexualized, and disillusioned characters in *Dance of the Happy Shades*: Lois, that "mystic of love" in "Thanks for the Ride" (*Dance*, 57) and Patricia, "[t]hat *singer*" in "The Time of Death" (*Dance*, 99) – who are marginalized and disadvantaged by class and family background. A celebrity singer on the local radio station, Sadie is, according to the father, "a godsend" (263), doing housework in the Munro household of three young pre-school children. From the mother's perspective, Sadie is less a godsend than a dangerous influence. "'You and Sadie talk together a lot'" (262), says the mother, which alerts the five-year-old narrator to an unknown danger: "I knew something was coming that I should watch for but I didn't know what" (262). While going about her chores, Sadie tells the narrator seductive stories about her life, stories that involve dance halls, fending off the grabbing hands of dance partners, and knowing advice about paying your own way, looking out for yourself, and not getting "caught" (262). Without really understanding what was at stake for her mother in this contest for influence, the five-year-old narrator starts to become aware of her own resistance: "something in me was turning traitorous, though [my mother] didn't know why, and I didn't know why either" (263).

Following this slow mapping of fault lines, the second half of the story is condensed into the span of an afternoon visit. For this scene, Munro returns to territory first presented in "The Time of Death": the gathering of the community at the house of a bereaved family for ritual expressions of mourning. Sadie has been killed by a car that hit her at night when she was walking home alone from the Royal-T dance hall. In late autumn, the mother takes the narrator, who is dressed up in her good coat "with the dark velvet cuffs and collar" (264), on a ceremonial visit to pay last respects. The narrator and her mother are led into Sadie's house by a "conducting woman" (266), who guides their progress past two young boys in the kitchen who are eating cookies and making faces, then towards Sadie's dazed parents who are sitting on a sofa, and finally towards the open coffin. The conducting woman now seems to be "conniving" (267) with the narrator's mother, whose softly spoken "'Come now'" sounded "hateful" and "triumphant" (268). This, the narrator recalls, was what she feared as "worse than anything. // Seeing Sadie" (267).

The narrator is drawn relentlessly toward the coffin by her mother who keeps her "hand tightly held in hers" (268). But then, as the narrator reports, "her hold on me weakened and I was able to get myself free of her. She was weeping. It was attention to her tears and sniffles that had set me loose" (268). Released from her mother's tight grasp, the narrator "looked straight into the coffin and saw Sadie" (268) and received a message – a flicker of Sadie's eyelid – "meant ... completely for me" (269). The legendary shape underlying these everyday details resembles the pattern in "Images," in which the narrator, leaving her mother behind, goes on a journey with her father, meets a man with an axe who represents her worst fears, is taken to his underground house, and returns home "dazed and powerful with secrets" but "never said a word" (*Dance*, 43). The second half of "The Eye" traces the narrator's descent to the underworld guided by a conductor, her temporary freeing of herself from her mother, her terrifying encounter with death, and her return to the ordinary world with the sense of having received a special message – a "special experience ... owing to myself" (269) that must not be spoken about.

With "Night," the second story, we begin to notice patterns that are present in all four stories. "The Eye" begins, "When I was five years old ..." (257). "Night" begins, "When I was young ..." (271). The third story, "Voices," begins, "When my mother was growing up ..." (286). And "Dear Life" begins, as noted, with "I lived when I was young at the end of a long road ..." (299). These opening sentences draw attention to the dimension of time and to the differences between then and now and between the child's experience as remembered and the adult narrator's reflections on that experience. In qualifying her statements ("or a road that seemed long to me" – 299), the narrator acknowledges that reported events, as perceived in childhood, might seem different from an adult perspective. The narrator returns obsessively to significant childhood experiences to try to understand them. As the narrator notes in the third story, "Voices," "Some questions come to mind now that didn't then" (288). In "The Eye," having said that "the whole house was full of my mother, of her footsteps her voice her powdery yet ominous smell that inhabited all the rooms even when she wasn't in them," the narrator asks, "Why do I say ominous?" (257). She tries to capture the precise emotion through a series of denials and qualifications: "I didn't feel frightened. It wasn't that my mother actually told me what I was to feel about things. She was ..." (257-58). In the same story, the narrator recalls her father's statement that "Sadie was a godsend," but then reports the attempts by her five-year-old self to understand his meaning: "What did that mean? He sounded cheerful. Maybe it meant he wasn't going to take anybody's side" (263). Throughout the four stories in the "Finale," there is a layering of perceptions then and perceptions now.

There are other notable patterns that connect the stories. Cycles of the day and of the year, together with the passage of time and the narrator's growing older, emerge in the specific details of the stories. For example, in "The Eye," there is the beginning of a new school year and the falling of the red and yellow leaves (264). In "Night," there is the blizzard that closed the roads on the night when the team of horses was harnessed to take the fourteen-year-old narrator to the hospital to have her appendix taken out (272) and later there is "the heat of early June" when she begins to have trouble sleeping and spends her nights walking around outside the house (273). In "Night," the longer cycles of history, specifically the Great Depression and the Second World War, enter the story through their effects on the everyday lives of the characters: the economic collapse that permanently killed the market for the father's furs and triggered the bank's foreclosing on his loan (284-85) and the wartime gas rationing that prolonged the use of horses for transportation (271). In "Voices," Canada's role in the war is the back story behind the presence at the dance of the young British men in Air Force uniforms, who are training at the nearby airfield for bombing missions against Hitler's Germany.

Three of the stories feature dancing. Types of dances, dancing, and dancers are distinguished, one from another, by where they can be placed on the various scales of respectability, decency, sexuality, and risk. In "The Eye," Sadie told the five-year-old narrator about the dance halls, the one in town off the main street, and the Royal-T, just out of town, which had "a better class of dancer" (261) but you had to watch out for "where they wanted to get hold of you" (261-62). "Voices" begins with a recollection of the country dances the narrator's mother attended in girlhood, where the whole family participated in the "complicated patterns" of square dancing (286) – respectable dances, which contrast with the "shuffling or swaying in tight circles" (291) at the dance described later in the story. For the mother, who had been expecting "a nice decent dance within a neighbourhood" (295), the outing was ruined by the unwelcome presence of the local madam, Mrs. Hutchison, and one of her girls, Peggy. In "Dear Life," the prospect of the narrator's learning the Highland fling, otherwise acceptable to the mother, is similarly contaminated by its indirect connection with prostitution.

Each story includes, either directly or indirectly, an encounter with death: Sadie's body in the coffin in "The Eye"; the narrator's experience in "Night" of having her appendix (and an unexplained growth "the size of a turkey's egg" that may or may not have been cancerous) removed, which is described as "a kind of rite" that "set you apart, briefly, as one touched by the wing of mortality, all at a time in your life when that could be gratifying" (272); the Air Force boys in "Voices," who are training for "missions on which so many of them would be killed" (297); and Mrs. Netterfield with the hatchet in "Dear Life," about whom much more will be said later.

In an Alice Munro story, clothing is always important and notice is often given to the appropriateness of dress for the occasion. Wearing inappropriate dress can result in social exclusion and can sometimes signify eccentricity or that something is off kilter. For the narrator's mother, clothing is a marker of class aspirations (in "Dear Life," the narrator's mother "used to wear an afternoon dress, even if she was only washing things at the sink" – 312). On the day of the visitation, the mother was washing "a celebratory load of knitwear, ribbons, things to be washed carefully by hand" (311): fussy baby clothes acquired for a much-hoped-for first child after the disappointment of two miscarriages (307). Sometimes clothing is a clue to a person's intended activity. In "Night," the narrator recalls that her father, sitting on the stoop at dawn, was "dressed in his day clothes" (281). In adulthood, she wonders, "why wasn't my father in his overalls? He was dressed as if he had to go into town for something, first thing in the morning" (281) and speculates that this may have been the day when "he had a morning appointment to go to the bank, to learn, not to his surprise, that there was no extension to his loan" (284). Clothing, remembered in exact detail, becomes a way to establish significant contrasts and to sort characters by temperament, occupation, and class.

And sometimes clothing becomes a way to make unexpected connections, as is achieved by the contrastive pairing of the rival dresses worn by two women in "Voices" – women, different in so many ways, who are alike in being outsiders. In this story, the ten-year-old narrator is taken by her mother to a dance being held in "one of the altogether decent but not prosperous-looking houses on our road" (288). Her mother is dressed in her best dress, "too elegant for church and too festive for a funeral" (289). These precise distinctions – the "decent but not prosperous-looking" house, the "too elegant" / "too festive" dress – are characteristic of the way that an Alice Munro story locates characters as well as their accoutrements along various scales such as degrees of respectability, affluence, glamour, sexual generosity, and acceptability within the social structure of "town." The mother's dress is black velvet and "[t]he wonderful thing about it was a proliferation of tiny beads, gold and silver and various colours, sewn all over the bodice and catching the light" (290).

In the front room where the dancing is going on, there is another very noticeable woman. As the narrator was later to discover, this woman, Mrs. Hutchison, "was a notable prostitute" (292) and her dance partner was the owner of the town poolroom. She had brought along to the dance her girl Peggy, whom the narrator has observed crying on the stairway and being comforted by two Air Force boys in their soothing British voices. Mrs. Hutchison herself is wearing a dress of golden-orange taffeta, which the narrator thinks "would certainly put my mother's in the shade. ... // ... You could have called her brazen, and perhaps my mother later did – that was her sort of word" (291-92). In a self-reflexive aside, the narrator remarks "that if I was writing fiction instead of remembering something that happened, I would never have given her that dress," which was "[a] kind of advertisement she didn't need" (292).

When the narrator's mother spots Mrs. Hutchison in her golden-orange dress, she brings the dance outing to an abrupt halt, calling her daughter's name in a tone the narrator "particularly disliked" and demanding, "'Where is your coat?'" (293). Nevertheless, despite the narrator's negative response to her mother's intervention, the brave image of her mother is not entirely erased – she appears "thrillingly handsome" in her dress with tiny beads "catching the light" (290).

The stories in the "Finale" derive some of their strangeness and visceral impact from a feature of Munro's work evident right from the beginning in *Dance of the Happy Shades* (Ross 1983, 112-19, 125) and given full rein here: the eruption into the everyday world of another world informed by the patterns of fairy tales, myths, and legends. At the heart of a Munro story there is often a ceremonial or ritualized event such as a party, a dance, a homecoming, a funeral, a beating, or a visitation. Munro focusses on particular details of everyday life – of her own life – with such intensity that they appear extraordinary, charged with meaning.

"Night," which features the narrator's relationship with her father, is a story of demonic possession. Having recovered from her wintertime appendix operation and the simultaneous discovery and removal of an unexplained growth, the narrator has retained enough of her "invalid status" (275) that she is free to spend early June reading, sleeping in the hammock, and staying awake later and later each night. As her insomnia prolongs itself through the heat of June, the narrator becomes increasingly disturbed by fears of what she might do. The thought has come to her and won't be banished that she might strangle her little sister, who sleeps below her in the bottom bunk in the attic room of the house. (This sister is not called Sheila, which is Munro's own sister's name, but Catherine, the name of Munro's daughter who lived less than two days).

In "Night," the narrator has been taken over – she is possessed. She is no longer herself, but thinks (wrongly) that "nobody knew there was a thing the matter with me" (273). She says, "Something was taking hold of me and it was my business, my hope, to fight it off" (276). As the house changes from the daytime world to darkness, "it became a stranger place" (276). The narrator recites rhymes, then real poetry, and finally "the silliest random speech" (276) as a charm against the wicked spell she feels herself falling under, which is the thought, "Why not try the worst?" (277). To avoid the worst, night after night the narrator walks up and down until dawn in the nighttime world outside the house – like those dancing princesses in the fairy tale who go on nightly journeys to the underworld – until the next night when "[t]he demons got hold of me again" (280).

How to break the spell? On her nighttime perambulations, she sometimes paused at the stoop outside the kitchen in order "to look towards town, maybe just to inhale the sanity of it" (280). One night she encountered her father, who has been waiting for her on the stoop. Her father asks no questions, but the narrator realizes, "I had to break the silence out of my own will" (282). When the narrator reveals her secret and obsessive fear, the father responds calmly and matter-of-factly, calling it "An effect of the ether" and "No more sense than a dream" (283). He brings her back to the everyday world by saying, "'People have those kinds of thoughts sometimes'" (283). Her father's words were "just what [she] needed to hear" (284). It was a gift that drew her back from the demonic, nighttime world of obsession and restored her to the ordinary, daytime world: "It set me down ... in the world we were living in" (284).

"Dear Life"

"Dear Life," the last and most complex of these "not quite stories," re-engages with material introduced in "The Eye," "Night," and "Voices." Moreover, longtime Munro readers are likely to experience "Dear Life" as a journey that returns to its starting point – to concerns, images, and themes first presented in *Dance of the Happy Shades* and taken up again in later stories – but goes deeper, connecting strands treated separately in previous stories. Structurally "Dear Life" is divided into seven sections, separated in the *New Yorker* version by a large bolded initial letter for the first word of the new section and separated in the collected volume by spaces. These sections can be considered rooms, if you like – connected enclosed spaces, each one with its own thematic furnishings. I have assigned a heading to each of these sections that highlights what I see as its most significant concern.

The temporal sweep included in "Dear Life" extends for some 150 years, starting with the building of Lower Town in the 1860s by the first settlers. We see a family over time: the marriage of the narrator's parents and the arrival of their three children; the father's building up and later dismantling the silver fox business; the mother's progression from hopeful teacher to ambitious young mother to paralyzed invalid; the narrator as a babe-in-arms, a school-age child, a rebellious adolescent, a busy mother and writer in Vancouver, and finally a person in old age who is trying to make sense of remembered events from the past. Scenes present key episodes in the lives of the characters, but not in chronological order, and there are big jumps and gaps.

In an *Atlantic* interview with Cara Feinberg (2001), Munro answered a question about "break[ing] the rules" of short story writing with this comment about the handling of time in her stories:

In my own work, I tend to cover a lot of time and to jump back and forward in time, and sometimes the way I do this is not very straight-forward. ... [I]t's a way of saying whatever it is that I want to say, and it sort of has to be done this way. Time is something that interests me a whole lot – past and present, and how the past appears as people change. ... Maybe I should say that memory interests me a great deal, because I think we all tell stories of our lives to ourselves, as well as to other people. ... What interests me is how these stories are made – what is put in at different times in your life, what is left out at different times, and how you use the stories to see yourself, or sometimes just to make life bearable for yourself.

"Dear Life" directly and explicitly takes up the theme of "what is put in" and "what is left out" of the stories we tell ourselves to make life bearable.

"Dear Life" unfolds slowly, with postponements, deferrals, and a rich build-up of details. Certain remembered events – notably the mother's plotting, interventions, and illness and the father's beatings – reappear almost obsessively. The same material is cross-cut into the story from one section to another, each time presented in different contexts and with slightly different shadings of meaning. Important events, motifs, and themes are introduced briefly – sometimes in what seems to be an incidental or throwaway detail – to be picked up and elaborated later in a variation that invites a reassessment of the previous treatments. Magdalene Redekop (1992, x) has drawn attention to "the circling and apparently repetitive movement of Alice Munro's fiction," a description that applies at the micro level of the individual story as well as to Munro's work as a whole. "Dear Life" begins slowly with four lengthy sections but then speeds to a gallop in the last three sections that get shorter and shorter until all the previously established details come together into a new pattern in the heart-stopping ending.

1. Sequins

The opening section of "Dear Life," which I am calling "Sequins," offers that leisurely unfolding – the delay and deferral – that is characteristic of Munro's most complex stories. This section introduces the theme of class and gender differences and the divergent life outcomes associated with staying in versus dropping out of school. The sequins in question were sewn onto an outfit worn for a restaurant job in Toronto by a childhood friend, whom the narrator says she will call "Diane" (301). Many years earlier, Diane had briefly been the narrator's only friend at the country school in Lower Town attended by the narrator for her first two years of schooling. This rural school is remembered in this section as a place of brutal chaos. In an interview with Eleanor Wachtel (2015, 98), Munro described how, for a long time, the memory of that rural school was "so painful" that she didn't think about it or about the class differences between the rural school and the school in town over the bridge. But then she found herself wanting "to write about it, the way it was." Munro herself had been raised as a middle-class child – and for her first five years as a much-cherished only child – when she was suddenly plunged into the much rougher and more violent world of that rural school. In an unpublished interview with me (Ross 1991), Munro said:

> There was real violence in that first school, which was in a rural ghetto. People got beaten up. I got beaten up. Before I went to that school, life was cozy and protected. Then at the Lower Town school, no one liked me. And there was the violence and the unpleasantness of things like the outhouse, which I never went into. Since my home was sheltered, things like that would make me feel sick. So those were a tumultuous two years.

Halfway through the narrator's second year at that school, Diane appears. Motherless, she has come to live with her grandparents on the Lower Town side of the river. Diane offers to teach the narrator the Highland fling, which requires a visit to her grandparents' house so that the narrator can borrow her "clicking shoes" (301) for the lesson. "But then, too soon, my mother was outside" (301), says the narrator. "I told her about the Highland fling, and she said that I might learn it properly sometime, but not in that house" (302).

In this first section, the narrator's mother stages two significant interventions. In the first, she extricates her daughter from "that house" with its contaminating association with sexual ruin, just as she whisked her away in "Voices" from the presence of the notorious Mrs. Hutchison and her girl Peggy. In the second intervention, she instigates her daughter's release from the routine victimization of the rural school and gets her enrolled in the town school, where she might have some chance of learning something and making suitable friends. Long afterwards, the narrator's mother told her the reason for the first intervention. In the voice that the narrator had come to hate "of shuddering, even thrilled, conviction," her mother told her "that Diane's mother had been a prostitute," that she "had died of some ailment it seemed that prostitutes caught," and that the text at her funeral service, held at the narrator's family's own church, was: "The wages of sin is death" (302).

The linkage between these two interventions becomes evident in the last four paragraphs of this section, which introduces the theme of education's key role in the direction that a life takes. In two separate episodes, wonder is expressed over the length of time the narrator is staying in school. In the first version, Diane's grandmother reports that Diane, "who also continued at school for a notable time" (302), was working as a waitress at a Toronto restaurant in her sequin outfit. The narrator comments, "I was old enough at that point, and mean enough, to assume that it was probably a place where you also took the sequin outfit off" (302). In the second version, Waitey Streets, "a one-armed veteran of the First World War" (302-03) marvels over how long it was taking the narrator to get through school and makes jokes about what a pity it was she "could never pass [her] exams and be done with it" (303). Pointing out that she took the normal five years to graduate from grade thirteen, the narrator observes accurately that of the students who started high school "in those days," only about one quarter graduated: "Girls got married and had babies, in that order or the other" (303).

Although the narrator strenuously resists her mother in so many ways, in the matter of education her mother prevails. Alice Munro's mother had fought for her own education when her mother, crazed by religion and by an enormous sense of self-sacrifice, had tried to discourage her daughter from going to high school. Like Del's mother in *Lives*, Annie Clarke Chamney passed her High School Entrance exams, ran away from home, made herself a dress, and put herself through high school. The exemplary story of her self-invention is so standard a part of the mother's repertoire that in "Red Dress – 1946" the narrator remarks, "I was afraid she was going to start again on the story of her walking seven miles to town and finding a job waiting on tables in a boarding-house, so that she could go to high school" (*Dance*, 149). The narrator's mother in "Dear Life" is very aware of two divergent paths open to women: education, which offers choices in life and expanded opportunities; and sexuality, which curtails choices and was associated too often, in those days, with entrapment and sometimes death. Hence the strength of the mother's opposition to Sadie in "The Eye," to Mrs. Hutchison and her girl Peggy in "Voices," and to Diane in "Dear Life." All these characters are seen, in one way or another, to be "asking for trouble" (267).

In "Dear Life," Diane serves as what Douglas Glover (2016, 51) has called "a dipole" for the narrator, just as Naomi does for Del Jordan in *Lives of Girls and Women*. Del and her friend Naomi started off together in elementary school but then diverge as Naomi transfers to the commercial stream, leaves school to work in the creamery, becomes pregnant, and is trapped into a forced marriage. Glover (2016, 48) has pointed out that Munro often develops her stories this way by "setting up these parallel contrasts: characters, families, ways of speaking, even homes and neighbourhoods." The sequins section ends with the narrator's awareness of how far she has travelled from her classmates, including Diane in that rural school: "I felt as if I were a lifetime away from most of the people I had known in grade nine, let alone in that first school" (303). Diane disappears from the story at this point, but her inclusion in this first section draws attention to the role played by mothers in shaping the choices and opportunities available to daughters.

To turn from thematic concerns to Munro's literary style, this section provides, in its deployment of the "one-armed veteran of the First World War" (302-03), a good example of what Coral Ann Howells (2016, 90) has identified as Munro's characteristic use of apparent digressions to divert attention. Notice is drawn to the odd name, Waitey Streets, his one-armed status, his sheep, his little-seen wife, and the way his jokes about prolonged time at school illustrate how "you knew people on the road" (303). But, under the radar, the hardly noticeable reference to his house "on a small hill" (302) on the narrator's own street has been planted here in section one, like a seed.

2. Golf bag

"In a corner of our dining room was something that always surprised me a little" (303), says the narrator at the beginning of the second section. It was "a very new-looking golf bag, with the golf clubs and balls inside" (304). This unexpected golf bag provides the starting point for considering another aspect of class differences – not education this time, but what Pierre Bourdieu has called "cultural capital." A way of speaking, tastes in cooking and in style of dress, and chosen ways of spending time – all these locate the culture of a family within a social structure. Here the golf bag, with its connotations of middle-class leisure, brings into focus differences between the socially ambitious mother and the "fitter-inner" father, who turns down opportunities that might expose him to ridicule or rejection. The mother "had managed to get herself off a farm ... much more hopeless than the one my father came from – and she had become a schoolteacher, who spoke in such a way that her own relatives were not easy around her" (304). The narrator's mother had perhaps "convinced herself that certain boundaries were not there" and that she and the narrator's father "were going to transform themselves into a different sort of people, people who enjoyed a degree of leisure. Golf. Dinner parties" (304). The father, who felt comfortable in overalls, could hardly be imagined in "the sporty kinds of clothes you would have to wear" (304) to play golf. He "had other ideas" (304), and in this instance the father prevailed. As the rest of this section makes evident, in order to hang on to the idea of an idealized life of gentility and leisure, much needs to be overlooked: notably financial disaster, illness, and death. The narrator remarks about the fox farm, "There was quite a lot of killing going on, now that I think of it" (305). A strong theme in this second section is the gulf between aspirations for an idealized life, as represented by the golf bag, and the everyday reality of things as they are on a failing fox farm with a mother whose shakiness is only going to get worse.

The golf bag has been on Munro's mind for a long time. It was featured in a draft fragment, "Old Mr. Black," that Robert Thacker (2005, 106-07) thinks was likely written in the late 1970s, perhaps just after Robert Laidlaw's death. The fragment, which was recorded in one of Munro's longhand notebooks that are held in the University of Calgary *fonds*, describes the wedding photo of Alice Laidlaw and Jim Munro that has been included in three biographies of Munro (Ross 1992, 50; Sheila Munro 2001, 15; Thacker 2005, opposite 135). The photograph was taken in the Laidlaw house in 1951. It shows a very young-looking bridal couple standing immediately in front of the stone fireplace in the living room and flanked on either side by Munro's seated father and mother, the men together on the left of the photo, mother and daughter on the right. In the draft fragment from the notebook, the description of the wedding photo leads directly to details about the fall in the family fortunes:

> My wedding had come at a time when our family had had a patch of ill-luck so shocking that it makes other people turn away in embarrass-ment, my mother sick with an incurable disease (there she is with her slightly crazy eyes and her stiff pose and her beautiful Irish skull), my father with his business in ruins trying to support us by working as a night-watchman in the local foundry, our skid into poverty coinciding naturally with a skid from the middle class through the bottom of the middle class into the working class. And it was not as if there hadn't been hopes and possibilities. My father owned a set of golf clubs. (Munro qtd. in Thacker 2005, 106-07)

In an unpublished interview with me (Ross 1991), Munro described a friend who grew up on the next farm and became an anthropologist: "She claims that we were the privileged poor, because there was this weird thing of books in the house, nice furniture, dishes that had some-how survived, and *no cash flow*. Literally no cash flow." "It made you feel special," I suggested, to which Munro's response was: "It made you feel special. It also made you feel more ashamed, because the element in this kind of household is the fall from some kind of golden age when there has been gentility in all matters. And now there are very desperate sorts of measures." This second section captures these diverse and con-tradictory elements: the golf bag representing hopes and possibilities; the shocking ill-luck that involved a fall from some kind of golden age, with an accompanying sense of shame; and the shifts and desperate measures that are forced upon the family.

Following the introduction of the unused golf clubs, a long paragraph about the hopefulness of the parents' buying the twelve-acre plot of land and the father's building pens for the captive foxes briefly recapitulates material first presented in "Boys and Girls." The long paragraph ends with two sentences holding in tension two contrasting realities. The penultimate sentence invokes the father's world of the fox farm with its blood, violence, and death – the cutting up of old horses for fox food and the culling and pelting of the foxes. The next sentence, which describes a pastoral landscape, is: "The pasture ran right down to the river and had twelve elm trees shading it" (305). This side-by-side juxtaposition of routinized death and pastoral nature is the set-up for a reflection by the narrator on perception and on her early apprenticeship as a writer. "There was quite a lot of killing going on" (305), the narrator remarks, right before redirecting attention to something quite different: the idealization of nature as it was modelled for her by the heroines in the L.M. Montgomery books that she enjoyed in childhood.

Like the young Anne who rhapsodizes over blossom-covered apple trees, the narrator "had the help of the elm trees, which hung over the pasture, and the shining river, and the surprise of a spring that came out of the bank above the pasture, providing water for the doomed horses" (305). She says she was able to ignore the killing by "constructing for myself a scene that was purified to resemble something out of the books I liked, such as *Anne of Green Gables* or *Pat of Silver Bush*. ... Fresh manure was always around, but I ignored it, as Anne must have done at Green Gables" (305). The manure that is everywhere but ignored makes another appearance in section five, in which the idea of selective perceptive is elaborated in the context of choices made by writers about what to include in and what to leave out of their writing.

Some things prove resistant to any form of idealizing, notably the beatings. In this second section, what might appear to be an incidental reference to the beatings is embedded in a description of the father's important outdoor work. When the mother would summon the father from the barn to discipline an outburst of talking back, "he'd have to interrupt his work to give me a beating with his belt," after which the narrator would "lie weeping in bed and make plans to run away" (306). The narrator returns obsessively to the fact of these strappings in sections three, four, and five, each time adding small differences in detail and shadings of meaning. Tentative explanations and justifications – talking back had hurt her mother's feelings; such punishments were "much more common in that period" (Munro in Awano 2013) – are never satisfactory and never enough. In "Night," the narrator speculates that her father, if he remembered the beatings at all, might have explained them as a necessary correction of "a mouthy child's imagining that she could rule the roost" and thinking that she was "too smart" (284).

These strappings previously appeared in "Royal Beatings" in *Who Do You Think You Are?* and earlier still in "The Ottawa Valley," where the narrator's cousins, who were beaten until they howled, forgot about their punishment "five minutes, three minutes, afterwards" (*Something*, 232). In contrast, the narrator of "The Ottawa Valley" experienced the beatings as an unforgettable wound: "With me, such a humiliation could last for weeks, or forever" (*Something*, 232). The father's punishments are the other side of the mother's plotting to change the daughter's identity. In "Fathers" in *The View from Castle Rock*, the narrator explains why the beatings were an existential threat: "I was being punished at those times for some falling-out with my mother, some back talk or smart talk or intransigence. ... I felt as if it must be my very self that they were after, and in a way I think it was. The self-important disputatious part of my self that had to be beaten out of me" (194).

Section two ends with an abrupt shift to the brick house and to the nineteenth-century settlement of Lower Town in the 1860s. "That early village soon had a sawmill and a hotel and three churches and a school, the same school that was my first, and so dreaded by me" (306). And then comes an apparent digression about the dating of the house that becomes important later: "Our house would not have been one of the very first houses in that early settlement, ... but it had probably gone up not long afterwards" (306). Unexpectedly the final paragraph closes with the description of "another house" located "on another hillside" that long ago had seemed to her "like a dwarf's house in a story" (307). Why this doubling, this counterpart to the narrator's own house on a hill? This other house was lived in by Roly Grain, who "in spite of his troll's name" has no further part, says the narrator, "in what I'm writing now ... because this is not a story, only life" (307). Nevertheless the reference to "a dwarf's house" on the hill and the "troll's name" introduces an element of mystery and strangeness and heightens the reader's attention to references about houses on hills.

Douglas Glover's article on Munro's style provides a clue to the function of the doubling, even the tripling, of houses, characters, and scenes
that happens throughout "Dear Life" (Glover 2016, 54):

> Munro is not just telling a story but creating a complex pattern of repe-
> tition and contrast over and above the mere story. Although she is con-
> cerned with what comes next, the chronological thread of narrative, she
> clearly also composes with an eye to elaborating this system of repeti-
> tions, parallels, reflectors, and contrasts. Munro deliberately juxtaposes
> similar or parallel scenes to add a dimension of meaning not contained
> in the mere story. Similar things – characters, scenes, locations, fami-
> lies – are contrasted, and different things are stamped with unexpected
> similarity, creating a complex structure of inter-relation, cross-reference,
> and identity not, perhaps, reducible to a single simple theme.

3. Hatchet

The third section opens with a statement about the family's satisfaction
with the arrival of a first-born daughter: "My mother had two miscarriages before she had me, so when I was born, in 1931, there must have
been some satisfaction" (307). The topic of babies, both lost and celebrated, is dropped for now, but is picked up again later in this section
with the reference to the "celebratory load of knitwear, ribbons" (311),
which the mother washes at the sink, while her long-hoped-for baby
is outside asleep in the baby carriage. In the second sentence of this
section, the narrator veers off into a consideration of the challenging
economic times in the 1930s, the encouraging flurry at the end of the
war, and the short-lived optimism during which the father renovates
the house, adding a bathroom, replacing the unused dumbwaiter with
kitchen cupboards, and changing "the big dining room with the open
stairway … into a regular room with enclosed stairs" (307-08). Why mention the dumbwaiter and the enclosing of the stairway? Because this
renovation changed the room that had been the locus for the beatings,
making it "hard even to imagine such a thing happening": "That change
comforted me in some unexamined way, because my father's beatings

of me had taken place in the old room, with me wanting to die for the misery and shame of it all" (308).

And there were other changes. The fox farm failed and was pulled down; the father got a job as evening watchman in the local foundry; and then something worse: "Something had come upon us that was even more unexpected and would become more devastating than the loss of income, though we didn't know it yet. It was the early onset of Parkinson's disease, which showed up when my mother was in her forties" (308). In the space of barely two pages, Munro has returned to "the real material" of her two breakthrough stories: "Royal Beatings" about the father and "The Peace of Utrecht" about the mother. In the remainder of section three, she begins to link this "real material" into something new that relates to stories and storytelling and, in particular, to a special two-part story that the narrator's mother used to tell about a crazy old lady, a hatchet, a protective mother, and a threatened baby.

In "What Is Real?" Munro described how her stories often develop from a seed, a very vivid scene ("What," 224). The major task of writing is to get this initial scene adequately housed in the story that builds around it, which Munro achieves through the layering of details and remembered material chosen to convey the emotional reality that is "the soul of the story" ("What" 224). The seed for "Dear Life" is the vivid scene of a vulnerable baby being snatched away from danger and held tight by her mother. And the emotional reality? The deep, contradictory, and troubled relationship of a daughter and a mother that begins with the mother's love and close protection and evolves over a lifetime through gradations of resistance, refusals, distancings, and guilt.

But before the narrator gets to her mother's stories featuring crazy old Mrs. Netterfield, she establishes, in broad sweeps, the new reality that had overtaken family life: the mother is initially able to "get dressed in the mornings with some help, and ... do occasional chores around the house" (309); the narrator as oldest daughter takes on the responsibilities of most of the domestic work, making lunches and dinners and bossing her brother and sister about; and the father is glad to escape the house to join other men at the foundry, who are doing dangerous, satisfying work.

The description of domestic life during the narrator's high-school years is the backdrop for a scene of pleasure reading that is part of a thread in "Dear Life" that concerns the narrator on her path to becoming Alice Munro, the writer. This thread is woven through the story in scenes that develop different facets of the topic: the staying-in-school material in section one; the references to L.M. Montgomery as a model for constructing idealized scenes in section two and as a rejected model in section five; the account here in section three of the narrator's omnivorous reading; the self-description in section six of the grown-up narrator in Vancouver, who is "so busy with my own young family and my own invariably unsatisfactory writing" (318) – in the *New Yorker* version, "my own invariably torn-up writing"; and finally the narrator's self-reflexive references to "what I'm writing now" (307) and to the family's cascade of misfortunes, which "wouldn't do in fiction" because it would be "just too much" (309).

In "this precious time" (310) after all the chores are done, the narrator would sit with her feet in the warming oven and "read the big novels [she] borrowed from the town library" (309-10): Laxness's *Independent People* about the hard life in Iceland, which had "a hopeless grandeur to it," or Proust's *Remembrance of Things Past*, which was baffling but "not on that account to be given up on," or Mann's *The Magic Mountain*, which contained "a great argument between ... a genial and progressive notion of life and ... somehow thrilling despair" (310). Summing up this period, the narrator says, "Against several odds, I believed myself a lucky person" (310).

A brief statement about the changed relationship between mother and daughter provides the bridge to the narrator's retelling of two of her mother's stories: "Sometimes my mother and I talked, mostly about her younger days. I seldom objected now to her way of looking at things" (310). The stories that people choose to tell each other, especially stories that are often retold, have been a longtime interest for Munro. "The Shining Houses" from *Dance of the Happy Shades* starts with a description of how the main character used to explore "the lives of grandmothers and aunts – by pretending to know less than she did, asking for some story she had heard before; this way, remembered episodes emerged each time with slight differences of content, meaning, colour, yet with a pure reality that usually attaches to things which are at least part legend" (*Dance*, 19). In the interview with Awano (2013) that is focussed on *Dear*

Life, Munro suggests that a particular story is important to its teller because it illustrates "some strangeness about life":

> I listen a lot to stories people tell and get the rhythm of them and try to write. I think, Why is this sort of story so important to people? I think you still hear lots of stories that people tell which are maybe supposed to illustrate some strangeness about life.

In "Dear Life," the two related stories that the narrator's mother used to tell are examples of embedded stories, or stories within a story. They are what Isla Duncan (2011, 16-17), following Gérard Genette, has called the "sustained use of hypodiegetic or metadiegetic narrative, one that is embedded within the primary narrative." The stories about Mrs. Netterfield, as presented in sections three and four, are a blend of details given in the remembered voice of the mother (e.g., "One day ... the grocer forgot to put in her butter" – 310) overlaid, in the primary or frame narrative, with additional information, comments, and questions from the narrator (e.g., "The story was not about [Waitey Streets] but about someone who had lived in that house long before he did, a crazy old woman" – 310).

Munro has used this story-within-a-story structure before, most memorably in "Friend of My Youth," which is of interest because the relationship of the frame story to the embedded story appears to be handled very differently in "Dear Life" than it was in "Friend of My Youth." In "Friend," the narrator recalls one of her mother's stories about a family in the Ottawa Valley with whom the mother boarded when she was a young school teacher. When, as a teenager, the narrator first hears her mother's account of Flora's being engaged to Robert and then being twice displaced as a bride by more sexy rivals, she feels bound to resist her mother's view of things. The narrator rejects her mother's version of long-suffering, saintly Flora and imagines instead the melodramatic counter-story that she herself would make from the same materials. In a merging of the imagined counter-story she would tell about Flora with her mother's actual life story, Flora gets her comeuppance when she ends up "crippled ... with arthritis, hardly able to move" (*Friend*, 21).

Here the imagined defeat of crippled Flora is part of a larger program of the teenaged narrator's resisting "an incontestable crippled-mother power, which could capture and choke me" (*Friend*, 20). In particular, the narrator rejects her mother's "gloomy caution" (*Friend*, 22) about sex. The narrator describes how the "solemn thrill" in her mother's voice alerted her to "a personal danger" (*Friend*, 20), which her teen-aged self resisted by deflating and undercutting her mother's story. In what Deborah Heller (1998/1999, 64) has called a harsh judgment of her former self, the older narrator comments, "I was no comfort and poor company to her when she had almost nowhere else to turn" (*Friend*, 20). In "Dear Life," the mother is sick enough and the narrator is old enough that she seldom objects to her mother's "way of looking at things" (310). So, at the time, she didn't question or contradict her mother's two-part story about Mrs. Netterfield. Recalling the story many years later, her pressing goal is ostensibly to understand the story and get it straight. But, by the end of "Dear Life," it turns out that here too the narrator has rewritten her mother's version, turning the original story on its head.

In introducing the first story that she is about to retell, the narrator says that it "had to do with the house that now belonged to the war veteran named Waitey Streets – the man who marvelled at the length of time it was taking me to get through school" (310). So this is a story that has to do with a house, but it is also a story about an old woman with a hatchet and the alarmed reaction of the delivery boy who was trying to deliver her grocery order to her house. When the delivery boy opened the back of his truck, Mrs. Netterfield noticed that butter was missing from the order and she became upset. But "she was prepared, in a way. She had her hatchet with her and she raised it" (310). So threatened did the grocery boy feel that he drove off in a rush "without even closing the back doors" of his truck (310). The details about the butter, the delivery boy, the hatchet, and the truck are told in the voice of the mother, but then the narrator comments on the story from her much later perspective: "Some things about this story were puzzling, though I didn't think about them at the time and neither did my mother" (311). This puzzlement leads, in the frame narrative, to a series of questions about Mrs. Netterfield's preparedness to punish "before she knew there was any fault to find": "why would she have come equipped with a hatchet…? Did she carry it with her at all times, in case of provocations in general?" (311).

And what are we to make of this hatchet? Longtime Munro readers have encountered this figure with the hatchet before. Previously they have all been men, associated, in one way or another, with death. In the first appearance of this figure in "Images," the young narrator goes on a walk with her father to check the traplines and sees Old Joe Phippen coming toward them down the hill carrying in his hand "gleaming where the sun caught it – a little axe, or hatchet" (*Dance*, 37). Commenting on "Images," Munro ("Colonel's Hash," 1972, 182) has said that this story "started with the picture in my mind of the man met in the woods, coming obliquely down the river-bank, carrying the hatchet, and the child watching him, and the father unaware, bending over his traps. For a long time I was carrying this picture in my mind, as I am carrying various pictures now which may or may not turn into stories. Of course the character did not spring from nowhere. His ancestors were a few old men, half hermits, half madmen, often paranoid, occasionally dangerous, living around the country where I grew up.... I had always heard stories about them; they were established early as semi-legendary figures in my mind."

Decades later, Munro was still carrying in her mind the picture of the menacing axe-man when she wrote "Vandals," a story in which Ladner, a taxidermist who works with piles of animal skins and eyeless animal heads, turns out to be a child-abuser. The first time that the six- and seven-year-old Kenny and Liza saw Ladner, we are told, "He came out like a murderer on television, with a little axe, from behind a tree" (*Open*, 285). In the conclusion of "The Love of a Good Woman," Rupert, who may or may not be a murderer, walks ahead of Enid toward a boat waiting by the bank of the Maitland River – "he had brought a little hatchet from the woodshed, to clear their path" (*Love*, 77). And now the threatening figure with the hatchet is an old woman.

It turns out that this story about Mrs. Netterfield and the hatchet is a preamble to the main event: "another story about Mrs. Netterfield that had more interest because it featured me and took place around our house" (311). However, the inclusion of this preliminary story has done its work, establishing Mrs. Netterfield as a likely source of trouble when she enters the second story on "a beautiful day in the fall" (311). The narrator, then a baby, was outside, asleep in her baby carriage. Her father was away. Her mother was inside doing some hand-washing of knit baby clothes at the sink on the opposite side of the room from the window. Home alone!

In this third section of "Dear Life," we are taken to the threshold of the main story with the detail of the mother's crossing the room to look out the north window that gives onto the driveway leading up to the house. The section ends with a series of questions about the mother's motivations that resemble the previous series of questions about Mrs. Netterfield's hatchet but are more detailed and more searching. Note the structure: a question, two statements of reasons denied, two statements of alternative possibilities, and the final denial: "Why did my mother decide to leave her washing ... to look at the driveway? She was not.... My father wasn't.... Possibly she.... She was ... more so, in fact, than.... // ... Or it may have had nothing to do with ... but.... // She never said afterwards why she had done it" (311-12). The narrator's question about the mother's motivation for looking out the window has generated two explanations rejected outright as incorrect, a hypothetical possibility relating to the mother's fancy cooking, and a second hypothetical possibility relating to the mother's sewing her own dresses, and then the denial, "She never said afterwards why ..." (312). This sequence of denials and alternatives has the effect of acknowledging the uncertainty of ever knowing other people's reasons.

These concluding paragraphs ending in "She never said afterwards why ..." are a striking example of Munro's style of deferral through statements, qualifications, counter-statements, and the accumulation of details that deliberately slow down the forward movement of the narrative. What did the mother see through that kitchen window? In her frame narrative, the narrator chooses instead to provide supplementary details about the mother herself "in those days" (311) and report misgivings felt by the father's female relatives about the mother's style of fancy cooking and dressing: "Her fault was that she did not look like what she was. She did not look as if she had been brought up on a farm, or as if she intended to remain on one" (312). So why these details? Because the story that Munro is telling is more than an account of Mrs. Netterfield's visitation.

By the end of section three, it is evident that the story is about two women and two houses and the lines of connection between them. But it is also a story about the narrator's mother and the differences that set her apart from her neighbours and from the family of the father who administered the royal beatings. And finally it's about the narrator herself who is going back to the very beginning in order to make sense of her own life and her family of origin.

4. The visitation

What the mother saw coming down the lane was "the old woman, Mrs. Netterfield ... [who] must have walked over from her own house" – the house that later belonged to Waitey Streets, the one-armed war veteran who teased the narrator about her lengthy time in school; the same house from which Mrs. Netterfield "had pursued the delivery boy with a hatchet" (312). After the postponements in section three, we finally get the story that lies at the very heart of "Dear Life" – the story of "[t]he visitation of old Mrs. Netterfield" (315) and the mother's panicked protection of her cherished baby. Even so, the narrator delays as she works through a series of hypothetical constructions about the mother's previous relationship with Mrs. Netterfield: "My mother must have.... Maybe.... It's possible, though, that.... My mother might have.... It might even ... was ... probably" (313). As we discover in section five, the most significant connection between the mother and Mrs. Netterfield was probably not known to the mother and is only discovered by the narrator by accident years later in a letter to the hometown paper.

And then: "But now.... Now she was running out the kitchen door to grab me out of my baby carriage" (313). The tempo picks up as we hear, in the voice of the mother, these details about running and grabbing. But there is another delay as the narrator mentions "a problem with the kitchen door" (313), which lacked a proper lock and was barricaded at night with a chair under the doorknob, a detail previously mentioned in "Night" (279). The thought of the insecure kitchen door leads in the frame narrative to a whole new series of unanswerable questions: "Did my mother think of any weapon...? Had she ever picked up a gun, or loaded one, in her life? // Did it cross her mind that the old woman might just be paying a neighbourly visit? I don't think so. There must have been ..." (313). These two delaying sequences of questions, possibilities, and denials repeat the pattern already noted in section three and lead to the same sense of uncertainty and inconclusiveness. A striking feature of the narrative style here is the high ratio of frame to embedded story: the narrator's questions, speculations, provision of supplementary information, and commentary make up the majority of the text.

A new urgency and sense of menace emerge from the selection of details in this section: the hatchet remembered from the first story, the insecure kitchen door, the unloaded rifle and shotguns, the absence of any really satisfactory hiding place in the house, and the intruder's beeline for the baby carriage. The effect of menace is intensified because of the doubling here: the narrator is both the person retelling the story and the story's central object. She is the innocent baby who had been sleeping outside in her baby carriage until her mother grabbed her up and rushed with her back into the kitchen to wait out the invasion "in the hiding place by the dumbwaiter" (314).

First Mrs. Netterfield checks out the baby carriage, flinging away the blankets. Next comes the looking: "She was walking around the house, taking her time, and stopping at every downstairs window.... She could press her face against every pane of glass" (314). "How did my mother know this?" (314) wonders the narrator, immediately jumping to a counterfactual construction of what is *not* the case. She conjures up the grotesque image of two women peering at each other through the windows, a young mother looking out and an old woman looking in: "It was not as if she were running around with me in her arms, hiding behind one piece of furniture after another, peering out, distraught with terror, to meet with the staring eyes and maybe a wild grin. // She stayed by the dumbwaiter. What else could she do?" (315).

The narrator explains that this visitation story was not part of her mother's standard "repertoire" of stories, which included her "struggle to get to high school," her friends at normal school, the Alberta school where she had taught before her marriage, and so on (315). But she had told it often enough that the narrator can refer to different versions. The "earlier versions" ended "with Mrs. Netterfield pressing her face and hands against the glass" (315) while the mother hid. In "later versions," after the looking came more alarming displays: "Impatience or anger took hold and then the rattling and the banging came. No mention of yelling" (315). And it's not just what the mother in her earlier and later versions includes or chooses to embellish that invites attention. Also of significance is the narrator's own practice of inclusion and embellishment.

Through repetition, the narrator gives special emphasis to partic-ular story elements, such as the windows and the dumbwaiter. The mother was looking out the window when she saw Mrs. Netterfield; she didn't take the time to pull down the window blinds "but stayed with [her baby] in her arms in a corner where she could not be seen" (314);

because the storm windows were not on in summer, the visitor could look in every window, "pressing her face and hands against the glass" (315). The dumbwaiter appears three times in this section. It was introduced in section three as "the unused dumbwaiter" (307), which had been replaced by kitchen cupboards during the home renovations. Here in section four, the narrator's speculation about why the mother may *not* have chosen to hide in the rooms upstairs leads to the statement that "to get there my mother would have had to cross the big main room – that room where the beatings would take place in the future, but which lost its malevolence after the stairs were closed in" (314-15). The narrator returns again and again to this place by the dumbwaiter because it has two associations for her that are a matter of life and death: it is where her mother kept her hidden and safe and it is also where the never-to-be-forgotten beatings took place.

And Mrs. Netterfield – what of her? This section ends with the mother's saying, "'They took her away.... Oh, I think so. She wasn't left to die alone'" (316). In the story's original version in *The New Yorker*, the break between sections four and five came earlier, with section four ending with the chair kept under the doorknob until the father came home. Munro is known to revise stories right up to, and often after, their first magazine publication. As Munro told Awano (2013), "I do rewrite a lot, and I rewrite and then I think it's all done, and I send it in. And then I want to rewrite it some more. Sometimes it seems to me that a couple of words are so important that I'll ask for the book back so that I can put them in." This edit to move the section break – not a matter of altering even a few words but of changing the spacing – is one of those crucial Munrovian post-original-publication changes. Putting the mother's statement in the key position at the end of the section gives extra weight to the figure of the old woman and to themes of dementia, illness, and dying alone.

5. Manure

Section five begins with a chronological leap forward some fifteen or more years to when "After I was married and had moved to Vancouver, I still got the [hometown] weekly paper" (316). The narrator's mother's death is referred to indirectly in the second sentence, which is about how the subscription to the paper had been provided by "somebody, maybe my father and his second wife" (316). When the narrator happens to look at one of the weekly papers, her eye is caught by the name Netterfield, which turns out to be the maiden name of someone who has written a letter to the editor. This letter-writer, now living in Portland, Oregon, used to live in the narrator's hometown and has her own subscription to the paper. Her flowery letter includes a poem about her childhood home, "'written from memories of that old hillside'," which she hopes "'are worthy of a little space in your time-honoured paper'" (316). The poem of several verses begins, "*I know a grassy hillside / Above a river clear*" (316). Section five takes up the theme of writing and asks questions about what gets included in literary texts and what – like the manure in the farmyard – often gets left out.

This section contains much to note, but let's start with the letter. It often happens in a Munro story that the contents of a letter unsettle the story in which it appears. Some letters, such as the mother's exchange with Flora in "Friend of My Youth," precipitate, and mark, the ending of a relationship. Some deliberately leave out almost everything of importance, such as Corrie's one-sentence letter to her blackmailing lover Howard at the end of "Corrie" in *Dear Life*. Some letters, when they are found and read years later by the letter-writer herself, reveal that "some shift" has taken place, as was the case in "Soon" in *Runaway* (124-25). In "Soon," the shift concerns "where home was. Not at Whale Bay [on the West Coast] ... but back where it had been before, all her life before" (125). Some letters provide new information that changes what we thought we knew, as does the letter from the Oregon woman to the hometown paper.

While the narrator reads the letter in the paper, a recognition scene unfolds, detail by detail, and the narrator's attention narrows in from the river landscape to the house itself. The narrator realizes that the "*river clear*" in the poem is the narrator's own Maitland River – the letter-writer "was talking about the same river flats that I had thought belonged to me" (316). And "*the other bank*" with its "*blossoms wild and gay*": "That was our bank. My bank" (317). And finally the house on the "*grassy hillside*" (316) – what of it? The letter-writer said that her father, whose name was Netterfield, "had bought a piece of land from the government in 1883, in what was later called the Lower Town. The land ran down to the Maitland River" (317). In short, the letter contains the crucial information that the Netterfields had once lived in the narrator's family's house. Mr. Netterfield, who bought that piece of Crown land in 1883, presumably built the brick house, described in section two as "not ... one of the very first houses in that early settlement, ... but it had probably gone up not long afterwards" (306). Over the course of section five, the focus pulls in tightly from broad landscape panorama to the house itself. The narrator's full recognition of the identity of the letter-writer's childhood house is deferred till the last two-word paragraph: "Our house" (318).

The poem included in the letter to the editor features Nature with a capital N: consciously poetic descriptions of *"ceaseless sparkles"* of sun on water, *"the Iris-bordered stream,"* and white geese that fed *"on the river's watery field"* (317). Another verse described "a stand of maples," but the narrator believes that the letter-writer "was remembering it wrong – they were elms, which had all died of Dutch elm disease by now" (317). The narrator remarks, "She had left out, just as I would have done, the way the spring got muddied up and soiled all around by horses' hooves. And of course left out the manure" (317). The addition of a few words to the two-word *New Yorker* version ("And manure.") puts more emphasis on the central theme of perception and what gets included and what left out of literary writing. The reference to manure takes us back to section two, in which the narrator says that, growing up, she could ignore the killing going on by constructing a scene purified to resemble something out of the books by L.M. Montgomery: "I had the help of the elm trees ... and the shining river.... Fresh manure was always around, but I ignored it" (305).

In "Lying Under the Apple Tree" from *The View from Castle Rock*, the narrator similarly describes herself as "secretly devoted to Nature" (*View*, 198). She says that as an adolescent, her model "came from books, at first. It came from the girls' stories by the writer L.M. Montgomery, who often inserted some sentences describing a snowy field in moonlight or a pine forest or a still pond mirroring the evening sky" (*View*, 198). The narrator of "Dear Life" acknowledges that she, like the letter-writer, "had once made up some poems," now lost, that had "commended Nature, then were a bit hard to wind up" (317). These early poems were written, says the narrator, "right around the time that I was being so intolerant of my mother, and my father was whaling the unkindness out of me. Or beating the tar out of me, as people would cheerfully say back then"

(317). These two sentences highlight the triad of linked elements that lie at the heart of "Dear Life" – the narrator's developing identity as a writer; her need to resist her mother's view of things in order to become herself; and the violence of the father's beatings. In this fifth and last reference to the beatings, a new explanation for them is suggested, relating to kindness. The father, who in "The Eye" seemed to the narrator as maybe not "going to take anybody's side" (263), takes the mother's side in the furious rows that erupt when the daughter refuses to back down.

In the "Finale," the narrator has represented her adolescent self as being acutely aware of her own emotional life but largely unconscious of other people's concerns. In "Night," the older narrator says about her egotistical younger self's response to her appendix operation, "I don't suppose it ever crossed my head to wonder how my father was going to pay for this" (272). In "Dear Life," at the time of the beatings the narrator has an adolescent's acute sense of what Sheila Munro (2001, 152) says her mother felt was the unfairness in "never [being] allowed to tell her side of the story." For the older narrator, the injustice and the humiliation of the beatings are still vivid, but she is also more aware of the wider context of the mother's illness and the father's role to protect. The beatings take place when the mother is just "starting to get sick, overtaken by mysterious attacks of lethargy, but before she had any inkling that she was in the early stages of Parkinson's disease" (Sheila Munro 2001, 151).

6. The lost baby

This brief section, less than a page long, takes up two themes of continuing interest to Munro that are brought together here as the narrator puzzles over the visitation episode and what may, or may not, explain it. One theme is dementia, with its confusions, wanderings, disorientation, and catastrophic losses of memory and identity (see, for example, "Spelling" in *Who Do You Think You Are?*, "The Bear Came Over the Mountain" in *Hateship, Friendship, Courtship, Loveship, Marriage*, and "In Sight of the Lake" in *Dear Life*). And the other is the lost baby. One such lost baby was Alice Munro's own second daughter, Catherine Alice, born on July 28, 1955 (Thacker 2005, 125). Without functioning kidneys, she lived less than two days.

For the next two years, until her second daughter Jenny was born, Munro was haunted by a recurring dream. In an unpublished interview with me (Ross 1991), Munro said, "I was doing something and had the feeling I was forgetting something very, very important. It was a baby. I had left it outside and forgotten about it, and it was out in the rain. By the time I remembered what it was, the baby was dead. This dream stopped when Jenny was born." In "My Mother's Dream" in *The Love of a Good Woman*, the dream was transferred to another mother, Jill, who dreams that it is full summer, but there has been "a heavy fall of snow" (*Love*, 293). Jill "remembered that she had left a baby out there some-where, before the snow had fallen. ... She had left her baby out overnight, she had forgotten about it. ... // ... // The sorrow that came to [her] was the sorrow of the baby's waiting and not knowing it waited for her, its only hope, when she had forgotten all about it" (*Love*, 294). In both these dreams of the lost baby, the child is innocent and vulnerable and the mother feels intense guilt and sorrow.

Here in section six of "Dear Life," the pattern of innocence and guilt begins to be reversed, as a new possibility emerges of a mother suf-fering from dementia who is desperately seeking her lost baby in the house that used to be hers and a child, now grown up and living on the West Coast, who has distanced herself. Section six begins with another one of those questions about what the narrator's mother knew: "Is it possible that my mother never knew this, never knew that our house was where the Netterfield family had lived and that the old woman was looking in the windows of what had been her own home? // It is possi-ble" (318). This sequence differs from those in sections three and four that pose questions, make denials, suggest alternative possibilities, and end inconclusively because the mother "never said" (312). This third sequence doubles down on uncertainty by affirming the possibility that the mother not only never said but also never knew.

The narrator herself, who in her "old age" (318) has taken to looking up things in old records, now understands the confusing business of the succession of different families living for a time in certain houses and moving to other houses in the same neighbourhood – a game of musical houses. After the Netterfields sold the brick house, several other families had lived in it before the narrator's parents bought it. And when the

[70] Alice Munro Everlasting: Essays on Her Works II

narrator was a baby in that house, Mrs. Netterfield was living in a house on the same road that many years later belonged to Waitey Streets.

It's not just houses on a hill that are doubled – or tripled, if you also include that other house on a hill, "like a dwarf's house in a story," lived in by Roly Grain with "his troll's name" (307). Daughters are doubled as well, despite the difference in age of some fifty-five years between the letter-writer and the narrator. Both daughters lived on the West Coast far away from their families and hometown; both had subscriptions to the hometown paper; both wrote about the landscape of their childhood home; and both were babies in that brick house at the end of a long road. Crucially, the mothers are also doubled: two mothers seeking lost daughters, who are distant. These mothers are mirror images of each other, like the narrator's grotesque image of the two faces on either side of the glass window in section four.

The narrator transfers to the reader the job of wondering what happened to Mrs. Netterfield: "You might wonder why [the brick house] had been disposed of when that woman still had years to live.... And who was it who came and took her away, as my mother said" (318). The narrator muses, "Perhaps it was her daughter.... Perhaps that daughter, grown and distant, was the one she was looking for in the baby carriage. Just after my mother had grabbed me up, as she said, for dear life" (318).

A variant of the "grown and distant" daughter can be found in the third-person story "Soon" in *Runaway*. Here, the mother Sara, who is very ill and will die in a few months without seeing her daughter again, tells her daughter, Juliet, who is on a brief visit home from the West Coast, "'When it gets really bad for me – when it gets so bad I – you know what I think then? I think, all right. I think – Soon. *Soon I'll see Juliet*'" (*Runaway*, 124). Sheila Munro's memoir *Lives of Mothers & Daughters* includes the only letter by Anne Laidlaw that Sheila has been able to find. "Undated, unsigned, and written in pencil" by Anne Laidlaw to her daughter Alice "a few weeks before she died" (Sheila Munro 2001, 135), the letter begins: "Dearest dear, // I am just so full of love and good wishes that my letter will I fear it will burst at the corner. Please write soon (just for me) everything.... Please write soon" (Sheila Munro 2001, 135-36).

At the very end of section six, after a series of phrases suggesting uncertainty – "Is it possible ...?" "It is possible," "You might wonder why ...," "Who knows?", "Perhaps," "Perhaps," "I could have ..." – comes a reversal with the one definite statement in the entire section: "But the person I would really have liked to talk to then was my mother, who was no longer available" (318). All along, the stories in the "Finale" have represented a narrator who is trying to increase the distance between herself and her mother. Now, when the narrator wants to close the distance and talk to her mother, she is "no longer available."

7. *The person I would really have liked to talk to*

The six-sentence section that ends the story opens with, "I did not go home for my mother's last illness or for her funeral" (319). Elizabeth Hay (2016, 191) has called this "the central haunting fact of [Munro's] life." Each key word in the short opening sentence is resonant with meaning that has been carefully built up through her multiple uses of the word in previous contexts. Home is the brick house of the narrator's childhood "at the end of a long road" (299). The motif of the departure from home and the return was introduced at the outset of the story, but so unobtrusively that it barely registers: "Back behind me, as I walked home from primary school, and then from high school, was the real town" (299).

In the stories in the "Finale," the journey out from home and back again is repeated at different scales of distance, starting with the childhood journey to school and home again and eventually including the move to Vancouver. In each of "The Eye" and "Voices," the young narrator is taken on a journey by her mother, who brings her home again. The central episode in "Dear Life" involves the baby being placed outside and the frantic rush back into the safety of the house when the mother grabs up the narrator from her baby carriage "for dear life" (318). Only one journey is mentioned where there is no return: the narrator, living in Vancouver with her husband and two small children, "did not go home" (319). In an interview that followed the release of *Runaway*, Munro acknowledged to Eleanor Wachtel (2015, 100) that her sense of guilt over her mother "has become my subject." This final story about guilt ends on a note of calm reflection.

The quiet, restrained register of this conclusion succeeds through subtraction. So many previous stories have been journeys to reach the mother. The narrator in "The Ottawa Valley" said she "wanted to find out more, remember more ... to bring back all I could" (*Something*, 246). But, in the case of this ending, less is more. There is none of the heightened language or harrowing details to be found in "The Peace of Utrecht." The *New Yorker* version includes a final paragraph recalling details presented in "Peace," but this paragraph was cut: "When my mother was dying, she got out of the hospital somehow, at night, and wandered around town until someone who didn't know her at all spotted her and took her in. If this were fiction, as I said, it would be too much, but it is true." In the final version, "Dear Life" ends quietly, undramatically, and ambiguously:

> We say of some things that they can't be forgiven, or that we will never forgive ourselves. But we do – we do it all the time. (319)

Readers will draw their own conclusions on how to interpret this statement about self-forgiveness. First, two folk expressions deny the possibility of forgiveness for "some things" that "can't be forgiven" and for which "we will never forgive ourselves." And then the reversal. The statement, "But we do – we do it all the time" may be an acknowledgement and an acceptance of flawed human nature, similar to the father's gift to the narrator in "Night" when he said, "'People have those kinds of thoughts sometimes'" (283). By the end of "Dear Life," with the shift to the pronoun "we," individual guilt is subsumed in the general human condition. The two statements – "we will never forgive ourselves" and "we do it all the time" – don't cancel each other out. Like many apparent contradictions in the Munro world, both are true.

Works Consulted

Primary Sources

Fiction

Munro, Alice. 1968. *Dance of the Happy Shades*. Foreword by Hugh Garner. Toronto: Ryerson.
Munro, Alice. 1971. *Lives of Girls and Women*. Toronto: McGraw-Hill Ryerson.

Munro, Alice. 1974. *Something I've Been Meaning To Tell You*. Toronto: McGraw-Hill Ryerson.

Munro, Alice. 1978. *Who Do You Think You Are?* Toronto: Macmillan of Canada.

Munro, Alice. 1990. *Friend of My Youth*. Toronto: McClelland & Stewart.

Munro, Alice. 1994. *Open Secrets*. Toronto: McClelland & Stewart.

Munro, Alice. 1998. *The Love of a Good Woman*. Toronto: McClelland & Stewart.

Munro, Alice. 2001. *Hateship, Friendship, Courtship, Loveship, Marriage*. Toronto: McClelland & Stewart.

Munro, Alice. 2004. *Runaway*. Toronto: McClelland & Stewart.

Munro, Alice. 2006. *The View from Castle Rock*. Toronto: McClelland & Stewart.

Munro, Alice. 2011. "Dear Life: A Childhood Visitation." *The New Yorker*, September 19. <https://www.newyorker.com/magazine/2011/09/19/dear-life>.

Munro, Alice. 2012. *Dear Life*. Toronto: McClelland & Stewart.

Author's Commentaries

Munro, Alice. 1972. "The Colonel's Hash Resettled." In *The Narrative Voice: Short Stories and Reflections by Canadian Authors*, 181-83. Edited by John Metcalf. Toronto: McGraw-Hill Ryerson.

Munro, Alice. 1974. "Everything Here Is Touchable and Mysterious." *Weekend Magazine* [*The Globe and Mail*], May 11: [33].

Munro, Alice. 1982. "What Is Real?" In *Making It New: Contemporary Canadian Stories*, 223-26. Edited by John Metcalf. Photographs by Sam Tata. Toronto: Methuen.

Munro, Alice. 1997/1998/2015. "Introduction to the Vintage Edition." In *Selected Stories*, xiii-xxi. New York: Vintage. Rpt. as "Introduction" in *Selected Stories*, ix-xvii. Toronto: Penguin. Rpt. as "Introduction" in *A Wilderness Station: Selected Stories 1968-1994*, xiii-xxi. Toronto: Penguin.

Interviews

Munro, Alice. 1971. "Alice Munro Talks with Mari Stainsby." *British Columbia Library Quarterly* 35, no. 1: 27-31.

Munro, Alice. 1972. "A Conversation with Alice Munro." With John Metcalf. *Journal of Canadian Fiction* 1, no. 4: 54-62.

Munro, Alice. 1981. "What Is: Alice Munro." With Alan Twigg. In *For Openers: Conversations with 24 Canadian Writers*, 13-20. Madeira Park, BC: Harbour.

Munro, Alice. 1982. "An Interview with Alice Munro." With Geoff Hancock. *Canadian Fiction Magazine* 43: 74-114.

Munro, Alice. 1983. "The Real Material: An Interview with Alice Munro." With J.R. (Tim) Struthers. In *Probable Fictions: Alice Munro's Narrative Acts*, 5-36. Edited by Louis K. MacKendrick. Downsview, ON: ECW.

Munro, Alice. 1984. "Interview with Alice Munro." With Thomas E. Tausky. Transcribed by Catherine Sheldrick Ross. Unpublished interview recorded in London, Ontario.

Munro, Alice. 1986. "Alice Munro." With Kevin Connolly, Douglas Freake, and Jason Sherman. *what*, September-October: 8-10.

Munro, Alice. 1991. "Interview with Alice Munro." With Catherine Sheldrick Ross. Unpublished interview recorded in Goderich, Ontario.

Munro, Alice. 1991. "An Interview with Alice Munro." With Eleanor Wachtel. *Brick* 40: 48-53.

Munro, Alice. 1994. "Alice Munro: The Art of Fiction CXXXVII." With Jeanne McCulloch and Mona Simpson. *The Paris Review* 131: 226-64.

Munro, Alice. 1994. "Layers of Life: No More 'Single Paths' for Alice Munro." With Stephen Smith. *Quill & Quire*, August: 1, 24.

Munro, Alice. 2001. "Bringing Life to Life." With Cara Feinberg. *The Atlantic*. Available at: <https://www.theatlantic.com/magazine/archive/2001/12/bringing-life-to-life/303056/>.

Munro, Alice. 2004/2005/2015/2016. "Interview with Eleanor Wachtel." *Writers & Company*. Broadcast on CBC Radio One on November 7, 2004. Rebroadcast on CBC Radio One on July 8, 2016. Audio interview available at: <https://www.cbc.ca/radio/writersandcompany/alice-munro-on-writing-about-life-love-sex-and-secrets-1.3668382>. Printed (abridged) in 2005 as "Alice Munro: A Life in Writing: A Conversation with Eleanor Wachtel" in *Queen's Quarterly* 112: 266-81. Printed (in full) in 2015 as "Interview by Eleanor Wachtel, *Writers & Company*" in *Alice Munro: Writing for Dear Life*. Edited by Corinne Bigot. *Commonwealth Essays and Studies* 37, no. 2: 89-104.

Munro, Alice. 2012. "On 'Dear Life': An Interview with Alice Munro." With Deborah Treisman. *The New Yorker*, November 20. <https://www.newyorker.com/books/page-turner/on-dear-life-an-interview-with-Alice-Munro>.

Munro, Alice. 2013. "An Interview with Alice Munro." With Lisa Dickler Awano. *Virginia Quarterly Review*. Available at: <https://www.vqronline.org/vqr-portfolio/interview-alice-munro>.

Munro, Alice. 2013. "Nobel Prizewinner Alice Munro: 'It's a Wonderful Thing for the Short Story'." Interview with Lisa Allardice. *The Guardian*, December 6. Available at: <https://www.theguardian.com/books/2013/dec/06/alice-munro-interview-nobel-prize-short-story-literature>.

Other References

Berthin, Christine. 2015. "Of Wounds and Cracks and Pits: A Reading of *Dear Life*." *Alice Munro: Writing for Dear Life*. Edited by Corinne Bigot. *Commonwealth Essays and Studies* 37, no. 2: 79-87.

Bigot, Corinne, and Catherine Lanone. 2014. *Sunlight and Shadows, Past and Present: Alice Munro's* Dance of the Happy Shades. Paris: Presses Universitaires de France – Cned. Série Anglais.

Buchholtz, Mirosława. 2015. "Alice Munro's Legacy: The 'Finale' of *Dear Life*." *Alice Munro: Writing for Dear Life*. Edited by Corinne Bigot. *Commonwealth Essays and Studies* 37, no. 2: 69-77.

Duncan, Isla. 2011. *Alice Munro's Narrative Art*. New York: Palgrave Macmillan.

Glover, Douglas. 2016. "The Style of Alice Munro." In *The Cambridge Companion to Alice Munro*, 45-59. Edited by David Staines. Cambridge, England: Cambridge University Press.

Hay, Elizabeth. 2016. "The Mother as Material." In *The Cambridge Companion to Alice Munro*, 178-92. Edited by David Staines. Cambridge, England: Cambridge University Press.

Heller, Deborah. 1998/1999. "Getting Loose: Women and Narration in Alice Munro's *Friend of My Youth*." *Alice Munro Writing On....* Ed. Robert Thacker. *Essays on Canadian Writing* 66 (1998): 60-80. Rpt. in

The Rest of the Story: Critical Essays on Alice Munro, 60-80. Edited by Robert Thacker. Toronto: ECW.

Heller, Deborah. 2009. *Daughters and Mothers in Alice Munro's Later Stories*. Seattle, Washington: Workwomans.

Howells, Coral Ann. 2016. "Alice Munro and Her Life Writing." In *The Cambridge Companion to Alice Munro*, 79-95. Edited by David Staines. Cambridge, England: Cambridge University Press.

Ładuniuk, Magdalena. 2015. "'Autobiographical in Feeling but Not in Fact': The Finale of Alice Munro's *Dear Life*." *Studia Anglica Posnaniensia* 50, nos. 2-3: 141-53.

May, Charles E. 2011. "Alice Munro's 'Dear Life'." *Reading the Short Story*, October 1. <may-on-the-short-story.blogspot.com/2011/10/alice-munros-dear-life.html>.

Munro, Sheila. 2001. *Lives of Mothers & Daughters: Growing Up with Alice Munro*. Toronto: McClelland & Stewart.

Redekop, Magdalene. 1992. *Mothers and Other Clowns: The Stories of Alice Munro*. London: Routledge.

Ross, Catherine Sheldrick. 1983. "'At Least Part Legend': The Fiction of Alice Munro." In *Probable Fictions: Alice Munro's Narrative Acts*, 112-26. Edited by Louis K. MacKendrick. Downsview, ON: ECW.

Ross, Catherine Sheldrick. 1992. *Alice Munro: A Double Life*. Toronto: ECW. Canadian Biography Ser. 1.

Struthers, J.R. (Tim). 2016. "Traveling with Munro: Reading 'To Reach Japan'." In *Alice Munro:* Hateship, Friendship, Courtship, Loveship, Marriage; Runaway; Dear Life, 163-83, 231-44 passim. Edited by Robert Thacker. London: Bloomsbury.

Thacker, Robert. 1983/2016. "'Clear Jelly': Alice Munro's Narrative Dialectics." In *Probable Fictions: Alice Munro's Narrative Acts*, 37-60. Edited by Louis K. MacKendrick. Downsview, ON: ECW. Rpt. as "'Clear Jelly': Alice Munro's Narrative Dialectics (1983)" in *Reading Alice Munro 1973-2013*, 23-44, 271-72. By Robert Thacker. Calgary: University of Calgary Press.

Thacker, Robert. 1998/1999/2016. "Introduction: Alice Munro, Writing 'Home': 'Seeing This Trickle in Time'." *Alice Munro Writing On....* Ed. Robert Thacker. *Essays on Canadian Writing* 66 (1998): 1-20. Rpt. in *The Rest of the Story: Critical Essays on Alice Munro*, 1-20. Edited by Robert Thacker. Toronto: ECW. Rpt. as "Alice Munro, Writing 'Home':

'Seeing This Trickle in Time' (1998)" in *Reading Alice Munro 1973-2013*, 145-65, 285-300 passim. By Robert Thacker. Calgary: University of Calgary Press.

Thacker, Robert. 2005. *Alice Munro: Writing Her Lives: A Biography*. Toronto: McClelland & Stewart.

Thacker, Robert. 2017. "'This Is Not a Story, Only Life': Wondering with Alice Munro." *Alice Munro's Miraculous Art: Critical Essays*, 15-40. Edited by Janice Fiamengo and Gerald Lynch. Ottawa: University of Ottawa Press. Reappraisals: Canadian Writers 38.

Ware, Tracy. 2006. "Tricks with 'a Sad Ring': The Endings of Alice Munro's 'The Ottawa Valley'." *Studies in Canadian Literature / Études en littérature canadienne* 31, no. 2: 126-41.

Uncanny Tracks in the Snow; or, Alice Munro as Assemblage Artist

Michael Trussler

[E]very single person needs to be reconciled to a world
into which he was born a stranger and in which, to the extent
of his distinct uniqueness, he always remains a stranger.
— **Hannah Arendt,**
***Essays in Understanding: 1930-1954* (308)**

"When you read a canonical work for the first time," Harold Bloom observes, "you encounter a stranger, an uncanny startlement rather than a fulfillment of expectations" (3). Although Alice Munro doesn't mention being startled when she describes her initial encounter with two canonical modernist texts (*Remembrance of Things Past* and *The Magic Mountain*, the former re-translated as *In Search of Lost Time*) in the "Finale" section of *Dear Life*, it's noteworthy that the four works comprising the "Finale" are especially concerned with the uncanny. (I will take up Munro's response to Proust and Mann shortly; for now, let me observe that their continual presence in her work is sometimes manifested as a direct allusion, frequently a shared thematic interest, but more often as a subtle flickering: it's as if a story such as "Powers" recasts *The Magic Mountain* as a dream distills and reworks a day experienced consciously.)

Of the "Finale," this *"unit ... that is autobiographical in feeling,"* Munro claims that these texts *"are the first and last – and the closest – things I have to say about my own life"* (*Dear Life* 255; emphasis in orig.). A beginning that's simultaneously an ending, this autobiographical text published in her early eighties recalls primarily childhood experiences that embody dislocating strangeness. In perhaps the most overt instance of such an estrangement, a corpse seems deliberately to single out the young Munro in "The Eye" and look at her with a slightly open eyelid. As she becomes an adolescent, this memory stays with her "the way you might believe and in fact remember that you once had another set of teeth," though when she eventually rejects this memory's accuracy it leaves "a dim sort of hole in [her] insides" ("The Eye" 270). If adult teeth occupy the physical space once held by baby teeth, the latter persist as a kind of ghostly memory regardless of their material absence, signalling the kind of uncanny blurring of temporal horizons that so fascinates Munro.

By mentioning her early reading of Proust and Mann, Munro reminds us of how so many of her characters are serious readers, a trait that is likely shared by those of us who keep returning to her work. It's noteworthy that the act of reading itself (and subsequent rereading) engages the uncanny: recall Juliet, in "Chance," looking at her marginalia in the Dodds book, "an orgy of underlining"; however, "what she had pounced on with such satisfaction at one time now seemed obscure and unsettling" (65). In-between my first encounter with *Dear Life* and subsequent revisiting of this and other collections, I read *The Magic Mountain* to discover a Munro that then became new to me. Her comment in "Dear Life" that the novel contains "a great argument between what on one side seemed to be a genial and progressive notion of life, and, on the other, a dark and somehow thrilling despair" (310) is accurate enough but hardly speaks to what likely retained her interest.

Obsessed with how time can't be measured, not even by narrative, *The Magic Mountain* is particularly attentive to the experience of historical change, involving a shift in perception that doesn't survive into the future, subject matter of considerable importance to Munro. When for instance the novel's characters listen to a gramophone for the first time, they find the technology not only astonishing but also unnerving. Because "[t]he singers he listened to, but could not see, had bodies that resided in America, in Milan, in Vienna, in Saint Petersburg" (Mann 633), the novel's central character, Hans Castorp, intuits that his previous notions of communal proximity have been usurped by this new technology; this sudden shift summons the uncanny: "[t]he ghost of a world-famous violinist played as if behind veils" (Mann 629).

That this sensibility is limited to the time of the machine's early twentieth-century invention seems clear; one can assume that someone possibly listening to The Beatles in Munro's story "Haven" (117) would not only be unperturbed by the technology but would also be entirely immune to the uncanny sensation experienced by Mann's pre-World War One characters. Film is another crucial technological invention whose original reception embodies an instance of the uncanny that is now lost to us; when Castorp and some friends watch a movie, Mann writes: "The actors who had been cast in the play they had just seen had long since been scattered to the winds; they had watched only phantoms, whose deeds had been reduced to a million photographs" (311). Mann then intriguingly relates this experience with the abject: "Once the illusion was over, there was something repulsive about the crowd's nerveless silence" (311).

Munro's description in "Leaving Maverley" of how Ray, the night policeman (a man with a Lacanian sense of "lack"), doesn't follow the plots in movies parallels her own reading habits; more importantly, Munro's description of the "bits and pieces" (72) of the movies Ray watches are an instance of surreal list-making that parallels Mann's similar technique of describing filmic images. While neither openly distinguishes between what Proust calls voluntary and involuntary memory, Mann and Munro both share his desire to investigate the "anaesthetic effect of habit" (Proust I, 11), an effect whose simplifying, corrosive power is manifested in both individual lives and culture at large. While powerful, habit isn't necessarily all-encompassing however; alternate possibilities are sometimes glimpsed, if not necessarily acted upon.

In her essay on "Vandals," the concluding story of Munro's 1994 collection *Open Secrets*, Nathalie Foy comments on the "many-layered" (149) nature of the story not only by showing how it is linked to others in the same volume, but also by noting that Munro's characters sometimes stumble upon the possibility that their lives might have taken various trajectories; when they "bump up against parallel, unerased narratives, they experience a kind of vertigo" (159). We might expand on this sense of "vertigo" by relating it to the condition of contemporaneity itself.

Observing that the present contains something that "we are absolutely incapable of living," Giorgio Agamben explains:

What remains unlived therefore is incessantly sucked back toward the origin, without ever being able to reach it. The present is nothing other than this unlived element in everything that is lived. That which impedes access to the present is precisely the mass of what for some reason (its traumatic character, its excessive nearness) we have not managed to live. (51)

Many of Munro's characters intuit that parts of their lives remain "unlived."

Munro frequently complicates her characters' sense of the "now" by showing them writing letters (or diaries) to addressees who necessarily cannot be present at the time of writing; and in fact, very often don't receive the original compositions. In Agamben's terms, then, through Munro's frequent use of the epistolary form, with its existential drive to speak from a continuously vanishing and almost unrealizable isolation, her characters brush up against an "unlived element" that is instantly eroded. Alongside the technique of deploying personal correspondence, however conflicted or misconstrued these letters may become, Munro has repeatedly used Alzheimer's disease to depict (literally and figuratively) the collapse of potentiality, a situation deftly described by N.R. Kleinfield's feature-length examination in *The New York Times* of the way the disease affects a family: "It was how one got to a moment in life when possibility ends."

To intimate how closely Munro interrelates Alzheimer's to phenomena beyond an individual patient, consider Grant's reaction in "The Bear Came Over the Mountain" to the notes Fiona leaves to identify objects in their kitchen:

> Cutlery, Dishtowels, Knifes. Couldn't she have just opened the drawers and seen what was inside? He remembered a story about the German soldiers on border patrol in Czechoslovakia during the war. Some Czech had told him that each of the patrol dogs wore a sign that said *Hund*. Why? said the Czechs, and the Germans said, Because that is a *hund*. (276)

While imagining words in spatial terms goes back as far as "Royal Beatings," and continues into *Dear Life* when the narrator of "The Eye" ponders the word "caught" and sees "a big wire net coming down ... choking you so you could never get out" (262), this passage implies quite incommensurate juxtapositions. A passage that refers to Alzheimer's capacity to defamiliarize domestic space in conjunction with the behaviour of Nazi soldiers during the Reich Protectorate (their peculiar behaviour seemingly involving a kind of cultural and linguistic aphasia) is writing that operates in several distinct and disjunctive registers simultaneously. When one further considers that "The Bear Came Over the Mountain" presumably takes place after Czechoslovakia dissolved in 1993, one recognizes how Munro overlays multiple temporalities almost invisibly.

Discussing the scene when Greta discovers her daughter Katy in-between train cars in "To Reach Japan," the initial story of *Dear Life*, J.R. (Tim) Struthers clarifies how this technique often signals trauma. Struthers detects how this single moment evokes "a sinister suggestion of what, metaphorically speaking, the future might hold for Katy. Not to ignore what *will very likely happen*, what *is already happening*, what *has already happened* to Greta and to Peter" (179). These various registers and temporalities aren't harmonized; rather, as Theodor W. Adorno describes such combinations: "Artworks synthesize ununifiable, nonidentical elements that grind away at each other" (176).

It is in homage to this kind of radical heterogeneity that the present essay includes standard literary criticism along with forms of paratactic discourse and quotation. In what follows, my attention will be devoted primarily to "Vandals," the last story in *Open Secrets*. But throughout these fragmented sections I will also refer to "Powers," the last story in *Runaway*, and the "Finale" of *Dear Life* because they function as a kind of prism through which other stories refract.

***

On Taxidermy and Literary Assemblage: Alice Munro's "Vandals"

> For Thucydides, the fullness of history doesn't lie either in
> what men did or what they said, what we could see and describe
> or what we could hear. It seeps through the cracks
> between hearing and seeing, speaking and acting.
> — W.J.T. Mitchell, *Picture Theory* (106)

Munro has often described artistic form by using spatial analogies. In the early story "Material," the narrator compares her memory of a former acquaintance with this woman's subsequent depiction in a short story written by the narrator's husband: "There is Dotty lifted out of life and held in light, suspended in the marvelous clear jelly that Hugo has spent all his life learning how to make" (43). Art – I'm paraphrasing Arthur Schopenhauer here – has the capacity to isolate material, to pluck the "particular" out of reality's plenitude and hold it up for "contemplation" (I, 185), and this distillation creates an alternate way of knowing. In her oft-cited essay "What Is Real?" Munro rejects linear narrative – when reading, she explains, "I don't take up a story and follow it as if it were a road.... It's more like a house ... [which] encloses space and makes connections between one enclosed space and another and presents what is outside in a new way" (1072). This spatial simile implies that art is more phenomenological than precisely representational: art "presents what is outside in a new way." Munro later clarifies this phenomenological component of art in her introduction to the Penguin edition of *Selected Stories*; returning to her earlier house comparison, she adds:

> You go inside and stay there for a while, wandering back and forth and settling where you like and discovering how the room and corridors relate to each other, how the world outside is altered by being viewed from these windows. And you, the visitor, the reader, are altered as well by being in this enclosed space.... You can go back again and again, and the house, the story, always contains more than you saw the last time. It has also a sturdy sense of itself, out of being built out of its own necessity.... (xvi-xvii)

If the art object has phenomenological qualities – both the reader and the external world are "altered" within its presence – the art object is also vigorously autonomous: it has "a sturdy sense of itself" that is independent of its reception. If we take Munro's house analogy – with its useful figuration of a three-dimensional object that is poised between an inside and an outside – and extend this analogy in two directions, we can gain a better understanding not only of her story "Vandals," but also of her recent writing generally. The first direction shows the resemblance to the assemblage work done by Joseph Cornell, Robert Rauschenberg,

and Edward Kienholz; and the second picks up on taxidermy's confluence between realism and open artifice as a further analogy for Munro's
notion of artistic form. Given the relatively benign, lyrical nature of
Cornell's boxes and the frequently semiotically-inclined Rauschenberg
assemblages, it's most valuable to link Munro's story with the potentially
violent, so-called "environmental" pieces of Kienholz. One can easily
imagine Munro rendering his mixed media tableau *The Wait 1964-65*
(which is part of the Whitney Museum's collection) into a narrative.

***

The Wait illuminates the poignancy of passing time and the sorrowful
isolation of the elderly in a life-size domestic tableau. The figure of an
old woman, constructed of cow bones and encased in plastic coating,
clutches a taxidermied cat and sits beneath a framed portrait of a young
man who was presumably her beloved. In place of her face is a glass jar
with a photograph of a young, attractive woman on the front and a cow
skull set inside. She wears a necklace of glass canning jars containing
crosses and gold figurines that represent her memories as imagined by
the artist: "her childhood on a farm and move on to girlhood, waiting
for her man, marriage, bearing children, being loved, wars, family, death
and then senility, where everything becomes a hodgepodge." She awaits
her imminent death to the song of a live parakeet in a nearby cage, a
disparity that renders the melancholy of the woman's situation all the
more evident.
     — Whitney Museum of American Art

***

Similar to Munro's house simile, the Kienholz piece defamiliarizes – and
yet maintains – the ordinary; additionally, its combination of a human
figure, cloth, photographs, and a stuffed cat near a live bird imply several
discontinuous narratives while comingling ontologies, a technique
shared by Munro's "Vandals," a story offering three temporal horizons:
when Bea writes (though doesn't complete) the letter; the earlier February afternoon when Liza and her husband, Warren, trashed the house;
various scenes from not only the courtship of Bea and Ladner, but also

their interaction with Liza and Kenny when they were children. What links all three temporal horizons is the uncertainty as to whether Bea is aware that Ladner had sexually abused both children and whether the vandalism is therefore an act of deferred revenge. If pedophilia and its aftermath form the primary narrative trajectory of the story, this particular narrative is only one component of a text that compresses within it much of Western philosophy and aesthetics alongside references to an almost apocalyptic range of military violence that defies conceptualization. Put differently, in a house composed of numerous rooms, sexual violation saturates the mood in only one of these rooms. "Vandals" is a kind of assemblage piece, a literary installation that, in intimating a collector's drive for totality, provides an allegorical rendering of Munro's more recent poetics that expands upon the earlier simile of short story as house. Let me mention a few of the various materials Munro uses to *assemble* the story.

***

"Powers" begins as a diary, but we can't identify the diarist's name until the story shifts into third person in the next section. March 13, 1927 was a Sunday, though Nancy couldn't intuit that her future husband, Wilf, with his love of music, would likely be interested to know that on the next day, March 14, 1927, Stravinsky would finish his score for the opera *Oedipus Rex*. What she does record is that, after she'd walked down a street in snowshoes because of an unexpected storm, her tracks quickly "were entirely filled in" (270). But tracks appearing in the snow (the same snow that hides a corpse) are what a diary's ink places upon a white page and if Nancy is still alive as I write this sentence, she's 89, and she might not remember the person who wrote those diary pages (effectively filling in the tracks) just as the nineteenth century somehow disappears (as if it had never been) as the story drifts into the late twentieth century, a disorienting place that finds Nancy's children worried that she has "taken to Living in the Past," yet "what she believes she is doing, what she wants to do if she can get the time to do it, is not so much to live in the past as to open it up and get one good look at it" (330). But how to succeed in doing this broad and intricate thing when there's this "feeling of something being out of kilter" (303) that accompanies human experience and when, unavoidably, "'The mind's a weird piece of business'" (308)? Eavesdropping on Nancy's unfulfilled wish to tell Ollie about the incidents of her life, the reader might surmise that Nancy is one of Munro's most emblematic characters, someone who never finds the narratee whom her life seemingly requires.

***

Apart from being a taxidermist, Ladner is a physically scarred World War Two veteran with a propensity for reading: "There were books in the house – a small section of books on taxidermy, the others mostly in sets. The History of the Second World War. The History of Science. The History of Philosophy. The History of Civilization. The Peninsular War. The Peloponnesian Wars. The French and Indian Wars. Bea thought of his long evenings in the winter – his orderly solitude, his systematic reading and barren contentment" (273). Systematic reading indeed (and odd to find an almost identical library belonging to Dr. Fox, the acerbic suitor who rejects the narrator of "Amundsen," a story that is playfully reliant on *The Magic Mountain*). It's worthwhile to ponder all of the words, details, events, people, and ideas that Ladner has mentally concretized over the years while he has gone through these books. Let's consider only one text. In *History of Peloponnesian War*, Thucydides cautions that, when trying to understand the past, one "must not be misled by the exaggerated fancies of the poets...[; rather, one's] conclusions [must rest] upon the clearest evidence which can be had" (13-14). That Munro's story also cites Aristotle, who saw history and poetry somewhat differently, is less important than what Thucydides says about the way soldiers view their personal military experience: "though men will always judge any war in which they are actually fighting to be the greatest at the time, but, after it is over, revert to their admiration of some other which has preceded, still the Peloponnesian, if estimated by the actual facts, will certainly prove to have been the greatest ever known" (14). Remembering what it felt like to be wounded at Caen during World War Two, Ladner presumably read Thucydides with a degree of irony. If we consider that the story also refers to the possibility of nuclear Armageddon, we must wonder at the range of this text's references to destruction. What's most noteworthy, however, is Thucydides' observation that, when people participate in events, they believe those events to be definitive of human experience. What is the relation between temporality and knowledge?

To say that Munro is curious about the intersection between temporality and the vagaries of the mind is an obvious understatement: usually in a Munro story, the present is in many ways unknowable and the past remains equally difficult to ascertain. Most often, Munro uses characters as a device to embody the mystery of temporality. But the psychology of individual characters is only one component of the house that Munro asks us to inhabit when we read her work. Remember the Kienholz installation with its heterogeneous registers of meaning. Deeply interested in what survives into the future – consider the title story from *Too Much Happiness* – Munro frequently creates stories that are a kind of time capsule, but a time capsule that's self-consciously decaying. Raymond Williams' notion of "structures of feeling" (128-35) is useful here. By "structures of feeling," Williams means those aspects of contemporary consciousness which exist apart from taxonomies. Intuitively at hand to those living during a specific moment, these "structures of feelings" won't be visible to future historians. If we see "Vandals" as an installation, we can say that the contemporary horror of child abuse forms part of the installation's response to the collection's treatment of the present, a structure of feeling, that links "Vandals" with other stories in *Open Secrets* such as "Spaceships Have Landed" and the title story. In its efforts to explore what constitutes the present, "Vandals" also pays close attention to the nature of mimesis itself.

***

"In reality," states Marcel towards the end of *In Search of Lost Time*, "every reader is, while he is reading, the reader of his own self" (Proust VI, 322). If this is accurate, what, then, took place in Munro's mind when she was reading Proust? I often imagine her reading – in ways similar to how she describes Juliet engaging in an "an orgy of underlining" ("Chance" 65) – paying exuberant attention to several sections in Proust. For those of us who continually return to Munro over our reading lives, reading Proust becomes quite strange. We frequently come upon passages in Proust where, yes, we may actually read ourselves, but reading in this way is especially uncanny because it's almost as though we are also reading

Proust over Munro's shoulder. To give one example that illuminates Munro's characterization of Nancy late in "Powers," here's Proust on change and viewing the past: "For a man cannot change, that is to say become another person, while continuing to obey the dictates of the self which he has ceased to be. ... But, as a rule, with this particular period of his life from which [Swann] was emerging, when he made an effort, if not to remain in it, at least to obtain a clear view of it while he still could, he discovered that already it was too late" (Proust I, 537). When I read these sentences I can well imagine them being underlined in Munro's own hand so the passage I read has been transformed by her: "what she believes she is doing, what she wants to do if she can get the time to do it, is not so much to live in the past as to open it up and get one good look at it" ("Powers" 330). I could offer numerous other instances where one can read Proust specifically through Munro as a lens; let me simply invite the reader to look at what Proust says on multiple selves and imagine reading these passages with Munro's writing in mind (Proust, V 660 and 803).

***

When one considers Aristotle's claim that "from childhood it is instinctive in human beings to imitate" (*Poetics* 47), one has to wonder what he would have made of the following tableau in "Vandals": near some live geese and swans swimming in a pond, "was a glass-fronted case containing a stuffed golden eagle with its wings spread, a gray owl, and a snow owl. The case was an old gutted freezer, with a window set in its side and a camouflage of gray and green swirls of paint. // 'Ingenious,' said Bea. // Ladner said, 'I use what I can get'" (271). While Aristotle might have judged Ladner to be insane, Munro's audience is used to the mimetic conventions of the diorama as a form, enjoys optical illusion and is obsessive about boundaries and borders.

Taxidermy is uncanny as it flickers between numerous boundaries: science and art; culture and nature; realism and open artifice. As the text states regarding Ladner's craft: "Ladner fitted the skin around a body in which nothing was real" (286). Taxidermy also partakes in our culture's overall concern for the funereal and the ethos of commemoration. Yann Martel's taxidermist in *beatrice and virgil* claims: "When I work on an animal, ... [w]hat I am actually doing is extracting and refining memory from death. In that, I am no different from a historian" (96). If the story's taxidermy mirrors its subdued emphasis on historical knowledge generally and the loss of human life through conflict specifically, the mimetic impulse that animates taxidermy extends to the way that "Vandals" is curious about the implications of imitation.

Just before the text introduces us to Liza's secret collection, her private *Wunderkammer*, "Vandals" turns us into voyeurs as we watch Ladner splash around in the pond, "imitating Bea" (288). This spectacle of momentary cruelty confuses Liza: "Part of her wanted to make Ladner stop ... before the damage was done, and part of her longed for that very damage, the damage Ladner could do, the ripping open, the final delight of it" (288). Mimesis might be natural to our species; it might be an activity with pedagogical value – as a teacher, Bea has often helped out with class field trips, some of them going to the Royal Ontario Museum, others to Stratford so that students can have "their annual dose of Shakespeare" (264), but in the instance when Ladner imitates Bea, mimesis-as-parody becomes a weapon, one that induces *schadenfreude* in its audience. The story's pronounced fascination with mimesis is an important component of the assemblage piece Munro creates. As I suggested earlier, another part of this "installation" includes materials that "decay"; numerous references in the story embody the deterioration of cultural memory.

When Liza and her husband trash Bea and Ladner's house, this act recalls the Vandals sacking Rome and invading northern Africa; that Liza has doctrinal issues with her kind of Christianity reinforces this connection (though there's no evidence she accepts the Arian heresy). While Liza destroys Ladner's stuffed animals, Warren turns on the black-and-white TV: most of the channels show "nothing but snow or ripples. The only thing he could get clear was a scene from the old series with the blond girl in the harem outfit – she was a witch – and the J.R. Ewing actor when he was so young he hadn't yet become J.R." (279-80). This seemingly minor reference to a 1960s TV show is key to Munro's engagement with the deteriorations of cultural memory. As a kind of "built-in-obsolescence" – how many of Munro's future readers will recognize the *I Dream of Jeannie* rerun? – the reference significantly blurs historical fact with irony. Barbara Eden played a genie, not a witch;

however, Warren is bang on insofar as the show was NBC's rip-off of ABC's hit *Bewitched.*

If we contemplate the history of the Germanic Vandal tribe that is the background to the mess being made in the living room in the story, we find the horrific violence of almost two hundred and fifty years of conflict that spread over two continents, influencing presumably millions of lives, becoming reduced to a black-and-white TV screen that pinpoints a moment in Larry Hagman's career. As an aside: a visual artist such as Kienholz might render such a range of reference with equally sharp irony by juxtaposing a faded photograph of a couple getting a hot dog at a diner alongside a copy of the statue of the flag raising at Iwo Jima near an actual trash can that alludes to Beckett (*The Portable War Memorial 1968*).

After turning on the TV and seeing the *I Dream of Jeannie* rerun, Warren wants Liza to share in his discovery – "'Look at this,' he said. 'Like going back in time'" (280) – but she ignores him; she is too busy destroying things. Look at this, says a taxidermist; it's like going back in time. Look and learn, says Thucydides to the future. But we very rarely look at the past and perhaps we can't learn much about anything: both human activity and time are too busy destroying things. On that note, it's quite disturbing to read Thucydides' account of Greek POWs incarcerated in quarries (186-87) by the Syracusans; the conditions there resembled the Nazi quarries at Mauthausen. I'm not trying to make Munro into a moralist precisely. But a story such as "Vandals" requires us, as we wander from room to room in its structure, to recognize how little we know about what constitutes the fabric of human experience.

***

Oft him ānhaga   āre ġebīdeð,
Metudes miltse,   þēah þe hē mōdċeariġ
ġeond lagulāde   longe sceolde
hrēran mid hondum   hrīmċealde sæ,
wadan wræclāstas.   Wyrd bið ful ārǣd.
— *The Wanderer*, ll. 1-5

Fate is inexorable. Though irony is quick as footsteps isolating and then erasing memory and desire alike – until fear quickens Kant himself and Wordsworth's beloved sister too into dying most likely of Alzheimer's disease, a diagnosis no one then could have foreseen.

***

Literary assemblages often employ quotation, but as we have seen regarding the allusion to *I Dream of Jeannie*, these quotations can be reworked with irony. Selective quotation can provide a different kind of irony. When Ladner cites Aristotle on a sign – *"Nature does nothing uselessly"* (271) – he ironically castigates the human proclivity for waste, but Munro's story undermines Ladner's didactic intentions. Ladner has omitted Aristotle's essential idea: Nature, Aristotle argues in *Politics*, may indeed make "nothing in vain" (250), but his point is that by giving humans the capacity for speech, Nature intends for us to use speech to articulate the difference between "the just and the unjust" and "good and evil" (250). Certainly "Vandals" is concerned with the differences between good and evil: from the text's subdued reference to nuclear war, which is abstract, to the singularities of child abuse, "Vandals" charts the immense complexity of guilt, inheritance, and ethical choice. That Ladner uses a kind of Procrustean rhetoric – selective quotation – reinforces what I see as one of the primary techniques of the literary assemblage: in the desire to encapsulate the urge toward totality, irony becomes as necessary as the compression of various discourses that operate in different registers.

An essential component of the story's urge towards totality arises when Bea makes an off-handed remark in her letter to Liza. Confused about her dream that involves people waiting around a Canadian Tire store every seven years to receive the bones of their dead, Bea asks of this practice: "Is it pagan or Christian or what?" (263). While this unsent letter makes it clear that Bea suspects it was Liza who vandalized her house, and thus perhaps her Christianity is less pure than it should be, the story uses this question to accomplish several objectives. It implicitly raises the problem of hermeneutics: can a culture whose primary relationship to reality is through TV have any substantial understanding of pagan reality? It opens up the overall problem of the relationship between the unconscious and the rational and their links to the corresponding world views – pagan; Christian – that might be used to adjudicate between these two parts of the mind. Bea's question also points to what will become an ongoing thematic exploration in *Runaway*, which continually sets Greek against Christian thought. Let us consider Munro's choice to introduce this story with someone writing down the details of a dream in a letter.

In the attempt to answer the question of who it is that is present when we dream, Maurice Blanchot notes that when we dream we "often have the impression that we are taking part in a spectacle that was not intended for us" (144). Because the disconcerting state of dreaming unsettles subjectivity, upon waking we often reach out to share this vibrant but often isolating experience with others. Hence when Bea describes her sense of estrangement – "A woman ... seemed to know me but I didn't know her and I thought, Why is this always happening?" (262) – she confirms Blanchot's treatment of dream mechanics. After establishing the unstable relationship that dreaming fosters between the individual and the community, Blanchot then compares the oneiric state, which is a "refusal to sleep at the heart of sleep" with the "neutral vigilance" of writing itself (147). Munro's story certainly embodies Blanchot's sense that our dreams result in a seesawing between isolation and community. That Bea describes her dream in a letter that she decides not to send implies that Liza isn't the right narratee for her dream.

More importantly, this scene underscores a surprising parallel between Munro and Blanchot's connecting writing with insomnia and being "suspended between being and non-being" (147). Trying to include her narratee, Liza, within her dream experience and its repercussions upon waking, Bea adds that she still feels Ladner's presence:

> "Then I have to realize that isn't so, every morning, and I feel a chill. I feel a shrinking. I feel as if I had a couple of wooden planks lying across my chest, which doesn't incline me to get up. A common experience I'm having. But at the moment I'm not having it, just describing it, and in fact I am rather happy sitting here with my bottle of red wine."
> This was a letter Bea Doud never sent and in fact never finished. (221)

While it may be common for the bereaved to know and yet not feel that a loved one has died, it is less common for people to differentiate between description and ontology, which is a distinction made most often by writers and other artists. Thus, "suspended between being and non-being," Bea is reduced to silence.

Assemblage artists, though, often create their works from this place; in fact, the awkward and precise and yet blurred division between representation and actuality is what these installations embody. Literary assemblage can't employ physically heterogeneous objects, such as Kienholz constructing a woman out of cow bones who is seemingly oblivious to her own memory. Through juxtaposition of divergent discourses, subject positions, a wide-ranging irony and insinuation, a story such as "Vandals," however, can create an art object that alters the "outside world" as much as it does the reader.

***

> All this time [Nancy] had been waiting for [Ollie] to say one true word. All this afternoon or maybe a good part of her life. She had been waiting, and now he had said it.
> No.
> — Munro, "Powers" (328)

> Molly Bloom: "and yes I said yes I will Yes."
> — Joyce, *Ulysses* (933)

***

Looking into a café window, Nancy "stopped to read what they were advertising. // *Bless the grass*. And behind these scrawled words there was an angry-looking, wrinkled-up, almost teary creature," somehow showing "an elderly gentleman in a dressing-gown and a travelling cap … [and] I at once realized to my dismay that the intruder was nothing but my own reflection in the looking-glass" (Munro, "Powers" 314; Freud, "The 'Uncanny'" 371). Upon unexpectedly seeing their reflections, both Nancy and Freud are alienated from their own images as aging beings, creating what Jean Améry calls a "shudder" in which "the thin everyday layer is ruptured ... [and] then we are suddenly confronted with the horror that we are both ego and non-ego and as this hybrid can call our customary ego into question" (29).

***

Footsteps in the snow; sentences beneath or overtop other sentences: "She said that the reason the Dark Ages were dark was not that we couldn't learn anything about them but that *we could not remember anything we did learn*, and that was because of the names" (Munro, "The Jack Randa Hotel" 164; emphasis added) and perhaps worse, because we can't ever entirely remember stepping into the tracks of others.

***

"[T]hat word – *home* – seemed slightly off kilter to [Grace]"; [Ollie's] "off-kilter attraction" [to Tessa]; "[t]he feeling of something being out of kilter"; "some people not so old but just off kilter" (Munro, "Passion" 173, "Powers" 293, 303, "In Sight of the Lake" 229). The words "dear life" from the title story of Munro's last collection envelop that phrase's precious quality, but also panic as a mother grabs her baby "for dear life" (318) to save her, and then the narrator discovers from an elderly woman peering into the narrator's own childhood home (which had once been the old woman's) that we don't live inside our own lives; this life of ours has been inhabited by others before.

***

Is Nancy from "In Sight of the Lake" an incarnation of Nancy from "Powers," newly arrived in a setting designed by Giorgio de Chirico, with its stopped clocks and a boy riding his bicycle backwards, a setting in which random, everyday objects take on an uncanny incoherence? Seemingly from out of nowhere she notices "[a] jacket flung in such a way that you could not see – or she cannot see – what is wrong" ("In Sight of the Lake" 222). And yet this story seems to be spun from Hans

Castorp's hallucination as he barely escapes freezing to death in the Alps while he recognizes a Mediterranean landscape he has never visited although "he *remembered* it" (Mann 481) and then he hallucinates his own inner *Zeitgeist*:

> We dream anonymously and communally, though each in his own way. The great soul, of which we are just a little piece, dreams through us so to speak, dreams in our many different ways its own eternal, secret dream – about its youth, its hope, its joy, its peace, and its bloody feast. (Mann 485)

Tessa in "Powers" as an emanation of Mann's Elly Brand with her "extraordinary, sensational, unseemly" abilities (Mann 646).

***

> Remember how long you have been putting off these things, and how often you have received an opportunity from the gods and yet have not used it. You must now at last perceive of what kind of a universe you are a part, and the true nature of the lord of the universe of which your being is a part, and how a limit of time is fixed for you, which if you do not use for clearing away the clouds from your mind, it will go and you will go, and it will never return.
> — Marcus Aurelius, *Meditations* (20-21)

***

When Greta, the poet from "To Reach Japan," the opening story of *Dear Life*, enters a room at the Vancouver Art Gallery, she'll see a wall divided into a triptych streaming from three video projectors: first, the films move forward in chronological time and then the same scenes are rewound backwards in slow motion, only to start again from a different beginning:

In one, the characters from "Leaving Maverley" ("They had not ordered the snowstorm, after all ... a runaway ... as they tackled poor old Dante ... 'That's when it can start to feel weird' ... What an excellent word – 'remains'.' Like something left to dry out . in sooty layers in a cupboard"); in the middle, Joyce's Gabriel Conroy swooning into falling snow; in the third, Nancy from "Powers" becomes Dante to Wilf as senile Virgil: "Gently, inexorably leading her away from what begins to crumble behind her, to crumble and darken tenderly into something like soot and soft ash." Volcanic and Anglo-Saxon: darkening livestories of snowflakes falling.

***

Ulrich Baer's *Spectral Evidence: The Photography of Trauma* critiques the dominant Western historiographical practice of expressing temporality in a continuous, endlessly developing narrative. His study examines Jean-Martin Charcot's photographs of hysterics, the work of two photographers who've returned some fifty years later to record sites of Nazi atrocities, and Dariusz Jabłoński's *Fotoamator*, a documentary film created from slides originally taken by a Nazi official of Jews confined to the Lodz ghetto. Baer's starting point is that the West developed its way of thinking about time from Heraclitus's metaphor of time as a continuous river. From this metaphor, we've devised the narrative of historical progression. But Baer maintains that there was an alternative approach to temporal experience, an atomistic response that he ascribes to Democritus, which, as opposed to the steady river stream observed by Heraclitus, conceives

> of the world as occurring in bursts and explosions, as the rainfall of reality privileges the moment rather than the story, the event rather than the unfolding, particularity rather than generality. ... [Photography] is also an attempt to acknowledge that for uncounted numbers of individuals, significant parts of life are not experienced in sequence but as explosive bursts of isolated events (5-6).

To Baer, we haven't yet understood how photography actually functions; more important to his argument, we haven't learned what's entailed in the creation of and response to atrocity photographs. For him, we must attempt the difficult task of trying to understand how trauma's "'immediacy' must be studied as it unfolds according to its own dynamic, at once *outside of* and yet *inside of* the same moment" (10-11; emphasis in orig.). Nancy doesn't refer to Baer, but she very well might because his account of Democritean perspective elucidates some of the problems she is trying to ponder, namely life's penchant for showing her unintelligible images.

***

George Steiner became mystified by simultaneity because of places like Auschwitz; describing two men tortured to death in the camps, he writes: "Precisely at the same hour ... the overwhelming plurality of human beings ... were sleeping or eating or going to a film or making love or worrying about the dentist. This is where my imagination balks. The two orders of simultaneous experience are so different, so irreconcilable to any common norm of human values, their coexistence is so hideous a paradox" (156). One of these human beings, safely havened in North America, could easily have been the mysteriously self-aware / self-effacing narrator of Munro's story "Pride," a man who cannot sleep one night during the war and must walk the streets because he has heard on the radio of a civilian boat sunk off Newfoundland:

> I had to think of the people gone to the bottom of the sea. Old women, nearly old women like my mother, hanging on to their knitting. Some kid bothered by a toothache. ... I had a very strange feeling that was part horror and part – as near as I can describe it – a kind of chilly exhilaration. ... // Of course this feeling vanished when I got used to seeing things, later in the war. Naked healthy buttocks, thin old buttocks, all of them being herded into the gas chambers. (139-40)

These sentences are some of the most compelling, bizarre sentences Munro has ever written, blurring as they do a rare empathy, then a discharge enjoining the sublime and *schadenfreude*, and finally creating something else utterly strange because no photos exist of people being "herded" into gas chambers: all that remains are four photographs the Polish underground managed to smuggle out of Auschwitz-Birkenau in 1944: mostly out-of-focus, two show women in a small field forced to run to a crematorium and two show *Sonderkommando* at the fire-pits.

***

"But good use can be made of everything, if you are willing."
— Munro, "Pride" (134)

***

That Munro as a young woman seemed somehow attuned to continental philosophy and the new psychology: the prostitute on the stairs between two men in "Voices" appearing as if divined from Freud himself because, according to him, "staircases (and analogous things) were unquestionably symbols of copulation" (*Interpretation* 472); more surprisingly, Munro, suffering insomnia – noting "I was not myself" ("Night" 276) – links this sleeplessness with the mad, uncanny desire to kill her sister in their bedroom, "the most familiar place, the room where we had lain for all of our lives and thought ourselves most safe" ("Night" 277). Not herself, then, during insomnia, Munro would seem to have sensed what Emmanuel Levinas calls the "*il y a*" (46), the primordial, inescapable emptiness that is terrifying, the ground of all existence, a state that he believes is analogous to insomnia, a condition in which "[t]he present is welded to the past, is entirely the heritage of that past: it renews nothing" (48).

***

Sadie, whose dead eyelid would fasten upon Munro, playing guitar for a local radio show, singing a song of her own: "'Hello, hello, hello, everybody –'" ("The Eye" 258). Then "half an hour later it was, 'Good-bye, good-bye, good-bye everybody'" ("The Eye" 259).

This greeting, Munro's microcosm of what stands in for our lives.

Note

I would like to thank Medrie Purdham who suggested the phrase "built-in-obsolescence" to me and Ben Salloum who brought to my attention the image of Nazi soldiers with signs identifying a *hund*.

Works Cited

Adorno, Theodor W. *Aesthetic Theory*. Ed. Gretel Adorno and Rolf Tiedemann. Trans. Robert Hullot-Kentor. Minneapolis: U of Minnesota P, 1997. Theory and History of Literature 88.

Agamben, Giorgio. "What Is the Contemporary?" *What Is an Apparatus? and Other Essays*. Trans. David Kishik and Stefan Pedatella. Stanford, CA: Stanford UP, 2009. 39-54, 56. Meridean: Crossing Aesthetics.

Améry, Jean. *On Aging: Revolt and Resignation*. Trans. John D. Barlow. Bloomington, IN: Indiana UP, 1994.

Arendt, Hannah. *Essays in Understanding: 1930-1954*. Ed. Jerome Kohn. New York: Harcourt Brace, 1994.

Aristotle. *Poetics. Aristotle's Poetics*. Trans. and introd. James Hutton. New York: W.W. Norton, 1982. 43-79.

---. *Politics*. Based on the trans. by Benjamin Jowett. *On Man in the Universe*. Ed. and introd. Louise Ropes Loomis. Roslyn, NY: Walter J. Black, 1943. 244-414.

Aurelius, Marcus. *Meditations. Marcus Aurelius and His Times: The Transition from Paganism to Christianity*. Based on the trans. by George Long. Roslyn, NY: Walter J. Black, 1945. 11-133.

Baer, Ulrich. *Spectral Evidence: The Photography of Trauma*. Cambridge, MA: MIT, 2002.

Blanchot, Maurice. *Friendship*. Trans. Elizabeth Rottenberg. Stanford, CA: Stanford UP, 1997. Meridian: Crossing Aesthetics.

Bloom, Harold. *The Western Canon: The Books and School of the Ages*. New York: Harcourt Brace, 1994.

Foy, Nathalie. "'Darkness Collecting': Reading 'Vandals' as a Coda to *Open Secrets*." *The Rest of the Story: Critical Essays on Alice Munro*. Ed. Robert Thacker. Toronto: ECW, 1999. 147-68.

Freud, Sigmund. *The Interpretation of Dreams*. Trans. James Strachey. Ed. Angela Richards. London: Penguin, 1991. Vol. 4 of *The Penguin Freud Library*. 15 vols. 1990-93.

---. "The 'Uncanny' (1919)." *Art and Literature*. Trans. James Strachey. Ed. Albert Dickson. London: Penguin, 1990. 335-76. Vol. 14 of *The Penguin Freud Library*. 15 vols. 1990-93.

Joyce, James. *Finnegans Wake*. Harmondsworth, Eng.: Penguin, 1976.

---. *Ulysses*. Introd. Declan Kiberd. Toronto: Penguin, 1990.

Kienholz, Edward. *The Portable War Memorial 1968*. <https://artmuseum. princeton.edu/collections/objects/18741>.

---. *The Wait 1964-65*. <https://whitney.org/collection/works/822>.

Kleinfield, N.R. *Fraying at the Edges*. *The New York Times* 1 May 2016: Special Section. <https:www.nytimes.com/interactive/2016/05/01/ nyregion/living-with-alzheimers.html>.

Levinas, Emmanuel. *Time and the Other [and additional essays]*. Trans. Richard A. Cohen. Pittsburgh, PA: Duquesne UP, 1987.

Mann, Thomas. *The Magic Mountain*. Trans. John E. Woods. 1995. New York: Vintage, 1996.

Martel, Yann. *beatrice and virgil*. Toronto: Alfred A. Knopf Canada, 2010.

Mitchell, W.J.T. *Picture Theory*. Chicago: U of Chicago P, 1994.

Munro, Alice. "Amundsen." *Dear Life*. Toronto: McClelland & Stewart, 2012. 31-66.

---. "The Bear Came Over the Mountain." *Hateship, Friendship, Courtship, Loveship, Marriage*. Toronto: McClelland & Stewart, 2001. 274-322.

---. "Chance." *Runaway*. Toronto: McClelland & Stewart, 2004. 48-86.

---. "Dear Life." *Dear Life*. Toronto: McClelland & Stewart, 2012. 299-319.

---. "The Eye." *Dear Life*. Toronto: McClelland & Stewart, 2012. 257-70.

---. "Finale." *Dear Life*. Toronto: McClelland & Stewart, 2012. 255-319.

---. "Haven." *Dear Life*. Toronto: McClelland & Stewart, 2012. 110-32.

---. "In Sight of the Lake." *Dear Life*. Toronto: McClelland & Stewart, 2012. 217-32.

---. Introduction. *Selected Stories*. Toronto: Penguin, 1998. ix-xvii.

---. "The Jack Randa Hotel." *Open Secrets*. Toronto: McClelland & Stewart, 1994. 161-89.

---. "Leaving Maverley." *Dear Life*. Toronto: McClelland & Stewart, 2012. 67-90.

---. "Material." *Something I've Been Meaning To Tell You.* Toronto: McGraw-Hill Ryerson, 1974. 24-44.

---. "Night." *Dear Life.* Toronto: McClelland & Stewart, 2012. 271-85.

---. "Open Secrets." *Open Secrets.* Toronto: McClelland & Stewart, 1994. 129-60.

---. "Powers." *Runaway.* Toronto: McClelland & Stewart, 2004. 270-335.

---. "Pride." *Dear Life.* Toronto: McClelland & Stewart, 2012. 133-53.

---. "Royal Beatings." *Who Do You Think You Are?* Toronto: Macmillan of Canada, 1978. 1-22.

---. "Spaceships Have Landed." *Open Secrets.* Toronto: McClelland & Stewart, 1994. 226-60.

---. "To Reach Japan." *Dear Life.* Toronto: McClelland & Stewart, 2012. 3-30.

---. "Too Much Happiness." *Too Much Happiness.* Toronto: McClelland & Stewart, 2009. 246-303.

---. "Vandals." *Open Secrets.* Toronto: McClelland & Stewart, 1994. 261-94.

---. "What Is Real?" *The Norton Reader: An Anthology of Expository Prose.* Gen. ed. Arthur M. Eastman. 8th ed. New York: W.W. Norton, 1992. 1071-74.

Proust, Marcel. *In Search of Lost Time.* Trans. C.K. Scott Moncrieff, Terence Kilmartin, and Andreas Mayor. Rev. D.J. Enright. 6 vols. 1992. New York: Modern Library, 1998.

Schopenhauer, Arthur. *The World as Will and Representation.* Trans. E.F.J. Payne. 2 vols. New York: Dover, 1969.

Steiner, George. *Language and Silence: Essays on Language, Literature, and the Inhuman.* 1967. New York: Atheneum, 1970.

Struthers, J.R. (Tim). "Traveling with Munro: Reading 'To Reach Japan'." *Alice Munro:* Hateship, Friendship, Courtship, Loveship, Marriage; Runaway; Dear Life. Ed. Robert Thacker. London: Bloomsbury, 2016. 163-83, 231-44 passim.

Thucydides. *History of Peloponnesian War: Selections.* Trans. not mentioned. Chicago: Henry Regnery, 1948. A Great Books Foundation Edition.

The Wanderer. Introduction to Old English. By Peter S Baker. Malden, MA: Blackwell, 2003. 195-200.

Williams, Raymond. *Marxism and Literature.* Oxford, Eng.: Oxford UP, 1977.

"The Music Itself":
Musical Representation and Musicality
in the Short Stories of Alice Munro

Megan LaPierre

Introduction

Classification of the arts into separate categories further specifies the progression of genre: to divide based on relations to technique and medium. Preoccupations with the "creation, performance, and consumption" of literature and music, as distinguished from other arts, prevail "in all cultures," Diana Omigie argues, possibly because of their shared temporal development and resulting sense of narrative (1). Accordingly, the interdisciplinary intersection of music and literature remains certain – and paradoxically elusive in provoking controversial terminology such as "musicality," despite the centuries-long interplay between the two art forms. By way of music and literature having been mutually shaping forces on each respective artistic landscape, it is unsurprising for musicologists and composers to indicate the arcs in the storytelling of musical works, and likewise for critics and writers to refer to the intensely music-like qualities of literature. Music is, in and of itself, fluid in meaning and through the process of translating it to language, the waters become even murkier. As Emilie Crapoulet proposes, musicality in the context of literature inevitably reads, in Mieke Bal's terminology, as a 'travelling concept' (80).

Linguistic description of a musical work of performance (including but not limited to literary representation) often reaches an impasse so that commentary, as Roland Barthes argues in "The Grain of the Voice," "unfailingly takes the most facile and trivial form, that of the epithet" (179), instead of operating on a serious and detailed level. Similarly, there is a hesitancy in the literary representation of music, a sense that literature may be an insufficient vehicle to encompass affective qualities that transcend language. The imperfection in translating any single vernacular into another parallels the self-limited rendering of musical experience into prose. However, as Stephen Benson notes, this inarticulacy often paradoxically becomes a fundamental component of the text, if not its core resolution (46).

It could be argued that the affective resonance of both music and literature is what binds them. This is also what imparts the corresponding difficulty in the crossover between the two art forms. Omigie suggests that the notion of empathy, as understood in contemporary neuroscience and psychology, may be an underlying mechanism that contributes to the shared affective impact of these arts (1). Empathy is thought to comprise two components: a cognitive embodiment of perspective-taking (via Theory of Mind and mentalizing) and an emotive expression of shared visceral feeling (through emotional contagion) (Omigie 2). A growing body of research, Omigie explains, has shown that reader identification with literary characters and emotion invoked by music supports the belief that empathy processes may be a key contributor to the affective experience of both reading literature and listening to music (3). Smaller-scale investigation reminds us that discrete elements arranged by sets of principles (i.e., syntax) comprise both music and language: "In the field of cognitive neuroscience, a comparative approach has revealed similar electrophysiological signatures to irregular or unexpected events in the context of music and language" (Omigie 3).

Using expectations and their subversion to formulate tension or conflict is fundamental in the composition of both music and fiction, and Alice Munro's short stories are rife with such suspense. This essay focusses on musical representation and the musicality of the prose narrative in Munro's short stories "Dance of the Happy Shades" (*Dance of the Happy Shades*, 1968) and "My Mother's Dream" (*The Love of a Good Woman*, 1998) and beyond, glancing forward to the four-story "Finale" of Munro's apparently last collection, *Dear Life* (2012). The career-long span in the publication of these works encourages investigation of these motifs, as well as their evolution. Furthermore, all serve as the *dénouement* in their respective collections, undoubtedly purposeful in scoring a multitude of endings into one final coda. Alice Munro becomes a musical practitioner of what Eileen Baldeshwiler has termed 'the lyric short story' through Munro's use of rhetorical devices such as leitmotif, intertextual referents, performativity, narrative space, punctuation patterns, and (subverting) expectation.

Lyric & Leitmotif

The short story is a particularly interesting vessel for musical representation and musicality if we consider what Baldeshwiler points to as the historical development of the modern short story, dividing the larger mass of narratives into an "epical" vein differentiated from a smaller group which are more "lyrical" (443). While epical narratives are marked by external action, the lyric short story "concentrates on internal changes, moods, and feelings, utilizing a variety of structural patterns depending on the shape of the emotion itself, relies for the most part on the open ending, and is expressed in the condensed, evocative, often figured language of the poem" (Baldeshwiler 443). Its formal emergence can be traced back as early as an explicit naming by Conrad Aiken in a 1921 review of Katherine Mansfield's *Bliss and Other Stories*, with its initial practitioner being Ivan Turgenev in *A Sportsman's Notebook* (Baldeshwiler 443). Other stylistic pioneers, Baldeshwiler notes, include Anton Chekhov, A.E. Coppard, D.H. Lawrence, Virginia Woolf, Sherwood Anderson, Katherine Anne Porter, Eudora Welty, and John Updike (444-53), many of whom Munro has named as direct influences on her craft. Multiple scholars have indicated the intertextual interplay of "Dance of the Happy Shades" and Welty's "June Recital" (Cam; Victor; Duplay). In the case of Chekhov, D.S. Mirsky even goes as far as depicting the emotional architectonics of his stories in musical terms: "An infinitesimal touch, which at first hardly arrests the reader's attention, gives a hint at the direction the story is going to take. It is then repeated as leitmotif, and at each repetition the true equation of the curve becomes more important, and it ends by shooting away in a direction very different from that of the original straight line" (qtd. in Baldeshwiler 445).

Matthew Bribitzer-Stull explains that the Wagnerian term 'leit-motif' was coined by August Wilhelm Ambros in his 1860 descriptions of the German composer's operas (later termed 'music dramas') to highlight what was deduced as the central contributing factor to the expressive potency and lucidity of the works (22). The term was not popularized, however, until Hans von Wolzogen's 1876 publication of a thematic catalogue for Wagner's masterwork *Der Ring des Nibelungen* (Bribitzer-Stull 22). As a device, the leitmotif seeks to establish a larger sense of unity across the whole of the work. It is to be distinguished from other musical-associative constructs, or 'associative themes,' which do not provide a foundational principle, whereas the leitmotif conceptually blends the musical and the associative (Bribitzer-Stull 7, 11).

According to Bribitzer-Stull, there are three fundamental aspects that denote the leitmotif: 1) a bifurcated nature (encompassing both emotional connection and "a musical physiognomy"); 2) a developmental motivation resonating in "new musico-dramatic contexts"; and 3) a functional place "within a larger musical structure" (10). A leitmotif in literature may be considered, in the words of Calvin S. Brown, "a verbal formula which is deliberately repeated, which is easily recognized at each recurrence, and which serves, by means of this recognition, to link the context in which the repetition occurs with earlier contexts in which the motive has appeared" (211). While this device might be thought to lend itself more readily to longer fictional works such as novels, it is certainly also possible, in the case of a writer like Munro, to read leit-motifs across single stories or individual short story collections or an entire body of work.

Works Cited

Not one to shy away from overt mentioning of intertextual referents, Munro is specific in her designation of the musical works woven into her stories. In "Dance of the Happy Shades," the narrator performs the minuet from George Frideric Handel's opera *Berenice* (1737) and the girl from the Greenhill School brings the bewildering presence of actual music into Miss Marsalles' party with the titular "*Danse des ombres heureuses*" from the French version, *Orphée et Eurydice* (1774), of Christoph Willibald Gluck's opera *Orfeo ed Euridice*. Mathieu Duplay points out the implications of the reference to Gluck, whose reform operas are linked to eighteenth-century aesthetic debates, showing Munro's choice to be far from arbitrary (205-09). France stood apart from mainstream Italian operatic fashions, enabling Gluck's embrace of a Jean-Jacques Rousseau-inspired philosophy, which championed loosening the restraints of convention in favour of "the simple and untrammelled expression of human feelings" (Duplay 208). "My Mother's Dream" strays from the operatic as Jill decides to master Felix Mendelssohn's "Violin Concerto in E minor, Op. 64" (1845) for her conservatory examination, despite Ludwig van Beethoven's "Violin Concerto in D Major, Op. 61" (1806) being the piece "which she more passionately admires" (324).

The separation of more mainstream selections from operas and the technical challenge of violin concertos underscores the different musical approaches in the two narratives – domestic and public. The disappearing amateur in "Dance" ("[p]iano lessons are not so important now as they once were; everybody knows that" [213]), as Roland Barthes puts it in "Musica Practica," is "a role defined much more by a style than by a technical imperfection," whereas the virtuoso, an unsullied specialist, is one "whose training remains entirely esoteric for the public" (150). Most notably differentiating the minuet and the dance are their respective levels of public familiarity; while in time the overture-derived minuet from Handel's *Berenice* became highly popular (Blakeman 170), the piece from Gluck's *Orphée et Eurydice* played by Dolores Boyle "is not familiar" (222).

The Handel interpretation is among a slew of pieces that are heard throughout the years at Miss Marsalles' parties, fitting the dominant soundflow of the space. Gluck's minuet brings something foreign into the cultural isolation of the usual subjects (that is, the students and their mothers), 'rupturing' convention, as Ulrica Skagert says of Munro's technique, with its bearing of "a great unemotional happiness" (222). The aesthetically unfamiliar (both the piece and Dolores' disabled corporeality) feels out of place to the party guests. However, the strange beauty of what has been heard permeates, its aural quality less culturally taboo than the visual spectacle of the performer: "and so they speak gratefully of the music itself" (223). Duplay notes that, however beautifully played, Gluck's music (as re-created by Dolores) does not do as intended and

create an ineffable unified affect: "the resulting tension cannot be over-
come – 'the facts are not to be reconciled'" (213).

In "My Mother's Dream," Jill's selection of the Mendelssohn concerto
over the Beethoven is significant for a few reasons. It could be confidently shown off "without the least fear of catastrophe. This is not a work
that will trouble her all her life, she has decided; it is not something she
will struggle with and try to prove herself at forever" (324). Jill's choice
implies that Beethoven's piece might be that sort of lifelong challenge,
alongside motherhood (cf. the domesticity of Miss Marsalles' students
and their mothers), over both of which she struggles to make the decision that she will not be troubled by them evermore. Beethoven's concerto is notorious for its employment of virtuosic cadenzas (Stowell 90),
and Jill, knowing "she was not a great violinist, she had no marvellous
gift or destiny" (339), feels inept to take on the work.

It is also worth noting that Mendelssohn's is in E minor, a key commonly associated with grief, and the piece itself is described as having
a prominently elegiac first theme that supposedly haunted the composer, giving him "no peace" (Mendelssohn 155). This characterization
is concurrent with Karen Smythe's designation of Munro's fiction as
"fiction-elegy," the poetic term in this compound signifying elements
such as "a defined loss, meditations on the past, digressions, a focus
on the self (as a survivor and as an artist-figure, an elegist), temporal
fluctuations, consolation" (494). These elements are clearly present in
"My Mother's Dream," including the culminating moment of survivalist
consolation:

> [...] I believe that it was only at the moment when I decided to come
> back, when I gave up the fight against my mother (which must have
> been a fight for something like her total surrender) and when in fact I
> chose survival over victory (death would have been victory), that I took
> on my female nature.
> And to some extent Jill took on hers. (337)

As Naomi Morgenstern writes, the mutual femininity in the decision
to give up – the choice of survival, of accepting the Freudian enigma of
lack – allies mother and daughter (80-81, 87-88).

Aptly, E minor would seem a much more affectively Munrovian key than the triumphant-sounding D Major of Beethoven's heroic concerto, a trajectory that Jill was unwilling to spend her whole life trying to master.

Performance & Perception

In "Dance of the Happy Shades," music and musical performance are distinguished as two separated entities: "We are accustomed to notice performances, at Miss Marsalles' parties, but it cannot be said that anyone has ever expected music" (222). This discrimination reflects a musicological perspective dating back to assertions made by composers such as Igor Stravinsky and Arnold Schoenberg towards the act of performing as an execution of a translation of a score – as what Nicholas Cook terms "in essence the reproduction of a text" (204) – to an audience that likely would not be able to read it. However, while we have scores and, in more recent cases, recordings of compositions being played by their composers (and therefore exactly as they were intended), in most instances we are not able to experience Western 'art' music directly as it was written; we are left merely with interpretations. These oftentimes contradictory treatments give different impressions of the same work that, even when considered together, do not fully embody the identity of the piece. Considering this music as performance is what gives the original works such an ineffable resistance to the constraints of time: "the extraordinary illusion," as Cook states, "that there is such a thing as music, rather than simply acts of making and receiving it, might well be considered the basic premise of the Western 'art' tradition" (208).

Thus, Dolores' performance at the party is to be compared to the rest, including the narrator's own "lumpy interpretation of Handel" (221) – but it is unmistakably different, for the "freedom of a great unemotional happiness" carried within the music can be felt by the reluctant audience, "even in Miss Marsalles' living room on Bala Street on a preposterous afternoon" (222). Jean-Marc Victor notes the significance of the pieces mentioned being transcriptions or adaptations, not having originally been composed for piano (197). The unfamiliar melody played by the capricious girl bears a nostalgic reminder "of something that they had forgotten they had forgotten" (222), to the point where "the performance begins to seem [...] like a trick" (223). A similar reflection of aesthetic anxiety appears in "My Mother's Dream" when the narrator describes her father's and his family's feelings towards 'classical' music, their intolerance stemming, they thought, from "strength of character[...]. As if music that departed from a simple tune was trying to put something over on you" (317). The family's united front against Jill through this shared hostility demonstrates the innate sociability of musical performance, even in "concerts that put people to sleep" (317). Social context is evidently more prevalent, though, in "Dance," in which the intersubjectivity of the acts of making music (as a performer) and receiving it (as an audience) afford a certain claim to what Stephen Benson describes as "an ethics of being equal" (139).

Despite the representational difficulty of music, Benson argues, fictional narrative may in fact present a privileged method of embodying its sociability (Benson 140). Consider the insider-outsider dynamic between the annual attendees of Miss Marsalles' parties and the disruptive presence of the Greenhill schoolchildren. While it is not explicitly stated anywhere in the text, we are given the impression that these 'special' students are disabled in some way: "'They're nice little things and some of them quite musical but of course they're not all there'" (221). Disabled bodies are regarded as inherently lesser and unequal to those with no mental and/or physical defects, but in the performance context music acts as an equalizer. The performative body presents an issue of repulsion, "[f]or it is a matter of politeness surely not to look closely at such children, and yet where else can you look during a piano performance but at the performer?" (222). It is only by way of the music Dolores brings into the room that the focus is changed from visual to aural, fictional motives described by James Guetti as enacting opposite functions: the former, "progress," and the latter, "stasis" (5). Yet again, the music moves outside time and outside all things of this world and delivers an affective takeover, suspended in a moment, allowing the 'othered' to become equal: "it is that one communiqué from the other country where [Miss Marsalles] lives" (224).

Narrative Space

As with many of Munro's stories, the social nucleus of the narratives is women – namely mothers, daughters, and sisters. According with convention, the setting is primarily within the domestic sphere, enabling the author's metaphoric use of the house as edifice. The habitation of space underlies the stories, but rooms in houses are tangible spaces that may be grasped, and both "Dance of the Happy Shades" and "My Mother's Dream" extend their occupation to other narrative dimensions.

The enigma that is Miss Marsalles' living room manages to stay the same across the years and changes in address, "a room whose dim impersonal style [...] was at the same time uncomfortable and reassuring" (214-15). Nostalgic ritual draws together these mothers and daughters, hereditarily previous and current pupils of Miss Marsalles' piano lessons, to the annual party where they express "a familiar, humorous amazement at the sameness of things" (215) time after time. The persistence of the space and its musical proceedings interrupts their evolving daily lives once every year by transporting them back "to a more exacting pattern of life which had been breaking apart even then but which survived, and unaccountably still survived, in Miss Marsalles' living room" (215). Everything has been reduced to infantile states in these instances, where guests dined on "dressed-up nursery food" (213) and where the narrator is "greeted, as always, as if [she] were around five years old" (217). Through music and its performance context, an immortal childlike innocence is somehow maintained in this narrative space, which keeps patrons (ever reluctantly) returning. The life cycle is implicated by the degeneration of Miss Marsalles' sister and their shared tendency (and hatred) to forget, alongside the narrator's disgust at being "'the oldest girl [t]here'" (219), with the aging process inevitably resulting in an infantilization that will follow you outside of the mystic space of that living room.

Miss Marsalles' living room exudes "an atmosphere [...] of some freakish inescapable dream" (222), a quality that is extended in "My Mother's Dream," as the title would suggest. Mark Levene notes the balance between retrograde and concurrent or immediate narration: "Here Munro counterpoints the eerie, layered dream which suggests the death of the child with the raucous comedy of the daily life surrounding the very much alive infant" (858). Indeed, Munro's presenting of the contrast between the now-survivalist trajectory that Jill eventually chooses for her life and the valiant status conferred on her husband George by his early death in the war – together with the third important story line, the baby's – suggests the way in which "My Mother's Dream" works exactly like counterpoint in music: providing, as Walter Piston says, the coherent combination of two or more distinct melodic lines heard at the same time, thereby fulfilling the aesthetic principle of unity in diversity (9).

In music prior to the twentieth century, this effect was achieved through the rules of voice-leading in the resolution of consonances and dissonances, and in post-tonal music, the varied lines may follow principles of symmetry and complementarity (Piston 9). While Calvin S. Brown writes that the pun comes close to the conception of 'literary counterpoint' through the pun's presentation of one thing with two aspects or denotations ("a word can easily have a literal meaning plus a sustaining background of suggestions, and hence can be something analogous to a chord" [42]), he does not speak to the utilization of two simultaneous narrative dimensions – reality and dreams, as well as the past and the present. This technique could expand our sense of the literary possibilities of counterpoint, and Levene's well-founded use of the term may prove to be more suggestive than it first seems. Yet again, time collapses in this matriarchal narrative space, and the life cycle is implicated not only by the birth of the child on the day of her father's funeral, but also by the disintegration of her "'senile'" (299) grandmother. The temporal evasion that is encompassed is difficult to disassociate from the musical manifestation of this space, especially when the baby is found tucked beneath the sofa with the violin (333).

Punctuation & Expectation

The quality referred to when discussing the musicality of prose is as intangible as the word 'musicality' itself; all that is certain is that some writing unquestionably has this factor. Perhaps it is an inherent gift in some great writers, or perhaps it is something meticulously thought-out and rewritten dozens of times over to achieve its musicality, or perhaps it is both. Where the struggle for musical representation lies in a lost-in-translation pitfall, language possesses its own musical representation at the crux. As William H. Gass writes in "The Music of Prose," "language is not the lowborn, gawky servant of thought and feeling; it is need, thought, feeling, and perception itself" (319). In music, phrases are formed by sounds, and in prose, the opposite holds – sounds are formed by phrases (Gass 321). Even in our library training to read only to ourselves, the sounds of the words still rise and fall in our heads as we follow their patterns. Prose is an integrally auditory medium even when read silently.

In "Punctuation as Score" John Metcalf addresses punctuation's contribution to the structure of prose's musical qualities, citing the use of "quotation marks, italic, ellipsis, and paragraphing" as methods of scoring (97). Apart from ellipsis (but with the arguable addition of dashes), Munro employs these punctuation strategies in her short stories, aiding in their musicality. For example, in "Dance of the Happy Shades" she readily forgoes the use of quotation marks in some of the dialogue, usually in the narrator's mother's directly spoken questions, which would typically warrant double quotation marks: "My mother, very pleasant but looking a little uncomfortable, asks about Miss Marsalles' sister; is she upstairs?" (218). Corinne Bigot notes the variation in how one of Munro's favourite devices, the dash, is used across her catalogue of stories, but seemingly burgeons in cases describing intense emotion and lost control (33). Oriana Palusci points towards an embodiment of Bigot's argument in a line from "My Mother's Dream" where death and conception saturate the same sentence, "disjointed grammatically by dashes" (54).

Italicization is also used in "Dance of the Happy Shades," as well as in "My Mother's Dream" during Iona's psychotic break over the perceived death of the baby: "Words come out of her between fresh groans of recognition. // *Baby. Love my. Darling. Ooh. Oh. Get the. Suffocated. Blanket. Baby. Police*" (328-29). Metcalf contends that the utilization of these devices in ways that are on the margins of conventionality "is only effective *because the convention exists and is expected*" (100). The implication of expectation is some form of mental representation – codes of convention that are followed and subverted in both music and literature. David Huron refers to the representation process as "a sort of feedback loop: representations are used to form expectations, and the accuracy of these expectations is used to select among the various alternative representations" (109). The confirmation of expectation, when perceived to have come into fruition, can give rise to a response of satisfaction. However, it also inexorably makes things predictable. A balance of satisfying predictability and the eventual learned expectation of the unexpected is crucial to the composition of both fiction and music.

That Munro is hardly a writer who would ever garner the label of 'predictable' is manifest not only in the events and the structuring of her stories, but also in her characters and their sociocultural positioning. Evidently, "Dance of the Happy Shades" and "My Mother's Dream" are no exception, as their respective subverting of expectation has already been alluded to. "Everything was always as expected" (214), reports the narrator of Miss Marsalles' parties before noting that the piano teacher's new house "gives the impression of being better than we expected" (216), foreshadowing the unexpected presence of the children from the Greenhill School and their musical prowess. The fact of social conventions and codes of conduct not being met by the new disabled students, as well as Dolores Boyle's remarkable talent, is a subversion so pervasive that the guests leaving behind the newly impossible parties are unable to utter "– as [they] must have expected to say –" (224) pitying remarks about Miss Marsalles any longer.

From the beginning "My Mother's Dream" is said to be set in the middle of a change in seasons "unexplainable, unexpected" (293). Similarly, George liked that Jill was a musician because it made her an unexpected choice. Yet George's own early death was entirely predictable: "he was just the sort you always knew would be killed" (297). And the infant's acceptance and coming back after the near-death that her mother caused – and her mother's consequent acceptance of motherhood – is far from an expected trajectory, just as much as Jill's initial struggle with mothering her child and her unfulfilled expectation "to be happy – grateful and happy – when her mind caught up with [the] physical and social reality" (306) of her marriage to George.

Finale

As is characteristic of Munro, both "Dance of the Happy Shades" and "My Mother's Dream" feature unresolved endings, but ones that invite a more palpable glimmer of hope than several of the others included in the collections that they conclude. The musical conception of 'finale' was first presented by eighteenth-century composers (notably, Haydn and Mozart) in association with a light, tuneful movement, Michael Talbot notes (12). Later in the century, and continually developing into the next, the finale increased in dimension and musical weight, eventually allotting review or even development of thematic material (Talbot 12). "Finale" is also what Munro names the final four stories in her most recent and likely last collection, *Dear Life* (2012), making a case for their structural inspiration being derivative of a variation of the sonata form that final symphonic movements often take on. As its core, Scott Burnham explains, sonata form is about tension or conflict, resolution, and return (in other words: exposition, development, recapitulation [and coda]); "the natural expression of tonality" (111). It is an abstraction nonetheless, with no textbook configuration and many variants; still, as Burnham contests, sonata form may be "the closest analogue of music to the function of an overarching, archetypal plot in literature" (112). Burnham also notes James Webster's designation of the double return (of both the tonic key and the first theme) as the form's central aesthetic event or syntactic climax (113).

The role of the symphonic finale in Western 'art' music evolved, Talbot observes, "from early-eighteenth-century lightness to late-nine-teenth-century monumentality" (12). The shift from the "front-weight-ing" of the Renaissance, Baroque, and Classical periods "towards end-weighting – or, at least, to the abandonment of extreme forms of front-weighting –" can be attributed to "steadily increasing movement length" in the eighteenth century, together with "changing aesthetics and cultural style" (Talbot 47). As Talbot explains, "musical weight is a product of many factors, including bulk, duration, fullness of scoring, and 'tone,' but is validated primarily by structural properties" (46). However, some of the techniques and characteristics of final movements have stayed the same from the Renaissance until the present day (Talbot 14).

Influenced by the Agnus Dei conclusion to the Mass prominent since the late fifteenth century, two structural properties of the modern concept of the finale came to be formed: what Talbot terms "culmination" and "regression" (37-38), which are utilized either separately or together to develop the movement. Fundamentally, "[t]he finale comes laden with a charge that, at its end, when it delivers the work back into the void, it will have to discharge" (Talbot 6).

Talbot delineates three main types of finales: the relaxant finale (52-80), the summative finale (81-105), and the valedictory finale (106-26). Upon reading the valedictory form as a deviant variant of the summative, it becomes clear that the valedictory would most appeal to Munro. The valedictory finale is a departure – slow, calm, introverted, soft – favouring regression over culmination. According to Talbot, it expresses "a range of feelings, running from melancholia to nostalgia, from abstention to exhaustion, from fading out to passing away, that we easily identify with the twentieth-century condition. [It] represent[s] a retreat from the public into the private sphere" (107). This form has especially appealed to marginalized composers and, Talbot adds, is associated with the late Romantic aesthetic valorization of fragments and any other sense of incompletion (113). In *Dear Life*, like all Munro collections, satisfaction can only stem from the incomplete; "Finale" serves as a finale not only to the collection itself, but also, since this is likely Munro's final book, to her entire illustrious career's complete *oeuvre*. As she notes, *"[t]he final four works in this book are not quite stories. They form a separate unit, one that is autobiographical in feeling, though not, sometimes, entirely so in fact. I believe they are the first and last – and the closest – things I have to say about my own life"* (255).

The first not-quite story, "The Eye," begins with an end, paralleling the "inevitable duality about the opening of a final movement" that Talbot discerns in music (7). Sadie's death and subsequent wake prompt feeble attempts at reassurance by the protagonist's mother: "'Now then. It's over'" (269). This sentiment carries on into the loss of appendix and innocence (with the development of psychosis) in "Night," where the protagonist's mother once again tries to soothe her: "But don't worry, she said, it's all over now" (272). In "Voices" we get the thematic recapitulation of the daughter taking on her mother's views when they leave the dance as a result of an appearance there by a notable local prostitute:

"The Air Force boys were all right. It was Mrs. Hutchison who was the disgrace. And the girl" (295). The protagonist decides to blame Mrs. Hutchison ("for no particular reason") for having upset the girl crying on the staircase, comforted by the two Air Force boys, who "seemed to be unable to open their mouths without uttering some kind of blessing" despite their futures being "all bound up with disaster" (297). But as Linda M. Morra points out, the escapism from the social censure uncovered in the intimacy of this moment – the voices of the Air Force boys that the protagonist goes on to summon in consolatory fantasy – is illusory, given the soldiers' expected ill fates (211).

A finale within a finale, the titular "Dear Life" also begins with death. The passing of the protagonist's friend Diane's mother, also a prostitute, is expectedly not met with much compassion from the protagonist's own mother: "The wages of sin is death" (302). In reflecting back on her life, the grown-up protagonist/narrator mentions her parents' plans to prosper by raising foxes (reminiscent of background plot details in multiple stories in the *Dance of the Happy Shades* collection and other works by Munro), and the death that seemed to haunt her life: "There was quite a lot of killing going on, now that I think of it" (305). She recounts her mother's two miscarriages prior to her birth (307) and claims that the surplus of tragedy riddling the story (her mother's ill health, the demise of her father's business) "wouldn't do in fiction" (309). Referencing fictional literary works – "the big novels I borrowed from the town library" (310) – punctuates this statement and engages three intertexts: Halldór Laxness's epic *Independent People* (1934-35; trans. 1945), the multi-volume *Remembrance of Things Past* (1913-27; trans. 1922-31) by Marcel Proust, and Thomas Mann's monumental *The Magic Mountain* (1924; trans. 1927). These texts were not to be given up on, despite their tyrannical breadth.

"Dear Life" brings to a close one of the opening (and recurring) themes raised early in "The Eye": "Up until the time of the first baby I had not been aware of ever feeling different from the way my mother said I felt" (257). By the final story, the protagonist decides to give in to her deteriorating mother's perspectives, "seldom object[ing] now to her way of looking at things" (310). Still she tries to make sense of the ludicrous Mrs. Netterfield narrative her mother tells. Although deductive reasoning does not gain the protagonist any clarity, a poem enlightens her much later on. Finally, not being in attendance at her mother's funeral is a subverted recollection of the viewing of Sadie's casket and her flitting eyelid, a special sign meant "completely" (269) for the protagonist. It is safe to presume that no such glimmer would grace her mother's lifeless face. That's what the grown-up protagonist/narrator supposes, contemplating the so-called unforgivable and how routinely we exonerate ourselves – "for dear life" (318).

Coda

What is implied by the musical presence in "Dance of the Happy Shades" and "My Mother's Dream" and the stories' use as the final instalments in their respective collections? Perhaps it is a matter of resolution without the complete satisfaction that would enable readers to move on without giving the narratives a second thought: an indeterminacy contributing to what Ailsa Cox denotes as "a poetics of absence" (187). Or perhaps it is a chance for all the various leitmotifs and thematic elements, including expectations (and their subversion), female relationships, representation, domesticity, motherhood, performance, intersubjectivity, memory, aging, grief, humour, nostalgia, narrative spaces, punctuation patterns – among others – to be presented again as common threads solidifying their entanglement and pervasive presence. Or perhaps it is that these stories act as a sort of cadence, containing the essence of the musical language that characterizes Munro's writing, with the dominant preceding the conceivable perfect return home to the tonic or, possibly more accurately, the half-close of the semi-cadence resonating like a comma, suspended. This is the sort of catharsis achieved by Munro's fiction, in which the emotional release may be different than expected, in which music may be found within the melopoetic contours of her narrative voicings.

The musical manifestation in "Dance of the Happy Shades" and "My Mother's Dream," as well as the sonata form "Finale" to the symphony that is *Dear Life*, helps us as readers to experience the empathy that accompanies taking these narratives on as our own and integrating them into our mental representations and cognitive-emotional schemas. While we only read this music with our eyes, we hear it translated through the voicings in our heads, tentatively letting it achieve the full force of its sonorous qualities. We are attuned to its structural patterns and the reprise of themes, altogether the same and different in the course of their developmental trajectories. Moreover, we listen; and although we may not know exactly what is expected of us as reader-listeners of Munro's literary music or how to describe its emergence, it is something that cannot help but be wholly felt.

And so we speak gratefully of the music itself.

Works Consulted

Bal, Mieke. *Travelling Concepts in the Humanities: A Rough Guide.* Toronto: U of Toronto P, 2002.

Baldeshwiler, Eileen. "The Lyric Short Story: The Sketch of a History." *Studies in Short Fiction* 6 (1969): 443-53. Rpt. in *Short Story Theories.* Ed. Charles E. May. Athens, OH: Ohio UP, 1976. 202-13. Rpt. in *The New Short Story Theories.* Ed. Charles E. May. Athens, OH: Ohio UP, 1994. 231-41.

Barthes, Roland. "The Grain of the Voice." *Image – Music – Text.* Trans. Stephen Heath. 1977. New York: Noonday-Farrar, Straus and Giroux, 1988. 179-89.

---. "Musica Practica." *Image – Music – Text.* Trans. Stephen Heath. 1977. New York: Noonday-Farrar, Straus and Giroux, 1988. 149-54.

Beethoven, Ludwig van. "Violin Concerto in D Major, Op. 61." 1806.

Benson, Stephen. *Literary Music: Writing Music in Contemporary Fiction.* Aldershot, Eng.: Ashgate, 2006.

Bigot, Corinne. "Discontinuity, Disjointedness: Parenthetical Structures and Dashes in Alice Munro's Stories from *Dance of the Happy Shades.*" *Stylistic Perspectives on Alice Munro's* Dance of the Happy Shades. Ed. Manuel Jobert and Michael Toolan. Études de Stylistique Anglaise 8 (2015): 17-35.

Bigot, Corinne, and Catherine Lanone. *Sunlight and Shadows, Past and Present: Alice Munro's* Dance of the Happy Shades. Paris: Presses Universitaires de France – Cned, 2014. Série Anglais.

Blakeman, Edward. "*Berenice*, HMV 38." *The Faber Pocket Guide to Handel.* London: Faber and Faber, 2009. 169-71.

Bribitzer-Stull, Matthew. *Understanding the Leitmotif: From Wagner to Hollywood Film Music.* Cambridge, Eng.: Cambridge UP, 2015.

Brown, Calvin S. *Music and Literature: A Comparison of the Arts.* Athens, GA: U of Georgia P, 1948.

Burnham, Scott. "The Second Nature of Sonata Form." *Music Theory and Natural Order from the Renaissance to the Early Twentieth Century.* Ed. Suzannah Clark and Alexander Rehding. Cambridge, Eng.: Cambridge UP, 2001. 111-41.

Cam, Heather. "Learning from the Teacher: Alice Munro's Reworking of Eudora Welty's 'June Recital'." *SPAN: Journal of the South Pacific Association for Commonwealth Literature and Language Studies* 25 (1987): 16-30.

Cook, Nicholas. "Music as Performance." *The Cultural Study of Music: A Critical Introduction.* Ed. Martin Clayton, Trevor Herbert, and Richard Middleton. New York: Routledge, 2003. 204-14.

Cox, Ailsa. "'First and Last': The Figure of the Infant in 'Dear Life' and 'My Mother's Dream'." *Alice Munro's Miraculous Art: Critical Essays.* Ed. Janice Fiamengo and Gerald Lynch. Ottawa: U of Ottawa P, 2017. 177-90. Reappraisals: Canadian Writers 38.

Cox, Ailsa, and Christine Lorre-Johnston. *The Mind's Eye: Alice Munro's Dance of the Happy Shades.* Paris: Éditions Fahrenheit, 2015.

Crapoulet, Emilie. "Voicing the Music in Literature: 'Musicality as a Travelling Concept'." *European Journal of English Studies* 13 (2009): 79-91. <https://doi.org/10.1080/13825570802708212>.

Duplay, Mathieu. "'The Other Country Where She Lives': Opera and Its Doubles in Alice Munro's 'Dance of the Happy Shades'." *The Inside of a Shell: Alice Munro's Dance of the Happy Shades.* Ed. Vanessa Guignery. Newcastle upon Tyne, Eng.: Cambridge Scholars, 2015. 200-16.

Gass, William H. "The Music of Prose." *Finding a Form.* New York: Alfred A. Knopf, 1996. 313-26.

Gluck, Christoph Willibald. *"Danse des ombres heureuses." Orphée et Eurydice.* 1774.

Guetti, James. *Word-Music: The Aesthetic Aspect of Narrative Fiction.* New Brunswick, NJ: Rutgers UP, 1980.

Handel, George Frideric. *Berenice.* 1737.

Huron, David. *Sweet Anticipation: Music and the Psychology of Expectation.* Cambridge, MA: MIT, 2006.

Kerman, Joseph. *Concerto Conversations*. Cambridge, MA: Harvard UP, 1999. The Charles Eliot Norton Lectures 1997-98.

Levene, Mark. "'It was about vanishing': A Glimpse of Alice Munro's Stories." *Images of Canadian Short Stories* / Aspects de la nouvelle québécoise et canadienne. Ed. Mark Levene and Michel Lord. *University of Toronto Quarterly* 68 (1999): 841-60. <https://doi.org/10.3138/utq.68.4.841>.

Mendelssohn, Felix. "To Concertmeister Ferdinand David, Leipzig." 30 July 1838. *Letters of Felix Mendelssohn Bartholdy, from 1833 to 1847*. Trans. Lady Wallace. Ed. Paul Mendelssohn Bartholdy and Dr. Carl Mendelssohn Bartholdy. London: Longman, Green, Longman, Roberts, & Green, 1863. 153-56. <https://archive.org/details/lettersoffelixm00mend>.

---. "Violin Concerto in E minor, Op. 64." 1845.

Metcalf, John. "Punctuation as Score." *Kicking Against the Pricks*. Downsview, ON: ECW, 1982. 95-116.

Morgenstern, Naomi. "The Baby or the Violin?: Ethics and Femininity in the Fiction of Alice Munro." *Literature Interpretation Theory* 14 (2003): 69-97.

Morra, Linda M. "'It Was[n't] All Inward': The Dynamics of Intimacy in the 'Finale' of *Dear Life*." *Alice Munro*: Hateship, Friendship, Courtship, Loveship, Marriage; Runaway; Dear Life. Ed. Robert Thacker. London: Bloomsbury, 2016. 203-16, 229-30, 231-44 passim.

Munro, Alice. "Dance of the Happy Shades." *Dance of the Happy Shades*. Fwd. Hugh Garner. Toronto: Ryerson, 1968. 211-24.

---. "Finale." *Dear Life*. Toronto: McClelland & Stewart, 2012. 255-319.

---. "My Mother's Dream." *The Love of a Good Woman*. Toronto: McClelland & Stewart, 1998. 293-340.

Omigie, Diana. "Music and Literature: Are There Shared Empathy and Predictive Mechanisms Underlying Their Affective Impact?" *Frontiers in Psychology* 6 (2015): 1-6. <https://doi.org/10.3389/fpsyg.2015.01250>.

Palusci, Oriana. "The Memory of Ghosts: Alice Munro's 'My Mother's Dream'." *Reading Alice Munro in Italy*. Ed. Gianfranca Balestra, Laura Ferri, and Caterina Ricciardi. Toronto: The Frank Iacobucci Center for Italian Canadian Studies, 2008. 47-57.

Piston, Walter. *Counterpoint*. New York: W.W. Norton, 1947.

Skagert, Ulrica. "The Rupture of the Ordinary as an 'Awkward Little Space': Evental Moments in Alice Munro's 'Dance of the Happy Shades'." *The Inside of a Shell: Alice Munro's* Dance of the Happy Shades. Ed. Vanessa Guignery. Newcastle upon Tyne, Eng.: Cambridge Scholars, 2015. 271-82.

Smythe, Karen. "Sad Stories: The Ethics of Epiphany in Munrovian Elegy." *University of Toronto Quarterly* 60 (1991): 493-506. <https://doi.org/10.3138/utq.60.4.493>.

Stowell, Robin. *Beethoven: Violin Concerto*. Cambridge, Eng.: Cambridge UP, 1998. Cambridge Music Handbooks.

Talbot, Michael. *The Finale in Western Instrumental Music*. Oxford, Eng.: Oxford UP, 2001.

Victor, Jean-Marc. "Happy Shades of 'June Recital' in 'Dance of the Happy Shades': Munro's Dance with Welty." *The Inside of a Shell: Alice Munro's* Dance of the Happy Shades. Ed. Vanessa Guignery. Newcastle upon Tyne, Eng.: Cambridge Scholars, 2015. 186-99.

Alice Munro and James Joyce

W.R. Martin

The question of influence is notoriously difficult to discuss. In the first place, almost any two things can be said to be in some sense alike. Then, what degree of likeness must there be in their elements before compounds can be said to be similar? If we agree that there is similarity, how do we decide whether the similarity is a coincidence or, in a work of art, the result of influence? If there is influence, is it unconscious, or is there sedulous imitation or deliberate theft? Then there is the question of the significance of the influence, and so on. I don't propose to answer or even to address myself to all these questions, but I shall point to some likenesses, starting with Munro's *Dance of the Happy Shades* and Joyce's *Dubliners*.

In each there are fifteen short stories, some of which are narrated in the first person and which might be in some sense autobiographical: in both, the early stories are about childhood, and then there is a roughly chronological arrangement (more erratic in the Munro than in the Joyce), the protagonists becoming older and on the whole more mature. The setting for all fifteen of Joyce's stories is, as his title proclaims, his native Dublin; three of Alice Munro's stories are set specifically in Jubilee, a fictional town, and about five of the others might be, because they have as background similar country towns and their environs in Southwestern Ontario, usually not far from Lake Huron.[1]

These similarities between the two collections of stories are likenesses in external feature and, even when taken together, don't amount to very much. Similarities in intention would be more significant. We happen to have a number of declarations by Joyce of his methods and aims because he had a long correspondence with Grant Richards, his reluctant publisher. For example, on 5 May 1906 he wrote: "... I chose Dublin for the scene because that city seemed to me the centre of paralysis" (*Letters II* 134) and on 23 June 1906, "It is not my fault that the odour of ashpits and old weeds and offal hangs round my stories" (*Letters* 63-64).

It is remarkable that most of the stories in *Dance of the Happy Shades* deal with lives that are mean, or barren, or – because circumscribed by poverty, provincialism, or other circumstances – unfulfilled. One thinks of Mary McQuade and Joe in "Images," all the characters in "Thanks for the Ride," the main characters in "The Time of Death," "Postcard," and "A Trip to the Coast," the man in "The Office," and the girls in "Day of the Butterfly." When the characters are better educated and more affluent, they are narrow-gutted ("The Shining Houses") or superficial ("Sunday Afternoon"). Even Nora, who is so amusingly, vividly, and sympathetically portrayed in "Walker Brothers Cowboy," is apparently condemned to a blank life on a remote farmstead.

Key phrases crop up with telling emphasis: "You see that judgment [that the world is absurd] on the faces of people looking out of windows, sitting on front steps in some little towns; so deeply, deeply uncaring they are, as if they had sources of disillusionment which they would keep, with some satisfaction, in the dark" ("Thanks for the Ride" 44-45); "comments of the sort you see ... in town hall lavatories in the little decaying towns where I grew up" ("The Office" 72); "the peculiar flesh smell of her grandmother ... was sweetish and corrupt like the smell of old apple peel going soft" ("A Trip to the Coast" 183); "I had forgotten certain restrictions of life in Jubilee ... and also what strong, respectable, never overtly sexual friendships can flourish within these restrictions and be fed by them, so that in the end such relationships may consume half a life"; "unconsummated relationships"; "the quiet, decaying side streets" in Jubilee ("The Peace of Utrecht" 194, 194, 196). The burden of these phrases is unmistakable.

And if we don't have any declaration from Munro *in propria persona* as we have from Joyce, there is that strange "Epilogue" to *Lives of Girls and Women* in which Del describes the novel she is planning in terms that might apply in part at least to the collection of short stories we are considering:

> For this novel I had changed Jubilee, too, or picked out some features of it and ignored others. It became an older, darker, more decaying town, full of unpainted board fences covered with tattered posters advertising circuses, fall fairs, elections, that had long since come and gone. People

in it were very thin ... or fat as bubbles. Their speech was subtle and evasive and bizarrely stupid; their platitudes crackled with madness. The season was always the height of summer – white, brutal heat, dogs lying as if dead on the sidewalks, waves of air shuddering, jelly-like, over the empty highway. (247)

It seems to me that we are not very far here from Joyce's "Air, musty from having been long enclosed, hung in all the rooms, and the waste room behind the kitchen was littered with old useless papers" ("Araby" 29).

Again, many biographers write of Joyce's passion for Dublin, even in his "exile." According to Constantine Curran, "If Dublin were destroyed, his words could rebuild the houses; if its population were wiped out, his books could repeople it," and "Joyce was many things, but he was certainly the last forty volumes of Thom's *Directory* thinking aloud" (qtd. in Magalaner and Kain 292); or as Joyce remarked to Cyril Connolly, "'I am afraid I am more interested, Mr. Connolly, in the Dublin street names than in the riddle of the universe'" (qtd. in Magalaner and Kain 292). Compare Joyce's attitude with Del's expressed in that same "Epilogue":

> It did not occur to me then that one day I would be so greedy for Jubilee. ...
>
> I would try to make lists. A list of all the stores and businesses going up and down the main street and who owned them, a list of family names, names on the tombstones in the Cemetery and any inscriptions underneath. A list of the titles of movies that played at the Lyceum Theatre from 1938 to 1950, roughly speaking. Names on the Cenotaph (more for the first World War than for the second). Names of the streets and the pattern they lay in.
>
> The hope of accuracy we bring to such tasks is crazy, heartbreaking.
>
> And no list could hold what I wanted, for what I wanted was every last thing, every layer of speech and thought, stroke of light on bark or walls, every smell, pothole, pain, crack, delusion, held still and held together – radiant, everlasting. (253)

The evidence for Joycean influence is still not conclusive, of course. More than external features and inferred intentions should be compared. Similarities in what one might call feeling, or the tone of emotion, would make the case stronger.

If there were an influence from *Dubliners* one would expect it to be, in part at least, from "The Dead," the fifteenth and final story in Joyce's book, and one that is by common consent a masterpiece. One might compare it with the fifteenth and final story in Munro's collection – the one from which the volume takes its title – "Dance of the Happy Shades." Immediately one recognizes certain external features that the two stories have in common. In both the central event is an annual party given by one or both of two spinster sisters, one or both of whom teach music: the Misses Morkan of Dublin, and the Misses Marsalles of (it seems) Toronto. At both parties there is some anxiety about whether certain guests will arrive, and the narratives give prominence to the food and drink prepared – "cut glass" appears in both – and to musical items offered. These last details show some similarity in type: for example, there is "Arrayed for the Bridal" in the Joyce, "The Gypsy Song" and "The Harmonious Blacksmith" in the Munro. All these are additional external features, however. As Shakespeare's Fluellen would say, "There is salmons in both."

In both stories the central intelligences (Gabriel Conroy in "The Dead" and the narrator in "Dance of the Happy Shades") feel at first a little condescending or constrained in an embarrassing situation: the hostesses, whose goodwill and generosity are only too painfully obvious, are patronized or secretly despised because their taste – despite high intentions and valiant efforts – is felt to be common, insipid, and even mawkish. One's confidence that there is a relation between the stories becomes firmer when one detects that the emotional tones of the two situations correspond. Consider, for example, this from "The Dead":

> Gabriel's eyes, irritated by the floor, which glittered with beeswax under the heavy chandelier, wandered to the wall above the piano. A picture of the balcony scene in *Romeo and Juliet* hung there and beside it was a picture of the two murdered princes in the Tower which Aunt Julia had worked in red, blue and brown wools when she was a girl. (186)

And compare it with this from "Dance of the Happy Shades":

> In the room where the mothers sat, some on hard sofas, some on folding chairs, to hear the children play ... there was a picture of Mary, Queen of

Scots, in velvet, with a silk veil, in front of Holyrood Castle. There were brown misty pictures of historical battles, also the Harvard Classics, ... and a bronze Pegasus. (214)

Obviously the Morkan household has more resources than that of the Misses Marsalles, but both pairs of old maids indulge the same taste for heart-rending sentiments embodied in well-worn icons that are hallowed in the popular imagination. Not only are these local tonal values similar, but there is also a similarity in what one might call the emotional structure of the two stories. Joyce's story is of course much longer and more complex, but there is in both stories a strong and dramatic reversal of attitude, as a result of which the spinster ladies are seen by the protagonists no longer in an unsympathetic light, but as having resources and virtues that were overlooked and undervalued.

In *Dubliners* the last two stories are juxtaposed in ironic counterpoint: Mr. Kernan's sensibility and progress in "Grace" are a parody of Conroy's. I believe the last two stories in Munro's book are also linked, though without irony. "The Peace of Utrecht," like "Dance of the Happy Shades," echoes "The Dead." "The Peace of Utrecht" has the same kind of strong dramatic reversal that I have remarked on, though by making the older pitiable woman a close relation, a mother, in fact – in "The Dead" they are aunts – Munro has played up the remorse felt by her narrator. Both she and Conroy judge their earlier attitude and behaviour to have been mean and cruel, and feel at the end a flow of generous sentiment, with the effect of self-rebuke and remorse. Here is a passage from the Munro story "The Peace of Utrecht":

Now I listen to them [the people of Jubilee] speak of her, so gently and ceremoniously, and I realize she became one of the town's possessions and oddities, its brief legends. This she achieved in spite of us, for we tried, both crudely and artfully, to keep her at home, away from that sad notoriety; not for her sake, but for ours, who suffered such unnecessary humiliation at the sight of her eyes rolling back in her head in a temporary paralysis of the eye muscles, at the sound of her thickened voice, whose embarrassing pronouncements it was our job to interpret to outsiders. So bizarre was the disease she had in its effects that it made us feel like crying out in apology (though we stayed stiff and white) as if we were accompanying a particularly tasteless sideshow. All wasted, our pride; our purging its rage in wild caricatures we did for each other (no, not caricatures, for she was one herself; imitations). We should have let the town have her; it would have treated her better. (194-95)

That passage has interesting parallels in theme, feeling, and imagery to this from "The Dead":

Gabriel felt humiliated by the failure of his irony.... While he had been full of memories of their secret life together, full of tenderness and joy and desire, she had been comparing him in her mind with another. A shameful consciousness of his own person assailed him. He saw himself as a ludicrous figure, acting as a pennyboy for his aunts, a nervous well-meaning sentimentalist, orating to vulgarians and idealising his own clownish lusts, the pitiable fatuous fellow he had caught a glimpse of in the mirror. Instinctively he turned his back more to the light lest she might see the shame that burned upon his forehead. (219-20)

There is yet another story in *Dance of the Happy Shades* that has a recognizable echo of "The Dead." One remembers the detail in Joyce's story: Conroy with "warm trembling fingers tapped the cold pane of the window" (192). It might be a mere coincidence that in Munro's "The Time of Death" – again there seems to be some similarity hinted at in the titles – Benny, who is so different from Conroy, "would stand for hours just looking out a window ... stroking his hands down the window-pane" (93). But consider the detail, and especially the tone, of the following passages. This is the final paragraph of "The Time of Death":

There was this house, and the other wooden houses that had never been painted, with their steep patched roofs and their narrow, slanting porches, the wood-smoke coming out of their chimneys and dim children's faces pressed against their windows. Behind them there was the strip of earth, plowed in some places, run to grass in others, full of stones, and behind this the pine trees, not very tall. In front were the yards, the dead gardens, the grey highway running out from town. The snow came, falling slowly, evenly, between the highway and the houses and the pine trees, falling in big flakes at first and then in smaller and smaller flakes that did not melt on the hard furrows, the rock of the earth. (99)

Here with it is the famous last paragraph of Joyce's "The Dead":

A few light taps upon the pane made him turn to the window. It had begun to snow again. He watched sleepily the flakes, silver and dark, falling obliquely against the lamplight. The time had come for him to set out on his journey westward. Yes, the newspapers were right: snow was general all over Ireland. It was falling on every part of the dark central plain, on the treeless hills, falling softly upon the Bog of Allen and, farther westward, softly falling into the dark mutinous Shannon waves. It was falling, too, upon every part of the lonely churchyard on the hill where Michael Furey lay buried. It lay thickly drifted on the crooked crosses and headstones, on the spears of the little gate, on the barren thorns. His soul swooned slowly as he heard the snow falling faintly through the universe and faintly falling, like the descent of their last end, upon all the living and the dead. (223-24)

One goes on to examine Alice Munro's next book, her first novel, *Lives of Girls and Women*, and Joyce's next book, his first published novel, *A Portrait of the Artist as a Young Man*, to be struck by the fact that, near the beginning of *A Portrait*, Stephen Dedalus writes out his address, the last items of which are "*Ireland / Europe / The World / The Universe*" (15). In much the same way, and near the beginning of *Lives*, Del writes out Uncle Benny's address for him, and it ends with "*Canada, North America, The Western Hemisphere, The World, The Solar System, The Universe*" (11). This neatly underlines the similarities, namely that each is a *Bildungsroman* and that the protagonists are thinking out their places in the scheme of things, and at the same time scores the difference that one child is European and the other North American. This points to another similarity, which in turn goes with another difference: both novels are particularly revealing – each perhaps breaking new ground in fiction – about the adolescence and the coming to sexual awareness and maturity of the individual who is an artist in a society not especially sympathetic to artists. The difference is that one is about coming to manhood, and the other about coming to womanhood. Obvious points, but important.

Some readers might feel that finding echoes of Joyce in Munro has the effect of diminishing her achievement, but that would be a shallow view. We should recall the dictum T.S. Eliot offers in his essay on Philip Massinger: "Immature poets imitate; mature poets steal: bad poets deface what they take, and good poets make it into something better, or at least something different" (114). Even in his maturity Virgil did not shrink from stealing from Homer, and Milton made his light more refulgent by catching reflections from them both.

I believe it is possible to see a difference between Munro's first and second books. In the first she took some rays from one of the brightest beams in modern literature and used them for her own purposes. In her second book the similarities are sunk in the differences, because her genius is alight and burning brightly with its own individual flame. In her progress she may again be compared to Joyce, who, on 26 April 1906, wrote to Grant Richards, "I have written my book [*Dubliners*] with considerable care ... and in accordance with what I understand to be the classical tradition of my art" (*Letters* 60). If Joyce has his Homer, his Shakespeare, his Ibsen, and others, Munro may have her Joyce.

Note

1. In Munro's next book, *Lives of Girls and Women*, Jubilee is the constant setting and in a sense a leading character. The fictional Jubilee shares at least one unusual feature with the town of Wingham, where Alice Munro grew up: both have a thoroughfare called "Diagonal Rd." (as well as a John St. and a Victoria St.). Other features of Wingham can perhaps be discerned: for example, in "Postcard" Jubilee has a radio station; in "Day of the Butterfly" – in which Jubilee isn't named – we read, "... I was walking up the school hill" (103).

Works Cited

Eliot, T.S. "Philip Massinger." *The Sacred Wood: Essays on Poetry and Criticism*. London: Methuen, 1920. 112-30.

Joyce, James. *Dubliners: Text, Criticism, and Notes*. Ed. Robert Scholes and A. Walton Litz. New York: Viking, 1969. The Viking Critical Library.

---. *Letters of James Joyce*. Ed. Stuart Gilbert. London: Faber and Faber, 1957.

---. *Letters of James Joyce: Volume II*. Ed. Richard Ellmann. London: Faber and Faber, 1966.

---. *A Portrait of the Artist as a Young Man: Text, Criticism, and Notes*. Ed. Chester G. Anderson. New York: Viking, 1968. The Viking Critical Library.

Magalaner, Marvin, and Richard M. Kain. *Joyce: The Man, the Work, the Reputation*. New York: New York UP, 1956.

Munro, Alice. *Dance of the Happy Shades*. Fwd. Hugh Garner. Toronto: Ryerson, 1968.

---. *Lives of Girls and Women*. Toronto: McGraw-Hill Ryerson, 1971.

Shakespeare, William. *King Henry V*. Ed. J.H. Walter. London: Methuen, 1954. The Arden Edition of the Works of William Shakespeare.

Class Act?: Status, Disability, and Tolerance in Alice Munro's "Dance of the Happy Shades"

Gwendolyn Guth

Early on in the eponymous final story of Alice Munro's Governor General's Award-winning début collection, *Dance of the Happy Shades* (1968), two suburban mothers are commiserating by phone about attending "a party" given by piano teacher Miss Marsalles (212). It is an annual ritual at which fewer and fewer students each year perform predictably banal pieces for their bored, "ex-Rosedale" mothers (Noonan 171), themselves former students of the now elderly and socially-embarrassing teacher. The two mothers "giggle despairingly" as they remember discomforts endured at the more recent of the gatherings, and the narrative voice remarks on the escalating sense that "Miss Marsalles' parties ... are getting out of hand, anything may happen. There is even a moment, driving in to such a party, when the question occurs: will anybody else *be* there?" (212; emphasis added).

This proves to be a pivotal question, a fulcrum on which Munro's decisions about narrative voice, structure, and theme can be seen to balance. The question's ostensible meaning concerns "the widening gap in the ranks of the regulars" (212) – in other words, how many other mothers will deign to make "the annual, sacrificial trek" this time? (Taylor 137) – yet the question also points forward in the story, proleptically, to the surprise arrival of Miss Marsalles' developmentally-delayed pupils from Greenhill School, who, to the astonishment of everyone but their piano teacher and themselves, participate in the recital, too.

"Will anybody *else* be there?" (to shift the emphasis) is thus answered positively in a way that unbalances both the mothers and the reader.

133

Indeed, the story intentionally confuses the reader by its point of view, conflating the narrating suburban mother(s) with the voice of an adolescent daughter and thereby cultivating an inter-generational condemnation of Miss Marsalles and her Greenhill students. It is a silent judgment bound up, as Héliane Catherine Daziron (subsequently publishing under the name Héliane Ventura) explains, with "scorn, pity, and irritation" (118), which can be likened to the notion of tolerance in one of its obsolete meanings: the practice of enduring or sustaining pain or hardship.

With an imperiousness that achieves near physical anguish at the arrival of the Greenhill students, the narrative voice conveys the women's collective outrage at the imposition that tolerance forces upon them. Yet tolerance proves to be as entirely wrong-headed a notion as prejudice itself, for it is one of the "*little idiots*" of Greenhill School who, inexplicably, provides the sole shining moment of musical feeling during the sweltering and "preposterous afternoon" (222). This is not merely judgment or joke (though it is both), but rather a kind of prophecy for those who do not, and will not, hear. Munro's final story, in her first published collection, combines real-life pretensions and prejudice with an overlay of mythology-via-music, thereby underlining divisions while suggesting an as-yet-unimagined – and probably impossible – social reality that accepts both poverty and disability.

"Dance of the Happy Shades" generates a complex present-tense voice that oscillates between daughter and mother(s), thereby establishing not the past-tense retrospective narration that we have come to associate with the majority of Munro's *oeuvre* but rather a comingled point of view in which there is often no clear temporal distinction between the past and the present experiences of separate narrative consciousnesses. Munro's use of voice in this story is perhaps best understood as coalescing around class and class's persistence over time.

As readers and critics have long observed, a deep class consciousness pervades Munro's body of work,[1] deriving from her childhood sensitivity to poverty and exclusion. Unlike most of the other stories in the 1968 collection, however, the narrative of Miss Marsalles' annual recital "does not much draw on personal material" (Thacker 162).[2] Munro herself describes the "*I* of the story" as a kind of experiment in ventriloquism: "a masquerade, ... a little middle-class girl I never was, an attempt to see the story through the eyes of the relative who told it to me" ("The Colonel's

Hash Resettled" 183). The story's first paragraph makes the unpropitious pronouncement that "Miss Marsalles is having another party" (211), and reinforces the mother's urgent attempts to decline the invitation with a five-fold use of the insistent adverb *now* (Daziron 117). What results, as Daziron argues, is a "pattern of opposition between a present and a non-present" that "juxtapose[s] the alternatives" and "builds up a sort of enigmatic or conjectural mood, in which the uncertain prevails and not the definite or factual" (117).

Among the uncertainties, Miss Marsalles' altered social status looms large. The story suggests that one of "several troublesome meanings" assigned to "*now*" ("Dance" 211) concerns Miss Marsalles' "downward slide" economically (Noonan 171), from Rosedale to increasingly unsavoury neighbourhoods. The party cannot possibly be held, the narrative voice suggests, "[n]ow that Miss Marsalles has moved from the brick and frame bungalow on Bank Street, where the last three parties have been rather squashed, to an even smaller place – if she has described it correctly – on Bala Street" (211). The reader perceives that such detailed knowledge of Miss Marsalles' steadily declining material circumstances, going back at least four years, can hardly be available to the adolescent daughter, and yet somehow the reader is given this information as if from that "little middle-class girl" that Munro has created. The uncertainty in narrative point of view is thus established.

In a similar way, the strained telephone conversation between the mother and Miss Marsalles masterfully generates a to-and-fro whereby the listening daughter cannot possibly be privy to the information that proceeds from private assumptions, unheard tones of voice, unspoken rejoinders, and complex facial expressions:

And [Miss Marsalles] asks how her June party could ever be too much trouble, at any time, in any place? It is the only entertainment she ever gives any more (so far as my mother knows it is the only entertainment she ever has given, but Miss Marsalles' light old voice, undismayed, indefatigably social, supplies the ghosts of tea parties, private dances, At Homes, mammoth Family Dinners). She would suffer, she says, as much disappointment as the children, if she were to give it up. Considerably more, says my mother to herself, but of course she cannot say it aloud; she turns her face from the telephone with that look of irritation – as

if she had seen something messy which she was unable to clean up –
which is her private expression of pity. (211-12)

This quotation, with its parenthetical qualification, "(so far as my
mother knows ...)," and its interpolation in dashes, "– as if she had seen
something messy ... –," aptly illustrates the story's tendency to qualify,
re-phrase, and escalate tension by means of parentheses and dashes. As
the story progresses, traces of the mother's memories, irritations, and
thoughts are similarly rendered by the narrative voice, yet the reader
recognizes that the daughter could not possibly command such knowledge; she appears to have no role other than participating in the recital
and complaining about being "'the oldest girl here'," for which she is
promptly shushed by her mother (219). This apparent incongruity of
viewpoint has caused at least one critic to criticize the point of view as
"apt but not believable" and to claim that the story subsequently "fails as
a memoir" (Osachoff 65). I would postulate, rather, that the blurring and
conflating of voices makes possible the rhetorical power of prolepsis: the
representing of something future as already done or existing; the young
daughter, in other words, as anticipating or indeed already possessing
something of her mother's exclusionary upper-middle-class view of the
world and bringing us along for the read.

The story's literal and figurative geographies ride the narrative voice's
inflected through-line in terms of both class pretensions and (as I will
discuss shortly) intertextuality. When we are told that Miss Marsalles has
descended "to an even smaller place – if she has described it correctly
– on Bala Street," the narrative voice continues, "(Bala Street, where
is that?)" (211). This tonally-laden question, rendered parenthetically
after an interjection between dashes, speaks as if in the voices of both
the daughter and the mother simultaneously. One might be tempted to
read the parenthetical question as the daughter's lack of geographical
knowledge, "(Bala Street, where *is* that?)," but the more likely emphasis is
the rhetorical adult one, the one overlaid with implicit judgment about
the place that will turn out to be "one of these half-houses" in the vicinity
of "the railway embankment" (216-17): "(*Bala* Street, *where* is *that*?)."

Readers might correctly view Bala Street as prefiguring other dis-
reputable streets and roads in Munro's fiction: the Flats Road in *Lives of
Girls and Women*, of course, and Pearl Street in "Meneseteung," among

others. *Pace* critic Jean-Marc Victor, who considers Munro's Bala to refer to the Muskoka-area cottage-country "town north of Toronto famous for its waterfalls" (190),[3] I would argue for the simpler explanation of Bala Avenue, a real place in the Mount Dennis area of Toronto, due west of Rosedale (hence figuratively appropriate to the final decline / sunset of Miss Marsalles' parties) and in the 1950s just beginning the transition "from a rural outpost to an urban neighbourhood" ("History of Mount Dennis"). Mount Dennis' high elevation might account for Munro's mention of "the railway embankment" (necessary to counteract the area's ravines when the CPR line went in), and its history of "sawmills, wool mills, the Mount Dennis brickyards and the Conn-Smythe Sand and Gravel Pit" could certainly account for the distaste with which the fictional suburban mothers regard this decidedly working-class area (Archer).[4]

For as Daziron correctly observes, the mothers in the story "constitute a collective role" and serve "the same collective function of opposition" (118) to Miss Marsalles. Metaphorically, their unwilling journey to Miss Marsalles' residence is figured as a nightmarish descent into an underworld of distasteful poverty. The mothers twice refer to the Bala Street address using the direction "down" ("It is a hot gritty summer day as we drive down into the city and get lost, looking for Bala Street" [216]; "the heat is particularly dreadful down here" [219]) – and in the infernal heat of the recital day, Bala Street strikes them as "the worst place in the city" (220).

An element of revulsion, introduced into the descriptions of almost every aspect of the Bala Street party, confirms the hellishness of the event. Mrs. Clegg, the neighbour, reveals the unseemly detail that Miss Marsalles' sister (a shadowy presence at past parties, but always there) lies ill upstairs, having lost not only "'her powers of speech'" but also "'[h]er powers of control generally'" (218). It is Mrs. Clegg, too, who verifies what the narrator-mother can already ascertain from the dry tops of sandwiches, the flat-looking punch, and the flies "crawl[ing] comfortably" over the cupcakes: that the food was set out too early and is festering in the heat (218).

Tensions escalate: the narrator-mother feels "the hideousness" of being privy to details of failed hostessing in a hostess's own living room; the daughter notices "with disgust" that she is "'the oldest girl here'"; when Mrs. Clegg leans over to speak, she "let[s] loose a cloud of warm unfresh odour from between her breasts" (219). Munro makes it clear that the social event is unravelling as surely as are Miss Marsalles' tawdry presents, tied with silver ribbon that is "not real ribbon, but the cheap kind that splits and shreds" (220).

Into this miasma the developmentally-delayed Greenhill students suddenly arrive, shocking the narrative voice which in turn displays the "[f]ear and disgust directed toward disabled bodies" that Munro would explore subsequently in "Child's Play" (Narduzzi 73). Upon the "unlooked-for" arrival of the children from Greenhill School (220), and their squeezing in, literally, behind the daughter as she plays her "lumpy" version of a Handel minuet (221), the mothers send out silent salvos that strike the daughter as indicative of "perhaps something disastrous; you can feel such things behind your back" (221). What the daughter notices, as she returns to her seat after playing, are the Down Syndrome facial features and the "infantile openness and calm" of the Greenhill students (221).

The strange children, with their insistent profiles, are both alluring and revolting. Their presence and their subsequent effect on the mothers seem to enact Sianne Ngai's theory that "desire and disgust are dialectically conjoined" (332-33). As the daughter notes, "My mother ... looks around the room and meets the trapped, alerted eyes of the other women, but no decision is reached. There is nothing to be done. These children are going to play" (221). The narrator-mother's revulsion here – to use Ngai's formulation – "seeks to include or draw others *into* its exclusion of its object, enabling a strange kind of sociability" (336). The women are thus united in their fascinated opposition to the children.[5]

Standing in contrast to the trapped mothers is the thrice-invoked figure of the absent Marg French: the fair-weather telephone compatriot who had promised to come but has failed to show – failed to suffer through the heat, the delay, "the complacent journeys of the marauding flies" (220), and failed, by her absence (recall the opening question, "will anybody else *be* there?" [212; emphasis added]), to share the intolerable affront of mentally-handicapped children performing alongside able-bodied children of privilege.

Building on the metaphorical sense of hell already established, Munro aligns the physical and emotional geographies in the story with the mythical resonances of Christoph Willibald Gluck's eighteenth-century opera, *Orphée et Eurydice* (1774), and in particular with the Act II, scene ii expanded ballet, "*Danse des ombres heureuses*," from which the short story takes its translated title ("Dance" 223).[6] Linking the piano recital to the mythological underworld setting of the Orpheus narrative, Munro has the mothers react to the repulsive otherness of the Greenhill children with what could be considered their own silent but ragingly kinetic Dance of the Furies – another extensive ballet, complete with flames-of-hell stage machinery, that Gluck added to the 1774 version of his opera in the scene directly before Orphée enters Elysium (Beaumont, "*Orphée*").

In Miss Marsalles' living room, the objects of the exclusion, the "unlooked-for" children (220), are also unlooked-at, as the mothers find "there is nowhere to look" (222), politely or otherwise, that will not bring them face to face with the "freakish inescapable dream" that has assailed them (222). In a replay of the audibly inaudible telephone conversation with Miss Marsalles at the beginning of the story, the daughter offers that

> My mother and the others are almost audible saying to themselves: *No, I know it is not right to be repelled by such children and I am not repelled, but nobody told me I was going to come here to listen to a procession of little – little idiots for that's what they are* – WHAT KIND OF A PARTY IS THIS? (222)

As against the earlier euphemism of the well-meaning neighbour, Mrs. Clegg ("'Sometimes that kind is quite musical'" [221]), the mothers' collective outrage is a wordless barrage that ramps up via conjunction-joined clauses to a declaration of roiling disgust: "*– little idiots for that's what they are –*" (222). The reader, battered by italics, dashes, and starkly capitalized letters – "WHAT KIND OF A PARTY IS THIS?" – registers the revulsion-that-passes-for-tolerance as acute physical discomfort, a Fury-ous dance of outraged eyes. As Daziron puts it, "The story implicitly denounces the institutionalized violence of the social ritual and its conventions ... by resorting to the violence of language" (124). This wordless viciousness, forged by the mothers as an affective link between disgust and tolerance, can not help but profoundly unsettle the reader.

It is possible that Munro, following the trajectory of Gluck's opera in her storyline, intended that the reader would experience the same transformation that Orphée does, when, directly following "the fiendish

Dance of the Furies – [he] stumbles out of the deepest circle of hell and is struck dumb by the beauty of the Elysian Fields" (Beaumont, "*Orphée*"). Gluck's Dance of the Blessed Spirits, an elegant, serene, sorrow-tinged minuet that occurs before Orphée is reunited with Eurydice, could not provide more of a "heightened juxtaposition" to the tempestuous Dance of the Furies (Beaumont, "*Orphée*"). The suburban mothers, however, listening to the piece being played with almost miraculous artistry by the gangly Greenhill prodigy, Dolores Boyle, react not with changed hearts but rather with "protest" and even greater "anxiety" (222).[7]

In the paradox of perspective that makes Miss Marsalles' living room, in that moment, as much an Elysian Fields for her as it is a Hades for the furious mothers, there is no final peaceful harmony and, likewise, no Gluckian happy ending. Eighteenth-century opera's rules demanded happy endings to tragic stories, and Gluck's librettist provided one in which, although Eurydice dies a second time – having forced Orphée to turn and look at her as they travel out of the underworld, which causes her to perish in his backward glance, plunging him into suicidal sorrow – the god Amour appears and announces that Orphée's constancy will be rewarded by the beloved Eurydice's being restored to life. The pair then joyfully celebrate in Love's temple before returning to the upper world.[8]

If the mothers have played the role of the Furies, they may also be considered a collective version of Orphée – reference their backward-glancing nostalgia for a distant past – with Miss Marsalles as their (rejected) Eurydice. The mothers have already consigned Miss Marsalles' economic shame to "that region of painful subjects which it is crude and unmannerly to discuss" (216). The final degradation of Miss Marsalles to a row house on Bala Street, next door to a grocery and confectionery store, decisively disrupts "the changeless ceremony" that has characterized past parties to this point (Daziron 119). In the end, although the reader continues to clasp Miss Marsalles firmly in imagination, the narrative voice decisively turns its back, leaving her behind, "quite certainly forever" (224).

Munro's intertextual play with Gluck's opera ventures beyond simple correspondences into sub-strata social commentary and criticism that now seems ahead of its time. The story makes it clear that the ultimate abandonment of Miss Marsalles by the suburban mothers and their children is directly caused by her foisting on them not just economic embarrassment but also the even more "painful" (216) and, to them, unspeakable normalization of mentally-handicapped children. It has been argued that the Greenhill students appear in Munro's story as a kind of displacement of the mental illness attributed to the piano teacher in the 1949 Eudora Welty story, "June Recital," that aesthetically underlies "Dance,"[9] but this contention seems to minimize the specific social realities that Munro challenges in her story.

The provenance of "Dance of the Happy Shades" – an unsigned story pulled from a slush pile by Gerald Taaffe at *The Montrealer* in 1960 as the only item worth publishing (the first of six Munro pieces published in that magazine between 1961 and 1965 [Thacker 162-63]) – makes it clear that it was written in the 1950s. Vanessa Guignery claims a more specific date: "the summer of 1959 when Munro was 28 (a few months after her mother died)" (6). At that time, as even a cursory search reveals, there were few resources available for mentally-handicapped children in Canada, and nothing as radical as Greenhill School existed. Munro's deliberate inclusion of the Greenhill children, at a time when Canadian society excluded them, clearly bears both textual and contextual importance.

Since "Dance of the Happy Shades" was written about Toronto but Munro herself was living in Vancouver for most of the 1950s,[10] both Ontario and British Columbia can be scrutinized for the resources that they offered to the developmentally-delayed. Melanie Panitch notes that both provinces (like other places in England and the United States) began to mobilize at the end of the 1940s by means of small groups of mothers coming together to find solutions for their mentally-handicapped children – solutions that did not involve institutionalization (3-4, 36-37). In April of 1955, provincial parent and volunteer Associations from across Canada met in Toronto "to consider forming a national organization," and one-and-a-half years later met again to ratify a constitution for the Canadian Association for Retarded Children, which "formally came into being on January 31, 1958" (Panitch 37). Individual chapters of the Association became known as ARC, with the city or province identified immediately afterwards in the name.

In neither British Columbia nor Ontario, however, did government yet accept the public responsibility of educating children with mental handicaps; in British Columbia, at least, the Department of Education lagged behind the Department of Health in that regard.[11] It was not until 1959 that the BC School Act was amended and public school boards agreed to educate "'moderately retarded' children," signalling "the first time in Canada that educating children with special needs was recognized as a public responsibility" ("The 1950's").

In Toronto, as is mentioned in the January 1959 issue of *The Rotarian*, initiative came from "[f]ive Rotary Clubs in the northern metropolitan area" which had begun to "promot[e] a campaign to build a school for mentally retarded children" ("Rotary Reporter" 47).[12] The June 1962 issue of the same magazine devotes four pages and multiple photographs to this "North Toronto School for Mentally Retarded Children" that had been up and running, by that point, for almost three years ("They Love to Learn" 34),[13] with construction having begun in 1958 (a year before Munro wrote her story), according to historian Edward Shorter (124).

Various pieces of evidence seem to prove that this school was Beverley Public School, of the Toronto District School Board – a school still in operation today that is uniquely designed for "students who have a developmental and/or physical disability" ("Welcome to Our School").[14] One wonders if Munro could have known about Toronto's Rotary Club initiative, and about the construction of Beverley Public School, in the months before her story was written.

Still more likely, especially given certain hints in "Dance" itself, is the possibility that Toronto's St. Christopher House, a long-standing fixture of community activity and inner-city support, was the model that Munro had in mind (if indeed she had any model in mind at all). Established in 1912 as part of the reformist settlement movement's focus on alleviating urban poverty,[15] "St. Christopher House was filled with children's activities" during the post-World War Two decades and began at that time to pay particular attention "to children with special needs and to youth" (O'Connor 26). By 1957, special groups had been created for "mildly retarded and emotionally disturbed children" (O'Connor 26).

In addition, from the 1920s until 1950, St. Christopher House ran a "Vacation Bible School," consisting of "games, sports, outings and Bible stories" (O'Connor 3, 18, 27). Significantly, Munro – who worked as a maid in the Forest Hill area of Toronto in the summer of 1948 (Thacker 81, Ventura 108-09) and could well have encountered such a group of children – echoes this particular nomenclature in "Dance of the Happy

Shades" when the daughter first perceives the Greenhill children arriving on Miss Marsalles' doorstep: "It must seem at first that there has been some mistake. ... Is it the wrong house, are they really on their way to the doctor for shots, or to Vacation Bible Classes?" (220).

A second possible link with St. Christopher House concerns Swiss-born Madame Madeleine Boss Lasserre who was hired in the 1940s, by the music director of St. Christopher House, "to introduce free classes in eurhythmics for small children" (O'Connor 27). Dalcroze Eurhythmics was the "method of music education using body movement" that Lasserre brought from her studies with Émile Jacques-Dalcroze in Geneva and pioneered at Toronto's exclusive Margaret Eaton School when she was hired there in 1925 (Landen Odom and Orford).[16] In 1927, Lasserre "joined the Toronto Conservatory of Music (Royal Conservatory of Music) where she taught eurhythmics, solfège, and improvisation for more than 50 years" (Landen Odom and Orford).[17] It would have been during her many years of teaching at the Royal Conservatory that Madame Lasserre also offered instruction to disadvantaged youth at St. Christopher House.

In terms of the Swiss-born music teacher's interactions with both privileged and lower-class students, her long music-teaching career, and her assonant surname composed of virtually the same letters as Miss Marsalles' surname, the real-life Madame Lasserre offers a tantalizing parallel to Munro's fictional Miss Marsalles. ("Marsalles" and "Lasserre" contain all of the same letters with the exception of the "M," but the "M" can be accounted for if one includes the initial of Lasserre's first name, "Madeleine."[18]) Whether or not this correspondence can be verified is, perhaps, less important than the fact that such details in Munro's stories encourage us to research and to contemplate the significance of the social, intertextual, and biographical dimensions of her fictional world.

In an early interview with J.R. (Tim) Struthers, Munro acknowledged that a title assumes, in Struthers' words, "different connotations" when used for a single story as opposed to the naming of a collection (Struthers 28-29). W.R. Martin has pointed out that "most of the stories in *Dance of the Happy Shades* deal with lives that are mean, or barren, or – because circumscribed by poverty, provincialism or other circumstances – unfulfilled" (120); there would therefore seem to be a good deal of intentional irony in Munro's agreeing to a book title which seems light and almost frivolously innocent. (Robert Thacker notes that Earle

Toppings advocated for *Dance of the Happy Shades* over *Walker Brothers Cowboy* as the title of Munro's first collection [Thacker 547n24].) The moniker "Dance of the Happy Shades" is, of course, inseparable from its intertextual meaning, its positioning in Gluck's opera, and as such assumes connotations of both fragile hope and the otherworldly "great unemotional happiness" of the happy dead (222). The references to dance and to "various modes of theatrical display" that can be traced through a number of stories in the collection proceed in a way that "culminates in the allusion to Gluck" (Duplay 203, 204). But this allusion is likely lost on many readers until the final story, making them not unlike the suburban mothers at Miss Marsalles' party.

Another party, earlier in the collection, revelatory of anything but "happy"-ness, resonates with the title story in terms of both characterization and an ironically innocent-sounding title: "The Shining Houses." Mrs. Fullerton, one young neighbour sarcastically remarks, "'isn't exactly a charming old lady'" (29), but her economic non-status in the story aligns her with Miss Marsalles, as do the attitudes of those residents of the subdivision against whom she, and the main character, Mary, struggle. In a sense, "The Shining Houses" presents the opposite impulse from "Dance": not an older generation's steady decline in economic prosperity but a younger generation's violent forcing of affluence out of effluence, planks over raw, running ditches, "The new, white and shining houses, set side by side in long rows in the wound of the earth" (23). Yet, as in "Dance," the notion of disgust focusses on the seemingly time-locked older woman who is the object of the others' "self-assertion and anger" (27). One might consider "The Shining Houses" as commenting proleptically on the power of the suburban mothers in "Dance." Mary notes that her resistance to signing the petition to evict Mrs. Fullerton will merely "serve [herself] up as a conversational delight for the next coffee party" (28). The residents of the subdivision – like the suburban mothers – "are people who win" (29), in practical, though perhaps not in ultimate, respects.

If it is true, as Lorraine McMullen once posited, that disparity, irony, the element of surprise, and the reader's superiority all work together to create humour (149-50), then the end of "Dance of the Happy Shades" is a grand guffaw. But at whose expense? And apropos of what thematic significance? Critics have generally focussed on the final paragraph of the story, the one that explains how, in the wake of the glorious music inexplicably played by Dolores Boyle, the daughter and the mothers (and note the fully harmonized "we" here) recognize that their superiority has been subverted:

> But then driving home, driving out of the hot red-brick streets and out of the city and leaving Miss Marsalles and her no longer possible parties behind, quite certainly forever, why is it that we are unable to say – as we must have expected to say – *Poor Miss Marsalles?* It is the Dance of the Happy Shades that prevents us, it is that one communiqué from the other country where she lives. (224)

This final sentence has been generally taken as explanatory, as a stand-alone "moral" (Taylor 137) or "message" (Noonan 169) about the triumph of art over life (and, by extension, of the eccentric Miss Marsalles over the judgmental mothers), or even as a kind of narrative epiphany for the daughter such that "everything has changed, and a different life begins" (Martin and Ober 138). I would suggest that such interpretations are perhaps too positive. The final musical performance at Miss Marsalles' party – both miracle and trick, as the narrative voice observes (223) – does not seem to transform anyone, most definitely not the mothers. As Mathieu Duplay notes, "However beautifully played, Gluck's music fails to make the intended impression; he sought a unity of effect capable of melting the most hardened hearts, but Dolores Boyle's performance is harshly criticized by Miss Marsalles' guests" (212). The mothers acknowledge the music but refuse the musician. "The facts are not to be reconciled" ("Dance" 223) and neither are the mothers reconciled to the socioeconomic and emotional challenges of the Bala Street recital. They will not be moved; they will not accept.

This judgmental response accounts for the "look of protest" on the faces of the mothers, "a more profound anxiety than before, as if reminded of something that they had forgotten they had forgotten" (222). Steadfast in their repudiation, the mothers can leave the party, and all future parties, "quite certainly forever" (224), returning to the self-styled supremacy of the suburbs after the music is finished, having convinced themselves that Dolores Boyle "is just the same as before, a girl from Greenhill School" (223), and that, because of her disability, her undeniable talent is "after all useless, out-of-place" (223). As a result, the mothers and presumably their children can comfortably settle back into a more conventional kind of tolerance – that "repressive tolerance" that maintains the class structures and the systems of exclusion in capitalist democracy (Marcuse qtd. in Ngai 340)[19] and renders the Dolores Boyles of the world, and the Miss Marsalleses, and, most chillingly, perhaps, art itself, "harmless and helpless" (Marcuse 94), forgettable, after all, for "people who live in the world" ("Dance" 223). The title of Gluck's piece – like the title of Munro's story, and of her first published collection – is an allusion lost on the audience that it most needs to impress, leaving "nobody any the wiser" (223), with the possible exception, Munro trusts, of the reader.

"Never mind," the narrative voice concludes, dismissively (223). The joke is on us.

Notes

1. Lorrie Moore's review of *Hateship, Friendship, Courtship, Loveship, Marriage* points out that "there is not one of her stories in this new book that does not put together characters with real if subtle class divisions between them" (qtd. in Thacker 505). Similarly, Aritha van Herk's review of *The Love of a Good Woman* asserts: "Snide class judgements are frequent" (qtd. in Thacker 484). Robert Thacker puts it this way: "Although Munro early achieved a middle-class way of living through family aspiration, study, and marriage, her Lower Town Wingham upbringing has never left her – it echoes throughout her work" (484).

2. As Thacker clarifies, the story "owes something to a music teacher named Miss McBain who taught [Munro's first husband] Jim's aunt Ethel; it derives its setting from Munro's summer as a maid in Toronto [in Forest Hill at age 17, in the summer of 1948 (Thacker 81; Ventura 108-09)] and her visits to Oakville, and it gets its characters from there and from Munro's time in suburban Vancouver" (Thacker 162). A recent study by Jean-Marc Victor has supplemented this list. Building on an earlier essay by Heather Cam, Victor has shown definitively how Munro's "Dance of the Happy Shades" is a re-writing of Eudora Welty's story "June Recital" from her 1949 story cycle, *The Golden Apples*.

3. Bala, for Victor, is a cypher for the Welty story that Munro's story "engages in an intertextual dialogue" (187). Victor considers the Muskoka-area cottage-country town of Bala to be significant in that it has a waterfall – this because Welty refers to Miss Eckhart's face as resembling "what might be seen behind the veil of a waterfall" (qtd. in Victor 190).

4. As the Mount Dennis Business Improvement Area website points out, "Mount Dennis sits atop one of the highest topographical plains in the City of Toronto and is surrounded by lush ravines and parkland. Bordered on the west by the historic Humber River and on the east by Black Creek, it was founded by shipbuilder and United Empire Loyalist John Dennis in 1797 for its access to the Humber River (through Black Creek)[.] [T]he neighbourhood has been home to sawmills, wool mills, the Mount Dennis brickyards and the Conn-Smythe Sand and Gravel Pit as well as the Kodak Company Plant (1916-2005). // Mount Dennis is one of the most culturally diverse neighbourhoods in the Greater Toronto Area, representing more than 30 ethnic groups" ("About Mount Dennis").

5. Collusion in order to exclude an outsider similarly occurs in Munro's 2009 story, "Child's Play," when two girls at a summer camp, Marlene and Charlene, intentionally, silently, and remorselessly drown the developmentally-delayed Verna, whom they have constructed as a monstrous other (222).

6. This opera was originally performed in Vienna, in Italian, in 1762, as *Orfeo ed Euridice* but was reworked twelve years later, in 1774, for a French audience, as *Orphée et Eurydice* (Beaumont, "Remixing"). Gluck significantly expanded the use of ballet in the second act. Beaumont explains how "the substantial Dance of the Furies" was added to the revised version of the opera in Act II, "sating Parisian desire for dance" ("*Orphée*"). In addition, near the end of Act II, "Gluck ended up tripling the length of the Dance of the Blessed Spirits, adding that mournful middle section and closing with a reprise of the original F major music. This move was again prompted by the expectation of his Paris audience for dance – but by this expansion Gluck also deepens our sensation of the blessed spirits, of their elegance but also their sadness, and the ache Orpheus must feel knowing his Eurydice is among them" ("*Orphée*"). Ildikó de Papp Carrington's

"Recasting the Orpheus Myth: Alice Munro's 'The Children Stay' and Jean Anouilh's *Eurydice*" demonstrates Munro's continued interest in the Orpheus story.

7.   There is, of course, an intentional paradox between the sublime music generated by Dolores Boyle's sensitive playing and the sorrow and physical ugliness implied in the girl's name – its associations, as Redekop notes, with the words "dolour" and "boils" (27).

8.   The preface to the French adaptation of the opera, *Orphée et Eurydice*, says this about the necessity of changing the tragic ending to a happy one: "Pour adapter cette fable à notre scène, l'auteur a été obligé de changer la catastrophe, et d'y ajouter l'épisode de l'Amour, qui réunit ces époux" (Moline 4).

9.   Victor argues that "the mental disturbance of Morgana's piano teacher is transferred on to the children from Greenhill School in Munro's story" (189).

10.   As Munro told Jeanne McCulloch and Mona Simpson in *The Paris Review*, "I got married [at] the end of 1951, went to live in Vancouver and stayed there until 1963" (247).

11.   According to Inclusion BC, the delegates at ARC BC's 1956 meeting were told by the Department of Education's representative, Dr. W.A. Plenderlaith, that "'Government does not wish to go into the field of education for retarded children and believes it is better to leave the matter in the hands of the organizations who are dealing with it'" ("The 1950's"). The article continues: "His counterpart from the Department of Health, Dr. A.M. Gee, was a bit more inspiring and for his time, somewhat visionary. 'Every child has the right to develop his potentialities to the maximum,' he said. 'Every effort should be made to prevent him being cut off, by the special provisions made for him, from his family, from other more normal children of his age, and from the community in general'" ("The 1950's").

12.   The news item continues: "The Rotary Clubs of WILLOWDALE, ARMOUR HEIGHTS, EGLINTON, FOREST HILL, and DOWNSVIEW hope to raise $50,000 for the school, which will accommodate 125 students" ("Rotary Reporter" 47-48).

13.   The June 1962 issue of *The Rotarian* notes how the $50,000 that the Rotarians needed for their share of the $125,000 project was raised within one month of the kick-off dinner, "and a bit more than a year

later Rotarians of the five Clubs gathered again, with others who had helped, this time to view opening-day classes in the gleaming new school their efforts had wrought" ("They Love To Learn" 35). One of several photographs of the school included in this issue features a famous cowboy twirling a lasso over the head of a young boy. The photograph is captioned as follows: "On opening day, cowboy star Roy Rogers dropped in to entertain the youngsters" ("They Love To Learn" 36).

14. Proof that the Rotarian school is Beverley Public School comes from several sources that corroborate the *Rotarian* articles. In *The Kennedy Family and the Story of Mental Retardation* (2000), Edward Shorter provides a direct link, although he does not name the school: "The Rotary Clubs of Toronto had traditionally been active on behalf of MR [mental retardation], building in 1958 a school for the mentally retarded in North Toronto" (124). Shorter outlines how the Toronto chapter of ARC informed a Rotarian, in 1960, "that no research was being done in the area of physical education and fitness for MR children" and that subsequently "[t]he five Rotary clubs of North Toronto then asked the head of the phys-ed department at the University of Toronto to conduct a research program, which the clubs would fund" (124). Shorter notes that "the University of Toronto hired a young Canadian named Frank Hayden" to carry out the research (124).

A Special Olympics website makes specific the connection between Frank Hayden and Beverley School. A photograph of Hayden with uniformed school children appears on the website, beside which the following explanation appears: "In the early 1960s, a group of students at Toronto's Beverley School, became the test group for Dr. Frank Hayden, a sport scientist at the University of Toronto. Dr. Hayden was studying the effects of regular exercise on the fitness levels of children with an intellectual disability" ("Our History"). The Special Olympics website goes on to make an interesting connection among Hayden, Beverley School, and the inaugural competition of the Special Olympics in Chicago in 1968 – an event spearheaded by Eunice Kennedy Shriver, sister of the famous Kennedy politicians – namely, that it was Beverley School students who competed as Canada's entry ("Our History").

Beverley School appears to have been built on the grounds of a residence owned by Senator George Brown, "a leading Liberal politician and co-founder of the *Globe* newspaper (now *The Globe and Mail*)" who died in 1880 (Mill). From 1920 to 1956, this residence, at the corner of Beverley Street and Baldwin Street, was occupied by the Canadian National Institute for the Blind (Mill). The Beverley School web page cites the school's address as 64 Baldwin Street, and offers the following history: "The school, originally used as a training site for the CNIB and Bell Canada, has been a school for students with intellectual and physical disabilities since the 1950's" ("Welcome to Our School").

15. The settlement house model was one in which "staff actually lived in residence in poor neighbourhoods," learning "first hand about the problems facing their neighbours and join[ing] them in seeking solutions" ("History"). Today St. Christopher House – now called West Neighbourhood House – continues "to engage [with] the community to find solutions to the current social problems of homelessness, youth unemployment, social isolation and challenges of an aging population" ("History").

16. The Margaret Eaton School was "an institution that attracted the attention of Canada's elite" from its inception in 1906 until its amalgamation into the University of Toronto in 1941; it proved to be "an influential fore-runner to the development of a Canadian theatrical tradition" (Fischlin). It was also "one of the few schools in Canada addressing the need for advanced education for women in the early twentieth century" ("Margaret Eaton School").

17. As stated in Selma Landen Odom and Emily-Jane Orford's *Canadian Encyclopedia* article on "Dalcroze Eurhythmics," "Lasserre taught many generations of Dalcroze educators until her retirement in 1977, including dancer-choreographer Saida Gerrard; pianist Donald Himes; Donna Wood (b Donna Jean Roblin, Saskatoon 4 Aug 1920, d Kitchener, Ont 10 Oct 2007), an international leader in early childhood music education; and artists Temma Gentles and Tim Jocelyn." Donna Wood, in fact, was the music director at St. Christopher House who hired Lasserre, her former teacher, in the 1940s (O'Connor 27).

18. In much the same way, as Dilia Narduzzi notes of Munro's story "Child's Play," which concerns a disabled child who is drowned by two able-bodied children, all of the letters in the fictional child's name, "Verna," appear in the name of the real-life South-Asian-Canadian child, Reena Virk, who was bullied and murdered for her otherness in 1997, a decade before Munro's story was published (Narduzzi 77n2).

19. Marcuse calls this "an ideology of tolerance which, in reality, favors and fortifies the conservation of the status quo of inequality and discrimination" (123).

Works Consulted

"About Mount Dennis." *Mount Dennis Business Improvement Area*. 2017. <www.mountdennisbia.ca>.

Archer, Bert. "A Possible Kodak Moment: Our Visit to Mount Dennis Finds a Storied Community at a Crossroads." *Yonge Street*. 2 May 2012. <www.mountdennisbia.ca/a-possible-kodak-moment-our-visit-to-mount-dennis-finds-a-storied-community-at-a-crossroads/>.

Beaumont, Rachel. "*Orphée et Eurydice* Musical Highlights: Dance of the Blessed Spirits and Dance of the Furies." *Royal Opera House*. 4 Sept. 2015. <www.roh.org.uk/news/orphee-et-eurydice-musical-highlights-dance-of-the-blessed-spirits-and-dance-of-the-furies>.

---. "Remixing in the Age of Baroque: How and Why Gluck Transformed *Orfeo ed Euridice* into *Orphée et Eurydice*." *Royal Opera House*. 11 Sept. 2015. <www.roh.org.uk/news/remixing-in-the-age-of-baroque-how-and-why-gluck-transformed-orefeo-ed-euridice-into-orphee-et-eurydice>.

Bigot, Corinne. "Alice Munro's 'Silence': From the Politics of Silence to a Rhetoric of Silence." *The Short Stories of Alice Munro*. Ed. Héliane Ventura. *Journal of the Short Story in English / Les cahiers de la nouvelle* 55 (2010): 123-38. <https://journals.openedition.org/jsse/1116>.

Bigot, Corinne, and Catherine Lanone. *Sunlight and Shadows, Past and Present: Alice Munro's* Dance of the Happy Shades. Paris: Presses Universitaires de France – Cned, 2014. Série Anglais.

Cam, Heather. "Learning from the Teacher: Alice Munro's Reworking of Eudora Welty's 'June Recital'." *SPAN: Journal of the South Pacific Association for Commonwealth Literature and Language Studies* 25 (1987): 16-30.

Carrington, Ildikó de Papp. "Recasting the Orpheus Myth: Alice Munro's 'The Children Stay' and Jean Anouilh's *Eurydice*." *The Rest of the Story: Critical Essays on Alice Munro.* Ed. Robert Thacker. Toronto: ECW, 1999. 191-203.

Daziron, Héliane Catherine. "The Preposterous Oxymoron: A Study of Alice Munro's 'Dance of the Happy Shades'." *Canadian Number.* Ed. Rosemary Sullivan and Frank Davey. *The Literary Half-Yearly* 24.2 (1983): 116-24.

Duplay, Mathieu. "'The Other Country Where She Lives': Opera and Its Doubles in Alice Munro's 'Dance of the Happy Shades'." *The Inside of a Shell: Alice Munro's* Dance of the Happy Shades. Ed. Vanessa Guignery. Newcastle upon Tyne, Eng.: Cambridge Scholars, 2015. 200-16.

Fischlin, Daniel. "The Margaret Eaton School of Literature and Expression." 2004. *Canadian Adaptations of Shakespeare Project.* University of Guelph. <www.canadianshakespeares.ca/essays/margareteaton.cfm>.

Francesconi, Sabrina. "Negotiation of Naming in Alice Munro's 'Meneseteung'." *The Short Stories of Alice Munro.* Ed. Héliane Ventura. *Journal of the Short Story in English / Les cahiers de la nouvelle* 55 (2010): 123-38. <https://journals.openedition.org/jsse/1115>.

Guignery, Vanessa. "Introduction: The Balance of Opposites in Alice Munro's *Dance of the Happy Shades*." *The Inside of a Shell: Alice Munro's* Dance of the Happy Shades. Ed. Vanessa Guignery. Newcastle upon Tyne, Eng.: Cambridge Scholars, 2015. 1-24.

"History." *West Neighbourhood House.* <www.westnh.org/about-us/history/>.

Howells, Coral Ann. "Intimate Dislocations: Alice Munro, *Hateship, Friendship, Courtship, Loveship, Marriage*." *Alice Munro.* Ed. and introd. Harold Bloom. New York: Bloom's Literary Criticism-Infobase, 2009. 167-92. Bloom's Modern Critical Views.

Landen Odom, Selma, and Emily-Jane Orford. "Dalcroze Eurhythmics." *The Canadian Encyclopedia.* 29 June 2009; last ed. 9 June 2014. <www.the-canadianencyclopedia.ca/en/article/dalcroze-eurhythmics-emc/>.

Marcuse, Herbert. "Repressive Tolerance." *A Critique of Pure Tolerance.* By Robert Paul Wolff, Barrington Moore, Jr., and Herbert Marcuse. Boston: Beacon, 1969. 81-123. <www.marcuse.org/herbert/pubs/60s-pubs/1965MarcuseRepressiveToleranceEng1969edOcr.pdf>.

"Margaret Eaton School Digital Collection: The School." 9 Mar. 2018. Redeemer College. <libguides.redeemer.ca/MES/home>.

Martin, W.R. "Alice Munro and James Joyce." *Journal of Canadian Fiction* 24 (1979): 120-26.

Martin, W.R., and Warren U. Ober. "Alice Munro as Small-Town Historian: 'Spaceships Have Landed'." *The Rest of the Story: Critical Essays on Alice Munro.* Ed. Robert Thacker. Toronto: ECW, 1999. 128-46.

McCulloch, Jeanne, and Mona Simpson. "Alice Munro: The Art of Fiction CXXXVII." *The Paris Review* 131 (1994): 226-64. <https://www.theparisreview.org/interviews/1791/alice-munro-the-art-of-fiction-no-137-alice-munro>.

McMullen, Lorraine. "'Shameless, Marvellous, Shattering Absurdity': The Humour of Paradox in Alice Munro." *Probable Fictions: Alice Munro's Narrative Acts.* Ed. Louis K. MacKendrick. Downsview, ON: ECW, 1983. 144-62.

Mill, Adam D. "A City Intersected: Beverley Street & Baldwin Street." *Torontoist* 21 Dec. 2007. <https://www.torontoist.com/2007/12/a_city_intersec_9>.

Moline, P.L. Préface. *Orphée et Euridice, Drame Héroïque en Trois Actes, Représenté pour la première fois par l'Académie Royale de Musique, le Mardi 2 Août 1774, et remis au même Théâtre le 23 Juin 1809.* Poëme de P.L. Moline. Musique de Gluck. Ballets de Milon. Sixième Édition, revue, corrigée et augmentée par l'Auteur. Paris: Roullet, 1810. 3-4. <http://www.archive.org/stream/orpheeteuridiced00calz?ref=ol#mode/2up>.

Munro, Alice. "Child's Play." *Too Much Happiness.* Toronto: McClelland & Stewart, 2009. 188-223.

---. "The Colonel's Hash Resettled." *The Narrative Voice: Short Stories and Reflections by Canadian Authors.* Ed. and introd. John Metcalf. Toronto: McGraw-Hill Ryerson, 1972. 181-83.

---. "Dance of the Happy Shades." *Dance of the Happy Shades.* Fwd. Hugh Garner. Toronto: Ryerson, 1968. 211-24.

---. *Lives of Girls and Women.* Toronto: McGraw-Hill Ryerson, 1971.

---. "Meneseteung." *Friend of My Youth*. Toronto: McClelland & Stewart, 1990. 50-73.

---. "The Shining Houses." *Dance of the Happy Shades*. Fwd. Hugh Garner. Toronto: Ryerson, 1968. 19-29.

Narduzzi, Dilia. "Regulating Affect and Reproducing Norms: Alice Munro's 'Child's Play'." *Journal of Literary and Cultural Disability Studies* 7 (2013): 71-88.

Ngai, Sianne. "Afterword: On Disgust." *Ugly Feelings*. Cambridge, MA: Harvard UP, 2005. 332-54, 403-05.

"The 1950's." <http://www.inclusionbc.org/about-us/history/1950s>.

Noonan, Gerald. "The Structure of Style in Alice Munro's Fiction." *Probable Fictions: Alice Munro's Narrative Acts*. Ed. Louis K. MacKendrick. Downsview, ON: ECW, 1983. 163-80.

O'Connor, Patricia J. "The Story of St. Christopher House 1912-1984." Toronto: Toronto Association of Neighbourhood Services, 1986. *West Neighbourhood House*. <www.westnh.org/about-us/history/838-2/>.

Osachoff, Margaret Gail. "'Treacheries of the Heart': Memoir, Confession, and Meditation in the Stories of Alice Munro." *Probable Fictions: Alice Munro's Narrative Acts*. Ed. Louis K. MacKendrick. Downsview, ON: ECW, 1983. 61-82.

"Our History." *Special Olympics / Olympiques spéciaux Canada*. <http://www.specialolympics.ca/learn/about-special-olympics-canada/our-history>.

Panitch, Melanie. *Disability, Mothers, and Organization: Accidental Activists*. New York: Routledge, 2008.

Redekop, Magdalene. "*Dance of the Happy Shades*: Reading the Signs of Invasion." *Alice Munro*. Ed. and introd. Harold Bloom. New York: Bloom's Literary Criticism-Infobase, 2009. 5-28. Bloom's Modern Critical Views.

"Rotary Reporter: 'Doc Rotary' Lends a Hand." *The Rotarian* Jan. 1959: 46-48.

Shorter, Edward. *The Kennedy Family and the Story of Mental Retardation*. Philadelphia: Temple UP, 2000.

Skagert, Ulrica. "The Rupture of the Ordinary as an 'Awkward Little Space': Evental Moments in Alice Munro's 'Dance of the Happy Shades'." *The Inside of a Shell: Alice Munro's* Dance of the Happy Shades. Ed. Vanessa

Guignery. Newcastle upon Tyne, Eng.: Cambridge Scholars, 2015. 271-82.

Smith, Rowland. "Wilderness and Social Code in the Fiction of Alice Munro." *Alice Munro*. Ed. and introd. Harold Bloom. New York: Bloom's Literary Criticism-Infobase, 2009. 153-65. Bloom's Modern Critical Views.

Staines, David. "David Staines Talks with Alice Munro." *Reading Alice Munro in Italy*. Ed. Gianfranca Balestra, Laura Ferri, and Caterina Ricciardi. Toronto: The Frank Iacobucci Centre for Italian Canadian Studies, 2008. 11-13.

Struthers, J.R. (Tim). "The Real Material: An Interview with Alice Munro." *Probable Fictions: Alice Munro's Narrative Acts*. Ed. Louis K. MacKendrick. Downsview, ON: ECW, 1983. 5-36.

Taylor, Michael. "The Unimaginable Vancouvers: Alice Munro's Words." *Probable Fictions: Alice Munro's Narrative Acts*. Ed. Louis K. MacKendrick. Downsview, ON: ECW, 1983. 127-43.

Thacker, Robert. *Alice Munro: Writing Her Lives: A Biography*. Toronto: McClelland & Stewart, 2005.

"They Love To Learn: Teamwork in Toronto, Ontario, Educates the 'Uneducable'." *The Rotarian* June 1962: 34-37.

Ventura, Héliane. *Alice Munro:* Dance of the Happy Shades. Neuilly, Fr.: Atlande, 2015. Clefs concours Anglais-Littérature.

Victor, Jean-Marc. "Happy Shades of 'June Recital' in 'Dance of the Happy Shades': Munro's Dance with Welty." *The Inside of a Shell: Alice Munro's Dance of the Happy Shades*. Ed. Vanessa Guignery. Newcastle upon Tyne, Eng.: Cambridge Scholars, 2015. 186-99.

"Welcome to Our School." *Beverley School*. <schools.tdsb.on.ca/beverley/>.

Welty, Eudora. "June Recital." *The Golden Apples*. 1949. New York: Harvest-Harcourt, Brace & World, 1962. 20-97.

Remembering "Every Last Thing": Alice Munro's Epilogue to *Lives of Girls and Women*

Neil K. Besner

But when from a long-distant past nothing subsists, after the people
are dead, after the things are broken and scattered, taste and smell
alone, more fragile but more enduring, more unsubstantial,
more persistent, more faithful, remain poised a long time, like souls,
remembering, waiting, hoping, amid the ruins of all the rest;
and bear unflinchingly, in the tiny and almost impalpable drop
of their essence, the vast structure of recollection.
— Marcel Proust, *Remembrance of Things Past* (I, 50-51)

The Novel and Its Stories

When J.R. (Tim) Struthers asked Munro in a 1983 interview about the order in which she wrote sections of the book, she replied:

> OK. I remember that quite clearly. "Princess Ida" was the first. It was going to be a short story. Then I saw it was going to work into a novel, and then I went on and on writing what I thought was a novel. Then I saw that wasn't working. So I went back and picked out of that novel "Princess Ida" in its original form – I had changed it to make it into the novel – and I picked out "Age of Faith," "Changes and Ceremonies," and "Lives of Girls and Women." Then, having written all those separate sections, I wrote "Baptizing." Then I went back and wrote the first two sections, the one about Uncle Benny, "The Flats Road" ... and "Heirs of the Living Body." And then I wrote the "Epilogue: The Photographer," which gave me *all* kinds of trouble. (Munro in Struthers 24-25)

In Munro's explanation we can see some of the reasons for the book's related claims as a novel and as a book of stories. These are not contradictory claims: a chapter in a novel is not the opposite of a story in a book of stories.

There are several elements of *Lives of Girls and Women* that pull towards the centralizing form of a novel: a single narrative voice (although this might be a deceptive way to describe Del's narration); a single central character (although at times she is defined more fully by her reactions to another character or to an event she observes rather than experiences); a relatively stable cast of surrounding characters, including Del's family (although Del's father and her brother Owen, like Uncle Benny, recede to the Flats Road for a good part of the time in which Del's experiences are centred in Jubilee, and each section of the book tends to focus on Del's experience with a different set of characters); a roughly chronological line of development, tracing Del's growth from childhood through adolescence; and a common setting in Jubilee and the surrounding countryside.

But many of the elements of *Lives of Girls and Women* pull in a different direction – towards the form of a book of stories (as distinct from a collection of stories). First, we might consider Munro's description of the way she wrote the book: as suggested in the book's title, which looks towards the lives of both girls *and* women, the connections and distances between mother and daughter radiate out from the centre of this narrative towards its beginning and its end ("The Flats Road" and the last two sections) as Del explores her evolving relationship with her mother, the "Princess Ida" that Munro began with. As her material grew under her pen, we can see how the shape of this relationship became so prominent in the book it informs. From the nucleus and the transformations of "Princess Ida," Munro tells us, came the three sections after it; then came "Baptizing," followed by the book's two opening sections; and finally, the closing "Epilogue."

The continuous narrative line that we follow through the novel is also reshaped by the alternating cadences of Del's voice. Not only does Del's voice convey the distances as well as the closeness between past and present, between a younger Del and an older Del recollecting her experiences; it also conveys another, still older Del's insight into that *whole* process of growth and change, and this is the voice of Del the writer, who speaks of and through all of the younger and the older versions of Del presented to us. In fact, we are invited to read Del the writer – and not Munro – as the creator of this book, as distinct from Munro, the author, who creates Del the writer, who speaks to us through her earlier and later reincarnations.

We hear this synchronicity of voice, which cuts across the chronology of events in this book, more fluently than we apprehend the events Del narrates; and the events that Del narrates tend to organize themselves into what could often stand as self-contained stories. From section to section, from chapter to chapter, Del often reminds her readers of who characters are, how settings signify, or what time frame we are reading in. But Del's voice always invites us to migrate easily with her across the borders between past, present, and future, so that our sense of what happens to her becomes more episodic than strictly linear.

In other words, the casual relations between events that usually form a plot line are strongly affected by the forces and forms of Del's voice. Her voice shapes the parts of the book into reports, stories, and insights into the experiences Del recalls in order to give herself shape, to define her life in ways that seem meaningful to her – to turn her life into a story so that she might learn its form. We follow Del's impulses to shape her experiences through the seemingly erratic rhythms of her narration – its leisurely pauses to linger over the details of a description, its abrupt shifts and turns to different scenes and episodes. Our process of reading this kind of narration immerses us in the kind of development Del imagines and creates: the shaping of an identity seeking to order incoherent experience into the forms of stories.[1]

Del's impulse to turn reality into fiction leads me to the importance of the many different kinds of stories in this book, and here we can begin to see one of the ways in which *Lives of Girls and Women*, like much contemporary writing, begins to look in towards its own nature, its own workings and significance as a fiction, just as much as it looks out towards the stages of Del's experiences growing up in Jubilee. Del's strong need to turn events in her life into episodes in a fiction – to transform her experiences into stories that might reveal the significance of both – suggests some of the connections between living a life and narrating a story, between hearing and recounting different versions of stories, and between understanding autobiography as truths about a life and autobiography as a life story.

We should be aware from the beginning not only that Del is telling us the story of her life – a story that changes its meanings for Del as she tells it to us – but also that she is fascinated with the various kinds and forms of stories that other characters tell about their own pasts and about each other. Consider Del's stories about Uncle Benny, and the stories that will be told by the community about Madeleine after her departure, in "The Flats Road"; Auntie Grace and Aunt Elspeth's stories about their youth, and Uncle Craig's history of Wawanash County, in "Heirs of the Living Body"; Del's mother's and her Uncle Bill's different stories about their childhood in "Princess Ida"; the versions of belief embraced or abandoned in "Age of Faith"; Mr. Chamberlain's stories of wartime Italy in the title story, and Del's private stories about her imagined romance with him; or the many luridly docudramatic, melo-dramatic, and pornographic stories told in the various texts that Del describes as she reads them.

This emphasis on the origins, the narration, and the significance of stories, for Del and for other characters, invites us to reflect with Del on the nature of fiction as it reports, informs, and recreates reality, work-ing its transformations so inconspicuously and yet consistently that we believe Del's stories as if they were "true" stories – true, that is, to their nature as fictions, and not only to the facts of Del's (or of Munro's) expe-rience. At this level, *Lives of Girls and Women* is not simply composed of Del's stories about her life; it is also Del's story about the composition, and the lives, of stories.

I don't propose to resolve the debate over the form of *Lives of Girls and Women* here, but rather to open up the question so that the book can be read plurally, through its several ways of conveying its stories, chapters, or episodes, with their several ways of meaning. Munro herself has called *Lives of Girls and Women* both "an episodic novel" (Munro in Gerson 4) and a book in which "the sections could almost stand as short stories" (Munro in Gibson 258), and the book's early reviewers, as John Metcalf recalls, identified it as "'[m]emoir, autobiography, novel, collec-tion of short stories'" (60). In its generous possibilities as a novel *and* a book of short stories, *Lives of Girls and Women* widens the resonances of both forms.

"Epilogue: The Photographer" – How Del Writes

The last and the shortest section of *Lives of Girls and Women* was the one that gave Munro the most trouble – to the point that she changed her mind several times about including it at all. As Thomas E. Tausky has shown in detail in "'What Happened to Marion?': Art and Reality in *Lives of Girls and Women*," the Munro papers collected at the University of Calgary, which include several earlier drafts of this section, provide a fascinating glimpse of Munro's difficulties and of her process of revision.[2]

The epilogue is also the part of the novel that has given readers the most difficulty. Some have found it an unconvincing or unnecessary justification of Del's, and perhaps of Munro's, purposes and techniques in writing fiction, while others have found it successful on both these counts; some have found it too autobiographical, too much in Munro's voice rather than Del's.[3] But the difficulties with this section, whether they are Munro's or her readers', need not obscure how this "Epilogue" is intended to function in relation to the whole book.

Throughout the novel, Del reflects on the sound and sense of individual words; on her various forms of reading, and on various kinds of writing; and on the stories that she hears, that others tell, that she herself shapes and tells. In this final section, Del tries to define not only what she writes, or why she writes, although she explores both of these areas, but also *how* she writes. That she fails to explain this fully is an eloquent illustration of Del's apprehension of fiction's ultimately mysterious nature. Although Del is left dissatisfied with her (unwritten) novel about Caroline and the photographer – and then further frustrated with the heartbreaking impossibility of writing fiction that will "really" render a setting, a character, an experience, or a life – we may be left more content with Del's necessarily inadequate explanation of her fictional techniques and purposes.

Like the earlier themes Del explores, writing itself will finally be revealed as an unknowable mystery, and this will be the final illuminating correction to her vision in this book. It is an insight that allows Del to close her narration and to begin her novel – because this section also begins to transform *Lives of Girls and Women*, the novel we have been reading, into the novel that Del is about to write – with an affirmation that is an awareness of any writer's limitations, an acknowledgement of mystery, and above all a declaration of independence and inheritance.

The first major question that Del explores in this closing section raises an issue that has troubled her throughout the book, and that sooner or later engages most writers and readers: what is "real" in fiction? Munro's original title for *Lives of Girls and Women* was "Real Life" (Munro in Struthers 29), and the question of what is real arises often and in many different guises throughout the book. Now, however, the question centres on the powers and the nature of fiction itself, and on how a writer conceives of her art. And because of Del's role in this section as an interpreter, a commentator on her own fiction, the question brings home to us its inevitable corollary: how do readers conceive of their art, of the fictions that they shape from the text?

The novel that Del carries in her head originates in two questions that she poses, questions that she will discover cannot be answered satisfactorily in fiction. One is the question she asks herself while talking to Bobby Sherriff on the porch of the Sherriff house: "*What happened to Marion?*" (251). The other is the question implied by Del's contemplation of Marion Sherriff's picture in the hall of the high school, and explored through Del's creation of the character of the photographer in her unwritten novel: what kind of representation of reality is a photograph, and how should we read photographs?

Neither the explanation provided by Fern Dogherty for Marion's suicide nor Del's mother's reasoned objection to Fern's analysis is enough for Del: she needs to write a novel which will comprise a different kind of explanation, one that takes as its points of departure the photograph of Marion and the inexplicable fact of her suicide. But the photograph – a seemingly documentary representation of Marion's appearance – and the suicide – an act which would seem to demand an explanation derived from the circumstances in Marion's life that might have led up to her death – do not inspire Del to write a novel that operates as *Lives of Girls and Women* seems to be doing. *Lives of Girls and Women* seems to be a piece of fine realist fiction, a novel that shows us a faithful, detailed representation of real life, of more or less plausible characters acting in plausible ways in recognizable settings. But Del's novel departs from these conventions.

Caroline, the character that Del creates, does not represent Marion physically in the least:

> ... *Caroline*! Her name was Caroline. She came ready-made into my mind, taunting and secretive, blotting out altogether that pudgy Marion, the tennis-player. Was she a witch? Was she a nymphomaniac? Nothing so simple! (246)

Del's creation, "wayward and light as a leaf" (246), is an enchantress who acts in ways unthinkable, inconceivable in the Jubilee we have come to know through Del's narration. She is a seductress, one who picks the most unlikely partners and who seems to act sexually rather than being acted upon sexually; but she is also, in ways somewhat reminiscent of Del's experiences in the title chapter and in "Baptizing," described as a passive agent:

> She was the sacrifice, spread for sex on mouldy uncomfortable tomb-stones, pushed against the cruel bark of trees, her frail body squashed into the mud and hen-dirt of barnyards, supporting the killing weight of men, but it was she, more than they, who survived. (246)

We might see elements of Del's experience as a girl growing up in Jubilee transformed in her creation of Caroline, so that the character not only blots out Marion, but affords Del herself a more richly ambiguous sexual life, one that allows her, and not the men with their "killing weight," to endure.

Regardless of what elements of Del's experience we might read into her creation of Caroline, though, we can see that Caroline and Marion are worlds and conventions apart. Marion (and her photograph) is a part of the Jubilee world that Del has recollected throughout *Lives of Girls and Women*, whereas Caroline belongs in a world that Del has created for her own fictional purposes, a world less mimetically reflective of Jubilee. The fictional world of Del's novel, she recalls, was "true" rather than "real" (248), and it revealed all of the depths and mysteries that she had always perceived to lie beneath everyday reality. Yet her description of this fictional universe opens with the same reference to mental imagery that evoked Del's confusion in "Changes and Ceremonies" over operetta director Miss Farris's different poses and gestures, and that now force-fully returns us to one dimension of a photographer's art:

> All pictures. The reasons for things happening I seemed vaguely to know, but could not explain; I expected all that would come clear later. The main thing was that it seemed true to me, not real but true, as if I had discovered, not made up, such people and such a story, as if that town was lying close behind the one I walked through every day. (248)

Del's description is not a realist's credo. The truth of her conception has little to do with realism's aims; the novel is "true" in that it presents what she imagines, what she sees in her "pictures" of Caroline, the Halloways, the Jubilee she has transformed for her own purposes. None of this is "real" in the same way that Del's evocations of her own Jubilee life have been, and will be in the novel Del will write and we have just read. The Halloway novel gives Del a coherent world, true to its own nature, true to her own intentions, but not "true" to the less predictable real world that her novel transforms in ways that are more apparent to us, and to Del, than the transformations necessarily produced in *any* work of fiction, including *Lives of Girls and Women*. The Halloway fiction is not necessarily worse fiction, or weaker fiction; it is only fiction that more visibly departs from the conventions of realism. In this way, it is just as "true" as *Lives of Girls and Women*.

It is tempting to read the role of the photographer in the Halloway novel as an important comment on the stance and function of the writer, particularly the writer of realist fiction. A more plausible photographer, taking photographs like the one of Marion that hangs in the main hall of the school, would practise an art more in keeping with our suppositions about realist fiction. His photographs would not transform their subjects to expose horrifying revelations. Real photographs, as Del is discovering about the photograph of Marion (and as we might discover, along with Del, about realist fiction), announce a paradox. On one hand, they seem to represent reality in images that read like documentary, literal transcriptions, so that when we see a face in a photograph, we are apt to say, that *is* the person it represents. In other words, we do not usually read photographs with much attention to their artifice, to their *re*presentation of reality. But on the other hand, a photograph, by virtue of its seemingly perfect rendering of a part of reality – a face, for example – becomes impenetrable, impossible to interpret, because it seems to offer no gap between that which it represents – the original face – and the *re*presentation, the photograph.

Realism, Del is in the process of discovering – and we have been discovering throughout this novel – performs a similar illusion. But her photographer only seems to wield the realist's instruments of perception; like Del's Caroline, he departs radically from convention, so that his photographs, like the "pictures" from which Del constructs her Halloway novel, reveal truths rather than "real" images. Of all Jubilee, only Caroline is not afraid of him; one way of understanding her impassioned pursuit of the photographer is to read it as her (and Del's) desperate search for the truth of her own nature, which this photographer (in a neat reversal of the failure of the Jubilee photographer who took Marion's picture to reveal in it any truth about Marion to Del) might be able to reveal. At this point Del's novel ends by returning to its point of departure, the mystery of Marion's suicide, the enigma of her photograph, just as *Lives of Girls and Women* will soon end by returning to its point of departure. The photographer vanishes, and Caroline, like Marion, walks into the Wawanash River (247).

Del's account of her first attempt at a novel may be completed, but the reality that she drew on for its creation remains to push Del into another inadequate attempt to recreate her past. When Del accepts Bobby Sherriff's invitation to have a piece of cake and some lemonade, she realizes, sitting on the Sherriff porch, that reality, in all of its ordinary, everyday, flat impenetrability, has persisted, in spite of her novel about it. Not only this: she sees that it is her novel, and not reality itself, that has lost power (251). The writer's art, regardless of its conventions, creates a reality which, regardless of its own truth, is *both* autonomous *and* related to the world it refers to, however diffuse or symbolic this connection may be. Paradoxically, it is in the Halloway novel that we (along with Del) may be able to see more clearly the relations between real world and fictional world. In *Lives of Girls and Women* itself, the relations are more mysterious, for all of realism's supposed mimetic properties; and Del is discovering this mystery at the heart of what will be her art as she sits with Bobby Sherriff, who is himself only the last of the several Jubilee eccentrics who have confronted Del with unknowable and yet alluring realities.

While Bobby Sherriff explains to Del (anticipating the title of Munro's 1978 book of stories) that he knows who she is ("'I know you.... Didn't you think I knew who you were?'" [251]), Del is confronted with the realization that whatever else it might do, fiction does not provide explanations of reality. This realization reaffirms the insights Del has been gaining about inexplicable but enduring realities throughout her story; as well, it helps her to see how she might write a novel like *Lives of Girls and Women*, and helps us to understand how we might read it:

> And what happened, I asked myself, to Marion? Not to Caroline. *What happened to Marion?* ... Such questions persist, in spite of novels. It is a shock, when you have dealt so cunningly, powerfully, with reality, to come back and find it still there. (251)

Reality is, indeed, "still there," and as Del muses on its pervasive, persistent, insistent presence, she returns for the last time to one origin of her novel about Caroline and the photographer – the photograph of Marion – and is led from there to her famous insight, which resolves for one luminous moment Del's lifelong experience of surface and depth, appearance and reality, flat ordinary details and the mysteries they proclaim, into an image announcing the presence and plurality of *all* these qualities:

> His [Bobby's] sister's photographed face hung in the hall of the high school, close to the persistent hiss of the drinking fountain. Her face was stubborn, unrevealing, lowered so that shadows had settled in her eyes. People's lives, in Jubilee as elsewhere, were dull, simple, amazing and unfathomable – deep caves paved with kitchen linoleum. (253)

It is important to notice, as Del does, that it is Marion's *photographed* face that hangs in the hall – that it is this *image* of her face that is "stubborn, unrevealing."

From this perception of what the photographer's art does *not* render, Del is able to reach her insight about people's lives everywhere, in and beyond Jubilee. The passage ends where *Lives of Girls and Women* begins: not with the mystery concealed by surfaces, but with the surface itself. It is the ordinary "kitchen linoleum" underfoot, usually faded, that covers the "deep caves." The passive agency suggested by the structure of the closing phrase – "paved" by someone, no one, or everyone – appears to offer us an indication of unconscious, ritualized, or unintentional behaviour; but the more explicit suggestion of intentionality and domesticating, civilizing concealment conveyed by "paved" offers us a fitting complementary reading, so that the syntax and vocabulary of the phrase enact at one more level the vision of complementary worlds, complementary visions that Del has been creating.

From recording this insight Del moves to the first of the novel's two conclusions, narrated from the vantage point of the adult Del, recalling that she did not realize, sitting on the porch with Bobby Sherriff, that she would "one day ... be so greedy for Jubilee" (253). In "Heirs of the Living Body," Del gains an important insight into the kind of mistake her Uncle Craig was making when writing his history of Wawanash County; now, she extends the compass of that insight to include her own "[v]oracious and misguided" impulse "to write things down" (253). This is an interesting formulation, suggesting that making fiction might depend on lists, on accuracy, on reporting, as Uncle Craig did, what took place, why, to whom, when, and where. But Del's process of correction and adjustment continues: writing things down will not give her what she wants, she now realizes, any more than Uncle Craig's history did. It is her recognition of what she really wants, of what fiction might really be capable of giving her, that will return Del in memory to her moment with Bobby Sherriff on the porch.

Del wants detail – the grainy particulars, all of the elements that all of her senses can apprehend – in order to read them into language and shape them through her imagination to give them the fictional form that will bring her past alive. This is the kind of list that Del realizes she needs, and this is what she writes down as her last insight:

> And no list could hold what I wanted, for what I wanted was every last thing, every layer of speech and thought, stroke of light on bark or walls, every smell, pothole, pain, crack, delusion, held still and held together – radiant, everlasting. (253)

With this passage we have reached the point closest in time to the present of Del the writer, looking back over her past and over the way she looks at her past, learning how she will write. *Lives of Girls and Women*

remains to be written, and Del takes us back to her younger incarnation, sitting with Bobby Sherriff, to show us Del's opening response, at
the beginning of her career as a writer, at the first end of our careers
as readers of this text. Presumably, Del will return to Bobby Sherriff's
gesture through language, through writing things down, because "the
only special thing" (253) he ever does for her appears to Del to have "a
concise meaning, a stylized meaning" (254) which is written, performed
in "an alphabet" (254) she cannot read.

Del's closing gestures invite at least two readings. His wishing her
luck in her life is a sincere and conventional gesture, to which Del might
have responded with the expected "Thank you." But Del's actual response
is more resonant, given that Bobby has just risen on his toes for her, in
the last theatrical act in the novel. Del's "'Yes'" (254) may well be the
bold affirmation that we expect from a narrator who takes "[p]eople's
wishes, and their other offerings," as if they were her due – "naturally, a
bit distractedly" (254). But it may also be an acknowledgement of what
she does not know, what she has just seen in Bobby's gesture – another
entrance into the "deep caves paved with kitchen linoleum" (253) that
are people's lives. "Thank you" would diminish Del's vocabulary, close her
novel, and return us to the world. "'Yes'" (254) opens out the possibilities
of her imagination, affirms the powers of her fiction, and returns us to
Lives of Girls and Women.[4]

Epilogue: The Reader, the Text, and the Real

Any reading of a text is partial. It will vary with the varying circumstances of each reader's cultural experience, including its historical,
national and regional, social and psychological dimensions. And a text
like *Lives of Girls and Women*, with what I have read as its complementary forms, its invitations to contemplate mysteries, and its narrative
intricacies, seems to multiply readings rather than consolidate them;
I have read this tendency as a good thing. No reading is complete; any
hope for such total authority is as "crazy, heartbreaking" (253) as Del's
hope for a total recapturing of her past, and probably a more serious
delusion. And just as there are no total readings, it may be that there are
no "true" readings; perhaps there are only "real" readings.

But if that were so, it would leave us with an obvious question: what is a "real" reading? This returns us to one of the central concerns of *Lives of Girls and Women*, and brings me to my conclusion by way of an essay of Munro's, "What Is Real?".

In the opening of her essay, Munro comments on the inevitable questions that arise when she is asked about her fiction:

"Do you write about real people?"

"Did those things really happen?"

"When you write about a small town are you really writing about Wingham?" (223)

These are questions that relate directly to the tendency of some readers to read *Lives of Girls and Women* as autobiography. Munro suggests that "People go on asking these same questions because the subject really does interest and bewilder them. It would seem to be quite true that they don't know what fiction is" (223).

Lives of Girls and Women may help us to refine our ideas of how we read fiction by dissolving, just as Del dissolves, any hard and fast distinctions we might want to draw between fiction and reality, or between fiction and autobiography, between a life story and a life. Novels do not stand in direct opposition to reality; they do not present mirror images of reality; they do not explain reality. There are autobiographical elements in *Lives of Girls and Women*, as Munro has freely admitted; and there are ways in which Jubilee resembles Wingham. But fiction does not draw on what is real in any straightforward way; rather, fiction may be a kind of enquiry into what is real, an exploration of what is. Beyond any such investigative purpose, then, fiction also *creates* reality, performs a kind of reality. And reading fiction requires the same kind of creation and performance.

Del Jordan's explorations of what is real are readings, constructions of the experiences she recalls and reshapes into a novel, so that her life becomes a story – not a true story, but a real one. Del's story traces and enacts her development as a person and as a writer, developments that are intimately connected with her growth as a reader. Our readings of *Lives of Girls and Women* may not be true, but if they encourage us to rediscover the texts of the book, the world, and ourselves, they are real.

Notes

1. I am indebted to Carlene Besner for this insight.
2. For an enumeration and detailed description of the Munro papers at the University of Calgary, see Jean M. Moore and Jean F. Tener, comps., *The Alice Munro Papers First Accession* and Jean M. Moore, comp., *The Alice Munro Papers Second Accession*.
3. See, for example, the reviews by James Polk, Clara Thomas, and Marigold Johnson, the interview by J.R. (Tim) Struthers, and the essay by Thomas E. Tausky.
4. For discussions of ways Del's "'Yes'" (254) represents an echo by Munro of the "Yes" that opens and closes Molly Bloom's monologue in James Joyce's *Ulysses*, see the essays by J.R. (Tim) Struthers (45-46) and Barbara Godard (69-71).

Works Cited

Gerson, Carole. "Who Do You Think You Are?: A Review-Interview with Alice Munro." *Room of One's Own* 4.4 (1979): 2-7.

Gibson, Graeme. "Alice Munro." *Eleven Canadian Novelists*. Toronto: House of Anansi, 1973. 237-64.

Godard, Barbara. "'Heirs of the Living Body': Alice Munro and the Question of a Female Aesthetic." *The Art of Alice Munro: Saying the Unsayable*. Ed. Judith Miller. Waterloo, ON: U of Waterloo P, 1984. 43-71.

Johnson, Marigold. "Mud and Blood." Rev. of *Plough Over the Bones*, by David Garnett, *Bring Larks and Heroes*, by Thomas Keneally, *Lives of Girls and Women*, by Alice Munro, and *Jane*, by Dee Wells. *New Statesman* 26 Oct. 1973: 618-19.

Joyce, James. *Ulysses*. 1922. The corrected text. Ed. Hans Walter Gabler. Student's Edition. Harmondsworth, Eng.: Penguin, 1986.

Metcalf, John. "A Conversation with Alice Munro." *Journal of Canadian Fiction* 1.4 (1972): 54-62.

Moore, Jean M., comp. *The Alice Munro Papers Second Accession: An Inventory of the Archive at The University of Calgary Libraries*. Ed. Apollonia Steele and Jean F. Tener. Calgary: U of Calgary P, 1987.

Moore, Jean M., and Jean F. Tener, comps. *The Alice Munro Papers First Accession: An Inventory of the Archive at The University of Calgary Libraries*. Ed. Apollonia Steele and Jean F. Tener. Biocritical Essay by Thomas E. Tausky. Calgary: U of Calgary P, 1986.

Munro, Alice. *Lives of Girls and Women*. Toronto: McGraw-Hill Ryerson, 1971.

---. "What Is Real?" *The Canadian Forum* Sept. 1982: 5, 36. Rpt. in *Making It New: Contemporary Canadian Stories*. Ed. John Metcalf. Toronto: Methuen, 1982. 223-26.

---. *Who Do You Think You Are?* Toronto: Macmillan of Canada, 1978.

Polk, James. "Deep Caves and Kitchen Lineoleum." Rev. of *Lives of Girls and Women*, by Alice Munro. *Canadian Literature* 54 (1972): 102-04.

Proust, Marcel. *Remembrance of Things Past*. Trans. C.K. Scott Moncrieff, Terence Kilmartin, and Andreas Mayor. 3 vols. New York: Random House, 1981.

Struthers, J.R. (Tim). "The Real Material: An Interview with Alice Munro." *Probable Fictions: Alice Munro's Narrative Acts*. Ed. Louis K. MacKendrick. Downsview, ON: ECW, 1983. 5-36.

---. "Reality and Ordering: The Growth of a Young Artist in *Lives of Girls and Women*." *Essays on Canadian Writing* 3 (1975): 32-46.

Tausky, Thomas E. "'What Happened to Marion?': Art and Reality in *Lives of Girls and Women*." *Studies in Canadian Literature* 11 (1986): 52-76.

Thomas, Clara. "Woman Invincible." Rev. of *Lives of Girls and Women*, by Alice Munro. *Journal of Canadian Fiction* 1.4 (1972): 95-96.

A Series of Metaphorical Epitaphs: Alice Munro's "The Ottawa Valley"

Louis K. MacKendrick

Some Opening Considerations

Alice Munro's stories have proven to be critical treasure troves whose riches sustain a growing number of appreciative and analytical approaches. The almost transparent accessibility of her narratives testifies in the first instance to a craftsmanship which is extraordinarily accomplished and seemingly unpretentious. On our first acquaintance with them, Munro's fictional environments seem lived-in, casual, accessible, very often familiar. Her fictions do not parade the skill behind their construction in self-conscious stylishness, but in the subtle arrangement of something like half-heard echoes.

Munro's ways of telling a story exploit the ambiguity and ambivalence of language. This means, most obviously, its natural potential for metaphorical and symbolic associations, its double entendres, its capacity for irony, and the ambiguities of narrators who may not be completely straightforward with their audiences. These kinds of prospects are complemented by an extensive vocabulary, and even by Munro's stylistic quirk of defining terms or concepts by several qualifying words. All this gives the impression, in any one short story, of a considerable universe both within and beyond that fiction: the story and its characters are usually larger than their technical confinement within several pages of narrative.

And yet, because of Munro's terrific sensitivity to the nuances of English, and the ways in which this allows the internal expansion of her fictions, her writing possesses an almost severe economy. A story sometimes reads as shorthand, as a sequence of emblems or symbols which stand for larger emotional and physical associations. These may be so implied in the story's language that strict exposition of such matters would be redundant, truistic, even banal. In effect, Munro's reader is, in the best of her work, forced to become involved as a creative partner, to work for the success of the story, to fill in narrative assumptions which the language of the story and its actors can, and do, understate.

"The Ottawa Valley"

"The Ottawa Valley," the concluding story of Munro's third volume, *Something I've Been Meaning To Tell You*, has a narrator who presumes upon the unwritten bargain with the reader. This tacit agreement (we should realize) concerns the acknowledgement of narrative objectivity, the maintenance of the proper distance of association, and the distinction between passive and active participation in a fiction. Particularly in the case of a first-person narrator there is the invariable danger of autobiographical identification: is this a character speaking/writing, or is it (for example) Alice Munro? Readers rarely allow for the existence of a persona in such instances, and the technical term needs its own reminder: it means the literary device of a character, through whom the author may voice at this one remove his or her personal concerns. James Joyce had his "Stephen Dedalus," Jonathan Swift his "Lemuel Gulliver," and Samuel Clemens his "Mark Twain," a persona who himself had a "Huckleberry Finn." Munro has said to J.R. (Tim) Struthers, "In 'The Ottawa Valley,' I'm looking at all this material, I'm looking at real lives, and then I not only have to look at the inadequacy of the way I represent them but my right to represent them at all. And I think any writer who deals with personal material comes up against this" (28).

In Munro's stories the "I" figure speaking with apparent straightforwardness to her audience about her models or techniques is the same kind of fictional creation, or persona. Munro's first-person narratives – a substantial portion of her work – are fictions, not memoirs. (It should go without saying that these characters have histories and attributes which have nothing to do with those of Alice Munro.) Certain recurring figures are not to be identified as the author's actual family, whose members and experiences may nonetheless contribute to whatever the writer is creating in a story. It is not difficult to find aspects of Munro's life in her stories, and we cannot be too often reminded that writers work from what they know. Munro has made this point in most of her interviews, affirming an emotional, rather than a factual, correspondence of her fiction and her life. We may have to be reminded of the narrator's cautionary words in the story "Winter Wind" from the same volume, "I have used these people, not all of them, but some of them, before. I have tricked them out and altered them and shaped them any way at all, to suit my purposes" (201). The illusion of life in any story by Alice Munro is a testimony to her successful technique, not to the successful verbal photography of her own life.

One problem with this concluding story is that it has the least "fictional" apparatus of any in this collection. What in Munro's fiction are relatively accessible themes and motifs – so acknowledging their answering to fictional demands and structures – are not here obvious, or implied. "The Ottawa Valley" has the form of a linear narrative, whereas Munro's fiction customarily takes liberties with the order of chronological time. Its narrator offers two endings, one more satisfactory from the perspective of art and the other not completely satisfactory for her personal need. This is the problem which is broached to the reader, though without inviting any decision. The image which concludes the narrative is, by no coincidence, that of a photograph, and through it Munro's narrator might imply some of the preceding distinctions. To arrive at this image, however, and the context within which it appears, requires a journey – another image from the same source.

We learn at the beginning that the narrator's mother had a "categorical way" (227), which perhaps explains why she is thought of by her daughter as being "in department stores" (227), where many categories are available. Yet the mother is presented as a relatively unbending and reserved individual, never completely committed to generosity of spirit: "Luck was not without its shadow, in her universe" (228). On the visit to the Ottawa Valley she manifested several contradictions. She claimed that she will not tolerate filth, but did not deny her cousin Dodie's risqué story about Allen Durrand. She did not forbid her daughter's taste of Uncle James's porter, though having insisted her husband not drink after they married. Splendidly outfitted for church, she still sacrificed her only strategic safety pin to the narrator's falling panties, so that her own slip "was showing in a slovenly way at one side" (241). When Dodie accused her cousin of not being repelled by the sight of Allen Durrand's frantic urination, the narrator observes, "She just looked as if there was a point at which she might give up" (236), and the remark has a double thrust. It is followed by a clinical description of Parkinson's disease and the degree to which the mother suffered from it, so that the juxtaposition with Dodie's rude accusation marks her defeat both by the disease and in her attempt to not put up with filth.

Much of the narrative, however, is about "Aunt" Dodie, the mother's cousin. Her remarks are often cynical and uncharitable, possessing a rural forthrightness and distrust of authority. Yet her condition seems predicated from the start on her desertion by her fiancé, a jilting in which she takes a masochistic pride. Instead of marriage, she milked the cows. "'Lots of girls would've cried, but me, I laughed'" (230), Dodie claimed, and the fact that now she "laughed at the end of every sentence" (228) perhaps marked her enduring disappointment. Her "bare" (229) house is virtually an emblem of how she had been emotionally marooned for years, of how functional her life was. Dodie's bitter obsessive song, "'There was I / Waiting at the church'" (231), further indicates her continuing fixation. She had none of the peace, *pacem*, attested on a gravestone in the grandparents' cemetery (239); the word is in Latin, a "dead" language like her prospects. (The narrator's mother confidentially reported Dodie's nighttime tears two years after the desertion.) Dodie did not speak to her sister, nor to Aunt Lena on the next farm. Metaphorically, her ice-house bespeaks her condition: it was "a roofed dugout where ice cut from the lake in winter lasted the summer" (231), not unlike her own regions of ice and denial. Lena's "remote unanswerable fury" (232) in beating her children is perhaps a public expression of what Dodie may have concealed beneath her brashness.

Dodie implied that Lena's incessant pregnancy was James's revenge for her abusive treatment of their many offspring: "'But he gets it back on her, doesn't he?'" (233). (The narrator's mother has also claimed, "'I will never listen to smut'" [236], so her association with Dodie must have been painful, but this is never stated.) Dodie's long anecdote about Allen Durrand and the lemonade had its own motives: sewing up the boy's fly is another metaphor, here for her later jilting. She relished the story, giving it effective dimension, order, and detail: it was, as it were, a turning of the tables on deceitful manhood, unknowingly overseen in "'full view'" (236). (A slight echo is anticipated here: Durrand's problem with his pants has its comic contrary in the girlish narrator's falling panties.) In "malice and kindness" Dodie told the girl one version of what Dodie called "'Life'" in the story of her mother's dropsy, part of her "threatening to let out more secrets than I could stand," and of her own generally mordant interests in life (243). Her mentioning the narrator's mother's little stroke reflects this slightly off-centre focus, but at another remove we may recall Lena's beaten and stroked children.

Yet in this catalogue of desertion and despair, in this feeding on hurt, Dodie managed one completely unselfish and generous act: she praised James's reciting of a verse from Wilfred Campbell's often-anthologized poem "Indian Summer." When she said, "'Good for you'" (245) harmony and community reigned; it was the only really unqualified positive reaction she has managed. She had "cheerfully" (245) recited some of Thomas Babington Macaulay's "Horatius," a poem about an admirable but fruitless defense against impossible odds – like that by the narrator's mother. Though the text is unclear, she may also have delivered some of Charles Wolfe's "The Burial of Sir John Moore after Corunna," another poem of doomed heroism – already encountered in the story "Tell Me Yes or No" earlier in the volume – with the same implicit application. Despite the mutual reciting and laughing, it is natural that Dodie caught the "'sad ring'" (246) that linked this informal contest of memory. At this point the story turns to the narrator's aesthetic comment.

One curious and informal motif is apparent in "The Ottawa Valley": the story deals somewhat incongruously with certain liquids. Dodie was seen in "her milking outfit" (229), a beggarly thing of fragments, laughing, cursing, and feeding a calf milk from a pail. The impression is of nothing quite coherent, of disruption of what the incident should look like. Lena obsessively feared her children's injury or deaths by water, snow, or ice. At Lena's the chamber pots were "not emptied every day" (231): the fastidious comment prepares for the joke at the expense of Allen Durrand. The story of the boy's discomfiture, neither smut nor filth, relies on the natural transformation of lemonade to urine; the lemonade leads to Uncle James's after-dinner porter and his song celebrating "*the water of the barley*" (238). The motif is given a Dodie-twist in her tale of her mother's dropsy, and the undescribed removal of unspecific "*Fluid*" from the woman "'by the pailful'" (243). This returns us in a grotesque circle to the feeding calf. The notion, which has no major function in the story, goes no further. It is better seen as one small example of Munro's attention to the minute through the sort of unpretentious detail which creates the convincing illusion of her fictions' reality. It represents the sort of element which helps to fill out her stories' self-contained authority, each its little convincing world.

The narrator's penultimate image of her mother, with herself significantly as a follower in growing darkness, is almost wholly metaphorical, with "her familiar bulk ahead of me turning strange, indifferent. She withdrew, she darkened in front of me" (244). The implication – deliberate, as will be evident – is of the unapprehended personality, a notion that has not preoccupied the narrator throughout this sequence of reminiscences. These images are followed by the qualification of the literal, "though all she did in fact was keep on walking along the path ..." (244). The metaphorical transformation has threatened to leave the girl behind; it concludes her relentless need to be assured that the woman will not get sick. The symbolic note has been struck: the mother was and remains a mystery; she did not answer; "For the first time she held out altogether against me" (244). This leads to the narrator's artistic and emotional inability to let her mother go, as she speaks to the reader out of her need and through the concluding flourish of leading poetic allusion and metaphor.

We return, then, to the final consideration of aesthetic effect: "If I had been making a proper story out of this, I would have ended it, I think, with my mother not answering and going ahead of me across the pasture" (246). The battle with the manner of the material is joined. The final scene, of the mother, James, and Dodie reciting and joined in laughter is, we infer, not "story" (246); somehow it spoils fictional closure, and the narrator's attempt to "reach" her mother is too large, and too undischarged, to be contained by the arrangements of fiction. The old cliché that life is stranger than fiction is borne out. This final incident of memory-work – by the adults, by the remembering narrator

– is not "major," but it must press her as much as she had been pressing her mother. "I wanted to bring back all I could" (246), she says, using the analogy of sepia snapshots in which the other characters are clear. What is the final picture in the narrator's album?

James, Dodie, and the narrator's mother engage in a spontaneous memory-work contest, and, characteristic of Munro's care with literary allusion, the recited items are meaningful. We have seen the relevance of Dodie's bits from Macaulay and Wolfe. The mother offers passages from Tennyson's *Idylls of the King*, specifically "The Passing of Arthur." The first, "*And all day long the noise of battle rolled*" (245), informally recalls the unspeaking antagonistic relationship between Lena and Dodie, and that the Arthurian battle is within the family makes the passage even more pointed. The second, spoken by Arthur in his final reception by three queens, is metaphorically in line with the description of Parkinson's disease, and the mother's presumptive death from it. James's recitation from Campbell is a marvel, saluted by Dodie, but its theme is of passage as well, though here, unlike the male focus of Dodie and the mother's pieces, the terms are purely natural and not military.

It may not be too forced to say that what the narrator has added to the picture of her mother may be seen as a series of metaphorical epitaphs for a fighter who has succumbed. The verses are variously elegiac, heroic, or nostalgic. The narrator makes her mother the focus of "this whole journey" (246), which is certainly literal: she journeyed, and here re-journeyed, to the Ottawa Valley. It is equally figurative: the journey through life, from innocence to experience, ignorance to knowledge, a standard archetypal literary figure.

The pictures we have seen, however, are as kinetic as the narrator's art has been able to manage, and in any event, "The problem, the only problem, is my mother": the narrator subsequently uses the words "looms" and "indistinct," which continue both the motifs of the darkening mother whose "edges melt and flow" (246). The photograph's normal clarity, and the borderless ambiguities of fiction, and even literary allusions, are not satisfactory renditions of the subject. The mother sticks to the narrator, whose terms are wonderfully revealing: "To mark her off, to describe, to illumine, to celebrate, to *get rid* of, her" (246). The ghost is unlaid, and the denial of connection – for so it appears – is not possible. The mother is not distinct enough to dismiss, "Which means she has stuck to me as close as ever and refused to fall away, and I could go on, and on, applying what skills I have, using what tricks I know, and it would always be the same" (246). Art cannot completely discharge the demands of life. The final message of "The Ottawa Valley," it would appear, is that art is not a completely satisfactory container for life – that is, life is more various and intractable than art can completely manage.

Some Closing Considerations

Munro's work is almost consistently read with "the shock of recognition" and with the pleasure taken in identifying the familiar and the familial. We are unusually comfortable with her characters: they are our sort, and often their experiences are not much removed from our own. To render these things credibly in fiction is no small accomplishment, and yet her narratives transcend regional associations – most specifically those of Southwestern Ontario. The particularity of these stories does not demonstrate, or imply, any narrowness: they prove the persistent literary claim that the universal is to be found in the local and immediate. They are interesting and appealing precisely because any readership can identify, and perhaps identify with, the accuracy of her portraits; that her protagonists are nearly exclusively female does not seem to matter. These stories are deceptively well told; through their limpid and poetic levels of narration they are appreciable both as the tellings of an accomplished storyteller, and as art.

The importance of Munro's collection *Something I've Been Meaning To Tell You* extended beyond its clear but not easily demonstrable evidence of her singular and wide appeal. It was not just that some of these individual stories have received the popular and critical respect and reception often accorded the novel. Her work is in the tradition of Canadian realist fiction, whose sometimes documentary clarity and implicit confirmation of the community's values has allowed it to be frequently identified – and confused – with sociological actuality. Munro's fiction, however, both honours this tradition and, through her extraordinary technical mastery, exposes and reasserts its possibilities. Her poetic understanding and deployment of language challenges what is implicit in the tradition; her work is not purposive, it contains no messages or declarations.

These fictions usually draw subtle, and at times blatant, attention to their narrative manners. They sport with those elements of fiction which normally remain unobtrusive, undeclared, invisible, and which realism rarely seems to propose. Munro's stories are often metafictional or self-reflexive, though without consciously straining after these contemporary manners in fiction, and without ever losing narrative's first obligation to the primary elements of character and event. With these fictions, style becomes an active partner in narrative. In this way Munro's stories have substantially transformed and illuminated the understanding of realistic narrative; they belong to and reassert the international craftsman's tradition in English of (for example) James Joyce, Katherine Mansfield, and Flannery O'Connor. They recover a broader tradition of short fiction for the contemporary literary consciousness, where denotation is not the end of expression.

By the time of her third volume Munro's work was already becoming a significant part of the Canadian literary continuum, a standard of reference. The evident maturation of her talent into full realization in *Something I've Been Meaning To Tell You*, the consistent excellence and variety of this collection, and the beginning of international attention to her work, signalled a literary rank which time would only confirm, and augment.

Works Cited

Campbell, Wilfred. "Indian Summer." *Canadian Anthology*. Ed. Carl F. Klinck and Reginald E. Watters. 3rd ed., rev. and enl. Toronto: Gage, 1974. 95.

Macaulay, Thomas Babington. "Horatius." *Lays of Ancient Rome. The Lays of Ancient Rome & Miscellaneous Essays and Poems*. Introd. G.M. Trevelyan. London: Dent, 1910. 418-34. Everyman's Library 439.

Munro, Alice. "The Ottawa Valley." *Something I've Been Meaning To Tell You*. Toronto: McGraw-Hill Ryerson, 1974. 227-46.

---. "Tell Me Yes or No." *Something I've Been Meaning To Tell You*. Toronto: McGraw-Hill Ryerson, 1974. 106-24.

---. "Winter Wind." *Something I've Been Meaning To Tell You*. Toronto: McGraw-Hill Ryerson, 1974. 192-206.

Struthers, J.R. (Tim). "The Real Material: An Interview with Alice Munro." *Probable Fictions: Alice Munro's Narrative Acts.* Ed. Louis K. MacKendrick. Downsview, ON: ECW, 1983. 5-36.

Tennyson, Alfred. "The Passing of Arthur." *Idylls of the King. Poetical Works.* London: Oxford UP, 1963. 434-41.

Wolfe, Charles. "The Burial of Sir John Moore after Corunna." *The Oxford Book of English Verse: 1250-1918.* Ed. Sir Arthur Quiller-Couch. New ed. Oxford, Eng.: Clarendon, 1939. 712-13.

Who Do You Think You Are?:
Alice Munro's Art of Disarrangement

Lawrence Mathews

Later on Rose would think of Franny when she came across the figure of
an idiotic, saintly whore, in a book or a movie. Men who made books and
movies seemed to have a fondness for this figure, though Rose noticed
they would clean her up. They cheated, she thought, when they left out
the breathing and the spit and the teeth; they were refusing to take into
account the aphrodisiac prickles of disgust, in their hurry to reward
themselves with the notion of a soothing blankness, undifferentiating
welcome. (26)

This passage, a few pages into "Privilege," the second story in *Who Do You
Think You Are?*, is jarring. The flow of the narrative has been disrupted by
what looks like gratuitous feminist pamphleteering. In fact, it is difficult
not to read this passage as an attack on Robertson Davies for his presentation of Mary Dempster in *Fifth Business*. The reader can be forgiven
for wondering whether Alice Munro is nervous about Davies' literary
intrusion into her Southwestern Ontario bailiwick. As a comment on
Davies' novel, the passage is singularly beside the point; Davies is clearly
not interested in the sort of realism which Rose demands. More importantly, the passage's function in "Privilege" remains unclear: in this story,
we hear nothing more on the subject of male illusions about women.

But this passage does introduce an idea which is reiterated again and
again as we follow Rose through the ten stories of *Who Do You Think You
Are?*: literature and, for that matter, art in general have nothing useful
to say to her. What they do say is either irrelevant or downright untrue,
as in the case of the unnamed books and movies about idiotic, saintly

whores. This point is made so insistently that its presence can hardly be accidental. In "Half A Grapefruit," for example, Rose finds that the English literature she reads in high school speaks of a world to which she does not belong. Katherine Mansfield's story "The Garden Party" makes her angry:

> There were poor people in that story. They lived along the lane at the bottom of the garden. They were viewed with compassion. ... She could not really understand what she was angry about, but it had something to do with the fact that she was sure Katherine Mansfield was never obliged to look at stained underwear; her relatives might be cruel and frivolous but their accents would be agreeable; her compassion was floating on clouds of good fortune, deplored by herself, no doubt, but *despised* by Rose. (48)

In "The Beggar Maid," Rose realizes that the painting *King Cophetua and the Beggar Maid* provides a false image of her relationship with Patrick. She cannot identify with the Beggar Maid's "milky surrender," her "helplessness and gratitude"; on the other hand, she knows that Patrick is completely unlike King Cophetua, who, Rose imagines, "could make a puddle of her, with his fierce desire" (77). But Patrick believes that Rose *is* like the Beggar Maid, and, in agreeing to marry him, she is in a sense agreeing to play the Beggar Maid's role. The result is, of course, disastrous. In "Mischief," Rose's ill-fated tryst with Clifford at Powell River coincides with a concert whose heavily Romantic programme (Glinka, Tchaikovsky, Beethoven, Smetana, Rossini) mocks her aspirations to enjoy a passionate affair. Clifford will not fulfil her desire to be "loved, not in a dutiful, husbandly way but crazily, adulterously" (124); he dismisses the idea as "'mischief'" (122). The Romanticism of the music finds no echo in Rose's life.

Such examples can be multiplied almost endlessly. In "Simon's Luck," there is a young woman who is writing a paper on the suicide of female artists – "She mentioned Diane Arbus, Virginia Woolf, Sylvia Plath, Anne Sexton, Christiane Pflug" (157) – but Rose has no desire to emulate these women: survival is what interests her, and, in the end, it is Simon who dies. In "Spelling," Rose is a member of the chorus in a television production of *The Trojan Women*, a play in which female suffering is raised to tragic dignity (185); in the same story, Flo slides pathetically into senility. In "Half A Grapefruit," *Macbeth* is irrelevant to the world of West Hanratty (49); in "The Beggar Maid," Patrick is misleadingly reminded of Rose by the title of *The White Goddess* (78); in "Mischief," Rose is baffled by a "symbolic" play (106); and in "Providence," Rose's daughter, Anna, likes two television programmes, *Family Court* and *The Brady Bunch*, neither of which reflects the life they are actually leading (140). In all of these stories, art – if that term might be defined broadly enough to include *The Brady Bunch* – bears no direct relation to reality, at least to the reality of Rose's life. Patrick is not a king; her "love" (124) for Clifford is not to be consummated in some dream world conjured up by the *Pastoral* (123); female artists who commit suicide have nothing to say to Rose – instead they excite the prurient interest of a woman who is herself "emaciated, bloodless, obsessed" (157). And so on.

But the most explicit outburst against art comes at the end of "Simon's Luck." Rose is acting in a television series; a scene involving a girl who seems about to commit suicide is being filmed:

> The girl didn't throw herself into the sea. They didn't have things like that happening in the series. Such things always threatened to happen but they didn't happen, except now and then to peripheral and unappealing characters. People watching trusted that they would be protected from predictable disasters, also from those shifts of emphasis that throw the story line open to question, the disarrangements which demand new judgments and solutions, and throw the windows open on inappropriate unforgettable scenery. (172-73)

Out of context, this passage looks even more quixotic than the apparent attack on Robertson Davies in "Privilege": a philippic against the conventions of prime-time television! But the next paragraph reveals that Rose has interpreted her own experience according to similar conventions:

> Simon's dying struck Rose as that kind of disarrangement. It was preposterous, it was unfair, that such a chunk of information should have been left out, and that Rose even at this late date could have thought herself the only person who could seriously lack power. (173)

Art not only bears false witness to life, but we tend (or at least Rose does) to impose equally mendacious aesthetic patterns upon our own experience. She is disconcerted by the "chunk of information" which shatters the neat pattern she has imposed upon her relationship with Simon. Rose's life has many such "disarrangements which demand new judgments and solutions," and art has nothing useful to teach her about how to cope with them.

Distrust of aesthetic pattern is not an entirely new motif in Munro's work at this point. In this respect, the most obvious forerunner of *Who Do You Think You Are?* is "Material," a story in *Something I've Been Meaning To Tell You*. But in "Material" the emphasis is, as Bronwen Wallace has pointed out, on the contrast between the way men (whether artists or not) order their experience by means of their perverse expertise in knowing "how to ignore or use things" ("Material" 44) and the way women do *not* do this, but rather see their experience in terms of "scraps and oddments" ("Material" 43), imposing no pattern, and thereby avoiding the comforting self-deceit to which men – if the narrator is to be believed – are inevitably subject (Wallace 61). In *Who Do You Think You Are?*, however, gender is no longer an issue. One of Rose's problems is precisely that she *does* continually succumb to the temptation to see her experience as ordered and must continually re-learn the lesson of "Material": it is, as the narrator of that story writes to her ex-husband, "*not enough*" ("Material" 44) to regard the chaos of experience as though it existed only to provide raw material for our fantasies of order.

Two questions, then. How does Munro herself deal with the problem of imposing an artistic form upon the raw material of Rose's experience? And what value does she expect these stories to have for her readers, whose experience is presumably as subject to "disarrangement" as Rose's?

The answer I should like to propose to the first question is that Munro supplies the reader with the missing "chunk of information," so that the stories in *Who Do You Think You Are?* do not give us merely an aesthetically successful ordering of Rose's experience. They also give us the information we need to be able to perceive that the aesthetic pattern is possibly, and often probably, "false," in the sense that it does not provide an adequate rendering of the full truth of that experience. Nor does the missing "chunk" allow us to devise a new, definitive pattern which yields the story's "real meaning." Instead, the presence of the new information raises questions about the validity of any pattern we might find in the story. It is not that our narrative expectations are reversed: they are neither reversed nor fulfilled. Each story arouses the need to interpret Rose's experience but does not satisfy that need.

Munro uses two principal means of conveying the new chunks of information. One is the use of the epilogue (in almost every story); the other is the use of characters, situations, and anecdotes which are not necessary to the development of the main strand of the narrative, but which seem to bear some thematic relation to it. Examples include Franny McGill in "Privilege"; the stories Flo tells in "Half a Grapefruit"; the anecdote of the undertaker at the beginning of "Wild Swans"; Dr. Henshawe, whose career represents a road Rose chooses not to take, in "The Beggar Maid"; the stories Simon tells Rose about his past in "Simon's Luck"; and the old woman whose pastime furnishes the title for "Spelling." These chunks of information and those provided by the epilogues all raise unanswerable questions about the meaning of Rose's experience. In order to demonstrate this point, I should like to look more closely at the technique of "disarrangement" as it is used in the book's first story, "Royal Beatings," in a later story, "Mischief," and in the book's last story, "Who Do You Think You Are?."

If Munro had chosen not to include the epilogue to "Royal Beatings," the story would still have all of the qualities for which her work is usually praised. The effect of the epilogue is to cause us to question the validity of Rose's perception of the past, as it has been delivered by the narrative. The anecdote of the horsewhipping of Becky Tyde's father by three men, including one named Hat Nettleton, has been inserted early in the story, apparently to say something about the psychology of cruelty which permeates the culture of Hanratty and environs, and this explains, in part, the psychology of the "royal beatings" which Rose receives at home. The horsewhipping, carried out by the "Three useless young men" at the instigation of "more influential and respect[ed] men in town" (7) was, ironically, a kind of revenge for the beatings the misshapen Becky was said to have suffered at the hands of her father. Perhaps this leads the reader to look for further parallels between Becky and Rose, but Nettleton is soon forgotten. The epilogue, however, thrusts him back into the limelight.

"Years later, many years later" (20), Rose happens to hear a radio interview with Nettleton on the occasion of his hundred-and-second birthday.

The interview reproduces the clichés of the genre so faithfully that Rose first thinks it is a scene from a play. Nettleton, at the interviewer's prodding, delivers what is expected of him: "*We worked and we was glad to get it. ... Didn't have no T.V.*," and so on (21). Rose, naturally enough, is struck by what she takes to be the falseness of the picture of Nettleton which the interview has given: "Horsewhipper into centenarian. ... Oldest resident. Oldest horsewhipper. Living link with our past" (22).

The reappearance of Hat Nettleton changes our understanding of the story. For Rose, of course, what he does in the interview is tantamount to denying his true identity, since, as far as she is concerned, the most important fact about him has been concealed. But in fact what he says is determined largely by the demands of the interviewer. As far as we know, he tells no lies, and he is hardly going to volunteer information about the horsewhipping, even if he does remember it. That Nettleton's version of his past so blatantly diverges from Rose's memory of it raises the question of the accuracy of Rose's account of her own past. Is her understanding of it as selectively based and misleading as that of the centenarian horsewhipper?

A sentence in the opening pages speaks unobtrusively to this issue:

> This was, of course, in the days before the war, days of what would later be legendary poverty, from which Rose would remember mostly low-down things – serious-looking anthills and wooden steps, and a cloudy, interesting, problematical light on the world. (5)

What Rose understands of the physical world is determined by her vantage point within it. Is it fair to make a parallel statement about her perception of human nature? Are the "royal beatings" the moral equivalent of the "low-down things" that she sees – not the whole truth (or even a metaphor for the whole truth) about her childhood, but the only *part* of the truth that she is equipped to perceive? And has her desire to interpret her childhood in terms of "legendary poverty" led her to omit, to falsify?

There is other evidence to suggest that this may be the case. Rose, listening to Flo's stories, gets the sense that "Present time and past, the shady melodramatic past of Flo's stories, were quite separate ..." (8), and Rose's imagination is stimulated by the thought of Flo's exotic and mysterious early life, "crowded and legendary, with Barbara Allen and Becky Tyde's father and all kinds of old outrages and sorrows jumbled up together in it" (10). Yet every time a situation in the story is coloured by someone's imagination, a more convincing, "realistic" account is presented along with it. Thus, Rose likes the phrase "royal beatings" because it conjures up the image of "An occasion both savage and splendid"; but she recognizes that "In real life they didn't approach such dignity ..." (1). Flo enjoys recounting the legend about Becky Tyde's illegitimate child: "'Disposed of,' Flo said. 'They used to say go and get your lamb chops at Tyde's, get them nice and tender!'" But she adds "regretfully" that "'It was all lies in all probability'" (7). The old men who congregate in front of the store believe that "a star in the western sky, ... the evening star," is "an airship hovering over Bay City, Michigan ... lit by ten thousand electric light bulbs"; Rose's father "ruthlessly" demolishes this myth by pointing out that the "airship" is really "the planet Venus" (20). Perhaps the relation between Rose's memory of the events of her childhood and the "truth" of those events parallels the relation between the imaginary airship and the real planet.

The prominence given to Hat Nettleton's account of the past certainly stimulates the reader to speculate along these lines. The irony of the epilogue seems to lack the sort of "point" we might expect it to have. Neither differences nor similarities between Rose and Nettleton are emphasized. Perhaps Rose, unlike Nettleton (insofar as she understands Nettleton), has a view of her past experience which is unromanticized, "balanced," "objective." Perhaps, on the other hand, she has, unwittingly, undergone a transformation as dramatic as Nettleton's ("Horsewhipper into centenarian"), and perhaps this has affected her view of the past. Certainly the question has been raised. In the epilogue, we have one of "those shifts of emphasis that throw the story line open to question."

The first story in the volume, then, alerts us to the possibility that any pattern that Rose perceives in her life (and that we perceive through her) is suspect. Every story raises pertinent but unanswerable questions about the "real" meaning of her experience (as opposed to the ostensible meaning towards which the story line has been leading us). "Mischief" provides a particularly convenient example of Munro's technique here because Rose's response and the reader's are clearly distinguished. As in "Simon's Luck," Rose comes to realize, at the end of the story, that yet another narrative has suffered "disarrangement." The reader can easily assimilate Rose's disorientation to his/her own pattern, but then *that* pattern is disrupted, too.

Rose's unconsummated affair with Clifford in the early fifties has ended badly. We enter the epilogue, set at some point in the seventies, prepared to dislike him. It is something of a surprise to find that we are meant to despise his wife, Jocelyn, as well, but the evidence is overwhelming. We listen to the banal trendiness of her speech – "'What is happening now ... is that Clifford is wide open'" – and the point is underlined immediately: "Was Jocelyn's talk a parody, was she being sarcastic? No. She was not" (127). As for Clifford, there is "Something obscene about his skinniness and sweet, hard smile" (129). To complete the unattractive family portrait, both husband and wife have, with success, become unabashedly materialistic.

At the end of the story, Rose and Clifford finally consummate their affair, with Jocelyn, ironically, an approving participant. Rose's feelings about this are complex: "curious, disbelieving, hardly willing, slightly aroused and, at some level she was too sluggish to reach for, appalled and sad" (132). In the morning, she decides that their friendship is at an end:

> She was angry at Clifford and Jocelyn. She felt that they had made a fool of her, cheated her, shown her a glaring lack, that otherwise she would not have been aware of. She resolved never to see them again and to write them a letter in which she would comment on their selfishness, obtuseness, and moral degeneracy. (132)

At this stage, the reader does not share Rose's sense of disarrangement; rather, he/she feels entitled to ruminate complacently about Rose's moral education. At last, Munro seems to be telling us, Rose has learned the lesson that she should have learned twenty years in the past. Certain people *are* selfish, obtuse, and morally degenerate, and it is best to avoid them.

But the story's last sentence changes all that: "Sometime later she decided to go on being friends with Clifford and Jocelyn, because she needed such friends occasionally, at that stage of her life" (132). What does this tell us about Rose? Are we to deplore her for needing Clifford and Jocelyn, or should we applaud her for having the maturity to recognize that she does need them? And what, exactly, does she need them *for*? This sentence gives us the "chunk of information" which disarranges our pattern and demands "new judgments and solutions," although it does not give us the basis for arriving at them.

Certainly our suspicions are aroused to the point that we want to re-examine Rose's behaviour in the epilogue. The unholy – and carefully chosen – trinity of "selfishness, obtuseness, and moral degeneracy" takes on new significance. There is something intrinsically selfish about Rose's notion of her friendship with Clifford and Jocelyn. Whether *they* need *her* is apparently not a question which interests Rose, and the fact that she needs them (only) "at *that* stage of her life" (emphasis added) suggests a sort of consumerism with respect to personal relationships: last year's model can, without qualms, be cast aside. As for obtuseness and moral degeneracy, Rose remains ironically unaware of the similarities between her moral attitudes and those of Clifford and Jocelyn, similarities stressed at one level by her participation in the previous evening's sexual activity.

The story of Rose's "love" (124) for Clifford lends itself to this sort of analysis as well. Selfishness: it is Clifford, not Rose, who thinks of the undesirable consequences for others that their affair would have – "It was being away from home for a month that had made him see everything differently. Jocelyn. The children. The damage" (122). Obtuseness: Rose ignores the signals warning of Clifford's withdrawal from her – his failure to write, the "businesslike" phone call from Prince George (116). Moral degeneracy: it hardly makes sense to say that Clifford is more "degenerate" than Rose; it is true that he betrays her, but Rose is willing to betray Patrick by having the affair in the first place. No doubt the evidence for the prosecution here is far from conclusive. But the point is that it is not until the last sentence of the story that one would even think of making the case.

What Munro gives us in *Who Do You Think You Are?*, then, is an art which is based on the disruption of pattern, an art which seems rooted in scepticism about, even hostility towards, the kind of "truth" which most literature claims to deliver. What value can be ascribed to this kind of fiction, which seeks to perform the literary equivalent of proving a negative? A clear, if implicit, answer to this question is provided by the last story in the volume, "Who Do You Think You Are?."

This story is partly about Rose's relationship with a high-school classmate named Ralph Gillespie, partly her reminiscence of a town eccentric with the archly literary name of Milton Homer: "Whatever it is that ordinary people lose when they are drunk, Milton Homer never had, or might have chosen not to have – and this is what interests Rose – at some point early in life" (194). It is tempting to write Milton Homer off as yet another of Munro's regional grotesques, and yet there is evidence that he is meant to be more than that. "Milton" and "Homer," taken together, suggest literary profundity and universality, and the fact that for whoever named him Milton – "after his mother's family," we are told, as was "common practice" – "there was probably no thought of linking together the names of two great poets" (194) only underlines for the reader that Munro has very deliberately done just that. In writing about this man, she seems to be saying, she is dealing not merely with Hanratty's mild equivalent of the village idiot, but with the basic stuff of human nature, the same *materia poetica* that Homer and Milton used.

Ralph Gillespie is the primary artist figure in the story. It is he who first alerts Rose to the possibility that Milton Homer can be related to a tradition of literary art when he shows her that he has changed the title of a poem in his high-school English book: "He had stroked out the word *Chapman's* ... and inked in the word *Milton*, so that the title now read: *On First Looking into Milton Homer*" (194). Later, Ralph develops a Milton Homer imitation, the means by which he achieves social acceptance: "He was so successful that Rose was amazed, and so was everybody else. From that time on Ralph began to do imitations ..." (200). After high school, he joins the navy. Years later, Rose hears from Flo that he has returned to Hanratty. His attempt to get a job at the Legion fails, Flo says, because of "'the way he carries on'," a phrase that refers primarily to his imitations:

> "... half the time he's imitating somebody that the newer people that's come to town, they don't know even who the person was, they just think it's Ralph being idiotic. ... Ralph don't know when to stop. He Milton Homer'd himself right out of a job." (202)

Ralph is an artist who does present an unambiguous "truth" about his subject. He has found a way to translate reality (Milton Homer and the others) into the artistic form of his mimicry. Those in his audience who know Milton Homer can appreciate the way in which he does this, but for the others, "the newer people," the line between art and reality blurs, and Ralph, for them, himself becomes the subject matter. In the same way, one might suggest, regional writers may come to be understood as doing no more than embodying the spirit of their regions, or feminist writers as having significance only in their "representative" quality. (It is easy to see why these possibilities might perturb Munro.) It is not that these kinds of writing are without value: Ralph does a very *good* Milton Homer. But the form he has chosen has severe restrictions – like Hat Nettleton's radio interview, like Rose's half-hour television programme, like the well-made short story which makes a clear thematic "point" about its protagonist. The problem is that each of these forms requires that too much be omitted. Ralph, for example, has no way of rendering Milton Homer's *inner* experience, although the possibility of his having chosen to act the way he does "is what interests Rose" (194).

For Rose, too, is an artist figure in this story. The central focus of the narrative is on her attempt to understand Ralph and her feelings for him. The "disarrangement" in "Who Do You Think You Are?" is caused by the way Ralph's version of Milton Homer parallels (or does not parallel) Rose's version of Ralph. To what extent, the story leads us to ask, does Rose's account constitute a parody of the "real" Ralph, and to what extent is it an accurate reflection of his true being?

Rose's artistic task is, of course, much more difficult than Ralph's, since she is interested in what lies behind the social façade:

> Her first impression of him, as boyishly shy and ingratiating, had to change. That was his surface. Underneath he was self-sufficient, resigned to living in bafflement, perhaps proud. She wished that he would speak to her from that level, and she thought he wished it, too, but they were prevented. (205)

In this scene, Rose meets Ralph for the first time in many years, but their encounter is characteristic of all their shared experience: Rose's perception of his inner self remains intuitive, unverified, and unexpressed, even to Ralph himself. Deciding not to reach out to him in this way, Rose observes that "There seemed to be feelings which could only be spoken of in translation ..." (205). Perhaps, then, her perception of Ralph is false or inadequate, and perhaps what truth there is in it cannot be articulated accurately.

Unlike Ralph's version of Milton Homer, her version of Ralph depends on the interpretation of that which cannot be defined in any "objective" way: attitudes, feelings, moral and psychological phenomena whose true nature can only be guessed at, however educated Rose's guess may be. Where Ralph's Milton Homer is recognizably a precise rendering of the surface, or public, Milton Homer, Rose's ambitiously conceived Ralph is a multidimensional being, the hypothetical nature of whom Rose is herself only too sure. Ralph tells us nothing of Milton Homer's internal reality; Rose tells us nothing verifiable about Ralph. The two approaches comment critically on each other, and neither is fully satisfactory. But Rose's way is superior, in the sense that it addresses that most deeply felt, if unfulfillable, of human needs: to know completely the person whose life is lived "one slot over" (206) from one's own.

In *Who Do You Think You Are?*, Munro successfully keeps these two approaches in balance. Surface detail is – as always in her work – brilliantly realized, and it may seem that a world which is, in one sense, so vividly accessible to the reader should easily yield its meaning to the reader as well. And the critic who wishes to prove that Munro, too, does a good Milton Homer, will find much that can be confidently labelled "regional" or "feminist." But the art of disarrangement reminds us that any significant truth that literature delivers is a partial and provisional one. Rose's thoughts on her own acting ability make the point concisely: "there was always something further, a tone, a depth, a light, that she couldn't get and wouldn't get" (205). The context here, it is important to note, is not one of despair. Similarly, the consciousness that there is "always something further" permeates these stories, but far from providing a reason for Munro to abandon her art, it has given her the impetus to create more of it.

The value of the art of disarrangement, it might be said, lies in its continual commentary on its own tentativeness, in the face of life's complexity and mystery. It is not that the artist should abandon her attempt to render experience fully and accurately, anymore than Rose should stop trying to make sense of Ralph Gillespie. The point is, rather, that one should proceed warily, in humility, even, in a sense, quixotically. Munro's engagement in this endeavour, in full awareness of its difficulties, points to what will prove to be of enduring interest in her work.

Works Cited

Davies, Robertson. *Fifth Business.* Toronto: Macmillan of Canada, 1970.

Munro, Alice. "Material." *Something I've Been Meaning To Tell You.* Toronto: McGraw-Hill Ryerson, 1974. 22-44.

---. *Who Do You Think You Are?* Toronto: Macmillan of Canada, 1978.

Wallace, Bronwen. "Women's Lives: Alice Munro." *The Human Elements: Critical Essays.* Ed. David Helwig. Ottawa: Oberon, 1978. 52-67.

"The Way the Stars Really Do Come Out at Night": The Trick of Representation in Alice Munro's "The Moons of Jupiter"

Timothy McIntyre

"The Moons of Jupiter" was one of a number of breakthrough stories for Alice Munro. In the late 1970s and early 1980s, "Munro burst forth" into the international literary world "with successive stories that create the feelings of being alive, that replicate for their readers the very sense of being itself" (Thacker 371). This sense of being in "Moons," this feeling of presence, owes much to the story's mimetic precision, yet, paradoxically perhaps, it also co-exists with and is even augmented by a profound scepticism about language and representation. "Moons" is at once highly stylized, highly self-conscious about language, and deeply involved in the real and representational. Its various meditations on consciousness, representation, and death, as well as its temporal disarrangement – its abandoning of a natural chronology in favour of a more stylized presentation – artistically perform a cathartic effect, though one that stops short of offering full consolation. "Moons," like much of Munro's writing that came out of her return to Southwestern Ontario from British Columbia, demonstrates how an understanding of words as more than mirrors for things or containers for thoughts can enable the creation of a powerful and sophisticated, if not absolute and transcendent, feeling of presence, or connection. Its cathartic effect – its movement from a sense of separation, to unity, to separation – draws on the power of language to connect and evoke pathos even as it dramatizes its limited ability to represent the world, and the ultimate failure of consciousness to comprehend fully the world, the other, and the self.

"Moons" was written after Munro moved back to Huron County, which put her once again "living in the midst of her material" (Thacker 378). The "enriched awareness of her home" that resulted seems to have driven her to draw more on the autobiographical (Thacker 368-69) while simultaneously increasing her attention to the problems of representation. Both trends – toward autobiographical resonances and the questioning of representation – are present in "Moons." Connections between Munro and the protagonist Janet are apparent: their careers as writers,[1] the deaths of their fathers, and even their visits to planetariums. Munro herself has written that this story "has something to do with [her] father's death," as well as a trip she made the following summer to the McLaughlin Planetarium (Introduction xiii), and both Robert Thacker and Magdalene Redekop note the significance of these autobiographical connections (Thacker 385; Redekop 155). However, running through "Moons" – from the heart monitor on the opening pages, which dramatizes "what ought to be a most secret activity" (217), to the planetarium scene, which Coral Ann Howells identifies "as the dominant narrative image of transcendent patterning which exceeds all human comprehension" (83) – is a sophisticated examination of how the act of naming and patterning at the root of representation and comprehension inexorably carries us away from the real.

Redekop skilfully articulates the unity and poignancy of the naming of the moons scene and adroitly tracks its refusal of an easy elegiac reversal. However, she reads Nichola's absence as "a way of showing respect for Nichola – a way of acknowledging that she needs no patron Saint Nicholas and no fussing mother to take care of her" (171). Ildikó de Papp Carrington, in her fine reading, departs from Redekop; Carrington notes that the death of the father and the departure of Janet's daughters are in fact a "double loss" and that "the story is not so much about what Janet gains in perspective as about what she loses from her life" (203). Ajay Heble details the process by which "Moons" (as well as many other Munro stories) displaces and defers the main issue at hand – death – and how its fictional world is subject to change and possibility (128-29). Karen E. Smythe accurately defines "Moons" as a cathartic fiction-elegy which offers a staged performance of grief work (138-42), while Howells offers a strong reading of the story's cosmological imagery as an inherently limited "attempt to map patterns of significance on to changing circumstances" (81). The discussions by these critics, however, tend to lack sustained attention to the story as a whole. Their readings, sophisticated as they may be, tend to be marshalled into some overarching rationale that encompasses Munro's body of work or situates the story in its collection. As a result, these readings tend to sacrifice some level of attention to the story's specific form.

By form, I mean not some static structure, easily separable from content or meaning, from its cultural or intertextual context, its author, or individual reader. Rather, I use form in Derek Attridge's sense of the word: not "empirical structure" (111) but "performed mobility" (111), the sequence of linguistic operations that "functions as a *staging* of meaning and feeling" (109), a staging of operations of referentiality, metaphoricity, intentionality, and ethicity, which is realized in the act of reading. Attridge is right to point out that "a creative achievement in the literary field is, whatever else it may be, a *formal* one" (107); it is "the selection and arrangement of words" (107) and the artistry that results, over and above any analytical or representational function of the language, that divides the literary from other modes of writing. Form, in this sense, does not exclude context or semantics. Contextual information – such as the death of Munro's own father – cannot help but inform our experience of the story and can by no means be ignored. "Moons" has an undeniable stake in the real and also in the realist form, even if its self-consciousness and stylized arrangement challenge any simplistic mimetic understanding of language. It is largely this combination of formal features, realist and metafictional, that gives the story its power.

The metafictive sensibility at work in "Moons" never overtly repudiates language's mimetic contract, such that it registers both the power and the futility of language. The key metafictive moment comes near the story's end, when Janet attends a planetarium presentation while trying to fill the time before her next hospital visit to see her dying father. This scene dramatizes an ambivalence regarding the ordering and patterning of meaning involved in reading and writing narratives, whether artistically or in an attempt to make sense of life. The planetarium presentation draws on, though it also exceeds, realist modes of representation. The show starts within the conventions of realism: the stars "came out not all at once but one after another, the way the stars really do come out at night, though more quickly" (230). The appearance of the stars, realistic though accelerated to suit the needs of the demonstration, produces what Roland Barthes has called a reality effect.

Following the appearance of the stars is a list of scientific, objective facts, which give the size of the universe and provide a sense of scale for the earth's place within it. The style of the presentation shifts abruptly when, as Janet comments, "realism [is] abandoned, for familiar artifice" (231). Here the presentation abandons its realist pretense for a stylized simulation with more drama and excitement. "A model of the solar system" appears, "spinning away in its elegant style," as does "A bright bug" that "took off from the earth, heading for Jupiter" (231).

Both the reality effect and the departure into stylized simulation, however, are part of the same process: both name and pattern the facts, make them familiar, intelligible, and dramatic, and work to evoke a false sense of awe. "The attraction of any pattern," as Redekop notes, "lies in the illusion of control and in the denial of chaos" (150), and the planetarium presentation provides such a pattern by essentially mapping the universe from the earth out. This naming and patterning bears more than a passing resemblance to the act of writing, which similarly arranges language into meaningful patterns and which mixes representation and stylized drama in an attempt to evoke significance. That Janet is a writer and makes her living by constructing artifice through language strengthens this connection.

Janet's reflections on this stylized naming and patterning demonstrate that she finds something inadequate and disingenuous about the presentation and, by extension, about any serene faith in the human ability to know and represent reality. In a line that prefigures the wholesale reorganization of the solar system in 2006 based on a new definition for the term "planet" ("Pluto"), she challenges the scientific basis behind these apparently objective facts. The new definition of Mercury's orbit, in which the planet rotates three times for every two trips around the sun, not once per orbit, leads Janet to ask "Why did they give out such confident information, only to announce later that it was quite wrong?" (231). As Heble writes of this moment, "even the world of science – which seems to concern itself with measurable facts, with reality – can open up to new possibilities, to alternative versions" (128). Even patterns constructed out of the authority of the scientific method, then, can be plain wrong.

Beyond this error of fact, Janet finds both the goal and the style of the presentation to be wrongheaded. Ostensibly an attempt to give school-children a sense of the scale of the universe, the presentation instead seems to Janet to use its powers of representation only to reduce the terrifying insignificance of human life to little more than a cheap thrill. When the presentation fails to tear the schoolchildren in attendance from their pop and chips, Janet states that it is "A good thing" (231). This effort to fix the children's attention "on various knowns and unknowns and horrible immensities" has failed: "Children have a natural immu-nity" to this sort of artifice which "shouldn't be tampered with" (231).

For Janet, at this point at least, the artistic pretensions of the presen-tation – "the echo-chamber effects, the music, the churchlike solemnity" (231) – serve only to give a comfortable artistic gloss to these "horrible immensities" (231), to simulate "the awe that they supposed they ought to feel" (231-32) at the size of the universe and humankind's relative insignificance, and to reduce this awe to something like "A fit of the shivers when you looked out the window" (232). These "shivers" come as much and perhaps more from the well-wrought artistic elements of the presentation than they do from the knowledge gained about the universe. Real awe, according to Janet, is something more sinister: "Once you knew what it was, you wouldn't be courting it" (232).

Our relative insignificance in the grand scale of time and space is actually terrifying, just as it is for the protagonist in another Munro story, "Walker Brothers Cowboy." The protagonist of "Walker Brothers" listens to her father describe the formation of the Great Lakes by the gradual movement of ice caps and finds that "The tiny share we have of time appalls" her, though interestingly her father "seems to regard it with tranquility" (3). Like the schoolchildren in the planetarium, perhaps, she does "not like to think of it" (3). These schoolchildren, thanks to the pop, the chips, and their own lack of interest in edutainment, are spared a confrontation with their own mortality, albeit a confrontation that could only have been domesticated and misrepresented by the artifice of the presentation.

Yet for all Janet's scepticism, and despite its failure to engage Janet and the rest of the audience, the presentation is not without its appeal. In a detail that in a linear story would have immediately followed the presen-tation, but here is deferred to the end, Janet states that "The planetarium show had done what I wanted it to after all – calmed me down, drained me" (233). Inadequate as it is for coming to terms with the awe-inspiring immensity of the universe and the finite span of human life, the show nonetheless provides real comfort to Janet. This show, this naming and patterning, is one of a list of distractions, or tricks perhaps, that ease the burden of grief weighing on Janet. Fashion, food, crossword puzzles – any trivial thing that allows "Attention [to narrow] in on something" and become "fanatically serious" (229) – can provide temporary respite from the more troubling matter at hand. Janet may recognize the futility of these obsessions, but her recognition does not rob them of their power.

As a whole, the stories in *The Moons of Jupiter*, as Redekop points out, "insist on a process whereby we are forced to confront false comforts and recognize them as such" (152). "The Moons of Jupiter" is no exception in this respect, yet as Tracy Ware has written to me, "We tend to swing too violently from full Christian consolation to a stark sense of its absence in sceptical contexts." He continues, "the importance of minor comforts" in this story "is by no means a commonplace." For Janet, meaning-making through naming and patterning provides comfort and helps lay the groundwork for a real emotional exchange with her father: something that neither food, nor drink, nor fashion can do. Such stylized representations might fail to evoke immanent meaning, but at the very least, they have the power to distract: to absorb consciousness and temporarily defer anxiety and grief.

The planetarium scene, then, might cast doubt on our power to know and represent, but the story as a whole demonstrates the power of language to connect people and evoke emotion. At first glance, this story appears to be a simple recital of events – a failed shopping trip, a show at the planetarium, a hospital visit – focalized through Janet's consciousness. But the narrative is not linear, and the pattern that emerges from its disarrangement provides a cathartic movement: from Janet's emotional separation from her father, to a poignant moment of unity, and finally, to the inevitable separation at the end, when Janet performs the hard work of mourning by letting her father go into death, and in a parallel process, letting her daughter go into adult life. This movement from separation to unity and then to a new and more mature separation is also tied to a process in which Janet's naming and patterning of her loved ones – the tricks she uses to keep them spinning neatly in their orbits around her star – collapses and is recognized for what it is: a series of convenient fictions, or representations, with only a tangential relationship to reality. Yet Janet's loss of faith in her ability to narrate her life and define those around her nevertheless exists within this powerful story.

The opening scene demonstrates Janet's desire to define her father as self-contained and resigned to his impending death. Seeing her father as facing death without fear or despair allows Janet to maintain her emotional distance and avoid her own grief. Initially, the father's anxiety regarding his health appears understated: he is merely "pale and closemouthed" (218) when Janet brings him to the hospital, and he seems more concerned with the cost of his room than with his failing heart (217). Janet, at this point, is "pleased" with herself "for taking it calmly" and feels none of "the protest [she] would have felt twenty, even ten, years before" (219). Her father's stoicism enables her own emotional distance from his impending death and allows her to believe she can accept his passing without trauma. A momentary lapse in this stoicism forces Janet to a greater emotional distance: when her father's "refusal" of death "leapt up in him as readily as if he had been thirty or forty years younger," she finds only that her "heart hardened" (219).

Then, the day after his admittance, when he says "reasonably" that he will "'Give in gracefully'" and live out his remaining days without gambling on a high-risk surgical procedure, Janet approves (220). It is what she "would have expected of him," that man of "independence," "self-sufficiency," and "forbearance," who "worked in a factory" and "in his garden," who "read history books" and "never made a fuss" (220). His return to her understanding of him as stoic and scholarly, resigned to his fate rather than afraid or desperate, allows her to continue to maintain her own sense of calm and acceptance. However, mention of her father's childhood and the physical fact of his body trouble her definition of him as ready to face death and momentarily weaken her resolve. "The thought of my father's childhood," Janet observes, "which I always pic-tured as bleak and dangerous – the poor farm, the scared sisters, the harsh father – made me less resigned to his dying" (219). Janet "didn't care to think of his younger selves," but "Even his bare torso, thick and white – he had the body of a workingman of his generation, seldom exposed to the sun – was a danger to me; it looked so strong and young" (220). Memories of a childhood long past and a body that still bears

traces of a vigorous adulthood testify to the possibility of multiple, competing narratives of this man's life and point out the self-interestedness
of her chosen definition.

The next scene, a flashback to Janet's arrival in Toronto, further
develops her concern with the ability of one's concept of a person to do
justice to the actual individual. Her daughters, she realizes, have fixed
her into their own definitions: "They would have talked about me. Judith
and Nichola comparing notes, relating anecdotes; analyzing, regretting,
blaming, forgiving" (222); Janet herself "did the same thing at that age"
(222). Janet now recognizes just how false these definitions are: "How
thoroughly we dealt with our fathers and mothers, ... how competently
we filed them away, defined them beyond any possibility of change. What
presumption" (222). After reflecting on the inadequacy of the child's
understanding of the parent, she goes on to question her own definitions of her daughters. She observes her daughter Judith's interaction
with her partner Don and can feel "her sad jitters, ... predict her supple
attentions" (223). Janet asks herself, "Why should I think she wouldn't
be susceptible, that she would always be straightforward, heavy-footed,
self-reliant? Just as I go around saying that Nichola is sly and solitary,
cold, seductive. Many people must know things that would contradict
what I say" (223). Such a dramatization of the arrogance and self-interest
behind these limited, one-sided definitions of loved ones comes just
before Janet begins to question, in earnest, her understanding of her
father, a questioning that ultimately leads to a genuine moment of unity.

Janet loses faith that her concept of her father is adequate to the full
reality of his existence and, shortly thereafter, experiences a moment
of connection with him. Back in the hospital, when Janet enters his
room, her father utters a seemingly random phrase – "'*Shore*-less seas'"
– which is in fact from a poem, Joaquin Miller's "Columbus," that he
had been trying to recall (225). As Redekop notes, this phrase is evocative of the endless oblivion of death, of "a seascape without horizon or
limit, something beyond comprehension like the 'horrible immensities'
[Janet] glimpses in the planetarium" (170). This non sequitur provokes
in Janet incomprehension and worry. She wonders "if he had found out
how much, or how little, time he could hope for[,] ... if the pills had
brought on an untrustworthy euphoria," or if he has decided he "wanted
to gamble" (225). This apparently nonsensical address, haunted by the

spectre of death, calls her to account in an almost Levinasian sense. The "said," or linguistic content, of this address is at this point largely immaterial, but its "saying," or the underlying relationship that linguistic communication presupposes, is undeniable. The father appears before her as other – helpless, thanks to his leaky heart, his consciousness completely opaque – but her love and concern for him is crystal clear. Janet realizes how partial and self-interested her understanding of him had been: "I used to tell people that he never spoke regretfully about his life, but that was not true. It was just that I didn't listen to it" (225).

The inscrutability of the connections his mind makes to recall the line, as well as the tabloid accounts of life-after-death experiences he had been reading, lead the father to reflect on the "'great temptation ... to make a mystery'" out of the inexplicability of human consciousness, "'to believe in – You know'" (226). Janet completes his sentence – "'The soul?'" – and feels "an appalling rush of love and recognition" (226). The father, like Janet, is haunted by his impending death, tempted, but wary of, as he says, "'playing tricks on yourself'" (226). The "tricks" here are religious, but given Munro's use of the word in *Something I've Been Meaning To Tell You* to refer to storytelling, the parallel between these tricks and those of fiction is interesting.

Tricks, in "Material" and "The Ottawa Valley," or being tricked out in "Winter Wind," are those narrative acts that shape the world into the satisfying patterns of fiction. They can be "honest" and "lovely" (43) as they are in "Material," even if they remain part of a way of seeing, using, or writing about the world that is enigmatically "*not enough*" (44). They can be part of a process in which a writer or narrator has "used" people, "tricked them out and altered them and shaped them any way at all" (201) as stated in "Winter Wind." Or they can refer to the techniques – "applying what skills I have, using what tricks I know" – that are part of the narrator's apparently failed attempt in "The Ottawa Valley" to make "a proper story" out of her mother in such a way as "To mark her off, to describe, to illumine, to celebrate, to *get rid* of, her" (246).

Tricks seem to fix the world into satisfying aesthetic forms that may be celebratory or may be disingenuous yet nevertheless are static, cut off from change and possibility and divorced from the complexity and uncertainty of reality. Religious tricks, perhaps, represent attempts to shunt the facts of life and death into a religious schema for which there is no apparent evidence in the material world. Here, Janet and her father's shared suspicion of, and perhaps longing for, tricks unites them in a moment of love and recognition.

This moment of unity and exchange, in which Janet's father breaks out of her definition and effects a more genuine connection, is not unambiguously positive. In this emotional moment, Janet's father sees fit to pronounce judgment on her life in a way she finds hurtful. He implicitly conveys his disapproval of Janet's divorce, and Janet is "surprised – not just at what he said but at his feeling that he had any right, even now, to say it" (228). She considers gently reproaching her father, but stops short when she looks at the heart monitor and sees "the line his heart was writing" (228). As Redekop, Heble, and others have noted, in the opening pages, the father's heart monitor marks a concern with exposure that has metafictive overtones (Redekop 168-73; Heble 129). Its activity is described in textual terms – "On the screen a bright jagged line was continually being written" – and its "dramatizing" of "what ought to be a most secret activity" (217), Janet believes, "was asking for trouble" (217-18). She considers reproaching him by reminding him of his low opinion of her ex-husband, but instead finds herself "looking at the line his heart was writing" – an "'Unfair advantage'," her father says (228). The ethical move, or perhaps simply the gracious move, is to avoid capitalizing on her knowledge and responding to him in kind. This chilly note complicates the previous sense of harmony, but the overall movement has nonetheless been from stoic separation at the beginning to a greater sense of connection.

The planetarium scene, which elicits Janet's scepticism at representation yet still "calmed" her and "drained" her (233), just as she had wanted, also prepares readers for the penultimate scene, the naming of the moons. Redekop notes that this scene is not without ambiguity. Naming the moons is a way of insisting "on the reality of the space out there" (Redekop 169): like the Copernican revolution, it unsettles our belief in the significance of our existence (Redekop 156).[2] However, the act of naming also re-appropriates the moons according to our own mythologies, so "we can pretend that they still do orbit around the earth, that we have mastered them with our classical narratives" (Redekop 156). Janet and her father name, pattern, and in a sense affirm the existence of the universe at large, even if this act of agency paradoxically recognizes that they remain in the open, expansive universe of Copernicus and Galileo, a universe in which no transcendent meaning or final purpose appears evident.

In spite of this ambiguity, the scene has an undeniable emotional resonance. Yet the source of this power is perhaps not readily apparent. Because the scene lacks any overt displays of affection or access to Janet's consciousness, the sense of unity provided can be felt only obliquely. Biographical resonances account for some of the scene's power: Munro's father, Robert Laidlaw, wrote his novel *The McGregors* just before he died in 1976, and Alice Munro was indispensable both to its writing (Laidlaw vii) and its posthumous publication (Thacker 338). As Redekop notes, that Laidlaw "was writing, so to speak, side by side with [Munro] just before his death adds a poignancy to the father-daughter dialogues in this collection" (155), and this poignancy is never more pronounced than in the naming of the moons. Thacker similarly calls connections to Munro's life "of real consequence to a reader's experience of her work" (385), which is no doubt the case.

However, there is no easy correspondence – and perhaps no correspondence at all – between the emotional resonance evoked by the story and whatever emotional response we might have to Munro's personal situation. Munro is explicit that this story is not an account of her father's death; such an account would be "quite different, not just in factual detail, in incident, but in feeling" (Introduction xiv). For her, this story and the others that come from personal experience, as they are crafted into art, "are carried inexorably away from the real," just as the stories based more on observation "lose their anecdotal edges" and are "invaded by familiar shapes and voices" (Introduction xiv). Regardless of Munro's process of artistic creation, readers of "Moons" are relating primarily to Janet, a fictional character, with her own textual history as established both in this story and in those connected to it.

The Janet and the father in "Moons" are also the protagonist and the father from the two-part story "Chaddeleys and Flemings," which opens the collection: the story of the father's upbringing, of "the poor farm, the scared sisters, the harsh father" ("Moons" 219) and of "running away to work on the lake boats" ("Moons" 220) is related in greater detail in part two of "Chaddeleys and Flemings" – "The Stone in the Field" ("Stone" 29-30). "Moons," the title story as well as the final piece in the collection, works with the opening pair. All draw on and refigure elements of Munro's family history and the class-based tensions in her first marriage (Thacker 28-29, 119) to create a feeling of presence, a feeling crafted in and stretching across each story. The fictional world Munro evokes may be importantly connected to the real, but what readers respond to is Janet, with her history and her relationship to her father.

Despite the sense that, as Munro writes, people read such "first-person, seemingly artless and straightforward" stories and "imagine that just about all you did was write down everything that happened on a certain day" (Introduction xiv), the power of "Moons," and the planetarium scene specifically, comes from the language itself, regardless of any foreknowledge of Munro's personal situation. The original version of "Moons" accepted by *The New Yorker* was not even first-person, but third-person: Munro later re-submitted it as a first-person story to create this greater feeling of intimacy (Thacker 385). "The Moons of Jupiter" is, after all, an artistic, textual achievement: its intricate pattern of flashbacks, its choreographed movement from separation to unity to separation, its oblique treatment of the act of loving and letting go, and its metaphoric take on the acts of writing and representing make it one of Munro's best. "Moons," like many Munro stories, might be embedded in her life, but it is by no means reducible to it.

The formal features at work behind the power of the naming of the moons scene specifically, however, are somewhat difficult to pin down. The text of the passage itself gives little indication as to how to read the scene. In marked contrast to the rest of "The Moons of Jupiter," this scene contains little narrative commentary. The passage is mostly dialogue, and though the narration contains some description and some self-consciousness about diction, it lacks description of Janet's feelings or the state of her relationship to her father. However, it is precisely this *lack* that gives the scene its power. The naming of the moons, shared by father and daughter, is the only comfort, the only distraction, that wholly absorbs the narration. There is none of the scepticism of the planetarium scene and no realization of the triviality of the moment as is the case for Janet's temporary preoccupation with fashion. There is also none of the strain on their relationship caused by the father's teasing, or more seriously, by his subtle condemnation of Janet's decision, years ago, to leave her husband. The scene instead provides an absorbing moment of unity before the inevitable separation. This shared naming connects Janet, her father, and the reader in a creative discovery of meaning. The father's recital of the moons of Jupiter, with Janet's encouragement, draws on the discourses of history, science, and mythology, and the solace that comes from insisting on the naming and patterning of the moons invests those discourses with human and secular, if not sacred and transcendent, significance.

The final scene moves definitively to separation. The story flashes back to Janet just after she leaves the planetarium. Sitting in the Chinese garden behind the museum, feeling "calmed" and "drained" after the planetarium show, she contemplates a woman who vaguely resembles her daughter Nichola and decides that if it were her, she "might just sit and watch" (233). The anxiety she has felt over her father's health and her daughter's absence is temporarily relieved as Janet experiences a moment of real detachment, feeling "like one of those people who have floated up to the ceiling, enjoying a brief death. A relief, while it lasts" (233). The intimate connections she has had with her father and her daughter are now severed. "My father had chosen and Nichola had chosen" (233), she says, the father choosing his life-threatening operation and the daughter choosing to remain incommunicado. Janet has withdrawn to survive – just as she withdrew from Nichola, "measured and disciplined" her love, during the moment in Nichola's childhood when it was feared she had leukemia (230).

The image of the Chinese garden underscores both Janet's determination to carry on and her continuing scepticism at "tricks" of representation. The Chinese garden is a construction of high culture. It is adjacent to the museum, contains stone camels, warriors, and a tomb, and is surrounded by evergreens and a "high grilled iron fence" (233). Yet the garden is also a simulacrum, a reproduction completely displaced from its temporal and geographic context. Significantly, Janet looks away from the garden, through the bushes and the fence to watch the people travelling by on the street. The image of the tomb is also relevant. In ancient China, weapons, clothing, and sometimes people were buried along with royals to accompany them into the afterlife (Bush 1). Janet, however, will not throw herself into her father's grave or into a state of despair over her estrangement from her daughter; she will not be, as Redekop puts it, a "keeper" (172), clinging to her attachment to her family, though it is not so much that she "escapes being trapped" (172) in this role as it is that she comes to accept these losses. The garden cannot hold Janet's interest and neither can the tomb, with its relief carvings and stone pictures. Janet "always mean[s]" to look at the tomb's intricate carvings, and yet she never has, "Not this time, either" (233).

In the final lines of the story, Janet leaves the garden to escape the cold and "to have coffee and something to eat" (233). For the most part in "Moons," representation seems to have a special power. At this moment, however, it fails in the face of food and drink. Like the children in the planetarium, for Janet, this kind of artifice is no match for the tangible pleasure and biological necessity of nourishment. Here is a final failure of representation, linked significantly to the severing, or at least the weakening, of her bonds with her daughter and her father.

Were the events of the story to be arranged chronologically, the Chinese garden would appear somewhere around the midpoint. The final scene would have to be the naming of the moons, the night before her father's operation, which Janet interestingly refers to as "his last night" (232). To end at this point would be to draw the story to a close on a note of powerful emotional connection, of love and mourning. Yet the final scene moves back to that afternoon to end on a note of separation and of letting go, so the staging of emotion – from separation to unity to separation – releases the reader into catharsis.

This chronological *dis*arrangement of the story – its jumbled timeline – is, then, as Rosalie Osmond might put it, not an embracing of randomness "as an end in itself" but rather "as part of a quest for new, more viable patterns" (85). Arranging the scenes in non-sequential order might in some sense violate the mimetic effect of the story, yet this stylization gives the story a cathartic emotional resonance it might not otherwise possess. For all Janet's ambivalence around representation, the cathartic power, in the end, depends on readers experiencing these characters and their relationships as somewhat real. In fact, the apparently disordered narrative may itself be a strategy that mirrors the disorder of life, or may also be part of "the rambling nature" of Munro's narrative that, along with "the suppression of overt moralizing or thematizing," has been "a mark of the realistic short story since Chekhov" (Canitz and Seamon 68).

David Crouse similarly locates Munro's reordering of chronology, as well as her use of multiple epiphanies, in the attempt to navigate the

tension between creating a vivid and lifelike world and creating characters who move and change without producing "a kind of neatness which
might not ring true to both writer and reader" (51). Munro, he says,
displays a consciousness of her "work as a fictional artifact" yet gives it
an "internal consistency the meta-fictionalists denied" – she "play[s] the
game of the realist, but use[s] many of the meta-fictionalist's tricks" (64).
"The Moons of Jupiter" registers the inadequacy of fiction because of the
gap between the representation and the thing-in-itself and because of
the futility of representation in the face of death, yet paradoxically it does
so while exploiting the power of fiction to engage its readers' emotions
and imaginations.

This play between the explicitly metafictional and the more traditionally realist also manifests itself in the complex publication history
of the book in which "Moons" was originally to be published. As Helen
Hoy and Robert Thacker have documented, "Moons" was one of several
stories, including "Chaddeleys and Flemings," initially slated to be part
of a more explicitly metafictional collection called "Rose and Janet"
(Hoy 59-70; Thacker 341-44). The result of "tortuous" evolution (Hoy
69), including multiple versions of multiple stories in several different
sequences, "Rose and Janet" was to consist of six third-person stories
about the protagonist Rose, an actress, and six first-person stories about
Janet, a writer (Hoy 60). This collection, edited by Douglas Gibson, was
for the Canadian market and publisher Macmillan of Canada; it was
distinct from an American version then under the auspices of Norton
and editor Sherry Huber, who were "making earnest attempts to turn
the same material into a novel" (Hoy 67). In the final pages of "Rose and
Janet," Rose would be revealed to be Janet's fictional creation, thereby
"transforming all that has gone before" (Hoy 71). Once Munro realized
that a new version of the story "Simon's Luck" and the revision of three
Janet stories – "Mischief," "Providence," and "Who Do You Think You
Are?" – into Rose stories gave her enough material for a strong collection
focused solely on Rose, she literally stopped the presses, at a personal
cost of $1,864.08 (Thacker 347-48, 350). The Rose stories would stand
alone in the collection *Who Do You Think You Are?*.[3]

"Rose and Janet," with its indirect dramatization of the transmutation
of life into art, would have been more obviously metafictional. Hoy calls it
"a provocative and complex arrangement" (78) that would require "more

engagement in deciphering the silences" (72), more attention to "the gap between and ... the interaction between one story and another" (72). Yet Munro backed away from it at the last moment, at significant cost to herself. Munro has said that she rejected this explicitly metafictional arrangement as "just too fancy," as "a little bit pretentious or precious" (Munro in Hancock 88). Hoy notes that "Munro has shown a growing impatience with overt metafictional strategies" such as those in "The Ottawa Valley" and "Home" (79). This move away from more open self-reflexivity by no means moves her closer to any naïve realism: shattering the reality effect, after all, can easily become a mere mechanical demonstration of a particular aesthetic of self-consciousness, one with no special dispensation from the regular rules of language to transcend the representational contract of language and pronounce on its inadequacy.

The scepticism of "Moons," which eschews "fancy" or "pretentious" metafictional displays, might well owe more to John Calvin and John Knox than to Roland Barthes and Jacques Derrida. While discussing *The View from Castle Rock* in an interview on CBC Radio, Munro stopped just short of drawing a straight line from Presbyterianism to atheism: John Knox's push for an educated peasantry, she said, led to the development of a critical, practical, intelligent people with no use for rituals or symbols, and their critical reading practice created some inevitable ambivalence toward the Bible (Munro in Rogers). This Protestant culture led to a belief in the value of reading and an experience of its power, as well as an eventual and unsettling suspicion that interpretation could not be fixed either by faith or the authority of the church.

Carrington has previously drawn a connection between this ambivalence toward language and Munro's rural, Protestant upbringing. She writes that for Munro's characters, "manipulating and controlling language – the imaginative act of writing itself – somehow becomes a form of shame or humiliation" (15), and she notes an interview in which Munro says that "although writing was 'the only thing' that she 'ever wanted to do,' she felt 'embarrassment' about 'doing something' that she could neither 'explain' nor 'justify' to her hard-working parents" (16). Yet as Thacker notes, Munro has said that her father "understood the artist in her" (315). "Always a reader, always a thoughtful man," Robert Laidlaw, in the last years of his life, "had become a writer himself," producing not just *The McGregors*, but also publishing "five memoirs, and a short story," between 1974 and 1976 (Thacker 315). Perhaps Laidlaw, then, felt a similar ambivalence about literature over the course of his life.

If Munro's cultural heritage bred such an ambivalence, then it might ultimately have been an enabling one. In "Moons," Munro relies on realism – on its capacity for characterization, compassion, and presence – yet does so with full comprehension of language's inability to represent perfectly either the world or the totality of being. Her sophisticated and even sceptical understanding of the ability of language to represent nevertheless forms an important part of the power of Munro's aesthetic, in the process offering us a reminder that viewing language as more than a vessel for conveying thoughts or reflecting the world is not the exclusive province of theorists and philosophers.

Notes

1. In the original publication of this story in *The New Yorker*, Janet was a painter – a change made at the suggestion of the magazine's editorial staff but reversed when Munro published the story as part of her own collection (Thacker 341). This decision indicates Munro at least sees Janet's career as a writer as important to the story, even if it does not necessarily strengthen any autobiographical connection.
2. The Copernican revolution, which held that the earth was not the centre of the universe around which all else orbited, was, incidentally, confirmed by Galileo's observation of the moons of Jupiter, the first heavenly bodies shown *not* to orbit the earth (Redekop 156).
3. *Who Do You Think You Are?* was titled *The Beggar Maid* for the US and UK markets.

Works Cited

Attridge, Derek. *The Singularity of Literature*. London: Routledge, 2004.
Barthes, Roland. "The Reality Effect." *The Rustle of Language*. Trans. Richard Howard. 1986. Berkeley, CA: U of California P, 1989. 141-48.
Bush, Richard C. *Religion in China*. Niles, IL: Argus Communications-DLM, 1977. Major World Religions Ser.

Canitz, A.E. Christa, and Roger Seamon. "The Rhetoric of Fictional Realism in the Stories of Alice Munro." *Canadian Literature* 150 (1996):
67-80.

Carrington, Ildikó de Papp. *Controlling the Uncontrollable: The Fiction of
Alice Munro*. DeKalb, IL: Northern Illinois UP, 1989.

Crouse, David. "Resisting Reduction: Closure in Richard Ford's *Rock
Springs* and Alice Munro's *Friend of My Youth*." *Canadian Literature*
146 (1995): 51-64.

Hancock, Geoff. "An Interview with Alice Munro." *Canadian Fiction
Magazine* 43 (1982): 74-114. Rpt. (rev.) as "Alice Munro" in *Canadian
Writers at Work: Interviews with Geoff Hancock*. Toronto: Oxford UP,
1987. 189-224.

Heble, Ajay. *The Tumble of Reason: Alice Munro's Discourse of Absence*.
Toronto: U of Toronto P, 1994.

Howells, Coral Ann. *Alice Munro*. Manchester, Eng.: Manchester UP, 1998.
Contemporary World Writers.

Hoy, Helen. "'Rose and Janet': Alice Munro's Metafiction." *Canadian Literature* 121 (1989): 59-83.

Laidlaw, Robert. *The McGregors: A Novel of an Ontario Pioneer Family*.
Toronto: Macmillan of Canada, 1979.

Miller, Joaquin. "Columbus." *The Complete Poetical Works of Joaquin
Miller*. 1897. New York: Arno, 1972. 253.

Munro, Alice. "Chaddeleys and Flemings." *The Moons of Jupiter*. Toronto:
Macmillan of Canada, 1982. 1-35.

---. "Home." *74: New Canadian Stories*. Ed. David Helwig and Joan Harcourt.
Ottawa: Oberon, 1974. 133-53.

---. Introduction. *The Moons of Jupiter*. Toronto: Penguin, 1995. xiii-xvi.

---. "Material." *Something I've Been Meaning To Tell You*. Toronto: McGraw-
Hill Ryerson, 1974. 22-44.

---. "The Moons of Jupiter." *The Moons of Jupiter*. Toronto: Macmillan of
Canada, 1982. 217-33.

---. "The Moons of Jupiter." *The New Yorker* 22 May 1978: 32-39.

---. "The Ottawa Valley." *Something I've Been Meaning To Tell You*. Toronto:
McGraw-Hill Ryerson, 1974. 227-46.

---. "Walker Brothers Cowboy." *Dance of the Happy Shades*. Fwd. Hugh
Garner. Toronto: Ryerson, 1968. 1-18.

---. "Winter Wind." *Something I've Been Meaning To Tell You*. Toronto: McGraw-Hill Ryerson, 1974. 192-206.

Munro, Sheila. *Lives of Mothers & Daughters: Growing Up with Alice Munro*. Toronto: McClelland & Stewart, 2001.

Osmond, Rosalie. "Arrangements, 'Disarrangements,' and 'Earnest Deceptions'." *Narrative Strategies in Canadian Literature: Feminism and Postcolonialism*. Ed. Coral Ann Howells and Lynette Hunter. Milton Keynes, Eng.: Open UP, 1991. 82-92.

"Pluto Loses Status as a Planet." *BBC News* 24 Aug 2006. 21 Nov. 2006. <http://news.bbc.co.uk/2/hi/science/nature/5282440.stm>.

Redekop, Magdalene. *Mothers and Other Clowns: The Stories of Alice Munro*. London: Routledge, 1992.

Rogers, Shelagh. Interview with Alice Munro. *Sounds like Canada*. CBC Radio. 12 Oct. 2006.

Smythe, Karen E. *Figuring Grief: Gallant, Munro, and the Poetics of Elegy*. Montreal, QC and Kingston, ON: McGill-Queen's UP, 1992.

Struthers, J.R. (Tim). "The Real Material: An Interview with Alice Munro." *Probable Fictions: Alice Munro's Narrative Acts*. Ed. Louis K. MacKendrick. Downsview, ON: ECW, 1983. 5-36.

Thacker, Robert. *Alice Munro: Writing Her Lives: A Biography*. Toronto: McClelland & Stewart, 2005.

Ware, Tracy. Letter to the author. 19 Oct. 2006.

Ending Things Well:
Alice Munro's "White Dump"

Karen Houle

"White Dump" is the final short story in Alice Munro's 1986 collection, *The Progress of Love*. The working premise of this project of Tim Struthers' is that Munro's choice of final stories – the story among stories that she tasked with closing each of her fourteen collections – is deliberate. In any collection, some one story, in addition to being a great stand-alone story, has to perform the special act of ending the book; of making an ending and of being an ending that actually fulfils this extra task of *being* The End. That is, not only that there are technically no further pages to read once it has been read, but that the reader has simultaneously been brought to a psycho-aesthetic-affective place where no further pages are needed or wanted. The last story *gets* the last word because it *earns* it. It earns it through a very quiet, non-incidental mereological orchestration of the whole and the parts in the whole. In this instance, the maestro is Alice Munro.

What that choice of last story involves – in the case of *The Progress of Love*, "White Dump" – is thus of real significance and worth exploring. What we learn from taking up the reading of the story and the collection from this angle of questioning may be of genuine interest, philosophically, psychologically, or semiotically, for Munro scholarship in particular, for fiction writing more generally. And, really, for all art production. The question entertained here is a close cousin of: *Why does this poem end here? How did the filmmaker decide/intuit/sense that no further space or sounds or images would add anything more to the meaningfulness and coherence of what had happened on the screen up to that very point when it goes black in front of our eyes? When and how did*

217

the composer realize that one beat more would detract from the symphony?
Don't all art-makings involve an event of choice-among-all-the-possible-
choices: the one that the artists actually make to make the things they
are making stop?

Caveat: I am not a Munro scholar. I've never published a single ink
blot about her work. It always seemed to me to be the most impossible
thing to do (but many do do it, and well) precisely because her stories,
each one of them, gets such a peculiar centrifugal finesse going inside
me that each one of them earns the last word: by that I mean, each
story is so darned right that it doesn't invite me to respond to them with
more words. I have read her stories for almost all of my life as a reader.
I guess that makes me not a Munro scholar but a Munro reader. In this
essay, therefore, I'll try to stick to speaking from that place, reluctantly
allowing myself to wonder out loud what Alice Munro might – *might*
– have been up to by ending my (and our) reading of *The Progress of
Love* with "White Dump" rather than "Eskimo" or "Miles City, Montana."
My intention in musing aloud on this question is not to teach anybody
anything about Munro's fiction but to try to learn something about how
to make good endings. Lord knows we all have to make them – and I'm
not talking about writing fiction – so better to be schooled by a pro than
make a botch of things, Euphemia might say.

This story – "White Dump" – is about the possible trajectories of modern
aircraft. By modern aircraft we mean mostly planes, but in this case a
space ship is included.

What can an aircraft do? If it's "large" (295) and assembled out of
excellently machined parts from Europe, and is manned by a trained
pilot, it will go up smoothly and quietly, and come down smoothly and
quietly, as though "Everything was always the same" (279) except you
are now in Canada rather than Germany or vice-versa. If it's a space
ship on July 20th, 1969, it is "thick-waisted ... silver-gold" like Magda
(275) and will head for the moon up in our shared night sky, and actually land on it, and be a wondrous spectacle for viewers far away. If it's
"a five-seater" (278) that is parked on a rural landing strip, piloted by
a ruggedly handsome dude who takes money for taking locals up for
weekend birthday whims, or parachuting, this kind of plane lurches up
off the surface of the Earth, having "a peculiar and distressing effect"

(296). When it levels off it seems "not to be moving at all" (295), and is experienced from inside the metal hull as unpleasantly loud, "making a terrible racket" (296). It is only between the distressing upward motion and the equally distressing downward motion that there is a pause, and in this pause is where such an aircraft can deliver its spectacle. The spectacle of vantage on life below that such a plane makes is equally likely to be "wonderful" (304), "most enjoyable" (305), as to be nauseating, like a "sickening dot" (297). Here, this is the aircraft that has been hired by the daughter, Denise, for her father's, Laurence's, birthday surprise: "a kid's dream – the most wonderful promising thing" (306), as Isabel says of the White Dump of her childhood.

Planes also crash but the one which stars in this story won't while the family is up in it, looking down on the Ottawa Valley lake system, because that would end the story then and there. Except it does crash. Three times.

The first time occurs on page 278 between these two lines:

"Is this the new in-joke?" says Magda. "What am I missing? Goat milk?"
Laurence says, "Magda, did you know that on my fortieth birthday Denise took me up in a plane?"

The second crash happens on page 287:

She sat at the table quietly burping and retasting the bacon, and hearing the terrible sound of a stranger crying in their house.
From the plane on her father's birthday, they had seen some delicate, almost transparent, mounded clouds in the western sky, and Denise had said, "Thunderclouds."

The third, possibly not a full-crash but a deeply disorienting whiteout complete with a scary pressure drop, happens on page 306:

"White marble," said Sophie, quoting. "Pretentious stuff. They've put it on all the park paths in Aubreyville, spoiled the park. Glaring."
Isabel said, "You know we used to have the White Dump? At the school I went to – it was behind a biscuit factory, the playground backed on to the factory property. Every now and then, they'd sweep up these

quantities of vanilla icing and nuts and hardened marshmallow globs
and they'd bring it in barrels and dump it back there and it would shine.
It would shine like a pure white mountain."

The story that Munro writes has a powerful internal engine of forward progress. And thus, after each of these three crashes, it instantly
rebounds and flows on, as if they did not occur at all. In each of these
three moments I've just isolated, there is no formal break indicated –
while other parts of the story, no less chronologically and substantively
disjunctive, are divided with I, II, or III, or given breathing space on the
page, so that the reader can take stock, and adjust to a sudden change,
breathe into the mask normally. Not in the three cases of sudden but
unremarked crashes, though. In fact, the compression around each
of these fault lines is so intense that the reader is not actually able to
breathe through them.

Every key element that makes up the shape and comprises the heart
of "White Dump" can be compressed to six points: (1) Magda, the beautiful and stylish step-mother of adult Denise, is trying to pull off a tasteful
and harmonious cottage evening, but is ruthlessly (cruelly?) exposed to
both the fact of, and the ridicule toward, the first wife, Denise's mother
(Isabel) because her husband (Laurence, very rich businessman) keeps
baiting Denise about Isabel's current "situation" as if he is just making
conversation; (2) The man-child money-maker Laurence has wives
and female children who spend a disproportionate amount of time
and energy pandering to him: "he had to be propped up, kept going,
by constant and clever exertions on her part, by reassurance and good
management" (304), "she seldom concerned herself about Laurence's
being happy. She wanted him to be in a good mood, so that everything
would go smoothly, but that was not the same thing" (304); (3) Denise
and her brother, Peter, as children become involuntary and uncompre-
hending witnesses to a drama that involves their mother, father, and a
barely-known-woman (the cake caterer for his fortieth birthday party),
but Peter pretends to neither hear nor care or really manages to neither
hear nor care; (4) that the weather was good but Denise saw something
foreboding; plus, she is educated and knows the proper names of things
whereas her mother, Isabel, is not and so does not – "'Those streaky ones
are okay,' said Isabel. 'It's the big piled-up white ones that could mean a

storm.' // 'Cumulus,' Denise said" (281); (5) that the caterer woman and her "slightly stupid-sounding country voice" (302) husband the pilot (the one whom Isabel has an affair with and thus crashes her marriage and is launched out of the family) are the kinds of people who think white driveways are lovely; precisely the kinds of people and tastes inviting the disdain of Sophie: here Munro gives us another crystalline moment of the kind of person in whom real and deep contradiction can live (love of The People, disdain of people); (6) finally, that Isabel, despite ample "proof of [her] intelligence" (303), despite being a beautiful "slim and brown" redhead (284), despite being married to affluent Laurence, thus ensconced in the bosom of the Vogelsang family, cannot repress or hide the fact she is "a poor, bright girl from the factory side of town, wearing a tight pink sweater that Laurence always remembered" (282): she is *white trash*.

Which means the story maps out the possible trajectories of women in rural Ontario in the late twentieth century. Aircraft with names: Magda, Denise, Isabel, and Sophie.

MAGDA. The first one we meet. On the first page. Magda is spiffing up the now-very-spiffy cottage for the arrival of dinner guests. She "is an Englishwoman, not a Hungarian as her name might suggest. She used to be a dancer, then a dancing teacher. She is a short, thick-waisted woman, still graceful, with a smooth, pale neck and a lovely, floating crown of silver-gold hair" (275). This is all we get to know about her, and Munro's point is that it's all we need to know since it's all Magda needs: good-enough looks and good-enough shape to have snagged and kept her rich husband, Laurence.

Magda, Denise's stepmother, is "style through and through" (275), by which I suspect we are meant to realize that whether she has anything more to want or to offer than style and stylishness – wifely and cottagely stylishness – is totally irrelevant. It is totally irrelevant because those attributes are enough for this former dancer to have attracted a mate, found herself in the bosom of a family, and maintained her position as mate by virtue of constant style-offerings – ginger pots, settees, chintz, opera, magazines, scarves – for the long arc of her adult life.

The offer is made in perpetuity to Laurence first, and to his guests, his children, his furniture only incidentally by virtue of the offer first to

Laurence. Hence, whatever gains Laurence or the cottage or the investment portfolio will make, Magda will also make, but also in the second-hand position, the grateful, mute recipient. In this it's not nuts to suggest that in the story's arc, Magda is actually twinned with the poorest and shabbiest creature in the whole story, one of two interchangeable unremarkable Bryce girls – "Rita or Annie" – in that, despite all the chintz and portico paint, neither does Magda "indicate a preference of any kind" (294).

What this kind of female must be is a parasitic plane – a glider. Either one that goes up with the big ship, and lines all its forces up with the forces that keep that rocket on target for glory, and thus won't ever come down (or we don't care about watching that part of the drama). Or one that never gets off the ground in the first place. Magda as female or plane is utterly without engine, thus utterly boring, and thus practically guaranteed to be a successful woman, which amounts structurally to Munro needing her to be part of the launch of the story but not needing her to do anything else, again. Nor do we the readers need her. And by this complete lack of giving a shit about the current Queen Bee, we learn (or more joltingly remember) something about the beginnings and not-beginnings, and about the endings and non-endings that we females are currently allowed to choose; we women readers with our own stylish or unstylish faces, pleasing or unpleasing shapes, and thus each our own aviation chart. Yes, a Magda enjoys a progress of love, but only in the mode of a tidy and unobtrusive parasite.

DENISE. Half of my roommates through my university years were *Denises*: white Ontario girls born into money that came through their father (never their mother); girls of enriched if not private education; girls who then live out their adult lives facing squarely and purposefully in the direction of social justice, or poverty alleviation, or women's rights, or immigrant services, or foster children, or the creative class. Of the many women I count among my adult good friends, most fit that bill. The many I know are very intentionally and nobly, honestly, trying to give back, to share power across privilege, to live authentically and on principle. To be born affluent was in no way, after all, their choice. They know that to have been born poor or sick or into a house of awfulness was also not the bad judgment and choices of the poor or the sick or those condemned to the awful.

In this case, "Denise runs a Women's Centre in Toronto. She gets beaten women into shelters, finds doctors and lawyers for them, goes after private and public money, makes speeches, holds meetings, deals with varied and sometimes dangerous mix-ups of life. She makes less money than a clerk in a government liquor store" (276). When Laurence, her rich father, states that "this is a typical pattern for a girl of affluent background" (276), readers know before he has even said that out loud that he is not, not right but also that he's a jerk for saying it out loud in the presence of Denise, or, well, anyone. It's the kind of thing he gets to say because, as Denise's lover thinks, Laurence is one of those "successful old men, in a capitalist industrial society," who "are almost purely evil" (277), but we already know that too.

What catches our attention in Munro's story about aircrafts-or-women are two other teeny but important details about Denise. First, that she is not pretty or not considered pretty enough for anyone in the story, or writing the story, or reading the story, to dwell on. Only once is her appearance described: she is "a tall, careful woman with a long braid, very plainly dressed" (288). In other words, unlike Magda, whom Munro lets us see well, and keep looking at, and unlike Denise's mother, Isabel, who also enjoys the lens of beauty, and makes a moon landing of her own, i.e., lands a husband because she has got fabulous equipment, plain Denise is neither looked at by us, nor seen making any such moves. Munro lets you squirm wondering if it were, would she have taken it? And then there is also the truth that adult plain-looking Denise – for all her effort to deny it and create moral, political, and economic distance from everything her father represents, is, or manufactures (fake stained glass sheeting you can put on a window to make a room suddenly glow with a loon and a sunset) – cannot be what she manages to be, a fighter for justice, at too much distance from Laurence.

  If she was not Laurence's daughter, she would not have been the kind of girl who imagined all her family up in a plane for a birthday whim – *her idea* – and thus a girl of action and consequence that had a hand in everything that this ride brought about; nor would she be the kind of woman who was very strongly inclined (an ideological reactiveness to his position which is also hers?) to take up and be able to continue to work in her "chosen" field. Yes, Laurence has the bait and "lays the bait" but just as surely she "snaps it up" (277). And that bait is going to be hers for the taking even long after Laurence is eaten by worms, whereas Magda's share of the inheritance (and probably Magda herself) will be diminished by the time the patriarch's body cools.

What kind of a plane or trajectory a woman like Denise is, then, is not so much a hard question to answer as one that this reader ends up not feeling very good about even wondering about. Backlighting the grotesque complicity between patriarchal capitalism and white feminist social justice, in Ontario, in the 80s: that's Munro setting out poison bait for us on the unspoken other half of the cynical equation Laurence sums up:

> He has said that the Women's Centre is a good idea for those who really need it. But he sometimes wonders.
>
> What does he sometimes wonder?
>
> Frankly, he sometimes wonders if some of those women – some of them – aren't enjoying all the attention they are getting, claiming to be battered and raped, and so on. (276)

ISABEL. The other half of my roommates in university were *Isabels*: smart enough to be at university; but hot enough to not have to be. Or, for very long. What does it take for a woman to move rapidly and steeply up out of one class and its set of possibilities into a wildly better one? At first glance, the answer Munro seems to give is: a progress (via) love: Isabel and Laurence. Then, read more globally, the answer Munro seems to give is: brains and hotness. But the final answer she leaves us with, in the early trajectories of Isabel, is that it's really just the hotness that counts. It's easy for any reader to picture Isabel's easy, natural beauty: tall, slim, perky notable boobs in a sweater, flat stomach, forever 29ish, long dark red hair, a tan dialled in by Laurence's desire for his wife to look a certain shade of brown. "'Who cares about fried brains if you've got a gorgeous brown body?' said Laurence" (285). That she has the brain power to catapult out of the orbit of the working class and aspire to something other than, well, being the working class, is known by the reader to be technically true but never once shown. But that she has the body power to sexually attract and move a man, and is aware of her power and uses it, is shown, and on three occasions.

First, we recall, in the story of the courtship of Laurence and Isabel: "Laurence and Isabel had met in the cafeteria of the university, where Isabel was working as a cashier. She was a first-year student, a poor, bright girl from the factory side of town, wearing a tight pink sweater that Laurence always remembered" (281-82). Second, the morning of Laurence's fortieth birthday, in bed together, she manages *both* to get him aroused so as to flatter/placate/bond with him as per his birthday morning wishes, *and* to get him off at just the right tempo that the kids come in just after he has come so Laurence and Isabel are not coitally interrupted (i.e., him, peevish) but so well that he is not aware of her having been in Family Strategist rather than in Sexy-Time Hot XXX Wife mode. Of course, the last good glimpse the readers have of that power, a power of female beauty at its zenith, is what we don't see coming and aren't allowed to see happening at the end: her "first extra love affair" (308) with the five-seater pilot.

It is the irrational, sudden, class- and world-destabilizing force of sexual attraction between people that is the epicentre of Denise's parents' marriage, and at an early age she senses that truth in all its visceral weirdness: "She thought that those two people, Laurence and Isabel, her father and mother, kept something hidden. Something between them. She could feel it welling up fresh and teasing, or lying low and sour, but she could never get to understand what it was, or how it worked. They would not let her" (282). What that something was turns out not to be the force of sexual attraction between two people so much as Laurence's sexual attraction for Isabel plus her "concentrating then on being in love with Laurence's good looks and wit and intelligence" (304), which, as any child or reader will soon notice, are not two halves of the same whole.

Likely what young Denise also senses is the precariousness of that bond as the parental glue at the centre of her life. Also, given that all bodies age into something quite spectacularly human though not at all "sexy" (I think this is one of the roles played by the scene with Sophie, naked, standing in full view of the family on the morning of Laurence's birthday), Denise "knows" the special precariousness of the female body – including the drooping body of Denise's grandmother, Sophie, including the lovely body of Denise's mother, Isabel, a body whose market value had levelled out, requiring a rebalancing of her personal portfolio: "She read a lot; she dieted and exercised seriously; she had become a good cook" (304). Plain Denise – not an inch of her body is shown to us by Munro – knows that all this will happen to her too.

Denise's mother, Isabel, might have been born into what is unpleasantly referred to as *white trash*. Not only poor but uncultured, hicks or townies who lick sugar dust off the schoolyard dirt. However, Isabel had two real assets, brains and beauty, and that meant she was never fully enclosed by that world and its ludicrously puny range of possibilities: "She had a reputation in her family for thinking she was special" (304). As we spied with silvery-golden Magda and the tarnished "Rita or Annie" (294), Munro pairs Isabel with another female in the story, the pilot's wife, the "catering woman": "a stout, dark-haired, rather pretty woman in her forties, with heavy green eye shadow and a perfect, gleaming, bouffant hairstyle" (283). Both are hot, but Isabel is also very smart, and that combo initially launched her like a rocket out of the gravitational pull of the working class into the sort of life with inherited cottages at a lake. And unlike the tempered ambitions of the pilot's wife, Isabel was a launch so steep and single-minded that it severed her connection to her roots and thus marked out, in principle, a zenith, the moment her arc would stall and start the fall back down toward the dirt.

What Munro shows us is that "rather pretty" women are grotesquely vulnerable on many levels: "When Denise saw the catering woman again, more than a year had gone by" and at first Denise did not recognize her, for "she was wearing a more youthful dress this time – a loose dress with swirls of red and blue and purple 'psychedelic' colors – and did not look as pretty" (285). Their lives are uniquely vulnerable to men and to time. What Munro also shows us is that, in rural Ontario in the late twentieth century, the selfish use of that beauty – in Isabel's case, to go back to the pilot the day after Laurence's birthday, and in his arms feel "rescued, lifted, beheld, and safe" (309), is not safe harbour at all but the beginning of the end. Such a re-use of one's own attraction initiates an equally steep decline back to the sort of life cobbled together with "a commercial fisherman who used to be a TV cameraman" (277-78) and who, Laurence jokes, is engaged with Isabel in "goat farming" (278): back to the same dirt she lifted off from, but with a nasty landing. Since the beginning and the ending are the same, this sort of aircraft, or woman, only enjoys the illusion of progress. And worse: only enjoys the illusion of love.

SOPHIE: THE "OLD NORSE" (280). Sophie is the only woman who has a life that anticipates a good ending. She began as a Vogelsang, that is, was born into money, old money, but as an adult "she didn't really care enough" (290) about the extra trappings that, in a capitalist economy, could have swankified the basics she inherited and loved: a home, books, a vintage oven, a lake to swim in, a cigarette lighter, a tatty bathrobe. In the Log House "Everything was always the same" (279).

Sophie began as a "rich man's daughter, now poor" (279-80), with "odd spending habits" (280), mostly thrift and ambivalence about upkeep and domesticity and style and progress-for-show. Hers is a slow downslope, slow enough for her to develop preferences and for those preferences to stabilize, to remain intact. Sophie also had brains: she went to university to study languages, where, like Isabel, she met a man who would shape part of her future. In this case, Laurence's father, "a teacher of German, whose attention she had first attracted by arguing forcefully, in class, for a Westphalian pronunciation" (295). Where Sophie and Isabel differ is that in the case of the former, "she was too proud to ask him to uproot himself, leave his wife, follow her to the Log House" (295); in other words, she had a child by her professor-lover, and then carried on without him.

Sophie clearly completed her studies, even with a young child, and became "an assistant professor of Scandinavian languages" (280). Hers is a slow upslope, slow enough for her to develop her competencies, and for those competencies to stabilize and remain intact. And what of her female wiles, her physical beauty? We don't know what she looked like as a young woman, but it's not insignificant that Munro tells us that as a young woman, "she had *first attracted* [him] by arguing forcefully" (295; emphasis added). She may or may not have been a knockout. What matters is the order of deployment.

Readers only get to see a "broad, strong, speckled old woman, with a crown of yellowish-white braids" (281). But then, too quick for us to look the other way, we (the readers, Laurence and his kids and wife) stare at the most bodily of all the females in the story: "Sophie appeared at the top of the bank, naked. She walked directly toward them across the mown grass" (299). The sight of "an old woman naked" is surprising: "The smoothness of the skin compared to the wrinkled condition of Sophie's face, neck, arms, and hands. The smallness of the breasts ... slung down like little bundles, little hammock bundles, from the broad, freckled chest. The scantiness of the pubic hair, and the color of it, was also unexpected; it had not turned white, but remained a glistening golden brown, and was as light a covering as a very young girl's" (300). Hers is a circle, where the beginnings of her body as a girl are both present in, and eclipsed by, her body as an old woman.

When you overlay this triumvirate trajectory – one slanting up gently, one slanting down gently, and one that makes a circle – you get an impossible figure. No aircraft could do all of these at the same time. But Sophie did, so now we know that she is not an aircraft. A person moving upward and downward cancels the progress in either direction, levels off, and seems "not to be moving at all" (295). But since, unlike Isabel, she was not "straining," "looking forward to" a "bonus" she was "hoping to get, when this, and this, and this, was over" (303), and unlike Denise, she was held up by the power of opposition to the very thing that kept her up, and unlike Magda, she was not dropping into nothingness the minute the captain stopped noticing her, Sophie is still aloft, so something is working well. Moreover, only this sort of a subject can be the contradictions everyone is, without precipitating disaster: in her case being "a pacifist and Socialist" (281) but loving the totalitarian gore of the Icelandic sagas. Sophie is a person living in her own skin, a person who can reach down and find the end still connected to the beginning, which might not be sexy but makes for a good swimmer.

This kind of a female person, a woman in rural Ontario at the tail end of the twentieth century, gets to live her life rather than borrow one, or rent one, with her Visa card or nice boobs, for spectacle and a temporary fun ride. This kind of a female character, a woman in rural Ontario at the tail end of the twentieth century, in the last story in Alice Munro's *The Progress of Love*, is a whole person who happens to be a female person, where the female part is a part – a good one, a stand-alone bit with occasional blasts of superpower – and not the whole. It is one story, and an amazing one, but not the entire collection. Yet, it somehow shows us what ending things well takes, and how ending things well feels.

Note

Page references are to *The Progress of Love* (Toronto: McClelland & Stewart, 1986).

A Comic Streak:
The Two "Fairly Happy" Heroines
of Alice Munro's "Wigtime"

Tracy Ware

The best account of *Friend of My Youth* (1990), Alice Munro's seventh book, is Deborah Heller's: "Most of the stories ... are about characters – principally, but not exclusively, women – who in one way or another 'get loose,' are not 'fastened down.' They get loose from the roles expected of them by other characters in their fictional lives and from the roles that readers may expect them to play in predictable plots. In crucial instances, characters also seem to get loose from the narrator's knowledge and control" (60). There is no single narrator in "Wigtime," the concluding story, but Anita and Margot get "loose" from all predictions; their stories reflect what Heller calls Munro's "newly focused interest in the construction of collaborative, shared narratives" (68).[1]

Like "Meneseteung" and "Friend of My Youth," the stories from this volume that are most often singled out in criticism, "Wigtime" involves conflict as much as collaboration,[2] but Anita is partially reconciled with both her old friend and, to a lesser extent, her mother when she returns to Southwestern Ontario after a long absence. The revival of their friendship fits Roxanne Gay's rejection of the idea that "all female friendships must be bitchy, toxic, or competitive"; "[t]his is not to say women aren't bitches or toxic or competitive sometimes," Gay adds, "but rather to say that these are not defining characteristics of female friendship, especially as you get older" (47). They are defining characteristics in "Differently," the previous story in *Friend of My Youth*, but "Wigtime" is a comedy, in its humour and its form.

Munro said in an early interview that "when you have made something funny, you've achieved some kind of reality. That's what I'm trying to get" (Munro in Gibson 252). Although her humour is "a largely unexamined critical topic," as W.H. New observes (135n16), there have been exceptions, especially the work of Magdalene Redekop, who argued in 1992 that "Munro's vision, like that of all comic writers, is one of the community rather than the individual" (236; see also Jones, Jr. 56). The plot of "Wigtime" involves two incidents of adultery; to adapt Marx's famous revision of Hegel,[3] if the first is not quite tragic, the second certainly approaches farce. As a character in Margaret Drabble's novel *The Middle Ground* thinks, "Adultery is in itself farcical.... Of course, these affairs caused a good deal of genuine suffering and jealousy, but they were also comic, if regarded in the right light" (52-53). Both Anita and Margot find "the right light" for their life stories, though each casts a shadow on the other.

"Wigtime" is also comic in Northrop Frye's sense. "A comedy is not a play which ends happily: it is a play in which a certain structure is present and works through to its own logical end, whether we or the cast or the author feel happy about it or not" (46). The story's structure fulfills Anita's and Margot's youthful faith that "They could never be deeply unhappy, because they believed that something remarkable was bound to happen to them. They could become heroines; love and power of some sort were surely waiting" (253). They do become the ironic heroines of their own remarkable stories, but their power was neither surely waiting nor involved with love in any way that they could have expected.[4] Since neither regards the other as heroic, their stories neatly qualify each other, laying "bare the chasm in understanding that each character has of the other," to adapt Isla Duncan's account of "Lichen" (48).

This distance is nicely captured in Anita's belief that Margot "kept back" the full truth of her life at home with her abusive father:

> According to her, it was all like some movie comedy. Her father beside himself, a hapless comedian, racing around in vain pursuit (of fleet, mocking Margot) and rattling locked doors (the granary) and shouting monstrous threats and waving over his head whatever weapon he could get hold of – a chair or a hatchet or a stick of firewood. He tripped over his own feet and got mixed up in his accusations. And no matter what

he did, Margot laughed. She laughed, she despised him, she forestalled him. Never, never did she shed a tear or cry out in terror. Not like her mother. So she said. (255)

The last phrase indicates Anita's reservations, which return at the end of "Wigtime," when they are echoed by Margot's response to her friend's life story. Because their stories could not be told to anyone else, the two women become each other's ideal audience despite their limited sympathies.

In the absence of more specific evidence about why "Wigtime" concludes *Friend of My Youth*,[5] I turn to Munro's account of the story's origin. Here is the note she provided when Richard Ford selected it (along with "Differently") for *Best American Short Stories 1990*:

"Wigtime" actually came from an anecdote: the woman going to a trailer park, in disguise, to spy on her husband. I thought about her a lot, this woman I knew only as the subject of an anecdote. What would she do if she caught him? What would happen to her marriage? What was she like as a girl? Her friend Anita appeared and then Teresa and Reuel, and old school days very like my own, and I got to know the story. It became Anita's and Teresa's story as well as Margot's – maybe even Anita's mother's story. ("Contributors' Notes" 352)

Munro's note reveals how an amusing anecdote became the source of a comic vision that centres on a fractious group of women. Since the other characters are richly entangled, I will begin with Anita's mother, the subject of the opening line: "When her mother was dying in the Walley Hospital, Anita came home to take care of her – though nursing was not what she did anymore" (244). Anita became a nurse in part because of advice received when she was hospitalized at the age of seventeen. When she married a doctor in the Yukon, "This should have been the end of her story, and a good end, too, as things were reckoned in Walley" (255), especially by her mother. Instead Anita got a divorce and started a Ph.D. in anthropology, following through on an "odd" childhood ambition "to be an archeologist" (255). She never returns to Walley until the time of the story. When she does, her mother reacts as follows:

Even in her present sunken, hallucinatory state, her mother had recognized her, and gathered her strength to mutter, "Down the drain."
Anita bent closer.
"*Life*," her mother said. "Down the *drain*." (256)

The next line qualifies her bitterness: "But another time, after Anita had dressed her sores, she said, 'So glad. So glad to have – a *daughter*'" (256).[6] However frail this reconciliation, it is enough to make this mother-daughter relationship less tense than others in Munro.

When Anita and Margot meet by chance, Margot's snort of laughter, which "seemed both aggressive and embarrassed" (244), foreshadows the unconventional comedy to follow. To Anita, Margot seemed to talk "without envy, as if speaking to somebody younger than herself, still untried and unseasoned" (245). Here Munro establishes the perspective used throughout the story: it is written in the third person, but Anita is the subject of the focalization, and so what we get is her understanding of her friend's words and actions. The envy in their history resides not in Margot but in Anita, who has an enduring if dubious sense of being less experienced and wise. This anxiety emerged "more than thirty years" ago (244), in "the winter of 1948-49" (247), when they were the only grade-twelve girls riding the school bus. Although Margot "spoke disparagingly" of the driver, Reuel, and his wife, Teresa, "'carrying on',"

> it had occurred to Anita that this very scorn of Margot's, her sullenness and disdain, might be a thing that men could find attractive. Margot might be attractive in a way that she herself was not. It had nothing to do with prettiness. Anita thought that she was prettier, though it was plain that Teresa wouldn't give high marks to either of them. It had to do with a bold lassitude that Margot showed sometimes in movement, with the serious breadth of her hips and the already womanly curve of her stomach, and a look that would come over her large brown eyes – a look both defiant and helpless, not matching up with anything Anita had ever heard her say. (251)

As with the earlier passage on Margot's lack of envy, we must allow for the focalization. Margot's "bold lassitude" and "defiant and helpless" look are to some extent imagined by Anita, however perceptive she might otherwise be.

Their obsession with Reuel makes for what René Girard calls "triangular" or "mimetic" desire; as Paisley Livingston explains, "Desire ... is said to be 'triangular', for its most basic structure involves at least three terms: the agent who desires, the object of this agent's desire, and the agent who serves as the 'model' or 'mediator' of the desire" (1). In "double mediation," to employ Livingston's notion, like the one in "Wigtime," "two agents serve reciprocally as each other's models or mediators" (71). Anita and Margot "discussed in detail, coolly, everything about [Reuel]," pretending to be indifferent: "Was he good-looking or was he not? ... Not good-looking, they decided. Queer-looking, actually" (251). For Girard, "Every desire that is revealed can arouse or increase a rival's desire; thus it is necessary to conceal desire in order to gain possession of the object" (153). The sexual desire that Anita conceals from her friend is explicit elsewhere. First, in a parenthetical reference to a fantasy: "(The thought of being scooped up in Reuel's arms caused such a pleasant commotion in Anita's body that in order to experience it she was almost ready to put up with the agony that Teresa said she had undergone [in her two miscarriages])" (248). Second, in this recurring disturbance: "when Anita was anywhere near [Reuel] she had a feeling of controlled desperation along the surface of her skin. ... This feeling was at its worst when she had to get off the bus and he was standing beside the step. The tension flitted from her front to her back as she went past him. She never spoke of this to Margot, whose contempt for men seemed to her firmer than her own" (251). That contempt is mainly in Anita's overactive imagination.

Anita is deceived by her friend's reaction to Reuel's obscene song when they were his only passengers: "'Big fat nerve he's got, singing that song in front of us. Big fat *nerve*,' she said, spitting the word out like the worm in an apple" (258). As the ironic reference to the apple suggests, Margot is tempted by what she pretends to dislike, and so the next day she sings the obscene verse back to Reuel. That night, Anita's appendix bursts; when she is hospitalized, she enjoys the family "drama" (259), "happy, in spite of weakness and lingering pain. Such a fuss had been made to prevent her dying" (260). She even dreams or imagines "that Reuel visited her. He showed a sombre tenderness, a muted passion.

He loved but relinquished her, caressing her hair" (261). When she hears that Reuel has run off with Margot, however, her happiness fades, and she projects her envy onto her mother:

> Anita had a feeling that her mother was angry at her not only because she'd been friends with Margot, a girl who had disgraced herself, but for another reason as well. She had the feeling that her mother was seeing the same thing that she herself could see – Anita unfit, passed over, disregarded, not just by Margot but by life. Didn't her mother feel an angry disappointment that Anita was not the one chosen, the one enfolded by drama and turned into a woman and swept out on such a surge of life? She would never admit that. And Anita could not admit that she felt a great failure. She was a child, a know-nothing, betrayed by Margot, who had turned out to know a lot. (262)

That understanding of her mother is distorted, as Anita's mother reveals when she gloats to her daughter: "'You always thought I wasn't fair to your friend Margot. I was never fussy about that girl and you thought I wasn't fair. I know you did. So now it turns out. It turns out I wasn't so wrong after all'" (261).

Anita's dubious envy is one of several details that align the middle of the story with Girard's dark psychology. Another is that Anita "was ashamed and regretful and at the same time she thought Reuel wasn't fair" (259) in lecturing them after Margot's singing. Her childish phrasing reveals her understandable confusion about Reuel's mixed messages; how could the man who sang an obscene song lecture them about how girls should behave? In her youthful vulnerability, Anita resembles Jessie in "Jesse and Meribeth," who is similarly alarmed by Mr. Cryderman's contradictions: "His hand rouses and his words shame me, and something in his voice mocks, mocks endlessly, at both these responses. I don't understand that this isn't fair" (184). As Ildikó de Papp Carrington argues, Mr. Cryderman is "a deeply ambivalent man who can communicate two diametrically opposed messages at the same time, especially to an adolescent girl whom he considers his social inferior" (130). Reuel is similarly duplicitous, though each story avoids retrospective moralization.[7]

Two other details reveal the persistence of Anita's "mimetic desire." First, the plan to become a nurse was originally Margot's. Livingston explains that "The person in the grips of the emulative variety of mimetic desire would like very much to become the kind of person exemplified by the model, and the ensuing episodes of imitation typically are part of a project aimed at precisely that goal" (51). Anita admits her imitation, though she suspects its futility: "And now Anita was the one who would become a nurse, not Margot. ... But she felt that it was second best. She would rather have been chosen. She would rather have been pinned down by a man and his desire and the destiny that he arranged for her. She would rather have been the subject of scandal" (263). She may have lost the battle for Reuel, but her career choice and lingering envy suggest that the rivalry persists long after Anita's being "betrayed" by Margot and Anita's own "great failure" (262).

Second, Anita's account of the end of her marriage contains a veiled but insistent reference to Reuel. In a narrative that she carefully crafts for Margot when the two exchange stories, she speaks of entering

> a roadside restaurant, and Anita saw there a man who reminded her of a man she had been in love with – no, perhaps she had better say infatuated with – years and years ago. The man in the restaurant had a pale-skinned, heavy face, with a scornful and evasive expression, which could have been a dull copy of the face of the man she loved, and his long-legged body could have been a copy of that man's body if it had been struck by lethargy. Anita could hardly tear herself away when it came time to leave the restaurant. She understood that expression – she felt that she was tearing herself away, she got loose in strips and tatters. (271)

Here Anita gets "loose" in Heller's sense of women breaking free of the "predictable plots" (60) of conventional gender roles. But Anita's nervous revision of "in love with" to "infatuated with" suggests an adolescent memory, and who else could that involve but the scornful Reuel, with his "tall, striding body" (249)?[8] It hardly matters that the man in the restaurant is at best "a dull copy" if Anita is really driven by her lingering rivalry with Margot.

The passage provides the kind of "key" that, according to Carol Shields, Munro takes care to leave: "A reader can almost always find in the closing pages of a Munro piece a little silver ingot of compaction, an insight that throws light on the story" ("In Ontario" 23). Anita could not identify

Reuel without conceding victory to Margot, but the reader understands the desire that changed her life: "if she could feel such a pain, if she could feel more for a phantom than she could ever feel in her marriage, she had better go" (271-72). She does not pursue the man seen in the restaurant, but she leaves her husband for "'somebody else, and somebody else'"; "She felt regret about some of them," she admits to herself but not to her friend, "but no repentance. Warmth, in fact, spread from the tidy buildup" (272). Margot has no idea that it is Reuel who changed her friend's life, for Anita has been selective in what she explains: "So she told Margot. It was more difficult than that, of course, and it was not so clear" (272). After Anita finishes her story, however, she has an unspoken thought: "She didn't need to see him, for years she hadn't the least wish to see him. A man undermines your life for an uncontrollable time, and then one day there's nothing, just a hollow where he was, it's unaccountable" (273). The words "uncontrollable" and "unaccountable" reveal the force of her youthful drives, but she has moved on, and she has no interest in seeing Reuel now.

Girard's theory of "mimetic desire" explains what drove Anita and why Reuel loses his aura – Anita never really desired him, she desired what her friend desired – but cannot explain her "accumulating satisfaction" (272) in remembering her many lovers. "Wigtime" moves far from what Girard describes as "the hell of reciprocal mediation" (104), for Anita no longer imitates her old friend. As usual, Margot shows no envy: "'Well, that's one way,' said Margot staunchly. 'But it seems weird to me. It does. I mean – I can't see the use of it, if you don't marry them'" (272). She feels instead "an ample satisfaction" (271) of her own in telling the comic story of the outrageous disguise of a "light-brown" wig and "tight pink denim pants" (265)[9] that enabled her to go undercover and detect her husband with a girl who was about the age that Margot had been when she had run off with Reuel.[10] At one point, Margot feels like a Hollywood heroine: spotting Reuel leaving a cabin at a campground, she thinks,

> if this was only a movie, he'd come springing across the road with a light, keen to assist the stray pretty girl. Never recognizing her, while the audience held its breath. Then recognition dawning, and horror – incredulity and horror. While she, the wife, sat there cool and satisfied, drawing deep on her cigarette. But none of this happened, of course none of it happened; he didn't even look across the road. (267)

Her story may not be like a movie, but it is never more carefully structured than when she becomes her own heroine by moving from disguised spectator to betrayed wife to avenging force. The focalization is Anita's, the comedy Margot's; when she is not quoted directly, her colourful self-deprecations appear in such passages as this one: "Nobody whistled or made remarks to her. There were lots of long-haired girls around showing off more than she did. And you had to admit that what they had was in better condition to be shown" (266).

In this way, the last part of "Wigtime" is a collaborative narrative like the one between the narrator and her mother in "Friend of My Youth." And, as Heller would say, it is also the story of a woman getting "loose": driving back from the campground after leaving angry notes on Reuel's car, Margot "felt that she had been cut loose, nothing mattered to her, she was as light as a blade of grass" (269). The more she thinks about it, however, the less she thinks of leaving: "What should she do first, what should she do next, how should her life go on?" (269). By the time that she confronts a queasy Reuel, Margot has turned from anger to pragmatism, forcing him to promise the new house that James Carscallen calls the "temple" of her "success" (483). She even boasts that she still draws on the power that she gained through her disguise: "'If he got balky about something later on, all I'd have to say was "Wigtime!" ... I still say it once in a while, whenever I think it's appropriate',' though only Reuel understands the allusion (270). She may also be claiming success over her old friend and rival, but Anita takes a different position:

> And what about Reuel – what had he given up on? Whatever he did, it wouldn't be till he was ready. That was what all Margot's hard bargaining would really be coming up against – whether Reuel was ready or not. That was something he'd never feel obliged to tell her. So a woman like Margot can still be fooled – this was what Anita thought, with a momentary pleasure, a completely comfortable treachery – by a man like Reuel. (271)

Anita can no longer be fooled by Reuel, but it is a triumph that she must keep to herself, along with the career that she never gets the chance to explain.

In her comment on the story, Munro said that "Wigtime" also became Teresa's story ("Contributors' Notes" 352). That constitutes the conclusion of Munro's story. Teresa was cruelly treated by Reuel even before he left her: he used her cherished wedding dress for rags (254), and Anita and Margot hear a "story," ominous if unconfirmed, that Teresa's second miscarriage "happened because Reuel told her he was sick of her and wanted her to go back to Europe, and in her despair she had thrown herself against a table and dislodged the baby" (250). Otherwise Teresa is largely overlooked, even though she once provided "a ramshackle haven" (247) for the young girls whom she admired: "What they did every day to get to school made them heroic and strange in her eyes, and a bit grotesque" (248). The ending of "Wigtime" reveals that Margot visits Teresa in the Psychiatric Wing of the County Home; Teresa started going there to help others, but now she needs help herself. As Margot says, "she's sometimes sort of working there and she's sometimes just *there*, if you see what I mean" (272-73). In her belated concern for the woman she betrayed years ago, Margot again gets "loose" from Anita's and the reader's expectations.

Margot's surprising concern enables Munro to achieve the balance described by Elaine Blair in a comment that bears on several aspects of "Wigtime":

> You might say that a revelation of adultery, shorn of its old consequences, is the smallest possible disaster that still registers on the personal disaster scale. As such, it is formally comical, and a novelist must recognize the comedy. If she also wants to take her characters' experience seriously, rather than reduce it to satire, she has to perform a delicate balancing act. (12)

Reuel's first act of adultery is a disaster for Teresa; his second is "shorn of its old consequences" and turned into a farce by Margot. When she remembers a distraught Teresa beating on the door, however, she balances laughter with the sadness that is also part of her own story: "It was awful. I don't know. I don't know – do you think it was love?" (273).

"Wigtime" ends with a tense shift. To this point, the reunion of Anita and Margot has been narrated in the past tense, like the stories of their youth. When the last three paragraphs shift to the present tense, the distance between the events and the narration collapses. First comes a concluding view of the lake that figures so prominently throughout Munro's work, especially in *Friend of My Youth*. In other stories in this volume, Lake Huron is sometimes menacing: in "Pictures of the Ice," "Waves have frozen as they hit the shore, making mounds and caves, a crazy landscape, out to the rim of the open water" (151); in "Five Points," Cornelius, who was injured in the salt mines, thinks of the machines used to deepen the harbour as "temporarily tame and useless monsters" (30), then "asks what a rough winter will do to all this changing and arranging if the lake just picks up the rocks and beach and flings them aside and eats away at the clay cliffs, as before" (31); in "Oranges and Apples," Murray notes that "People will sit and watch the lake as they'd never watch a field of waving grass or grain. Why is that, when the motion is the same? It must be the washing away, the wearing away, that compels them. The water all the time returning – eating, altering, the shore" (134). After earlier references to the "open water, ink-blue or robin's-egg" (246), that Anita and Margot glimpse on their way to school and the lake breeze that cools Margot as she drives north to the campground (265), "Wigtime" concludes with a picturesque scene:

> From up here on the deck the two long arms of the breakwater look like floating matchsticks. The towers and pyramids and conveyor belts of the salt mine look like large solid toys. The lake is glinting like foil. Everything seems bright and distinct and harmless. Spellbound. (273)

Because the lake reflects the contentment of the two women who behold it, the spell is as provisional as their mood. In the next paragraph, Margot threatens to break it when she returns to Teresa's now confused memories of crossing the Atlantic as a war bride:

> "We're all on the boat," says Margot. "She thinks we're all on the boat. But she's the one Reuel's going to meet in Halifax, lucky her." (273)

Since Margot and Reuel effectively ended Teresa's luck, she is being wistfully ironic when she calls Teresa "lucky." The last paragraph restores the contentment, which is not false even if it does not cancel the darker notes earlier in the story and in the collection:

> Margot and Anita have got this far. They are not ready yet to stop talking. They are fairly happy. (273)

We should remember that Margot's house usurps the "prize view" from the surrounding "handsome hundred-year-old houses" (244). The neighbours started a petition, Margot says in the opening, but her husband, Reuel, "already had the Committee sewed up" (245), much as he had the police on his side against Margot's father years ago (262). Now as the two ironic heroines drink sangria laced with vodka in the house that Reuel built to his wife's demands, each is satisfied with her own partial perspective. The comic structure is complete.

Notes

1. At this stage in Munro's career, it is sometimes difficult to identify the protagonist. In this case, it must be Anita, for she alone is the subject of the focalization, despite the importance of Margot's story. In "Pictures of the Ice" from this same volume, however, Austin and Karin are joint protagonists, and the story uses a shifting focalization.
2. Heller argues that the narrator of "Friend of My Youth" collaborates with her mother to tell the story of Flora, and that in "Meneseteung" the narrator collaborates with Almeda in recovering her work, but she concedes that in both stories "the narrator's treatment of material from a (literary fore)mother may be viewed as both competition and *hommage*" (70). For discussion, see my "'And They May Get It Wrong, After All': Reading Alice Munro's 'Meneseteung'." Andy Belyea argues that "The collection's title, *Friend of My Youth*, also has special significance in 'Wigtime,' for any inclination to believe that Anita and Margot can rekindle a friendship after thirty years must be tempered with consideration of the past that shattered it" (88).
3. "Hegel remarks somewhere that all facts and personages of great importance in world history occur, as it were, twice. He forgot to add: the first time as tragedy, the second as farce" (10).
4. In her brief discussion of "Wigtime," Heller notes that "the divergent youthful paths of Anita and Margot seem clearly to cast them as contraries in a traditional good woman / bad woman dichotomy, but their later choices invert and then effectively dissolve this opposition (a staple of more predictable plots)" (70). Where Heller finds a "renewed friendship" (70), James Carscallen finds enduring conflict:

comparing Anita and Margot with the siblings in such stories as "Memorial" and "The Peace of Utrecht," he argues that "The story of such siblings' relation to one another will mean betrayal again" (482). "At the high point of such a story," he continues, "the sibling who has chosen to claim success ... celebrates this in a temple dedicated to it," like Margot "in her gaudy new house by the lake" (483).

5. Robert Thacker informs me that Ann Close, Munro's editor at Knopf, is unsure why "Wigtime" became the concluding story; it was at the time, she says, a favourite story for both her and Munro, and "'different from all the other stories in the collection – hard to figure out what would come before or after it'" ("Re: 'Wigtime'"). My thanks to Close for this information, and to Thacker for many insights over many years.

6. Anita's mother's reaction has a precedent in "Accident" from *The Moons of Jupiter* (1982), in which Frances is relieved to have daughters, despite her difficulties with her mother (107).

7. The immoral if not criminal behaviour of these men is left for the reader to assess, though two of the notes that Margot leaves on her husband's car raise a legal threat: "YOU BETTER WATCH YOURSELF, / YOU COULD END UP IN JAIL" and "THE VICE SQUAD WILL GET YOU IF / YOU DON'T WATCH OUT" (268). Carrington notes the similarities among Mr. Cryderman, Mr. Chamberlain in *Lives of Girls and Women*, Rose's father in "Royal Beatings," and the man dressed as a minister in "White Swans" (130).

8. I am indebted to Ian Moy for this identification.

9. A passage in "Bardon Bus" from *The Moons of Jupiter* (1982) may derive from the same anecdote as "Wigtime": Kay "disguised herself as an old woman, with a gray wig and a tattered fur coat; she walked up and down, in the cold, outside the house of the woman she thought to be her supplanter" (116). Here Munro is more interested in "the limit" (127) of relationships than in the comic aspects explored in "Wigtime."

10. In the version of "Wigtime" in *The New Yorker* of 4 Sept. 1989, the parallel is more explicit. Attempting to excuse his behaviour, "Reuel said it was all innocent. An outing for the girl. As with Margot, he'd felt sorry for her. Innocent" (48). That wording concedes that he acted in similar ways with the two schoolgirls. In the version in *Friend of*

My Youth, Reuel pretends to share his wife's concern: "Reuel said it was all innocent. An outing for the girl. Like Margot, he'd felt sorry for her. Innocent" (270). In both versions, Margot's response exposes his duplicity: "'I said to him, "Innocent! I know your innocent! Who do you think you're talking to," I said, "Teresa?"'" (48; 270).

Works Cited

Belyea, Andy. "Redefining the Real: Gothic Realism in Alice Munro's *Friend of My Youth*." MA thesis Queen's University, 1998.

Blair, Elaine. "'The Smallest Possible Disaster'." Rev. of *Dept. of Speculation*, by Jenny Offill. *The New York Review of Books* 24 Apr. 2014: 10, 12.

Carrington, Ildikó de Papp. *Controlling the Uncontrollable: The Fiction of Alice Munro*. DeKalb, IL: Northern Illinois UP, 1989.

Carscallen, James. *The Other Country: Patterns in the Writing of Alice Munro*. Toronto: ECW, 1993.

Drabble, Margaret. *The Middle Ground*. New York: Alfred A. Knopf, 1980.

Duncan, Isla. *Alice Munro's Narrative Art*. New York: Palgrave Macmillan, 2011.

Frye, Northrop. *A Natural Perspective: The Development of Shakespearean Comedy and Romance*. New York: Columbia UP, 1965.

Gay, Roxanne. "How To Be Friends with Another Woman." *Bad Feminist: Essays*. New York: Harper Perennial, 2014. 47-50.

Gibson, Graeme. "Alice Munro." *Eleven Canadian Novelists*. Toronto: House of Anansi, 1973. 237-64.

Girard, René. *Deceit, Desire, and the Novel: Self and Other in Literary Structure*. Trans. Yvonne Freccero. Baltimore: Johns Hopkins, 1965.

Heller, Deborah. "Getting Loose: Women and Narration in Alice Munro's *Friend of My Youth*." *The Rest of the Story: Critical Essays on Alice Munro*. Ed. Robert Thacker. Toronto: ECW, 1999. 60-80.

Jones, Jr., Malcolm. "The Glory of the Story." Rev. of *Friend of My Youth*, by Alice Munro. *Newsweek* 12 Apr. 1990: 56-57.

Livingston, Paisley. *Models of Desire: René Girard and the Psychology of Mimesis*. Baltimore: Johns Hopkins UP, 1992.

Marx, Karl. *The Eighteenth Brumaire of Louis Bonaparte*. 3rd rev. ed. Moscow: Progress, 1983.

Moy, Ian. Seminar Presentation on "Wigtime." 1 Mar. 2017. Queen's University.

Munro, Alice. "Accident." *The Moons of Jupiter*. Toronto: Macmillan of Canada, 1982. 77-109.

---. "Bardon Bus." *The Moons of Jupiter*. Toronto: Macmillan of Canada, 1982. 110-28.

---. "Contributors' Notes." *The Best American Short Stories 1990*. Ed. Richard Ford with Shannon Ravenel. Introd. Richard Ford. Boston: Houghton Mifflin, 1990. 352.

---. "Five Points." *Friend of My Youth*. Toronto: McClelland & Stewart, 1990. 27-49.

---. "Jesse and Meribeth." *The Progress of Love*. Toronto: McClelland and Stewart, 1986. 162-88.

---. "Oranges and Apples." *Friend of My Youth*. Toronto: McClelland & Stewart, 1990. 106-36.

---. "Pictures of the Ice." *Friend of My Youth*. Toronto: McClelland & Stewart, 1990. 137-55.

---. "Wigtime." *The New Yorker* 4 Sept. 1989: 34-46, 48, 50. Rpt. (rev.) in *Friend of My Youth*. Toronto: McClelland & Stewart, 1990. 244-73.

New, W.H. "Re-reading *The Moons of Jupiter*." *The Cambridge Companion to Alice Munro*. Ed. David Staines. Cambridge, Eng.: Cambridge UP, 2016. 116-35.

Redekop, Magdalene. *Mothers and Other Clowns: The Stories of Alice Munro*. London: Routledge, 1992.

Shields, Carol. "In Ontario." Rev. of *Friend of My Youth*, by Alice Munro. *London Review of Books* 7 Feb. 1991: 22-23. <https://www/lrb.co.uk/v13/n03/carol-shields/in-ontario>.

Thacker, Robert. "Re: 'Wigtime'." Message to the author. 10 June 2017. E-mail.

Ware, Tracy. "'And They May Get It Wrong, After All': Reading Alice Munro's 'Meneseteung'." *National Plots: Historical Fiction and Changing Ideas of Canada*. Ed. Andrea Cabajsky and Brett Josef Grubisic. Waterloo, ON: Wilfrid Laurier UP, 2010. 67-79, 215-36 passim.

Encountering "Blocks of Solid Darkness" in Alice Munro's "Vandals"

Janice Fiamengo

"'The Wages of Sin is Death'" (283). In "Vandals," this biblical warning is scrawled on the living room wall of a man who will soon die, unexpectedly, during heart surgery. It is put there by a young woman, a born-again Christian, who takes judgment into her own hands, wrecking the house in revenge, it seems, for her lost innocence. The story opens some months later, with the man's bereaved partner drinking red wine and musing on his death, perhaps preparing for – even hastening – her own, and paraphrasing for comic effect a Bible verse discouraging the storing up of treasures on earth. Death, judgment, heaven, and hell – the four final things of Christian eschatology – are all at issue, some ironically, in this final story of *Open Secrets* (1994), which offers readers a hauntingly inconclusive meditation on death, evil, and redemption.

"Vandals" is a fitting final story for the collection *Open Secrets* because of the secret at its heart – which may or may not be an open one. An open secret is, of course, a contradiction in terms. It usually refers to something shameful or forbidden that is generally known, or suspected, but not acknowledged except in a coded manner. It is thus neither a proper secret, nor open; on the contrary, a large number of people often know of it, but none will take responsibility for their knowledge.

Alice Munro's stories have often focussed on mysteries, lies, and silences, emphasizing the frequently unsettling or even horrifying behind-closed-doors realities of women's lives in (mostly) small-town Ontario past and present: sexual unhappiness and brutality, disappearances and murders, unglamorous dysfunction and betrayal. Ajay Heble defines Munro's subject as the thematic territory of "concealments,

deceptions, and the role of language in various kinds of (re)construc-
tions" (187-88). In *Open Secrets*, such mysteries are, if anything, even
more bizarre than we have come to expect from Munro, including alternate realities, waking dreams, and visionary worlds half-glimpsed from
the corner of one's eye. Moreover, the stories' meanings are even more
emphatically uncertain: seeming epiphanies do not clarify, characters
are unknown even to themselves, and meanings are ambiguously suggested, but not confirmed, often through what Coral Ann Howells calls
"unexpected parallels between different people's lives" (122). "Vandals"
is part puzzle, with elements capable of being put together by any alert
reader, and part irresolvable mystery.

The primary puzzle of "Vandals" is the secret behind the at-first-
inexplicable act of vandalism committed by Liza (joined by her husband
Warren) against Bea and Ladner, whom Liza had known when she was a
little girl. "'What did they do that made you so mad?'" (283) Warren asks
her after her rampage of destruction, but Liza will not tell him. "'She sent
me to college!'" (283) is all she'll say. The two trash Bea and Ladner's house
thoroughly, emptying out drawers, smashing dishes, and pouring the contents of refrigerator and pantry over Ladner's collection of taxidermied
animals. They write threatening messages on the walls with tomato sauce
and magic marker. Liza breaks the large front window with a bottle of
alcohol. Then she phones Bea to report what they have supposedly found,
pretending commiseration and shock "in a soft, hurt, hesitant voice" (283).

Why should she do such a thing to the woman she had loved as a
child? As the story reveals the secret that makes the vandalism expli-
cable, namely, Ladner's molestation of Liza and her younger brother,
mysteries of knowledge and responsibility confront the reader. Just as
no character has full knowledge of what others in the story know and
feel, so the reader is denied any comprehensive perspective. At crucial
moments of near-revelation, the narrative focalization shifts, not to
give a fuller picture but to create gaps of understanding, alternative but
always partial explanations. The story moves backwards and forwards
in time towards a bleakly indeterminate conclusion, as Warren waits for
Liza at the house, watching the night come on.

At the story's beginning, Ladner has been dead for some months, and
is mourned in a "sadly pleasurable" (264) manner by Bea, his lover, who

has taken to drinking alone in her house in town. Apparently unaware of what Liza has done, Bea writes to thank her and her husband for checking on the house while Bea and Ladner were in the city for the fatal heart surgery. In a letter that she never sends (the first mystery – why not?), she confides how she misses Ladner's weight next to her in bed, his skin, his smell, the small sensual details of a happy sexual partnership: "I always know even before I am awake that Ladner's body is not beside me and that the sense of him I have, of his weight and heat and smell, are memories. But I still have the feeling – when I wake – that he is in the next room" (263-64). She also notes that the only sign of Ladner's getting older was his anxiety about such details as whether the water had been turned off in the house. Such an anxiety might be seen to betray psychological unease, a fear of bodily disintegration and approaching death (with the house read as symbol for the self), but Bea does not explore or appear to recognize that, claiming he "had not the least premonition of death on the night before his operation" (262).

Bea does, however, relate a dream that announces its own story of the sly, insistent retrievals and linkages of the unconscious, its preoccupation with mortality and unfinished human business. In the dream, it is (a biblically suggestive) seven years into the future, and Bea finds herself part of a group of people in the neighbourhood collecting the bones of their dead at the local Canadian Tire store. It seems to be a well-known spring rite – well-known to other members of the community at least, though not to Bea, who wants to know whether it is "pagan or Christian or what" (263) but is never told. There is a festive air as the residents collect the bones in plastic bags. But instead of receiving "Ladner's strong leg bones and wide shoulder bones and intelligent skull" (263) as she thinks of them, it dawns on Bea that she has been given instead the smaller bones of a child. "'Did you get the little girl?'" (263) someone asks. Then Bea thinks that perhaps she has a boy's bones. The reference to the boy – in what turns out to be the final moments of the dream – leads Bea to think of Liza's younger brother Kenny, who was killed in a car accident as a teenager some years earlier; Bea wakes herself up wondering if it has been seven years since. The letter concludes by emphasizing the shock of living without Ladner, of Bea's having to readjust to his absence upon every waking.

There is not much of a puzzle in this dream of death. With its emphasis on digging up the dead and dealing with their remains (and discovering that the person one had expected to mourn is not there, and instead one has to confront other bones, other acts of destruction and remembrance), the dream's representation of the perils of memory and the omnipresence of the dead seems almost too obvious. This is a story about emotional entanglements, about multiple forms of loss (and theft). It is also about resurrection, or at least about disinterment – about the necessary work of remembering – and about the possibility, as Bea phrases it, of memories and feelings being "purified" (263) or whitewashed. That Ladner's profession was taxidermy, the construction of eternal-life-in-death animal figures, makes the symbolic suggestiveness of the dream, at least in its general outline, impossible to miss.

The unsent letter in which Bea tells the dream to Liza, however, is elusive. As Maria Löschnigg has demonstrated, letters are a frequent narrative device in Munro's stories, often used "to multiply, defer, and condense meaning" (97). Letters in stories allow for the construction of imaginary worlds, the expression of the forbidden, the control or deflection of emotion, and the heightened manipulation of words. The doubled nature of Bea's letter is evident from the very first paragraph, when in mentioning the vandalism to Ladner's house Bea writes, parodying a Bible verse, "Lay not up treasure on earth where moth and dust not to mention teenagers doth corrupt" (261) and then states that she has heard "you are a Christian now, Liza, what a splendid thing to be! Are you born again? I always liked the sound of that!" (261). She doesn't explain why. Even knowing nothing of Bea yet – of her sexual indiscretions in an insular small town, of her enjoyment of "tributes and attention" (265) in her hunt for a "suitable" man (269) – the reader is likely to find her exclamations unconvincing, or at least forced.

Is Bea needling Liza, mocking her (as Ladner, we discover later in the story, often mocked Bea) for an act of such blatant self-invention, such craven need? As we recognize later, her Bible quotation is an eerily apt echo of the verse Bea has seen on the wall of Ladner's wrecked house (a second mystery – why? does she know that Liza wrote it?). All in all, there is something coy and theatrical about Bea's manner of addressing Liza, as when she insists half-apologetically, half-nostalgically that "Oh, Liza, I know it's boring of me but I still think of you and poor little

Kenny as pretty sunburned children slipping out from behind the trees to startle me and leaping and diving in the pond" (261-62). Given that the central revelatory scene in the story concerns Liza, her younger brother, and Ladner at the pond, and Bea's determination at the time and later *not* to be startled, not to see what is going on behind her back, this appeal raises unanswerable questions about Bea's knowledge of and complicity in Liza and Kenny's sexual abuse by Ladner.

Only half-answers can be derived from the narrative that follows, which flashes back to the scene of Bea's first meeting with Ladner. The scene emphasizes the dark source of her erotic and emotional attraction to him, and the silences at the heart of their relationship. In their first encounter, as she wrote to friends at the time in an attempt at explanation, she had to admit that she liked that Ladner "was rude and testy and slightly savage," even if her response "was very regressive and bad form" (268). She could tell from the beginning that living with him would be difficult, that it would mean being "surrounded by implacability, by ready doses of indifference which at times might seem like scorn" (269). Nonetheless, he offered something that turned her safer affections for Peter Parr, the science teacher and school principal she was involved with when she first met Ladner, into symbolic "dust and ashes" (268). Her words figure Ladner as a demon-lover who burns away former attachments and interests.

We do not learn if Bea's premonition of her life with Ladner was correct; we never have the full picture of that. Some time later – perhaps in her "period of musing and drinking" (264) and "slow decline" (264) – or perhaps in one of the letters she wrote in her head while Ladner was still alive (another mystery – why did she give up sending letters?), she summed up the condition of her life by saying, "*I am slit top to bottom with jokes*" (269). The line suggests that indifference and scorn may not have comprised the sum of her difficulties in the life she chose. Drawn from the practice of taxidermy that she comes to know well, the image evokes eviscerating cruelty masquerading as humour. We learn only that amidst bouts of "hard-hearted" sex (272), lessons in humiliation meant to cure her of sentimentality and vanity (as she reports – or rationalizes), and encounters with "*blocks of solid darkness*" (274), there is some genuine friendliness and intimacy between them, "a kinder comfort" (274). "On the night before the operation they lay side by side on the strange bed, with all available bare skin touching – legs, arms, haunches" (274). This final image of Bea and Ladner is surprisingly innocent, and poignant, providing a counterpoint to his cruelty.

The second part of the narrative, focalized through Liza rather than Bea, reveals that she too, as a young girl, has been the object of Ladner's seemingly irresistible sexual and emotional power. This part of the story is temporally divided into two, one segment describing the wrecking of the house, and the other providing flashbacks to a childhood summer scene many years previously, in which we see the complicated and perverse intimacy among Ladner, Bea, Liza, and Kenny. The scene begins with the four of them cooling off in the pond at the back of Ladner's house, "[l]ike a family" (286), as Liza thinks longingly. But the normality of the scene is disrupted by Ladner, who begins, from where Bea cannot see him, to mock Bea's movements in the water. "He was doing what she was doing but in a sillier, ugly way. He was most intentionally and insistently making a fool of her" (288). Liza is both horrified and thrilled, wanting to protect Bea but also drawn to Ladner's viciousness. "Part of her wanted to make Ladner stop, to stop at once, before the damage was done, and part of her longed for that very damage, the damage Ladner could do, the ripping open, the final delight of it" (288). A number of critics interpret the reference to "the ripping open" as a displaced description of Liza's rape by Ladner; if it is so, it is part of a pattern of subtle, disturbing suggestions only.

Nathalie Foy interprets the passage about Liza's longing for "the damage Ladner could do" (288) as showing that Liza fears Bea's discovering the truth about Ladner but also wants Bea to see what he is capable of and who he really is (Foy 162). This interpretation makes some sense, but it ignores what is most striking in the scene, Liza's obvious pleasure in Ladner's cruelty. Liza does want Ladner to stop, but she is also attracted by the same darkness in Ladner that compels Bea, delighted as well as hurt and ashamed by it. The scene makes clear, in other words, Liza's willing complicity with Ladner and her strong sense of guilt as a result. It is revealed that she has a "secret life" (289) with him in which "badness was mixed up with silliness" (290), and "You couldn't get out of it, or even want to, any more than you could stop an invasion of pins and needles" (290). The metaphorical implications are clear, if not the specifics: there is a seeming inevitability in Liza's response to Ladner, a shocking, inexplicable (to her) surrender. Again, the imagery connects Liza's seduction with the literal "pins and needles" of Ladner's taxidermic art.

The ending of the story juxtaposes past and present scenes: the little girl longing for Bea to see "[w]hat Bea has been sent to do" (293), as if she were a guardian angel authorized by God to rescue the children from their gothic confinement by a demonic figure; and the adult woman calmly surveying the trees around Ladner's house after the vandalism, telling her husband how Ladner taught her to distinguish cedar, wild cherry, birch, and beech. The only thing clear in this ending is that Liza no longer looks to Bea, or anyone, for rescue.

The implication is that Bea failed to save Liza from Ladner's sexual exploitation, thus disappointing a hope so profound that Liza, as a child, could not even articulate it precisely to herself: "Liza's love for Bea [...] was one of expectation, but she did not know what it was that she expected" (287). She had thought that "Bea could spread safety, if she wanted to[, ...] could make them all, keep them all, good" (293). Now it seems that Liza cannot forgive Bea's betrayal, and readers are left to ponder what kind of betrayal it was. Was it that Bea *could not* see, as Liza initially asserts (the final line of the pond scene being "Only Liza sees" [293])? Was Bea so caught up in her own problems with Ladner that she was incapable of recognizing what was going on? Or did she make a choice not to see?

Nathalie Foy is determined to find Bea innocent and absolved of responsibility, asserting that "she is free of complicity in Liza's abuse and the silence around it" (151). In fact, the story provides no clear evidence in support of this point; on the contrary, it is quite possible, even probable, that Bea *does* see but chooses to forget, as with Ladner's brutal teasing, which she had half-caught. Carrie Dawson thinks it likely that "Bea has agreed to forgive and forget a great deal more" (72) than Ladner's teasing. That two critics can be so completely opposed on such a basic matter of plot says something about the deep indeterminacy of the text.

Just as Bea's responsibility is left unclear, so Liza's judgment of her cannot be fully understood. After the pond scene, Liza goes home and returns with a gift for Bea – a gift, as she sees it, to make up for Ladner's cruelty and her own felt betrayal; she explains that it was a piece of her mother's jewellery. As Liza walks back towards the house, she sees Ladner and Bea "sitting under the plum trees right behind" it, and thinks that Bea

"had forgiven Ladner, after all, or made a bargain not to remember" (293).
The moment can be interpreted in two ways. Either it is the moment
when Liza begins to recognize correctly that Bea's bargains will always
put protecting herself (her version of her life) above protecting her young
friend; or it may be the moment when Liza wrongly projects onto Bea a
guilt that is solely Ladner's.

Subsequent events offer no confirmation. Long after Liza moved
away from the neighbourhood, Bea had sent her money to enable her
to go to college, an action which may indicate conscious guilt (a kind of
hush money, which is how Liza seems to see it), but may instead have
been simple kindness. Bea's heavy drinking may signal self-recrimina-
tion; it started when she lived with Ladner, but perhaps not in relation
to Liza. It is even possible that Bea knows and accepts that Liza was
the one who wrecked the house; perhaps she recognized Liza's personal
fury in the damage. Bea mentions, in the half-taunting, half-confessional
letter never sent, that the wrecked house "just looked natural to me"
and "seemed almost the right way for things to be" (262). Perhaps she
never sends the letter to Liza because the letter comes too close to an
admission. It is even possible that Bea blames Liza for what Ladner
did, considering Liza's complicity a betrayal (as Liza herself once did)
and drafting the letter, vindictively, to gloat about her long-term sexual
intimacy with Ladner. Almost nothing is too dark for this story.

Most commentators on the story focus on Liza as a survivor of sexual
abuse who finds ways to deal with her trauma. Some such as Nathalie
Foy see Bea as a victim also, as a woman "ultimately silenced" (164)
by her humiliating relationship with Ladner. According to Foy, Liza at
last – but not Bea – finds a way to "dispel the darkness around her"
(164). Similarly, Corinne Bigot, in a detailed analysis of the story as a
trauma narrative, agrees with Foy that the story is about Liza's successful
overcoming: "Liza's trashing of the house, therefore, can be seen as the
therapeutic re-enactment of the abuse, giving her the empowerment
that survivors experience when they remember and acknowledge the
abuse" (121). Héliane Ventura comes to a similar conclusion, reading
"[t]he sack of the house by Liza [...] as a performance and a psychic
process" that "purges her of the traumatic events which unfolded on the
premises during her childhood" (317). Carrie Dawson, however, in an
analysis of the trope of taxidermy as a warning about quests for truth in

nature, is sceptical about the extent to which Liza dispels her darkness, but affirms that her final "act of reading the natural world is represented as a means of staving off that darkness" (80).

The trouble with all these interesting interpretations is that the story's shifts in focalization drastically limit our knowledge to such an extent that we don't know what Liza thinks or feels at the story's end; we're not even sure that she does "remember and acknowledge the abuse" (Bigot 121). The story keeps us outside the characters' minds at crucial moments of potential insight. While not discounting interpretations that focus on Liza as survivor, I read the story as, typically of Munro, complicating victim/victimizer roles (it's called "Vandals" in the plural, after all), and suggesting the irresolvable and mysterious interrelations of pain, need, guilt, and responsibility in human relations.

Bigot notes that child victims of sexual abuse often blame the mother figure for the transgressions of the father (122), and Liza's anger at Bea can be understood from that perspective. But Liza's anger at Bea could also be a deflection of self-blame. While Bea could not, or did not, save Liza from Ladner, Liza was similarly unable, or unwilling, to save her younger brother Kenny, who was even more vulnerable to Ladner than Liza and whose death in a drunken car crash may be seen to express his own shame and powerlessness. As for Ladner, we don't know where his darkness came from, but the story provides enough detail to suggest that it didn't come from nowhere. He is scarred from war, likely psychologically as well as physically, and has built himself a carefully tended nature park (a perverse Eden) containing multiple territories, just as he himself contains multiple territories. He is the black bear with the "melancholy face" (271) – significantly the one that Liza looks for in the yard at the story's end – and a man who "could switch from one person to another and make it your fault if you remembered" (289).

Liza, it seems, has chosen to remember good parts of Ladner, just as Bea has, and her rage for order similarly masks a capacity for unpredictable violence. The young woman who has found religion, who does knee-bends while reading Bible verses every morning and is fixated on the letter of religious law, is a far cry from the vulnerable girl who saw in Bea a potential saviour. Like Ladner, she too has become multiple people, switching back and forth between her various guises with ease. Her conversation with Bea on the phone after she has destroyed the

house is a lavish indulgence in sadistic fakery, "describing things, commiserating, making her voice quiver with misery and indignation" (283).
Her husband Warren doesn't like watching because it reveals her talent
for pleasurable deception, hardly the behaviour of a self-aware survivor
confronting and resolving her past.

On the contrary, the scene at the house can be read as a re-enactment rather than a resolution of the abuse. Liza's treatment of Warren is,
though not overtly cruel, certainly contemptuous: "'Why don't you relax
and watch TV or something?'" she tells him, when he asks her what she is
doing, which she claims is not "'remotely any of your business'" (279). (She
learned as a child from Ladner that television was for "'dumb kids'" [285].)
He responds as if to trauma: "His whole body felt as if it was humming,
with the effort to be still and make this be over" (280). Liza has not been
honest with her husband about her past and is not being honest now.
His mounting panic in the house and his apprehension of the "darkness
collecting" (294) outside in the oncoming night show his anxious awareness of the darkness within Liza, which he can neither understand nor
vanquish. The darkness bodes ill for their future life together, especially
for any children they may have, who will be at the mercy of their mother's
voracious appetite for rules and her unexorcised anger.

***

If one were to read "Vandals" as an allegory, one might say that Ladner
is the Devil, and the story is about the damage he does to all those who,
knowingly or not, allow him into their lives. His corrupt pleasure park
is called Lesser Dismal, which as Héliane Ventura notes, combines the
Greek name *Dis* (Land of the Underworld) with the French word for evil,
mal (313). Liza imagines Ladner's orgasmic spasm as leaving "nothing
[...] of him but black smoke and burnt smells and frazzled wires" (292).
The story is not such an allegory, for Ladner is neither a toy monster nor
a real one, but it is a meditation on human helplessness before death
and cruelty, and on the attractions of darkness. Redemptive love is a
remote possibility at best. Nathalie Foy sees *Open Secrets* as marking a
change in Munro's writing from a preoccupation with the difficulty of
telling the story, of getting at reality, to a concentration on the inscrutability of reality itself, its seemingly bottomless provisionality (148).

Difficulties of knowing are highlighted through the emphasis on reading signs, including the actual signs in Ladner's park, and on the human propensity for misreading, intentionally or otherwise (which may also encode a warning to readers of the story not to assume too much).

"'Can you two read?'" and "'So did you read my signs?'" (285) are the demands Ladner makes of Liza and Kenny when the children first enter his property. Ladner's words are less questions than accusations: he assumes that the children have read but have disregarded the signs' clear messages to stay out. Ladner's property is filled with other signs as well, educational signs about animals, about "their habitat, their Latin names, food preferences, and styles of behavior" (271) and signs identifying different tree types. Ladner is willing to teach Liza and Kenny – in fact seems to take pains to do so – but denies any interest in educating members of the general public, whom he doubts can learn much. When Peter Parr suggests bringing a select group of students to the property to "[s]ee the difference one individual can make" (267), according to Peter's sentimental interpretation of Ladner's project, Ladner scoffs, doubting that teenage "'louts'" (267) could do anything but leer without comprehension. Even after Ladner has denied Peter his flattering request to "'have a look'" (268), Peter remains hopeful that the visit has been a good ice-breaker. Peter is a man who tends to see mainly what he wants to see, assuming others to be as well-intentioned and social as himself. It is a habit of perception that has ceased to appeal to Bea.

Ladner's property has other types of signage too, including the cryptic P.D.P. carved into a tree (which means either "'Proceed down path'" or "'Pull down pants'" [289] – probably both, encompassing Ladner's dual role as teacher and molester). There are also signs bearing philosophers' statements about nature: Aristotle's "*Nature does nothing uselessly*" and Rousseau's "*Nature never deceives us; it is always we who deceive ourselves*" (271). It's not clear whether the anti-social Ladner has set these signs up for himself – as reminders or daily affirmations – or for the general public he claims not to care about. We never hear about any actual visitors other than Liza and Kenny. For readers, questions about which characters are deceived and whether we as readers deceive ourselves as we interpret their motives and meanings are at the centre of the story's many mysteries. In fact, there are too many potential signs in "Vandals," too many possible meanings: the more one looks, the more possible interconnections and suggestions we find, none of them leading anywhere definitive. Like Bea with Ladner, we encounter "*blocks of solid darkness*" (274).

The extent of Bea's misreading of Ladner remains, as I've suggested, an open question. On the day he takes her on a tour of his property, she has trouble interpreting him and his surroundings with any confidence. She cannot keep track of where he takes her and cannot get a reliable sense of the size and layout of the grounds. She cannot locate what he directs her to notice and similarly has no idea of his attitude towards her. She is surprised to discover in him any human frailty or vulnerability. His only direct appeal – which comes just as she was about to finish her tea and escape from what she had come to see as a humiliating "joke" or "punishment" (272) – is an invitation to visit again on the pretext that "'There is always something to see'" (273), perhaps the most ironic line in a story filled with double meanings.

Nathalie Foy sees Bea as "naïve" (151), easily misled – but it might be more appropriate to see her as delusionally over-confident in her powers of perception. When she first met Ladner, she was a woman who had made "love affairs [...] the main content of her life" (265), and was primarily interested in interpreting her experiences as a sometimes sad and misguided but nonetheless significant romance quest. If she were to paraphrase Aristotle, Bea would likely say that "Love does nothing uselessly." She believes that the time and energy she has devoted to her many failed affairs, to waiting for letters, crying in bars, and disposing of tiresome hangers on, has not been "wasted" (265). We learn that "she felt the first signal of a love affair like the warmth of the sun on her skin, like music through a doorway, or the moment, as she had often said, when the black-and-white television commercial bursts into color" (265). The point is not the effectiveness or lack thereof of her romantic tropes – they certainly don't strike us as typical of Munro's style – but that Bea has "often said" them, making them her personal maxims. (Perhaps she would also paraphrase Rousseau and say that "Love never deceives us, though individual lovers always do.") With her master's degree in English and varied sexual career, she believes herself a superior interpreter of the reigning maladies of the female heart, a belief that seems ultimately more important to her than her own well-being.

Ladner exploits (and mocks) Bea's sense of herself while encouraging a similar response in Liza, who also believes herself to be exceptionally perceptive. She has learned early on "not to talk so much about all she knew" (286). In the pond scene, her guilty enjoyment of Ladner's mockery derives from her ability to see and interpret what Ladner is signalling without Bea's knowing. "See how vain she is, said Ladner's angular prancing. See what a fake. Pretending not to be afraid of the deep water, pretending to be happy, pretending not to know how we despise her" (288). Ladner's mockery invites Liza into a parallel mockery in which she must pretend not to see him, and must go on talking to Bea as if he weren't doing what he's doing. The scenario is a displaced version of the silly and bad (shameful but pleasurable) sexual deception in which Ladner has involved her. Earlier Liza had been sure that Bea was "[l]ying for Kenny's sake" (284) when she said that one of her first memories was the same as his, and Liza believes that "he doesn't even know it" (284). Liza's certainty that she can see into Bea's (faking) character is similar to Ladner's assessment of Bea though in a more charitable vein. Even while watching Ladner mock Bea for her vanity and deceptions, Liza cannot help but respond to his appeal to her vanity in a shared deception.

Fakery and deception are frequently linked to the natural in "Vandals," with the suggestion that it is often difficult to tell them apart. Bea is attracted to Ladner at least in part because of his masculine directness, his seeming refusal to perform for anyone. There is "no waste about Ladner, no extra size or unnecessary energy and certainly no elaborate conversation" (270). When he asks her if she would like a tour of the property, "That was what he said and that was what he meant" (270) – or so Bea thinks. Perhaps she should have taken him at his word when he claimed of a refrigerator turned taxidermic display, "'I use what I can get'" (271). But Ladner's seeming frankness is contradicted by "the art and skill of taxidermy" (274) which, as Carrie Dawson has discussed, is all about the appearance of the natural constructed through elaborate ingenuity (72-74). Even as Bea must learn, in living with Ladner, to cast off "all her froth and vanity" (274), she is learning another kind of cosmetic simulation, "how to color lips and eyelids and the ends of noses with a clever mixture of oil paint and linseed and turpentine" (274). Ladner's whole property, with its careful divisions of landscape, its damned-up ponds and planned pathways, its recreated habitats and posed animal inhabitants, its apple orchards and pine plantations and secret glades, is a laboriously planned environment in which Ladner lays out scenes of instruction, delight, and "shame in the grass" (291).

The natural is what is least within human control, what no amount of good intentions or rules, Bible verses or red wine, can fence out – one's own darkness. When Bea realizes, having seen Peter next to Ladner, that she can no longer go on dating Peter or deny her attraction to Ladner, she figures the decision as a reversion to her "nature" (268). "Even after years of good behavior, it was not her nature" (268) to try to behave as she thought she should. This nature, whatever it is, also allows her to go on living with a man who can slit her top to bottom with jokes, and makes her a woman who cannot "keep [anyone] good" (293). Similarly, Liza's husband Warren thinks of the "wild" (281) side of his wife, despite her interest in rules to keep them both safe, as the unalterable core of her. "That's what she's got in her, he felt like saying to them all" (281), when they attend a Christian rock concert and Liza's sexualized dancing disturbs the youth leader. Like Bea with Peter Parr, living "an orderly life" and thinking "she enjoyed it" (264), Liza has sought order through her religious conversion, in Wednesday-night laundry, and by counting the strokes when she brushed her teeth – all ways of staving off chaos. All the characters in "Vandals" seek to contain the beast within, to live with their shame and hatred.

Bea's adaptation of the first verse of Matthew 6.19-21, "Lay not up for yourselves treasures upon earth, where moth and rust doth corrupt, and where thieves break through and steal," can be read as a direct response to Liza's citing of "the wages of sin is death" (Romans 6.23). Both verses allude to forms of threat – loss of one's treasures, punishment for sin – in order to make a countervailing statement, not quoted in either case, about trust in God as the only ultimate security: "lay up for yourselves treasures in heaven" (Matthew 6.20) and "the gift of God is eternal life" (Romans 6.23). That neither Bea nor Liza quotes the reassuring completion of their respective verses suggests that both women are sceptical about the possibility of cosmic justice or heavenly reward. Both live in their different ways with "the wages of sin," and the story doesn't allow readers to know if either character has found a way to salve her wounds. In its final, unsettling (and possibly hellish) image of "darkness collecting, rising among the trees, like cold smoke coming off the snow" (294), "Vandals" gestures towards their unanswered, seemingly unanswerable, need.

Works Consulted

Bigot, Corinne. "'Locking the Door': Self-Deception, Silence and Survival in Alice Munro's 'Vandals'." *Trauma Narratives and Herstory*. Ed. Sonya Andermahr and Silvia Pellicer-Ortín. New York: Palgrave Macmillan, 2013. 113-26.

Dawson, Carrie. "Skinned: Taxidermy and Pedophilia in Alice Munro's 'Vandals'." *Canadian Literature* 184 (2005): 69-83.

Foy, Nathalie. "'Darkness Collecting': Reading 'Vandals' as a Coda to *Open Secrets*." *Alice Munro Writing On....* Ed. Robert Thacker. *Essays on Canadian Writing* 66 (1998): 147-68. Rpt. in *The Rest of the Story: Critical Essays on Alice Munro*. Ed. Robert Thacker. Toronto: ECW, 1999. 147-68.

Heble, Ajay. *The Tumble of Reason: Alice Munro's Discourse of Absence*. Toronto: U of Toronto P, 1994.

Howells, Coral Ann. *Alice Munro*. Manchester, Eng.: Manchester UP, 1998. Contemporary World Writers.

Löschnigg, Maria. "Carried Away by Letters: Alice Munro and the Epistolary Mode." *Alice Munro's Miraculous Art: Critical Essays*. Ed. Janice Fiamengo and Gerald Lynch. Ottawa: U of Ottawa P, 2017. 97-113. Reappraisals: Canadian Writers 38.

McCombs, Judith. "Alice Munro's 1994 'A Wilderness Station': Storytelling and Retelling of Historic, Biblical, Gothic, and Grimm Stories." *Critical Insights: Contemporary Canadian Fiction*. Ed. Carol L. Beran. Ipswich, MA: Grey House, 2014. 119-34.

McGill, Robert. "Where Do You Think You Are?: Alice Munro's Open Houses." *Mosaic: A Journal for the Interdisciplinary Study of Literature* 35.4 (2002): 103-19.

Munro, Alice. *Open Secrets*. Toronto: McClelland & Stewart, 1994.

---. "Vandals." *Open Secrets*. Toronto: McClelland & Stewart, 1994. 261-94.

Ventura, Héliane. "Aesthetic Traces of the Ephemeral: Alice Munro's Logograms in 'Vandals'." *Tropes and Territories: Short Fiction, Postcolonial Readings, Canadian Writing in Context*. Ed. Marta Dvořák and W.H. New. Montreal, QC and Kingston, ON: McGill-Queen's UP, 2007. 309-22.

Walls, Jerry L., ed. *The Oxford Handbook of Eschatology*. Oxford, Eng.: Oxford UP, 2008.

My Mother's Dream

Sandra Sabatini

I didn't want to read this story, or write about it. Motherhood is fraught. Everybody knows that. We spend money talking to professionals about the damage our mothers caused, about the damage we cause as mothers, about the damage our daughters cause us. Wreckage all around. When I think of my mother, I wonder whether she had any dreams for herself. About these, I never got to find out. I know she was sent to work in a factory at age 12 with a robust grade six education. I know she was impregnated by a man twenty-two years older than she was, my father, and was married in May in a silk satin gown with an empire waist and not a moment too soon. My oldest brother was brought home before Christmas. She bore five children, three of whom lived. I was last born and soonest orphaned. What are mothers' dreams to me?

Still, Munro's story, as everyone who has read it knows, is provocative and so dense as to provoke a feeling of urgent claustrophobia. It sticks to you like the hot weather sticks to Jill's skin when she is left alone, closed up in a house to care for the story's narrator, her own screaming baby, in the heat of the summer. But I'm jumping ahead.

The story is one established in dichotomies: takes place in summer, but the dream is of winter; inaugurated by a funeral, but insists on birth and survival; describes a dream that is actually a nightmare – negligence apparently resulting in the death of a baby and the dream itself providing no escape from the waking nightmare of a baby who, in a state of vociferous mutiny, rigidly rejects the embrace of its own mother. The baby is conceived by a dead man.

The biggest paradox of all resides with the mother, Jill, who thinks, as I did in the process of gestation, labour, and delivery, that the birth of her baby will bring "something to an end rather than starting something"

(298). I assumed that my life, all I enjoyed about my life, its autonomy, tidiness, peacefulness, its pursuits, and its pleasures would effectively be terminated and that a big part of the person I thought of as being actually me would be terminated as well. This describes the conundrum of any female artist who finds herself in a hostile environment where her independence is under threat, but particularly it is the conundrum of Jill, whose pregnancy "the Conservatory people" treat with their customary tact "as if it was a tumor" (298).

Far from conveying what Hannah Arendt has described in *The Human Condition* as a sort of gospel of glad tidings that announces "A child has been born to us" (247) with angels rejoicing and shepherds and wise men in attendance, Munro portrays Jill's experience of pregnancy and birth in subtly negative discourse. She describes Jill's ill-fitting dress, the tumour-like growth, the end of her artistic life, and a list of unusual pregnancy symptoms that include a voracious hunger for meat. Her condition reveals itself in diverse itchings, achings, and swellings, to the point where her capacity for playing the violin, her ability to move her fingers to play a piece she had practised to perfection, has been annihilated.

Munro's language is unequivocal, representing Jill as a victim of motherhood: in attempting and failing to play the Mendelssohn, she discovers herself to be "emptied out, vandalized. Robbed overnight" (325). As I've discussed elsewhere, it's clear "The experience of childbirth carries with it the sense of participating in ... profound forces to produce what claims us, what interpellates us as subjects of that which will master us through bonds of love" (Sabatini 4). Jill is no longer the master of Mendelssohn (or the mistress). She has been mastered. The fundamental dichotomy of motherhood, and one which Munro explores with her usual mercilessness, concerns "the psychic crisis" to which Adrienne Rich refers:

> No one mentions the psychic crisis of bearing a first child, the excitation of long-buried feelings about one's own mother, the sense of confused power and powerlessness, of being taken over on the one hand and of touching new physical and psychic potentialities on the other.... No one mentions the strangeness of attraction ... to a being so tiny, so dependent, so folded-in to itself – who is, and yet is not, part of oneself. (36)

How does a mother maintain a sense of self in the face of this over-whelming colonization?

The infant, I've said before, becomes a type of "enemy for women who want to live independently, a site of struggle for women between power and weakness, between joy and despair" (Sabatini 97). Munro navigates this territory opaquely and fearlessly. Jill doesn't actually dream of killing her baby, but she does imagine the baby waiting with a "look of patience and helplessness ... for its rescue or its fate" (294).

Munro arrives at this potent image through a series of negatives that build expectation. I'm drawn to these absences, especially when they accumulate: the telephone did not ring, the latch of the garden gate was not lifted, she could not hear traffic. The scene is rendered in an environment that seems absent of any human presence – everyone had gone away; the new-fallen snow shrouds the landscape. Munro builds a dream based on human and divine absence so that while the scene she sets might suggest a vignette from "O Little Town of Bethlehem," the stars had, in fact, gone out. No guiding light, no annunciation. Only the overnight snowfall whose whiteness "did not hurt your eyes as it does in the sunlight" (293). She writes of Jill's observation of the dreamscape: she "looked out from a big arched window such as you find in a mansion or an old-fashioned public building. She looked down on lawns and shrubs, hedges, flower gardens, trees, all covered by snow that lay in heaps and cushions, not levelled or disturbed by wind" (293).

The snow, unlike the dreamer, is undisturbed. It does not hurt your eyes and it covers everything totally, the entire "luxury of summer" (293) which has provoked a confusing "change of season unexplainable" (293). Munro builds the dichotomy, fabricating it with the reckless improb-ability permitted to dreams and to fictions, so that we are entranced, complicit in working out the puzzle of this dream, of this mother, of the cold soothing starkness of an illicit winter cooling the fevered reality of Jill's constricted life. What is she longing for, as she looks out that win-dow? There is exquisite foreboding here and a compelling upending of the usual miraculous and immaculate birth story that one might expect to see accompanied by angels. Instead, "something was wrong" (293).

The wrongness emerges from a variety of sources as the story unfolds, not the least of which is Jill's reluctance to amend her artist life once she is certain that George will not return from the War. Jill had made up her mind to raise the baby in her small room in the city and to continue at the Conservatory. This independence, flouting as it does the conventions of George's family, will not be tolerated, or even acknowledged. Against the description of Jill's pregnancy by way of ill-fitting clothing and bodily inconveniences, Munro builds the larger framework of the family's house, the small town culture, the social rigidity through her portrayal of the relationship of the spinster sisters, Ailsa and Iona, to Jill and to their little world.

Although Jill had found the wherewithal to buy "the basic things" (299) that her baby would need, Ailsa turns up to remove Jill to George's ancestral home where she can spend her days surrounded by a gallery of framed photographs that provides a veritable chronicle of George's youth. George is pictured on a wagon, a bicycle, even wearing a gold cardboard crown suggesting nothing less than his true stature as the bonnie prince of the household, "bright as a dollar" with "a sunny dip of hair" (305) – for even the sun appears to shine on George. There are no photos mentioned of his considerably older sisters. These sisters keep his memory and will keep his wife and baby up to a standard that includes embroidered guest towels useless for cleaning up amniotic fluid when Jill's water breaks at the funeral tea.

The concept of an artistic life is alien to the family in which Jill finds herself. She is among people who think that any departure "from a simple tune was trying to put something over on you, and everybody knew this, deep down" (317). Jill becomes a mother, a breathtaking enough alteration in the course of the life she expected to live, but worse, she becomes a mother among people whose opinion of "classical" music is manifested by the very "way they pronounced the word" (317). She is doubly alienated. Triply, really, when you consider evidence Munro provides regarding even George's choice of Jill as a wife: she is a musician, an artist, with wild hair, clothing that fails to conform to the sisters' standards, and an individual "way of living" (317), whatever that may be.

George's choice of Jill, his claiming of her at nineteen, she believed to be the result of her presenting some kind of "dull puzzle" (306) to him. There's a strong suggestion, however, that his choice of Jill stems from his desire to show townsfolk and his family "what he thought of them," to show "those girls who had hoped to get their hooks in him" and to show "Ailsa" (317) too. Jill is unaware of how far out of the range of normal she is in this town and for her sisters-in-law as a choice of wife for a celebrated son, how much George must have enjoyed imagining the shock of his choice, until she attempts to play the violin. When she "had closed the curtained glass doors of the living room" she begins once again, tentatively, to play some scales:

> It was true that her fingers were no longer puffy, but they felt stiff. Her whole body felt stiff, her stance was not quite natural, she felt the instrument clamped onto her in a distrustful way. But no matter, she would get into her scales. She was sure that she had felt this way before, after she'd had flu, or when she was very tired, having overstrained herself practicing, or even for no reason at all. (317)

Jill has endured an accumulating list of shocks. From being orphaned, alone, a studious musician, she moves in rapid succession to becoming a lover, a wife, a widow, a member of a family, and a mother, eventually losing the very skill that shaped each of her days as a single woman. Jill now finds herself in a small town among people who consider classical music to be pretentious trickery, among family members whose preferences constrain her days, and as the mother of a baby whom she cannot feed and who screams and stiffens in her arms. Munro's portrait of an artist who has been fleeced of all that formed her personality and inclinations is devastating. She is "stiff," "not quite natural," with a "distrustful" instrument pressed against her (317). Her fingers have finally lost their puffiness and her stomach has become flat (316), but her first effort to reclaim something of her old life unleashes "a waterfall of shrieks" (317) from the baby. Jill hears "a new flood of unsuspected anguish, a grief that punished the world with its waves full of stones, the volley of woe sent down from the windows of the torture chamber" (318). The intensity of the baby's protest compels Jill to "set her violin down" (318) and walk outside to take an inventory of the "hot backyards and hot walls ... three blocks east ... or five blocks west, six blocks south or ten blocks north" (318), directions which define the parameters of her current existence and comprise the total area available to her to escape the shrieking, comfortless baby behind her.

The scene is overheated and miserable. The perimeter of her world is delineated by the "walls of summer crops already sprung high out of the earth, fenced fields of hay and wheat and corn" (318-19) that create an impermeable boundary. For Jill, there is "Nowhere to breathe for the reek of thrusting crops and barnyards and jostling munching animals. Wood-lots at a distance beckoning like pools of shade, of peace and shelter, but in reality they were boiling up with bugs" (319). The environment is deceptive, constricted and constricting, bovine or porcine, verminous and stifling. Meant to stifle. Whereas in music Jill has found "a problem ... that she has to work out strictly and daringly, and that she has taken on as her responsibility in life," she now finds that this problem has been "removed from her" (319). As Naomi Morgenstern claims in her essay "The Baby or the Violin?", "It is with the violin, not the baby, that she has a seemingly natural rapport" (84). To give the violin up, physically to bend and set it down and abandon the instrument, leaves Jill with noth-ing more than "just the back step and the glaring wall and my crying. My crying is a knife to cut out of her life all that isn't useful. To me" (319).

Munro makes manifest the breathtaking, mind-numbing, irresistible colonization by the infant, who thrashes against any contact with its mother and who operates, in this story and in life, at the level of primary narcissism. I imagine that Dr. Freud might have wished he could have cap-tured this phase of life with such dimension and horror. Munro does this with one hand tied behind her back, deftly creating a tyrannical baby who wants, as Morgenstern states, "both to reject her mother and to make an absolute claim on her" (84). What's so interesting to me is that this is not unusual: this is what babies do. The dazzling work of Munro here is to write a mock-epic narrative whose plot amounts to nothing much more than a difficult night with a crying baby. Out of this conceit, the drama unfolds.

Layered on top of the unrelenting demands of this baby are the social concerns of Ailsa and Iona, which are equally confining. On the heels of the baby's encounter with music, and after Jill has made a feeble attempt to escape as far as the back porch, Ailsa demands that Jill come into the house because "'people will see'" (319). The greater humiliation for Jill comes when Ailsa tries to pass the screaming off as a light joke, remarking that "'Baby isn't a fan of the fiddle apparently'" (319). But Jill is at an impasse. She cannot mother her child; she cannot play her violin. Something will have to give in order for her to reclaim a self. She considers her situation while lying on her bed and reading a book from Ailsa's library (without asking Ailsa's permission), imagining that "In a fairy tale she would have risen off the bed with the strength of a young

giantess and gone through the house breaking furniture and necks"
(319-20). Munro, having begun the story with a saviour-less Christmas
scene, will conclude it with a fairy-less fairy tale. The baby in this story
will not save, but will require saving, an intervention that will occur by
means of a plot device so banal as an overtired mother.

Jill will find that no giant is required to re-order her world. Ever more
constricted, having yielded everything she values and with nothing left to
lose, Jill will set herself to mount an effective offense against her baby and
her family. All she needs is an opportunity, provided when Ailsa compels
Iona to come along on a trip to visit relatives in Guelph. Ailsa overrules
Iona's protestations, insisting that Jill is capable of spending "a day and a
half looking after her own baby" (320) while the sisters head off with their
mother. It's an assertion not exactly grounded in the reality that they have
inhabited for the six weeks of the baby's life and the claim consequently
provokes in the reader a shudder of dreadful anticipation.

Epic forces are gathering, Munro makes clear, and a battle will be
waged. The turbid mood of the weather, the blunt claim that the day
would be "the longest and the worst in Jill's experience" (321) juxtaposed
against Ailsa's cheerful "Goodbye little mother" (320), conspire to gener-
ate a sense of looming anxiety. Munro multiplies descriptors like "threat,"
"disruption," "nightmare" (320-21) to set the scene for what one senses
is a coming mock-apocalypse.

The battle's first engagement, as related by the baby, occurs when Jill
changes its diaper:

> I made it as hard as I could – I flailed my arms and legs, arched my back,
> tried my best to turn over, and of course kept up my noise. Jill's hands
> shook, she had trouble driving the pins through the cloth. She pretended
> to be calm, she tried talking to me, trying to imitate Iona's baby talk and
> fond cajoling, but it was no use, such stumbling insincerity enraged me
> further. She picked me up once she had my diaper pinned, she tried to
> mold me to her chest and shoulder, but I stiffened as if her body was
> made of red-hot needles. She sat down, she rocked me. She stood up,
> she bounced me. She sang to me the sweet words of a lullaby that were
> filled and trembling with her exasperation, her anger, and something
> that could readily define itself as loathing.
>
> We were monsters to each other. Jill and I. (321)

The battle is epic, the lines are drawn. The baby's best weapon is its cry, which it deploys throughout the day with "breaks of two or five or ten or twenty minutes," pausing only to return "to the assault" (322). The cry is "a meat cleaver." It is "so powerful, able to break down the order you depend on, inside and outside of yourself" (322).

The baby's shrieking constitutes the storm. Suiting the epic form, the cry is "insistent, theatrical, yet in a way pure and uncontrived. It is reproachful rather than supplicating – it comes out of a rage that can't be dealt with, a birthright rage free of love and pity, ready to crush your brains inside your skull" (322). It's a potent weapon and anyone who has had anything to do with an inconsolable baby knows the helpless rush of adrenalin as ineffective attempts are made to staunch the distress and restore peace. The battle depicted here may seem trivial and banal, but in the middle of such salvos of crying, nothing is more pressing or more courageous than stepping into the line of that fire and dealing with it. Munro's Jill can only "walk around" while the kitchen "clock tells her how slowly, slowly time is passing. She can't stay still to take more than a sip of her coffee" (322). She is in "a tempest or in a house whose beams are buckling in an awful wind" (323). This is one powerful baby.

Compounding the urgency of disaster and the powerful sense of isolation is the fact that "The house is shut up like a box" in service to "Ailsa's sense of shame" (323). Jill does not want the neighbours to know that she is "A mother who cannot appease her own baby" (323), a mother who needs to keep "the doors and windows shut" (323). Her one act of rebellion against the infant's loud assault is to play the violin, honouring her enemy, the baby, by giving up on any "counterfeit soothing" – "no more pretend lullabies or concern for tummy-ache, no petsy-wetsy whatsamatter" (323). This becomes a fair and face-on meeting of foes. The problem is that the violin itself betrays her. Against all her attempts to push through the Mendelssohn and then move on to Beethoven, Jill finds that "Everything is off" (324). Her attempt to persist through the Beethoven piece shows her that she is "completely defeated" (324), "Robbed overnight" (325) of her ability to play. Instead of making music, she appears to be "howling, heaving inside" (325) and all the while the baby is howling as well.

The critical engagements of this battle – the changing of the baby's diaper, the desperate feeding, the disastrous violin-playing to the

accompaniment of infant screams – are set against the calm silence
of the story's opening dream. In light of the noisy conflict, what is the
mother's dream? The mother's dream is of a barren landscape, insu-
lated, snow-covered, cool, and peaceful, a scene she looks upon from
the height and the safety of a large window in a rich mansion. Recall
that this is a dream within which Jill dreams she has awakened[1] – and
awakened to a sense of something being wrong. And it's a dream Jill
has after taking some of Ailsa's pain medication, prescribed to handle
menstrual cramps, so that she sleeps not only out of exhaustion, but
also with the help of what is likely a mild narcotic. After Jill has shaken
some of the shavings from the pills into the baby's warm milk and has
endured the baby's final resistance – its "immediately rigid body," its
"accusing mouth," and its spitting "back at her" (327) – she manages to
envelop both herself and the baby in a deep sleep and, at least as far as
the baby appears, in a vanquishing that resembles nothing so much as
death. Jill is submerged in the dream scenario. Peace finally descends,
but the cost verges on the terrible.

When Jill's sleep is interrupted by Iona's screaming, she wakes, confused, and believes that "Iona has got into the wrong part of the dream,"
the part that "is all over" (329). The baby is not dead, as she recalls from
her dream. She has already found it and it is fine. Indeed, this is the
only place in the story where Munro reverts to pleasant similes in her
representation of this infant:

> What a reprieve, then, to find her baby lying in its crib. Lying on its stom-
> ach, its head turned to one side, its skin pale and sweet as snowdrops
> and the down on its head reddish like the dawn. Red hair like her own,
> on her perfectly safe and unmistakable baby. (295)

Whatever Iona is frantic about, then, it is not the death of the baby and
Jill is not its murderer. As Ailsa, refusing to look at what she imagines to
be an infant corpse, indulges uncharacteristically in her own raving loss
of control, wailing against what she imagines will be the annihilation of
all the "investment she has made in this family's respectability and the
blows she's had to take, from her father's shabby career and her mother's
mixed-up wits to Iona's collapse at nursing school and George's going
off to get killed" (331), Jill struggles to place herself in time and space

after her deep medicated sleep. Finally, she is able to assert that "'The baby's all right'" (332).

After Iona hides the baby, it is Jill who follows the sound of its "faint cry" (333) and finds the baby under the sofa "pushed in beside the violin" (333). Jill secures the baby and she secures the violin. In this deft image, Munro collapses the distance between the woman as an artist and the woman as a mother. You can find the two in the same place and you can find the baby there too if you have the strength to fight for both. It's arresting. As a woman who is a mother of five and an artist, I find the image delightful and profound and I wish I'd thought of it.

Jill feels "a flash of joy" (333) that "sets her life going again, when just as in the dream she comes upon a live baby, not a little desiccated nutmeg-headed corpse" (333-34). I find that this joy comes almost as a shock. We have seen Jill at such odds with her baby that she must struggle to care for it. We have seen the two in fierce opposition where each party, Naomi Morgenstern claims, must "give up a fantastic omnipotence to find the other" (83). Moreover, this is not a story that is imbued with anything like happiness. However, in finding the baby alive, Jill finds joy and, I would argue, an irrevocable fusion of artist and mother rendered in Munro's claim that Jill held the baby "in the crook of her arm" (335) and then she "properly stowed away" (336) the violin.

The baby concludes: "It was Jill. I had to settle for Jill and for what I could get from her, even if it might look like half a loaf" (337). In giving "up the fight against [its] mother (which must have been a fight for something like her total surrender)" (337), the baby as the central character, agent, and narrator of its own story chooses "survival" (337). Only then does it take on a necessarily "female nature" (337).

In this female world, Jill conquers all. Iona is medicated and sent to a hospital; Ailsa for once holds her tongue – instead of telling Jill "to go and put a blouse on over her halter" she decides not to "say anything" (335); and the baby surrenders, as Jill herself does, to loving, because, as Munro writes, "the alternative to loving was disaster" (338). The notion so tacitly expressed here that Jill and the baby win while they lose is compelling. Jill surrenders total independence in the decision to love and the baby relinquishes absolute dominion over Jill in the desire to survive. Jill is able to reclaim her life, her body, her territory:

She got her diploma; she graduated from the Conservatory. She cut her hair and got thin. She was able to rent a duplex near High Park in Toronto, and hire a woman to look after me part of the time, because she had her war widow's pension. And then she found a job with a radio orchestra. She was to be proud that all her working life she was employed as a musician and never had to fall back on teaching. She said that she knew that she was not a great violinist, she had no marvellous gift or destiny, but at least she could make her living doing what she wanted to do. (339)

And the baby is able to claim a mother, able "to settle for Jill" (337) and, therefore, able to survive.

Given the trajectory of the story, we don't expect any sort of happy ending, but it is typical of Munro, it seems to me, that even a happy ending is modulated by a healthy dose of Southwestern Ontario practicality and plain modesty. Jill is not God's gift to music, but she is certainly adequate and pays her way doing what she wanted. Such a succinct statement might summarize the tempered aims of many women who are artists and mothers and if it is disappointing in its aspiration, it in fact reflects a general truth and a pervading desire. Imagine being able to do what you want.

The story leaves us at the kitchen table with Ailsa and Jill, who take up smoking, that classical mark of shared sophistication and individual independence, and who also acquire a mutual sense of having been comrades in arms, having become, "unaccountably," as Munro writes, "good friends" (340). Jill has fought through widowhood and motherhood to construct an artistic and practical self and to manage her own life, while Ailsa has successfully wrangled with her mother and sister and her own elusive attachment to Dr. Shantz to achieve some peace. Imagine waging and winning a war in that world of women, so conspiratorial, so complicit – even the neighbour's pool is populated by daughters and, although the doctor is a man, his wife is the one who hides the evidence of the knife on the counter and who sees immediately what needs to be done.

My mother died young and suddenly and my brothers and I were left to sort through her possessions. Among these were yards of fabric she had collected with some future project in mind, costume jewellery in her dresser that she had worn on Saturday nights with my father dancing at Paradise Gardens, lingerie she never wore after his death, and cartons of cigarettes she never had a chance to smoke. We found, interred in a crawlspace and labelled and ready that warm September, what would have been my Christmas present. I opened the box to find a set of blue luggage she had put away for me. A gift to grant me what I most wanted, which was to disappear, to live a bigger life than she did. These days, I think of my mother's dream of me, her only daughter, and I wonder about our mutual surrender. I can't ask her about the self she might have yielded to take me on, but I recall vividly my small self, giving way to weariness and bonded to her side after any sort of discord between us. I think of how I loved to lean against her. I think of Munro's story with its women's voices in a women's world and the pledge so quietly expressed in the final revelation of a daughter who wishes to be thought of as a ghost.

Note

1. See Ailsa Cox's book *Alice Munro* for a discussion of the story's "beginning with what first appears to be an awakening" (13). Cox also discusses the recurrence throughout the story of "temporal and spatial fluidity introduced by the dream passage" (14).

Works Consulted

Arendt, Hannah. *The Human Condition.* Chicago, IL: U of Chicago P, 1958.

Cox, Ailsa. *Alice Munro.* Tavistock, Eng.: Northcote House, 2004. Writers and Their Work.

---. "'First and Last': The Figure of the Infant in 'Dear Life' and 'My Mother's Dream'." *Alice Munro's Miraculous Art: Critical Essays.* Ed. Janice Fiamengo and Gerald Lynch. Ottawa: U of Ottawa P, 2017. 177-90. Reappraisals: Canadian Writers 38.

Morgenstern, Naomi. "The Baby or the Violin?: Ethics and Femininity in the Fiction of Alice Munro." *Literature Interpretation Theory* 14 (2003): 69-97.

---. "Seduction and Subjectivity: Psychoanalysis and the Fiction of Alice Munro." *Critical Insights: Alice Munro*. Ed. Charles E. May. Ipswich, MA: Salem-EBSCO, 2013. 68-86.

Munro, Alice. "My Mother's Dream." *The Love of a Good Woman*. Toronto: McClelland & Stewart, 1998. 293-340.

Rich, Adrienne. *Of Woman Born: Motherhood As Experience and Institution*. New York: W.W. Norton, 1976.

Sabatini, Sandra. *Making Babies: Infants in Canadian Fiction*. Waterloo, ON: Wilfrid Laurier UP, 2003.

The Skald and the Goddess: A Reading of Alice Munro's "The Bear Came Over the Mountain"

Héliane Ventura

Alice Munro's short story entitled "The Bear Came Over the Mountain" was first published in *The New Yorker* (27 Dec. 1999 and 3 Jan. 2000) before it was collected under the same title in her tenth book, *Hateship, Friendship, Courtship, Loveship, Marriage*, in 2001 and adapted for the cinema, to great acclaim, by Sarah Polley in 2006 under a different, shorter title extracted from Munro's text: *Away from Her*. The puzzling short story title reads like a close variant from an American folk song, "The Bear Went Over the Mountain," while the concluding paragraph in the story features a characteristic trait from the world of childhood, which is linked with language learning, since the main female character, Fiona, strives to find the correct irregular form of the verb "to forsake": "and forsook me. Forsooken me. Forsaken" (322).

Nevertheless this story does not belong in children's literature and neither does it highlight any specific events in the lives of fictional children. As pinpointed by Robert McGill, "Children are virtually nowhere to be found in 'The Bear Came Over the Mountain,' and because Fiona and Grant are not parents, the story offers no consolation in the glimpse of a younger generation's possibilities, no catharsis through a child or grandchild coming to grips with Fiona's institutionalization, no redemption through the passing on of memory. Any hope lies in the future of Fiona and Grant themselves" (103). Fiona is afflicted with a degenerative disease which is not named but presents the symptoms of Alzheimer's and she has to leave the house in the country, near Georgian Bay, where the couple had taken early retirement twelve years before, in order to

275

settle in a nearby nursing home. Framed as it is between a folk song title and the groping for the right form of an irregular verb in the last lines, the story seems to refrain wittily from pathos and self-pity in order to favour a playful, distanced, and ironic approach to the ravages of aging.

This analysis will focus on the ambiguities of the uses and misuses of language on two levels, that of a Nonsense charade and that of the parodic re-writing of mythology to demonstrate that, through the enduring power of poetic language, senile dementia is momentarily deferred and, if not defeated, at least challenged with "the spark of life" (275), as Munro resorts to the double hook of folk song and mock-epic aggrandizement in her reconfiguration of love at twilight.

At first sight, the American folk song that reports the actions of the adventurous bear going over the mountain is a far cry from the Mad Hatter, the March Hare, the Snark, or Tweedledum and Tweedledee:

The Bear Went Over the Mountain

The bear went over the mountain,
The bear went over the mountain,
The bear went over the mountain,
To see what he could see.

And what do you think he saw?
And what do you think he saw?

The other side of the mountain,
The other side of the mountain,
The other side of the mountain,
Was all that he could see.

The folk song reads like a morphological pun, a self-parodic play on words, which relies on the opening up of expectations only to frustrate curiosity with the platitude of a tautological closure. Because of its contradictory relationship with language, I would like to posit the hypothesis that "The Bear Came Over the Mountain" belongs in the tradition of Nonsense as evidenced in the writings of Lewis Carroll and

Edward Lear, and that, like Nonsense, it constitutes a logician's entertainment which explores the limits but also the redeeming possibilities of language.

Let us compare "The Bear Went Over the Mountain" with this limerick from Lear:

There was an Old Man of the Nile,
Who sharpened his nails with a file;
Till he cut off his thumbs,
And said calmly, "This comes –
Of sharpening one's nails with a file!" (qtd. in Lecercle 97; and see Lear in Rhys 35)

As demonstrated by Jean-Jacques Lecercle in his groundbreaking study of Nonsense from which I will quote extensively in my analysis of Munro's story, there is, in the British limerick, a down-to-earth attitude, a refusal to be surprised by the turn of events and to yield to emotion or become prey to a sense of pain or catastrophe (97). We find the same sense of restraint in the American folk song, a spelling out of ordinariness no matter what happens, which Lecercle shows as standing in sharp contrast to the marvellous (92). In the wake of analyses by Propp, Todorov, and Greimas of the structural and semiotic components of marvellous folk tales, we have been led to expect the bear who is engaged in a quest to come up against a number of qualifying ordeals, to reveal his heroic stature during a confrontation with a villainous character, and to complete his journey satisfactorily with the discovery of the object he is looking for. But the folk song Munro has selected is not marvellous; it seemingly defeats all our expectations of heroic aggrandizement and magic discovery. As theorized by Jean-Jacques Lecercle, the marvellous is ruined by parody, plays on words, and platitudes (Lecercle 100).

The world that the bear discovers is just as ordinary as the one he has just left. He goes on the other side of the mountain and discovers the other side of the mountain. Expression is reduced to tautology, and tautology is fraught with rhetorical power. It reinforces and guarantees the ideology we live by: boys will be boys. The other side of the mountain is the other side of the mountain. The assertion is extremely sensible at the same time as it refrains from conveying meaning. It confirms the real world, the existence of which is clearly posited: the other side of the mountain exists and the bear has been able to find its location which is to be accepted as part and parcel of the real world, but this real world is simultaneously questioned because it is reduced to a self-parodic play on words. The bear indulges in an anthropomorphic quest which reveals its self-referential dimension because instead of killing the serpent or marrying the king's daughter, it comes up against "the other side of the mountain," that is to say a self-reflexive textual construction which is the result of the constraints of a particular fiction or self-parodic verse. In the words of Lecercle:

> Le Nonsense utilise donc la longue tradition des jeux de langage de façon sélective: il ne retient que ceux qui prennent au piège la langue pour mieux la renforcer. Il s'agit de prendre celle-ci au pied de la lettre, de la forcer dans ses retranchements, en jouant par exemple sur les ambiguïtés syntaxiques. (49)

The literal-mindedness of Nonsense and its often tautological syntax reinforce its fictional dimension, its being circumscribed by allusions to itself or to other texts. Munro multiplies the indexes of fictionality in her own fiction. The title is a case in point but we can find several other references to fiction, for instance in the names given to Fiona's dogs. The Russian wolfhounds are called Boris and Natasha, which reads like a wink that Munro is directing at her readers. These names, which seem to come straight from a Russian novel, are in fact the names of fictional characters from an American animated cartoon which from the late 1950s to the middle 1960s ran under the title *Rocky and His Friends* and then as *The Bullwinkle Show* and featured spies called Boris Badenov and Natasha Fatale. The obvious puns in the spies' names wittily expose them as "bad enough" and "fatal."

In addition to indirect, witty, and self-denigrating allusions to children's fictions, Munro also multiplies self-parodic similes which make it possible to erase the difference between the world of children and the world of senior citizens. When Fiona catches a cold, shortly after being accepted in the nursing home, the nurse called Kristy reassures Grant using a tell-tale comparison: "'Like when your kids start school,' Kristy said. 'There's a whole bunch of new germs they're exposed to, and for a while they just catch everything'" (281). The nursing-home pensioners could not be more eloquently equated with children and the pragmatic nurse more eloquently ironized for her flat and unintentional put-down.

Once familiarized with her new life in the institution, Fiona starts developing a social network through playing cards with some of the inmates and she makes a comparison with her life at college: "'I can remember being like that for a while at college. My friends and I would cut class and sit in the common room and smoke and play like cut-throats'" (289). Grant's response to Fiona's simile is particularly remarkable because it reintegrates the young card players' activity into the world of children's fiction: "'Wreathed in smoke, Fiona and Phoebe and those others, rapt as witches'" (289). Through the play of similes, Munro blurs the frontiers between the world of childhood and the world of pensioners, the world of ordinary existence and the world of fabulous creatures. She allows her characters, and her readers, to go down the rabbit-hole and through the looking-glass as she erases the difference between one side of the mountain and the other.

In particular one can notice that she erases the boundaries between human beings and animals, birds, and fish. The similes which equate the characters with creatures are inescapable and all characters seem concerned with this potential transformation. Fiona is compared with her dogs: "The dogs' long legs and silky hair, their narrow, gentle, intransigent faces made a fine match for her when she took them out for walks" (278). Grant undergoes the same metamorphosis: "And Grant himself ... might have seemed to some people to have been picked up on another of Fiona's eccentric whims, and groomed and tended and favored" (278). Aubrey, the man Fiona attaches herself to in the nursing home, is compared with a horse: "he had something of the beauty of a powerful, discouraged, elderly horse" (290). The inmates are said to be "'happy as clams'" (280) in their new life in the nursing home. Fiona's outfits, in typical Munrovian fashion, are elaborately described and the one with which she leaves home is markedly suggestive of the bird and animal kingdom: she has "a fur-collared ski jacket," a "turtle-necked sweater," and "fawn slacks" (275).

Besides, by choosing the title of the American folk song for her story, Munro seems to have implicitly required the reader to compare the adventures of the bear with the actions of the main characters in the short story. Fiona, like the bear, engages in a journey which takes her to a different world called Meadowlake. The name of the nursing home inspires Fiona with a series of plays on words: "'Shallowlake, Shillylake,' she said, as if they were engaged in a playful competition. 'Sillylake. Sillylake it is'" (279). As demonstrated by Freud, puns are transgressions which create pleasure and the function of the present plays on words is certainly to reduce, through playful amusement and scorn, the dramatic intensity and trauma linked with confinement in the institution. It also fictionalizes the place; it inscribes it in a nonsensical enumeration, that is to say in fictional language, at the same time as in reality, further erasing the boundaries between the two realms and the experiences of the "fictional" bear and the "real" Fiona.

By choosing Nonsense verse for her title Munro draws attention to the opposition between sense and non-sense and by destabilizing the boundaries between fiction and real life, between senior citizens and infants, between people and animals, Munro implicitly paves the way for a more radical equivocation, that is to say the blurring of difference between sanity and dementia, between those who are on one side of the mountain and those who are on the other. She performs this radical blurring, or what in "Royal Beatings" she calls "the tumble of reason" (12; and see Heble ix-x), in a very subtle and ambiguous way, through Grant's disbelief in his wife's disease and through the impossibility of pinpointing the exact nature of the intermittent degeneration with which Fiona seems to be afflicted. The sentences expressing Grant's perplexity abound: "It was hard to figure out" (277). "'She's always been a bit like this'" (277). In his utter incredulity, Grant even goes as far as imagining that Fiona is indulging in some sort of charade and is playing a game with him. He resorts to hypothetical sentences and extended modal verbs:

Or was playing a game that she hoped he would catch on to. (277)

He could not decide. She could have been playing a joke. It would not be unlike her. She had given herself away by that little pretense at the end, talking to him as if she thought perhaps he was a new resident.
If that was what she was pretending. If it was a pretense. (291)

Grant is a professor of Anglo-Saxon and Nordic literature and the journey he undertakes to accompany his wife through the meanders of degeneration can also be equated with the bear's going over the other side of the mountain. Grant does not "forsake" Fiona in the institution. He phones the nurses every day during the first month of their forced separation (no visits are allowed for the initial thirty days) and finally settles on two visits a week. His repeated journeys to Meadowlake are indeed forays into the other side of the looking-glass, a descent into the world of senile dementia which, at times, mirrors in inverted fashion Alice's journey in Wonderland. Like the young Alice, the elderly Grant is an intruder in a territory which is not his and, like her, he meets with unmitigated hostility. For instance, when he goes to the common room to try to see Fiona who is sitting at the card table with her new friends, he can easily feel their opposition: "They all looked up – all the players at the table looked up, with displeasure. Then they immediately looked down at their cards, as if to ward off any intrusion" (288). The exasperation of the card players towards Grant transforms the generosity of his visits into a *faux-pas*.

The inversion of values that is characteristic of Nonsense is fully displayed in the itinerary of Grant who, from the beginning, manifests symptoms which, strikingly enough, mirror Fiona's loss of memory. Munro embeds into the depiction of his actions a series of apparently innocent anecdotes which pave the way for a subtle elimination of the frontier between Grant's sanity and Fiona's dementia. For instance, we find "Grant could not remember now" (278); "Or it might have been after her mother died" (278). When he visits Aubrey's wife, Marian, he cannot find the proper word to describe the swooping curtains with which she has decorated her windows. More importantly, he himself uses the term "unhinged" to describe his behaviour: "every once in a while it came to him how foolish and pathetic and perhaps unhinged he must look, trailing around after Fiona and Aubrey" (295).

Like Fiona, Grant has gone over the threshold which separates sanity from madness; yet one of the differences between them is that, unlike her, he has so far been able to conceal it from the rest of the world. The most eloquent sign of his potential insanity is the moment when he is represented as comparing himself with Christ through a sacrilegious quotation from Luke 2.52. After reciting and translating a majestic ode, in front of his students, he feels lionized:

All applauded…. Driving home that day or maybe another he found an absurd and blasphemous quotation running around in his head.

And so he increased in wisdom and stature –

And in favor with God and man.

That embarrassed him at the time and gave him a superstitious chill. As it did yet. But so long as nobody knew, it seemed not unnatural. (302)

Munro is particularly apt at representing university professors – like Hugo from the story entitled "Material" dating from 1974 – as "Bloated, opinionated, untidy men" surrounded by "soft-haired young girls awash in adoration" (24). Similarly, Grant is represented, in 2001, as a narcissistic and egomaniacal philanderer, with a major difference. Despite his having had a great many affairs, he has never left Fiona and the final act he indulges in acquires an ambiguously redeeming dimension.

Because of her degenerative disease, once Fiona is on her own at Meadowlake she forgets Grant, the husband she has lived with for nearly fifty years, and falls in love with another inmate whose stay in the institution is only temporary. After this man, called Aubrey, who is afflicted with paralysis, is removed from the institution by his own wife, Marian, Fiona falls into severe depression and Grant shows himself capable of the greatest sacrifice. Because he loves his wife with the utmost selflessness, he sacrifices his honour and his pride in order to arrange for Aubrey to return to the nursing home and live close to Fiona. He ambiguously rescues his wife by making possible her lover's return to her. This uncanny act of love is made even "curiouser" by an additional twist in the plot, at the end of the story. When the lover is about to be reunited to the forgetful wife by the selfless husband, Fiona temporarily regains her sanity, recognizes her husband, and suggests returning to their old farmhouse together, thus ruining the sacrificial gesture her husband had engineered.

Munro's *dénouement* is extremely flippant and destabilizing because it juxtaposes the farcical and the sublime, the weird and the noble, the heretic and the pragmatic, on the threshold between life and death, in a senior citizen's residence. This remarkably ironic *dénouement* could be envisaged as a self-parodic treatment of sacrificial love. By comparing himself with Christ, Grant indulges in an operation of self-aggrandizement and endorses the role of the redeemer. However, the type of sacrifice he engineers when procuring a lover for his wife turns redemption topsy-turvy since he simultaneously becomes the agent of her betrayal. Through his own selflessness, Grant confirms the reversal of her faithfulness into faithlessness. After a lifetime of skilfully managed deceptions, he proves true to himself by allowing her to reciprocate infidelity. As rightly pointed out, if erroneously spelt by Robert Thacker, Grant is eminently a "long-time r[o]ué" (502).

There lies the crux of what Coral Ann Howells, along with other critics, describes as Munro's "art of indeterminacy" (85): her highlighting of what W.R. Martin terms "[p]aradox and [p]arallel," her ability to examine human surroundings and human actions as simultaneously and reciprocally "touchable and mysterious" (Munro, qtd. in Thacker 2), "strange and familiar" (Martin 1), but also elevated and degraded or transcendent and immanent. One description caps the point in an unusually explicit way: "Through the window came a heady, warm blast of lilacs in bloom and the spring manure spread over the fields" (321). By compounding fragrance with stench, Munro conjures up a non-judgmental universe in which the absence of moralism is articulated upon an all-permeating irony. The ambiguity of her moral philosophy, which has yet to be documented substantially, lies in the constant reversal of one sensation into the other and the simultaneous reinforcing and ruining of the former by the latter.

Grant, whose love has been freely distributed among his students and who is capable of sacrificing himself for his wife's sake, ambiguously impersonates in a self-parodic mode the figure of Christ who died on the cross to redeem mankind. But because he is a professor of Anglo-Saxon and Nordic literature and reads Skaldic poetry aloud to his students, he is simultaneously allowed to cut the figure of the emblematic Icelandic poet or Skald. *The Encyclopaedia Britannica* reminds us that, contrary to anonymous Eddaic poetry, Skaldic oral court poetry, which originated in Norway but was developed chiefly by Icelandic poets from the 9th to the 13th century, could be attributed to single identifiable persons ("Skaldic Poetry"). The magnificent ode which is mentioned by the narrator as being read aloud in class by Grant is one of the most famous: the *Höfuðlausn* by Egill Skallagrímsson; his life and poetry are recorded in *Egil's Saga*, a work attributed to Snorri Sturluson ("Egill Skallagrímsson"). This allusion to Skaldic poetry is worth investigating because it throws additional light on the redeeming power of language that is highlighted in Munro's story.

Egill Skallagrímsson (b. *c.* 910, d. 990), one of the greatest Icelandic Skalds, was "headstrong, vengeful, and greedy for gold," *The Encyclopaedia Britannica* notes, "but also a loyal friend, a shy lover, and a devoted father." While still a young man, "he killed the son of King Eiríkr Bloodaxe (Erik I) and placed a curse upon the king, which he inscribed on a pole in magic runes." Years later, "shipwrecked off the coast of Northumbria, England, he fell into Eiríkr's hands (*c.* 948) but saved his own life by composing in a single night the long praise poem *Höfuðlausn* ("Head-Ransom"), praising Eiríkr in a unique end-rhymed metre" ("Egill Skallagrímsson").

Munro, who published in 1986 a short story, "White Dump," which relies allusively on Old Norse mythology ("White Dump"), takes up explicitly and literally, in 2001, the theme of the redemption brought about by the power of poetry. When referring to the *Höfuðlausn*, she highlights the miraculous transformation that poetry operates, its power to transform a death sentence into a gift of life:

> he risked reciting and then translating the majestic and gory ode, the "Head-Ransom," the *Höfuðlausn*, composed to honor King Eric Blood-axe by the Skald whom that king had condemned to death. (And who was then, by the same king – and by the power of poetry – set free.) (302)

By reciting aloud the *Höfuðlausn*, Egill saved his head because the beauty of his words moved the heart of the king who, in return, granted him his life. By taking up Egill's words and reciting them in front of his class, Grant turns into the Skald and, like him, he escapes scot-free, despite his repeated misconduct and improper behaviour.

The transformation of the character necessarily influences the story which relates his adventures. Thus the allusion to the Icelandic ode provides the story with a mixed inheritance in which learned references rub shoulders with popular culture. Reflecting as it does the Great Code as well as Nordic Mythology, British Nonsense, and American Folk Song, to mention some of its most prominent intertexts, "The Bear Came Over the Mountain" is a *mise en abyme* of the redeeming power of words and of the performativity of poetic language which ensures that an action is accomplished at the same time as it is uttered. Consider the ending of *Alice's Adventures in Wonderland*. To the Queen of Hearts who shouts to her, "'Hold your tongue!'," Alice replies, "'I won't!'" (95). When the Queen threatens to decapitate her, Alice finally retorts, "'Who cares for *you*? ... You're nothing but a pack of cards!'" (95). Alice's words do not have the majestic beauty of the Icelandic ode but they have the same power: they reach their target and reduce the Queen of Hearts to her rightful status, that of a card which dissolves into thin air and keeps Alice from losing her head. Alice's words, like the Skald's, are fraught with immediate efficacy.

It is this magic efficacy that Munro's stories strive to recapture. In "The Bear Came Over the Mountain" Grant is endowed with the power of a Skaldic poet who casts a spell over his students and ensures the remission of his sexual sins. He ironically acquires his truly heroic stature when he undertakes to rescue Fiona from the severe depression which would ensure the further degradation of her present condition. As if in a mirror, Fiona's fully-fledged dimension manifests itself through the use of language, in an equally ironic manner. Of her, Kristy the nurse says, "'She's a real lady'" (293), and she repeats the epithet to Grant several times in a tone that does not reassure him and leads him to form conjectures. In the institution, Fiona may have turned into a wanton old lady who does not want to sleep alone in her empty room but teasingly lifts the covers of an old man's bed:

> "You'd think it'd be the old guys trying to crawl in bed with the old women, but you know half the time it's the other way round. Old women going after the old men. Could be they're not so wore out, I guess." (293)

The mistaken use of the wrong past participle might be taken as an example of what J.L. Austin calls revelatory "infelicities" (Austin 224, qtd. in Lecercle 20), a Freudian slip of the tongue, through which Kristy unconsciously pinpoints Fiona's nature. Neither a lady nor a whore, Fiona embodies the Old Norse goddess of love Friia, also called Frigg, or, in various other languages and mythologies, Frija (Old High German), Frea (Langobardic), and Frige (Old English). She is the very same goddess who is called Aphrodite by the Greeks and Venus by the Romans. It is through this tell-tale crack of language that Fiona's goddess-like stature is indirectly established because it is powerfully "half-uttered" or "*mi-dit*" to use the pun that Lacan coined for such linguistic return of the repressed (Lacan 118).

In Munro's short story, the Skald is an untidy university professor and the Goddess is no longer a rosy-cheeked maiden. Fiona's "skin or her breath [gives] off a faint new smell, a smell ... like that of the stems of cut flowers left too long in their water" (322). There is definitely a sense of decomposition and rottenness which invades this family saga, a corruption which is repeatedly suggested through the simile linked to the depiction of Fiona and the heady odours wafting through the windows of her bedroom and which by implication comes to characterize Grant as well. The offering that Grant makes to his wife in the shape of a paralyzed lover destined to comfort her is the result of a shady deal that he has engineered with the man's wife. Grant has probably offered himself and his sexual services to Marian, in ironic sacrifice, in order to make her accept her husband's return to Meadowlake.

In her adaptation of the story for the screen, Sarah Polley renders this improbable trade-off explicit by allowing the spectators more than a glimpse into Grant and Marian's bedroom; in the short story we are not allowed to witness such *rapprochement*. Munro leaves unuttered the terms of Aubrey's return. This powerful ellipsis seals her art of the secret, as I describe that in the essay entitled "Alice Munro's Secret *Ort*." There I use the German term "*Ort*" which means place to define Munro's art of secreting secrets, making explicit reference to Heidegger's theory of the Quadriparti as developed in "Bâtir habiter penser." The secrets to be found in Munro's stories frequently make their presence felt through tell-tale errors or infelicities in language which represent exemplary *loci* of the coming into being of the self around whom a world is made to emerge. In "The Bear Came Over the Mountain," Kirsty's use of the wrong past participle and Fiona's recapturing of the right one constitute emblematic traces that simultaneously conceal and expose the unutterable secret of the self. This duplicitous art (or *ort*) highlights Munro's commitment to a moral philosophy which rises above conformity to the moral values of the community and commits itself to more complex and more covert ethical principles, of which silence, restraint, and reticence are significant components.

The sense of physical and moral degradation which permeates the story is far from being magically dispelled by the closing lines. It is simultaneously confirmed and ruined to remain in keeping with the Nonsense genre in which the story of the Skald and the Goddess is couched. In the last line of the story, there is a process of reparation of language and reparation of the self at the same time as a powerful alliterative pattern which conspicuously stresses the menacing repetition of the consonant "s":

"You could have just driven away," she said. "Just driven away without a care in the world and forsook me. Forsooken me. Forsaken."
He kept his face against her white hair, her pink scalp, her sweetly shaped skull. He said, Not a chance. (322)

Kristy, the uneducated nurse and the good Christian, degrades and upgrades past participles as she keeps watch over her patients. Fiona, the victim of Alzheimer's and the Goddess of love, repairs the irregularities of grammar, like a pink-scalped child learning language. Simultaneously, the negative last words and threatening sibilant alliterations confirm Grant's enduring love in the inverted mirror of Munro's weirdly ironic writing. The word "chance," which is to be found recurrently in her work and is used as the title of a later story in the Juliet trilogy published in *Runaway* in 2004, means a risk but it also means an opportunity: by using it negatively, Grant makes room for a rejuvenating impertinence, a challenging of fate which is also an acceptance of fate.

The coming of dawn at the end of night is a *topos* encapsulated in many works of art, *The Sun Also Rises* being paradigmatic of this final redemption. At the end of Jean Giraudoux's play *Electre*, the last lines make the audience reflect on the image's resonance: "Cela a un très beau nom, femme Narsès. Cela s'appelle l'aurore" (227). Similarly, in a poem by Emily Dickinson, which resembles a nursery rhyme and whose first line reads "I know some lonely Houses off the Road" (138), an old couple goes to sleep leaving the door ajar and the poetess, like a thief in the night, allows the reader into the intimacy of the old couple's home, until Chanticleer screams to welcome the sunrise. In Dickinson's poem, the sunrise is literally an offering which is made to celebrate Grace Abounding.

In Alice Munro's narrative, the reader is seemingly denied the lyrical coming of dawn at the end of the journey to the other side of the mountain because the elderly heroine is undeniably in the grip of Alzheimer's; yet the loss of language, the ruin which it entails, is itself ruined by the transgressions of the various thresholds which are enacted throughout the story. The ultimate threshold, that of life versus death, is itself destabilized in the dissolution of the boundaries between sanity and dementia as Munro stage-directs the confusion between life and illusion. She re-enacts the theme of the illusoriness of life à la Calderón (*Life Is a Dream*), Carroll ("Life Is but a Dream"), and the well-known nursery rhyme "Row, Row, Row Your Boat" ("Life is but a dream"). Thus she dissolves the boundaries between drama and poetry, romance and nursery rhyme to highlight a celebration of the power of language as, in the view of Jean-Jacques Lecercle, the place and the means of freedom. Her story does not herald the coming of dawn: it orchestrates the twilight of the gods and it provides the disquieting possibility of equating that with the sunrise.

Works Consulted

Austin, J.L. "Performative Utterances." *Philosophical Papers*. Oxford, Eng.: Clarendon, 1961. 220-39.

Away from Her. Screenplay by Sarah Polley. Dir. Sarah Polley. Capri Films, 2006.

"The Bear Went Over the Mountain." <http://www.canteach.ca/elementary/songspoems.html>.

The Bullwinkle Show. NBC. 1961-64. Television.

Bunyan, John. *Grace Abounding to the Chief of Sinners*. Ed. and introd. W.R. Owens. London: Penguin, 1987. Penguin Classics.

Calderón de la Barca, Pedro. *Life Is a Dream*. Trans., fwd., and introd. Edwin Honig. New York: Hill & Wang, 1970. A Mermaid Dramabook.

Carroll, Lewis. *Alice's Adventures in Wonderland. Alice in Wonderland: Authoritative Texts of* Alice's Adventures in Wonderland, Through the Looking-Glass, The Hunting of the Snark; Backgrounds; Criticism. Ed. Donald J. Gray. 3rd ed. New York: W.W. Norton, 2013. 1-97. A Norton Critical Edition.

---. "Life Is but a Dream." *The Hunting of the Snark and Other Poems and Verses*. Illus. Peter Newell. New York: Harper & Brothers, 1903. 199-200. <http://www.poetry-archive.com/c/life_is_but_a_dream.html>.

Dickinson, Emily. "I know some lonely Houses off the Road." *The Poems of Emily Dickinson: Reading Edition*. Ed. R.W. Franklin. Cambridge, MA: Belknap, 1999. 138-39.

"Egill Skallagrímsson." *The Encyclopaedia Britannica. Encyclopaedia Britannica 2007 Ultimate Reference Suite*. Chicago, IL: Encyclopaedia Britannica, 2008.

Freud, Sigmund. *Jokes and Their Relation to the Unconscious*. Trans. James Strachey. Ed. Angela Richards. London: Penguin, 1991. Vol. 6 of *The Penguin Freud Library*. 15 vols. 1990-93.

"Frigg." *The Encyclopaedia Britannica. Encyclopaedia Britannica 2007 Ultimate Reference Suite*. Chicago, IL: Encyclopaedia Britannica, 2008.

Giraudoux, Jean. *Electre*. Paris: Éditions Bernard Grasset, 1937.

Greimas, Algirdas Julien. *Du sens: Essais sémiotiques*. Paris: Éditions du Seuil, 1970.

Heble, Ajay. *The Tumble of Reason: Alice Munro's Discourse of Absence*. Toronto: U of Toronto P, 1994.

Heidegger, Martin. "Bâtir habiter penser." *Essais et conférences*. Trans. André Préau. Paris: Éditions Gallimard, 1958. 170-93.

Hemingway, Ernest. *The Sun Also Rises*. 1926. New York: Charles Scribner's Sons, 1954.

Howells, Coral Ann. *Alice Munro*. Manchester, Eng.: Manchester UP, 1998. Contemporary World Writers.

Lacan, Jacques. *L'envers de la psychanalyse 1969-1970*. Ed. Jacques-Alain Miller. Paris: Éditions du Seuil, 1991. Vol. 17 of *Le Seminaire de Jacques Lacan*.

Lear, Edward. "There was an Old Man of the Nile." *A Book of Nonsense*. Ed. Ernest Rhys. Introd. Roger Lancelyn Green. 1927. London: J.M. Dent & Sons, 1974. 35.

Lecercle, Jean-Jacques. *Le dictionnaire et le cri*. Nancy, Fr.: Presses Universitaires de Nancy, 1995.

Martin, W.R. *Alice Munro: Paradox and Parallel*. Edmonton, AB: U of Alberta P, 1987.

McGill, Robert. "No Nation but Adaptation: 'The Bear Came Over the Mountain', *Away from Her*, and What It Means To Be Faithful." *Canadian Literature* 197 (2008): 98-111.

Munro, Alice. "The Bear Came Over the Mountain." *Hateship, Friendship, Courtship, Loveship, Marriage*. Toronto: McClelland & Stewart, 2001. 274-322.

---. "The Bear Came Over the Mountain." *The New Yorker* 27 Dec. 1999 and 3 Jan. 2000: 110-21, 124-27.

---. "Chance." *Runaway*. Toronto: McClelland & Stewart, 2004. 48-86.

---. "Everything Here Is Touchable and Mysterious." *Weekend Magazine* [*The Globe and Mail*] 11 May 1974: [33].

---. "Material." *Something I've Been Meaning To Tell You*. Toronto: McGraw-Hill Ryerson, 1974. 24-44.

---. "Royal Beatings." *Who Do You Think You Are?* Toronto: Macmillan of Canada, 1978. 1-22.

---. "White Dump." *The Progress of Love*. Toronto: McClelland & Stewart, 1986. 275-309.

Page, R.I. *Norse Myths*. London: British Museum, 1990. The Legendary Past.

Propp, Vladimir. "Morphologie du conte." *Morphologie du conte suivi de Les transformations des contes merveilleux et de E. Mélétinski L'Étude structurale et typologique du conte*. Trans. Marguerite Derrida, Tzvetan Todorov, and Claude Kahn. Paris: Éditions du Seuil, 1970. 5-170.

Rocky and His Friends. ABC. 1959-61. Television.

"Row, Row, Row Your Boat." <https://www.nurseryrhymes.org/row-row-row-your-boat.html>.

"Skaldic Poetry." *The Encyclopaedia Britannica. Encyclopaedia Britannica 2007 Ultimate Reference Suite*. Chicago, IL: Encyclopaedia Britannica, 2008.

Skallagrímsson, Egill. ["*Höfuðlausn* ('Head-Ransom')."] *Egil's Saga*. [By Snorri Sturluson.] Trans. and introd. Hermann Pálsson and Paul Edwards. Harmondsworth, Eng.: Penguin, 1976. 158-62. Penguin Classics. <http://www.odins-gift.com/pclass/hoefudlausn.htm>.

Thacker, Robert. *Alice Munro: Writing Her Lives: A Biography*. Toronto: McClelland & Stewart, 2005.

Todorov, Tzvetan. *Introduction à la littérature fantastique*. Paris: Éditions du Seuil, 1970. Poétique.

Ventura, Héliane. "Alice Munro's Secret *Ort*." *Alice Munro: Writing Secrets.* Ed. Héliane Ventura and Mary Condé. *Open Letter* 11th ser., no. 9 - 12th ser., no. 1 (2003-04): 255-66.

Waters, Juliet. "Under the Munro Influence." Rev. of *Away from Her*, by Alice Munro, pref. Sarah Polley. *Montreal Mirror* 24 May-30 May 2007: 47. <www.montrealmirror.com/2007/052407/booksl.html>.

The Place of Wisdom, Divination, the Act of Reading, and Alice Munro's "Powers"

J.R. (Tim) Struthers

For William Butt, Marianne Micros,
Catherine Sheldrick Ross, Ron Shuebrook

But where shall wisdom be found?
and where is the place of understanding?
– The Book of Job 28.12

And did the Countenance Divine,
Shine forth upon our clouded hills?
And was Jerusalem builded here,
Among these dark Satanic Mills?
Bring me my Bow of burning gold:
Bring me my Arrows of desire:
Bring me my Spear: O clouds unfold!
Bring me my Chariot of fire!
– William Blake, Preface to *Milton*

Do you still seek to know? And what?
– *Vǫluspá* 60, trans. Ursula Dronke

PROLOGUE: *Give Realism a Rest for a While*

Alice Munro's novella "Powers" has all the amplitude, the complexity, the range in tone, the density, the force that Munro admired in the two examples of this form collected by Ethel Wilson in *The Equations of Love* and that readers including Munro have appreciated in classic examples of this form such as James Joyce's "The Dead." Moreover, like any other Munro story we might choose to study, "Powers" requires us to approach reading it, just as Munro handled writing it, *differently* – to recall the title of another work by her that also involves a witty beginning. For "Powers" invites us to imagine Munro drolly declaring, "Give Realism a rest for a while. Think of my stories as semi-abstract or abstract paintings. Think of me, ultimately, as writing Allegory." More precisely, consider "Powers" as a vigorous contemporary contribution to the centuries-old literary tradition of dream-vision allegory comprised of such original titles as William Langland's *Piers Plowman* and John Bunyan's *The Pilgrim's Progress* and Lewis Carroll's *Alice's Adventures in Wonderland*. Or, we could readily suggest, given the rich blend of theatricality and narrativity and lyricism throughout Munro's work, consider "Powers" as a dream play in five acts, like August Strindberg's *A Dream Play*. Or, alternatively, consider "Powers" as a dramatic poem in five acts, like Henrik Ibsen's *Peer Gynt*, to which Munro alludes meaningfully in the last section of the first part of the novella.

Each of the five parts of "Powers" possesses a suggestive and, we might at first be tempted to say (though as we keep reading, we might *not* be so inclined to say), a whimsical subtitle: "Give Dante a Rest"; "Girl in a Middy"; "A Hole in the Head"; "A Square, A Circle, A Star"; and "Flies on the Windowsill." Indeed just as Coral Ann Howells nicely observes that "putting pressure on story titles may offer new insights" (11), so may consideration of subtitles enhance interpretation. The first of these subtitles involves a playful and original twist on the popular or folk expression, "Give it a rest." In the context of the novella's action, the opening subtitle anticipates the moment in the first part when the work's focal character, Nancy, is preparing to settle in to her daily reading of Dante's *The Divine Comedy*, the first title selected for discussion by her small-town, lake-side, evidently Southwestern Ontario book group, and is interrupted by her next-door-neighbour and soon-to-be fiancé, Wilf. Having arrived to invite Nancy to go for a drive and upon being told initially that she can't go because she needs to keep up with her reading for their book group, Wilf affectionately chastises her, "'Give Dante a rest for a while'" (277). Wilf's statement advances an opposing or balancing position about the significance of honouring all parts of one's life instead of focussing on creating literature or reading it or for that matter writing about it.

The line "'Give Dante a rest for a while'" (277) addressed by Wilf to Nancy is casual and cordial in tone, an element of the conversational or oral dimension that Dennis Duffy rightly emphasizes as being crucial to Munro's writing from the first story, "Walker Brothers Cowboy," of Munro's first collection, *Dance of the Happy Shades* (1968), onwards ("Too Little Geography; Too Much History" 212). Wilf's line, therefore, can be said to be part of the realistic texture that many readers and critics expect of an Alice Munro story, even if that's not all we should expect. Seeing fiction in the light of Realism, indeed guided towards this view by the cover art chosen for the first Canadian editions of Munro's work starting with Ken Danby's *Sunbather, 1972* for *Who Do You Think You Are?* (1978) and by that chosen for other world editions, many readers and critics would agree that a perfect analogy to the form and technique and style of Munro's work can be found in the mode of painting identified by Paul Duval as "high realism." Or, to employ a term introduced in an essay by Hugh Hood: "super-realism" – with "super" being used, as Hood confirmed to me, in the Latin sense of "*super*" or "coming from above" (Hood in Struthers, "An Interview with Hugh Hood" 76). Specifically, work in the style of American painter Edward Hopper, an artist praised by Munro herself in early interviews by John Metcalf and Graeme Gibson, or in the style of Canadian painters including Southwestern Ontarian Jack Chambers and Newfoundlander Mary Pratt. Or work by George A. Reid, Munro's fellow Wingham-area-born artist and Principal from 1912 to 1918 of the Central Ontario School of Art and Design (later OCAD University), a catalogue of Reid's work having been produced by Christine Boyanski under the intriguing title *Sympathetic Realism*.

Yet as compelling in and of itself as we may regard such painting, and as apt an analogy to the form and technique and style of Munro's writing as we may regard it, the case needs to be made that at least as strong an analogy to Munro's writing can be found in painting designated as semi-abstract or abstract. To take an early-twentieth-century example:

the art of Southwestern Ontario-born David Milne, whose fascinating watercolour *Relaxation* (1916) – a semi-abstract metafictive painting that depicts two women engaged in two different artistic practices, one on the viewer's left reading and another on the viewer's right painting – is a work that I recommended, with the strong approval of John Metcalf, as the cover art for our anthology of short stories *Canadian Classics* (1993). Or to take an early-twenty-first-century example: the art of Guelph, Ontario resident, OCAD University President from 2000 to 2005, and my good friend of thirty years, Ron Shuebrook, whose powerful abstract paintings *Levels* (2017) and *Glimpse* (2017) I recommended as the cover art, respectively, for *Alice Munro Country* and *Alice Munro Everlasting*.

As Roald Nasgaard brilliantly observes in his study *Abstract Painting in Canada*: "Shuebrook's paintings open themselves up to imaginative visual wandering, to narratives of pictorial events and to associative content" (269) – a creative process just like the imaginative workings on us as we read Alice Munro's stories. Comments that Nasgaard quotes from artist John Clark, who describes Shuebrook's painting as "an abstraction *from* the world, a distillation *of* experience as distinct from purely formal investigations of structure and design, made with a detached attitude" (269; emphasis added), again bear closely on our understanding of Munro's writing. Nasgaard rightly emphasizes of Shuebrook's paintings, precisely as we recognize about Munro's stories, that they are "not preconceived but found in the making" (269). In like manner, we ourselves in our responses to such works can attain new knowledge, new understanding, even wisdom, not through depending on preconceived structures of ideas (call these "political positions," "theoretical approaches," what you will) but through our own new fully imagined forms of engagement and making.

To this end, Munro's choice of the subtitle "Give Dante a Rest" for the opening part of "Powers" provides a strong if ironic, a serious if witty metafictive direction to read her work *not* as Realism in the way that many readers including as deservedly esteemed a critic as George Woodcock or as deservedly esteemed a critic as W.J. Keith or even as justly renowned a scholar as Munro's biographer Robert Thacker have seemed inclined to do. That is, Munro's writing needs to be read *not so limitedly as* resembling the kind of painting presented in *High Realism in Canada* by Paul Duval (as much as Munro admires this mode), *but more expansively as* resembling the kind of painting presented in *Abstract Painting in Canada* by Roald Nasgaard. George Woodcock apparently approached the same conclusion, making arguments in two separate essays for the one view and then for the other: in the more well-known instance developing a case for seeing Munro as a Realist and then in a less well-known instance suggesting that her work could be viewed more like abstract painting.

Carefully considered, then, each of Munro's stories needs to be seen as being at least as much about, or certainly dependent upon, the equivalents to the lines, the shapes, the colours, the proportions, the organization in abstract or allegorical paintings such as Ron Shuebrook's *Levels* and *Glimpse* as it is about, or certainly dependent upon, anything of a supposedly realistic or representational nature in her stories. And I make that statement as a devoted Southwestern Ontario regionalist for whom travelling "Once More to the Lake" (as E.B. White first wrote) in order to resituate myself, to reclaim myself, in Alice Munro Country represents the supreme mythic and personal journey – except, of course for immersing myself in the still greater reality of Alice Munro Country that we experience through reading her work. Let us say, then, echoing the headings of several chapters in Francine Prose's wonderfully instructive book *Reading Like a Writer*, that Munro's art is essentially and profoundly about "Words," about "Sentences," about "Paragraphs," about "Narration," that Munro's art is about what, following modern short story theory pioneer Mary Rohrberger echoing Poe, we might call the sense of "Design" to which such elements, and our interactions with them, give rise.

Consequently I would argue that all of Munro's stories, including "Powers," need to be read *not simply as* Realism, but as examples of "visionary realism," to adopt the term used about William Blake's poetry and art by W.B. Yeats in an essay, appropriately in the context of Munro's "Powers," on Blake's illustrations to Dante's *The Divine Comedy* (Yeats 121). That is to say, Munro's stories need to be read as Allegory – the way that James Carscallen's epic study of Munro's *oeuvre* up to 1990, *The Other Country: Patterns in the Writing of Alice Munro*, seems to me to do, the way that such essays as Mirosława Buchholtz's "Pseudo-Longinus and the Affective Theory in Alice Munro's Stories about Childhood," William Butt's "Southwestern Ontario, the Narrator, and 'Words with Power' in Alice Munro's 'Meneseteung'," Miriam Marty Clark's "Allegories of Reading in Alice Munro's 'Carried Away'," Dennis Duffy's "Alice Munro's Narrative

Historicism: 'Too Much Happiness'," W.R. Martin and Warren U. Ober's "Alice Munro as Small-Town Historian: 'Spaceships Have Landed'," W.H. New's "Utrecht Allegory," and K.P. Stich's "Munro's Grail Quest: The Progress of Logos" do, and as I also propose in "Traveling with Munro: Reading 'To Reach Japan'." Every Munro story represents a many-levelled Allegory in which the literal, the autobiographical, the realistic, the dramatic serve as the base. Every Munro story moves in the way Ian Rae finds that "Walker Brothers Cowboy" (for Reg Thompson and many others, a key Munro work) moves as it proceeds: "from an empirical mode ... to a more ... mythopoeic mode" (61) – that is, from Realism to Mythopoeia. Munro *not as* – or certainly *not simply as* – Social Historian or Realist or Autobiographer. But rather: Munro as Symbolist, Mythopoeist, Allegorist. A conception that Northrop Frye's biographer, John Ayre, James Reaney, Catherine Sheldrick Ross, William Butt, and I would all associate with Frye's method for reading the Bible, Shakespeare, Blake, and Canadian writing. Ultimately, we need to read Alice Munro's stories in the way that James Reaney suggests we alter our reading of nineteenth-century Ontario newspapers from a search for facts to a search for myths. In short, we need to read Munro as we would read Joyce. Or, indeed, Dante.

ACT ONE: Give Dante a Rest

The first part of "Powers" is comprised of eight diary entries (L.M. Montgomery's biographer, Mary Henley Rubio, might very well call them "Montgomery-esque" diary entries) written by Nancy and dating from March 13, 1927 to June 11, 1927. The opening lines are solidly set in Realism, specifically in an all-too-Canadian complaint about a lengthy winter, a time of year, Hugh Hood and I used to say to each other only half-jokingly, that lasts six months, from 1 November to 30 April, Hugh's birthday, this being why the other three seasons seem so short, only two months apiece, because they are! The novella's initial sentences state: "March 13, 1927. Now we get the winter, just when we are supposed to be in sight of spring. Big storms closing off the roads, schools shut down. And some old fellow they say went for a walk out the tracks and is likely frozen. Today I went in my snowshoes right down the middle of the street and there was not a mark but mine on the snow. And by the time

I got back from the store my tracks were entirely filled in. This is because of the lake not being frozen as usual and the wind out of the west picking up loads of moisture and dumping down on us as snow" (270). For some readers, this passage may resemble, and may be thought to echo, the justly-renowned passage about "the snow falling faintly through the universe and faintly falling, like the descent of their last end, upon all the living and the dead" (194) with which Joyce ends his novella "The Dead," a work that I believe Munro revisits at various points from her first collection to her last, from the stories "The Time of Death" and "Dance of the Happy Shades" through to the story "To Reach Japan" – just as she alludes to Joyce's story "A Little Cloud" in her story "Differently."

The repeated emphasis at the opening of "Powers" on "snow," used to end two different sentences, then on "tracks," is designed to invite us to contemplate the significance of these two words as metaphors for the particular qualities of the novella's narration. In the first diary entry Nancy describes making a trek to the store on a day of heavy snow and meeting there a friend of hers from high-school days, Tessa Netterby, whom Nancy portrays in a way that underlines what Harold Bloom and Daphne Marlatt would call the true complex "ficticity," as opposed to any supposed simple "facticity," of Munro's writing. Tessa "was all wrapped up in a big shawl and she looked like something out of a storybook" (270-71), Nancy reflects, leading us to think not only of children's stories and very possibly fairy tales appropriate to this child-like figure but also perhaps of Cynthia Ozick's emotionally wrenching story "The Shawl," a work that I see Oriana Palusci views as having influenced Munro's later story "Dimensions" (112-13). And while Tessa certainly seems to be a child-like figure, at the same time she appears, as Wilf's cousin Ollie thinks, "old for her years" (290) – an ancient, even timeless, near-mythical, even allegorical figure.

Read as metaphor or symbol, then, the wording of the very beginning of Munro's "Powers" – the first complete sentence, "Now we get the winter, just when we are supposed to be in sight of spring" followed by the emphatic phrase that starts the next sentence, "Big storms" (270) – provides a disturbing omen of what Munro in the closing sentence of the last story, "Vandals," of her collection *Open Secrets* (1994) describes as "darkness collecting" (294). Even the use of the number 13 here in the first date given, March 13, 1927 (though that specific date did not fall on a Friday the 13th but on a Sunday), conveys ominous possibilities because the number 13 frequently symbolizes bad luck. The topic of good luck – and its dark alternative – is introduced frequently as the novella proceeds. In this first part, for example, Nancy describes herself, now as Wilf's bride-to-be, taking an appointed ritualistic turn stirring the mix for her wedding cake "for good luck" (279). Yet this action is followed by Ollie surreptitiously intervening when the fairy-tale-like or nursery-rhyme-like cake-maker isn't looking – this scene, significantly, being Ollie's first appearance in the work – in order to take a turn stirring the mix (both literally and metaphorically, we soon realize), leading Nancy to speculate, and us to wonder too, "What kind of luck that will bring I do not know" (279). Nancy's father considers Ollie's arrival in town to be "'a real stroke of luck'" (281), by which he means good luck. Yet Munro's deliberately ambiguous omission before "luck" of "good" or "bad" (the sort of pairing that encourages reading the novella as allegory), along with her use of the term "stroke" which medically speaking involves something wholly undesirable, leaves the nature of the luck Ollie brings with him at best uncertain and conceivably ominous.

Other details in "Powers" are purely funny, as in the passage where Munro describes the formation of the local reading club. One member opposes the group's beginning with *The Divine Comedy* because he mistakenly thinks it is in Latin, not translated from Italian into English, and wishes to avoid repeating his high-school experience taking Latin from a teacher whom Munro merrily names Miss Hurt. More seriously, however, *The Divine Comedy* is characterized by Nancy as "not much of a comedy" (273), thereby anticipating the darker colouring of much of Munro's novella, despite various instances of pronounced comedy. The description "not much of a comedy" represents a cautionary remark meant to guide us towards carefully assessing the ambiguities in tone of Munro's own work for further hints of "darkness collecting." Hence, even if the novella seems on the surface to maintain a generally comic tone, as in the series of April Fool's jokes reported by Nancy, we need to make sure to look beneath that. Accordingly, might we not look beneath the surface of Nancy's comment about her April Fool's joke on Wilf – "Now comes the part I am not so anxious to record" (274) – and see this as standing for something very serious, for a larger pattern of feelings that Nancy would rather conceal, even at times from herself?

Upon close examination, we are able to see deeper meanings lying beneath surface statements in this story like tell-tale tracks beneath the snow. Thus when Nancy at the start of her May 30 diary entry says "I have not written in here for so long because I am in a whirlwind of things that have to be done" (278) in the short time up to her marriage to Wilf on July 10, 1927 – an inside joke on Munro's part since that date coincides with her own birthdate four years later – are we meant to consider Nancy's statement to be the complete truth, or even the most important truth, about what she is feeling? Or could she have another reason for not writing in her diary for over six weeks from April 14 until May 30? Such as Nancy's not wishing to admit even to herself that she has been experiencing a far deeper concern – about whether she should have accepted Wilf's proposal, about whether she would have preferred to marry someone not so forbiddingly serious as he is, someone wishing, like herself, "to have a little fun" (275) in their life together, someone more like Ollie we might surmise – with the playful but devious nature of Ollie's character being suggested by the probable allusion, in the name chosen for him by Munro, to the widely known if sometimes varied line "Ollie Ollie in come free!" from the children's game of hide-and-seek. Ollie believes – and we may find ourselves agreeing – that, unlike himself, Wilf "in his stolid, ordinary way" (284) seems unable to enjoy and even to perceive what is most exciting about, most important about Nancy's being. Could foreknowledge of the difficulties, the darkness facing her in marrying Wilf be the true "whirlwind" (278) that is swirling around Nancy?

Further intimations of the darkness and the mysteriousness gathering beneath apparently ordinary events or human consciousness or the act of narration may be detected in the final diary entry dated June 10, where, in another effort by Munro to encourage us to look beneath the surface, we are presented with Nancy's observation that sometimes when Wilf comes over to her father's home in the evening "he goes and sits at the piano and plays by ear" (282). Munro then adds, hauntingly, "In the dark, maybe" (282) – a line which brings to mind a comment that Munro made about herself, "I work in the dark" (Munro qtd. in Ross, *Alice Munro: A Double Life* 84). Importantly, playing by ear, if considered metaphorically or symbolically, suggests that there is a level of human understanding on which art can operate that rises above the written or printed word. This higher level is symbolized and underlined in different collections by Munro, as Megan LaPierre convincingly argues, through the special emphasis that she gives to music in those books' last stories – "Dance of the Happy Shades," "My Mother's Dream," and, I would add, "Powers" – in no small part by placing those stories last.

Another time, we are told in this last section of "Give Dante a Rest," Nancy catches Ollie quietly singing the words to the piece that Wilf is playing: "'Morning is dawning and Peer Gynt is yawning'" (283), Ollie sings, something that Nancy does not recognize. And so "I made him spell it. P-e-e-r G-y-n-t" (283). This interchange would seem to have an above-ordinary significance, like Auntie's spelling of the word "C-E-L-E-B-R-A-T-E" in the story named "Spelling" from *Who Do You Think You Are?* (1978), if one associates casting a spell with individuals possessing magical powers, such as Tessa, or Munro herself. Very interestingly, Munro, unlike Nancy, knew Henrik Ibsen's five-act dramatic poem *Peer Gynt* (and, we may assume, the accompanying music, including "Morning Mood," composed by Edvard Grieg) extremely well. For while she was only an undergraduate student at The University of Western Ontario, Munro had written an adaptation of *Peer Gynt* for The Players' Guild – as Robert Thacker reports Munro's eldest daughter, Sheila Munro, describing (Munro 8; Thacker 97). As employed here, I would argue, the reference to the title character of *Peer Gynt*, whom others accuse of lying, and to the dramatic poem *Peer Gynt* itself, enhances our understanding of the complicated nature of the loveable but treacherous Ollie and our understanding of the complex world of Alice Munro's stories. As James McFarlane states of *Peer Gynt*, "All is an aspect of a single reality/fantasy continuum, wherein fact is a function of fiction, invention of experience, and lies and life are one" (xii).

Mysteriously, at the very end of "Give Dante a Rest," Munro has Nancy write: "Good-bye Diary at least for the present. I used to have a feeling something really unusual would occur in my life, and it would be important to have recorded everything. Was that just a feeling?" (283). Can Nancy's sense that she would experience "something really unusual" be dismissed as "just a feeling" – or will something of this nature be revealed to her or at least to us later, say in some final redemptive scene that, while reading, we co-experience with her? And will we be *shown* it or, more powerfully, will we be invited to *imagine* it?

ACT TWO: *Girl in a Middy*

The second part of "Powers" – except for a surprising last section that takes the form of four letters – is told in third-person-limited narrative point of view (limited in this case by and large to Wilf's cousin Ollie) – but expanding to include what is said by others such as Nancy and what is inferred by us from all of this. Of the reliability of filtering material through Ollie, probably all that needs to be said, as Munro herself jokingly but hardly jokingly has Nancy state good-humouredly but partly seriously, is "'Don't believe a word he says'" (289). "Girl in a Middy" begins like a number of other parts of the novella on a Sunday, in this instance with an afternoon walk into the country on which Nancy takes Ollie to meet her old high-school friend, Tessa, a walk evocative of journeys made in fairy tales or myth and passing between walls of wild roses. The reference to wild roses may recall the "garlands of roses" that Jay Macpherson tells us "decked all the house" where "the great marriage feast" of Cupid and Psyche was held (Macpherson in Frye and Macpherson 394), with the association suggesting the possibility of regarding Nancy and Ollie as corresponding to those mythical figures and as perhaps eventually enjoying a romantic relationship of their own.

The subtitle used here refers to Tessa, who is first seen wearing a schoolgirl-like "odd costume – a middy blouse and skirt" (289), which we subsequently come to see as being in stark contrast to the warlike attire she puts on in the dream-vision that Nancy has of Tessa and Ollie in the fifth and final part of the novella. Although Tessa is only later represented as a potentially tragic figure, the choice of her name at once recalls that of the tragic heroine of Thomas Hardy's *Tess of the d'Urbervilles*, a novel that I believe to be one of Munro's favourite literary works and a source for the title of her later novella "Too Much Happiness" (Struthers, "Song for Alice Munro" 94). As the innocent but prescient "Girl in a Middy," Tessa becomes renowned, first locally, then more widely, for her mysterious yet illuminating capacity as a seer; indeed as Marianne Micros has suggested to me, the "middy" of Tessa's apparel, a word highlighted by this part's subtitle, may very well be meant to evoke the term "medium." Understood fully, Tessa closely resembles the wise-woman or prophetess of Classical Myth and Biblical Myth, "the prophetic *vǫlva*" of Old Norse Myth to use Ursula Dronke's term (28), who possesses the powers to divine and to convey not only knowledge but also wisdom that others do not. As Nancy said of Tessa in the novella's first part, "she is not in the world that the rest of us are in" (271).

When Nancy and Ollie arrive at Tessa's house, she requests their indulgence – having previously been interrupted in her domestic work by a visitor requiring a "reading" of a different sort from the kind in which we are engaged, namely a psychic reading – in order that she can finish churning the butter. An everyday realistic activity, involving the transformation of one product, cow's milk, into another, butter, we first think before recognizing this detail's second function as a metaphor for the process by which Munro transforms life into art. Moreover, the place where Tessa has Nancy help her take the butter introduces a further key metaphor – one that Munro returns to and develops in the next part of the novella. For as Ollie continued to watch he saw that once the two women had finished making the butter, "Tessa lifted a door in the floor" so that they could carry the butter "down some cellar steps he wouldn't have known were there" (290) – exactly as we as readers do not at first see or understand various elements here. In addition to possessing a suggestive dramatic association with the trapdoor on a theatre stage, the "door in the floor" serves as a metaphor for how Alice Munro's stories – indeed individual passages or lines or phrases in her stories – work: opening to deeper registers, to unknown meanings. As we continue reading, we need to keep in mind the trapdoor in Tessa's kitchen floor as a metaphor for the novella's additional levels (to recall the title of one of Ron Shuebrook's paintings) only glimpsed (to echo the title of the other of Ron Shuebrook's paintings) by different characters and by ourselves later, if at all. Levels that involve the true motives for, or the possible implications of, what is said and done; levels that involve multiple ways in which Munro's writing can be interpreted other than on the surface level, the literal or dramatic level, the realistic or representational level, on which the words first strike us.

Ollie becomes involved in the visit when Nancy asks Tessa to demonstrate her psychic powers to him by revealing the contents of his pockets. Tessa's identification of one particular item, a clipping inviting contributions to a magazine, so distresses Ollie that he lies about how and why he acquired it, attributing interest in the clipping to someone else rather than telling the truth that he wants it for himself. As weeks pass, Ollie's

self-admitted albeit self-admired "Scientific Curiosity" (299) takes hold
of him, leading him to return frequently to visit with Tessa. He subsequently publishes in a national magazine, *Saturday Night*, what Munro
(with a nod to deliberate points of slippage in her own handling of genre)
describes as an "article or story or whatever you call it" (297) about Tessa.
But more dramatically – and one could add more insidiously – Ollie
entices Tessa to leave town with him to travel very possibly to the United
States where he has learned there are people with substantial funding
who, in the course of treating Tessa "as a research subject," might allow
Ollie to develop a career "as a scientific journalist" (299).

While we do not realize this on a first reading, the ensuing conversation between Nancy and Ollie as they return from visiting Tessa, in
which Nancy reprimands herself by saying metaphorically "'I should
have my head kicked in'" and Ollie replies "'Not quite'" (295), anticipates
the strong suggestion in the next part of the novella of how Tessa will
in the years ahead experience something "'Not quite'" like having her
"'head kicked in'" literally but something all too close to the equivalent.
Although Nancy's "burst of contrition" (296) is only temporary, along with
being only a parody of the religious act that Munro names and therefore
a moral indictment of Nancy, Ollie's attitude is seriously troubling. Ollie's
response supplies a preview of his subsequent refusal to take responsibility for how horribly he later treats Tessa. Nancy states "'I should go and
beg her pardon'," to which Ollie answers "'I wouldn't do that'" (295) – a
reply which at first appears to be compassionate advice for Nancy, but
which, at a deeper level, represents a disturbing admission of his own
self-centredness and, we might say, amorality. The contrast between
Ollie's character or behaviour and Nancy's more limited self-centredness or moral failings is underlined when she replies "'Wouldn't you?'"
and Ollie says "'No'" (295). Nancy's raising the matter this second time
through her question, "'Wouldn't you?'," signals her sense that there
are moral issues and decisions that need to be thought about carefully,
whereas Ollie's conversation-ending reply, "'No'," firmly underlines the
unsympathetic and inflexible nature of his attitudes and actions.

"Girl in a Middy" could have ended with the conversation that Nancy
and Ollie have as they walk back from visiting with Tessa; but rather than
being the end, this scene represents what Susan Lohafer terms a "pre-
closural point" (4). For instead of finishing the second part here, Munro

proceeds with another section, set that Sunday evening at the home of Nancy's father, where Wilf is described as "playing, by ear, *Eine kleine Nachtmusik*" (296). As noted previously of his playing the piano "by ear" in the first part of the novella (282), the description here of his playing the Mozart piece "by ear" means that he wasn't reading the music – a detail emphasizing the existence of a level of activity that surpasses reading in its capacity to achieve knowledge or even wisdom. And surely Wilf's reverence for the music of Wolfgang Amadeus Mozart (and Munro's own reverence for it, as she told me once in a phone conversation when describing the desired effect of her story "Spaceships Have Landed") is meant to be reinforced by Nancy's original choice and later use of the nickname "Wolfie" for her husband. A practice that Nancy engages in, we infer, bemusedly and affectionately – though perhaps, on a deeper level, also critically and resentfully. Nancy feels that "the name suited his long jaw and thin moustache and bright stern eyes" (307), characteristics that evoke the figure of the wolf in Charles Perrault's version of the fairy tale "Little Red Riding Hood," a comparison supported by the way Wilf's personality represents a threat to Nancy's innate vigour.

Again, Munro could have ended this second part of the novella here with this scene of Wilf playing Mozart but does not. Instead, she chooses to have this part end with what I view as a sonata-like series of three letters – the first from Nancy to Ollie, the second from Ollie to Nancy, the third from Nancy to Tessa – followed by a coda, a brief message from Tessa to Nancy. Such a sonata-like structure, I have long believed, was employed very early on by Munro in the two complementary framing stories of her first collection, *Dance of the Happy Shades* (1968), the opening genesis-style coming-of-age story "Walker Brothers Cowboy," which John Metcalf similarly regards as being "sonata-like" in form (Metcalf, *The Canadian Short Story* 507), and, especially appropriately, the closing revelation-style music story "Dance of the Happy Shades" – as well as being employed, Megan LaPierre astutely observes, to form the final group of four stories in Munro's *Dear Life* (2012). Here in this second part of "Powers," one important effect of concluding with this sonata-like series of four letters written or received by Nancy is to bring readers' attention back to her as the work's focal character and the author of the eight journal entries that form the first part of the novella.

Reading Nancy's letters closely, we are able to discover more about Nancy's true feelings and motives than her words are intended to suggest or than she would readily acknowledge that they mean. Hence in Nancy's first letter, the one to Ollie, when she complains about his neglect of Wilf and herself in not writing to them even at Christmas – one of many details that reinforce the possibility of viewing "Powers" in the context of Christian allegory – Nancy's response needs to be read as her offense not at Ollie's neglect of Wilf and herself but at Ollie's neglect of her. Similarly, when Nancy complains about Ollie's (mis)representation of her home town in his magazine piece about Tessa and goes on to remark that "The main problem however is Tessa and what this will do to her life" (297), we can again surmise that Nancy is not admitting to her own real feelings. Furthermore, in Nancy's question to Ollie whether he only chose to "make use of us Prosaic People here to embark on your Career as a Writer" (298), the very simple and near-hidden word "us," in which she includes herself, represents the means by which Munro subtly suggests that for Nancy "The main problem" (297) with what Ollie has done involves her. Nancy's true objection is not to the surface-level omission in Ollie's article of any reference to her role in introducing him to Tessa, but rather to the much more profound failure on Ollie's part to follow up on his feelings for Nancy. For beneath what we are told Nancy or Ollie says or thinks about each other, there exists, we come to suspect, a much deeper set of feelings: a sense that Nancy is angry with Ollie for limiting his attention to her rather than pursuing a more sincere and lasting relationship; a sense that Ollie is sorry to see Nancy spend her life with the man she chose to marry, his cousin Wilf, rather than with someone more like himself.

The overall intensity of Nancy's letter to Ollie betrays a far different and much more personal motive, as does Munro's deliberately vague but all-encompassing use of the word "this" when Nancy then says, "I just had to get this off my chest" (298). Nancy's true feelings are underlined when she remarks to Ollie, "but what about other people?" (298), a comment that, on the surface, seems to refer to her fully conscious awareness of Ollie's self-serving treatment of Tessa, but that, deeper down, undoubtedly refers to Nancy's half-conscious sense of the casualness of Ollie's treatment of herself. The admittedly "sarcastic" (298) tone that

Nancy takes throughout her letter to Ollie, a tone that she only pretends (to him and to herself) to apologize for, betrays the profound but largely hidden (from him and from herself) emotional pain she is experiencing. Even Nancy's seemingly snide letter-ending farewell, "Well good luck Ollie, I don't expect to hear from you again. (Not that we ever had the honour of hearing from you once.)" (299) can be read alternatively as a despairing, desperate, at most half-conscious plea by Nancy for Ollie to re-establish their near-severed connection.

Nancy's second letter, the one to Tessa, goes deeper than her first, the one to Ollie; or, rather, it brings what lies in Nancy's subconsciousness much closer to the surface for her and certainly for the reader. Early in this letter she apologizes to Tessa for a particular comment, saying, "I don't mean that to sound catty" (300) – a statement that does not deny or excuse the negativity but only claims the negativity wasn't consciously intended, though we suspect it may have been meant unconsciously. Nancy goes on to state, "I am expecting a baby ... and it seems to make me very touchy and jumpy" (300), as if that is an adequate explanation for the negativity in her tone, as if that is anything other than a rationalization or, we could say, a cover, like snow. The key word used by Munro here, as Wayne C. Booth would remind us, is "seems," for the real source of the resentment unfairly displaced onto Tessa by Nancy is her own unhappiness. Munro, by inviting us to liken Wilf not only to Wolfgang Amadeus Mozart but also to the wolf in "Little Red Riding Hood," makes clear that, along with Nancy's unfulfilled relationship with Ollie, the unsatisfying nature of Nancy's marriage to Wilf is what truly troubles her.

Continuing her letter to Tessa, Nancy raises a serious concern that she has about Tessa's future based on what Nancy has heard in the letter from Ollie about his arranging to have Tessa subjected to certain scientific testing: "I do not know what kind of research he means but I must say that when I read that part of his letter it made my blood run cold" (300-01). Nancy then goes deeper if perhaps not far enough, in that she remains partly blinded to Ollie's faults by her ongoing love for him, adding, "Another thing I feel I have to tell you though I don't know how to. It is this. Ollie is certainly not a bad person but he has an effect" on others; "it is not that he does not know about this but that he does not exactly take responsibility for it" (301). Thus in his relationship with Nancy, Ollie, other than at fleeting moments, fails to match the depth of feeling that Nancy in her letter to Tessa indirectly confesses to having for him. As Nancy now advises Tessa about Ollie, barely hiding the fact that she is actually describing her own failure to comprehend the true meaning of his behaviour towards her, "he will be very friendly and natural but you might mistake the way he acts for something more than it is" (301). It is at this point that Nancy advises Tessa (and effectively admits about herself) that "To put it frankly, I cannot think of any worse fate than falling in love with him" (301).

The cheerful coda-like message from Tessa to Nancy at the end of the second part of "Powers" is of special interest, partly for something it reveals that Nancy and the readers have not known: for by the time the note arrives, Tessa expects she will be married to Ollie and likely be in the United States. But Tessa's note, if read ironically as potentially foreshadowing the opposite of its surface optimism, is of equal interest for what it seemingly unknowingly hides – like the symbolic cellar concealed by the secret door in the floor of Tessa's kitchen. Here, if we could only see it, we are offered a premonition of something much darker that for now seems to be unperceived by the letter-writer, Tessa, as well as unperceived by the letter-readers, Nancy and ourselves. Here, Tessa reassuringly but it would appear all too blithely, that is, seemingly and surprisingly without the least foreknowledge, begins her note to Nancy by saying, "Please do not worry about me" (301). Tessa herself may in fact be oblivious to her future. Or she may foresee it and be content with it, whatever happens. We, on the other hand, if we have any inclination to read Tessa's declaration ironically, find ourselves worrying about her fate – a concern shortly confirmed when Tessa's life takes on an utterly different, in many ways horrifyingly dark tone as Nancy and readers alike find out in the novella's next part, "A Hole in the Head."

ACT THREE: A Hole in the Head

The third part of "Powers" jumps forward to the Fall of 1968, forty years in the future from the events recorded in the first two parts of the story. "A Hole in the Head" recounts in third-person narrative point of view limited to Nancy a drive she makes to central Michigan in order to visit a private hospital after receiving a letter from the institution explaining that she has been listed as the contact person for one of its patients. The individual whom Nancy travels to see has been a long-time "inmate," or, rather, "a resident, as they wanted you to say" (303) euphemistically – a use, or we might say an abuse, of language that Munro in her story "The Progress of Love" pinpoints, I would argue, by giving the narrator there the name Euphemia. Very interestingly, along with having prison-like "bars" (302) on some of the windows, the hospital has, as Munro has Nancy, and ourselves, discover upon her arrival, not only "a partly aboveground cellar" (302) but also "a lower cellar" (303) – a metaphor calculated to suggest the many-levelled nature of every Alice Munro story that we read.

Nancy begins her visit by talking with the Matron, who explains that in addition to providing a place "for those who were genuinely mentally ill, or senile, or those who would never develop normally," the hospital housed "people whose families could not or would not cope with them" (304). Furthermore – and the suggestion is that this statement applies to the individual about whom Nancy is contacted – "The Matron said that people had been here for years who perhaps didn't belong here" (304). The hospital is going to be shut down because of its long history of fraudulent use of public finances. And as a result, Nancy learns, "The serious cases were going to a big facility in Flint or Lansing ... and some could go into sheltered housing, group homes" (305). But also, the Matron states invitingly and not so subtly, "there were some who could manage if they were placed with relatives" (305). It is only at this point, nearly four pages into the third part of the novella, that Munro at last mentions by name the "inmate" or "resident" (303) whom Nancy's trip involves: "Tessa was considered to be one of these" (305).

Nancy was sent the letter because she was listed, the Matron says, in the hospital's records amongst "'the names that were given as relatives'," though Nancy promptly refutes this statement with the declaration "'I am not a relative'" (304), thereby establishing her distance, at least as Nancy sees it, from any responsibility for Tessa. Ironically in our view, this negative response by Nancy exhibits the same failing, morally, to "take responsibility" (301) for which Nancy had criticized Ollie in her letter to Tessa. Accordingly, when the Matron refers back to Nancy's assertion that she is not a relative of Tessa's and concludes, "'That means you don't intend to take her'," we are not altogether surprised, though we are dismayed, when Nancy seeks to excuse herself from this responsibility by claiming that she already has plenty of work of this kind taking care of the now deteriorating Wilf: "'I have a husband who is – he would be in a place like this, I guess, but I am looking after him at home'" (305). This dubious position Nancy weakly repeats when she talks with Tessa: "'It's not anything to do with you, Tessa. It's just that I've got Wilf'" (311).

When the Matron adds about Tessa, "'so I suppose you are not interested now in seeing her?'" (305), Nancy replies that the opposite is the case – with the key word spoken by the Matron being "now" in the sense that Nancy, having clarified to the hospital that she will not take responsibility for Tessa, is "now" ready to visit with her. Moreover, Nancy's statement – "'Yes, I am. That's what I came for'" (305) – leads readers to wonder if, metaphorically, the second part of the comment doesn't involve, like the two cellars in the hospital building, something "aboveground" (302) that is stated but false, along with something "lower" (303) that is unadmitted but true. Wasn't Nancy's main purpose in making this trip to find out, and to refute, any claims on Tessa's behalf that the hospital might try to impose on Nancy? And wasn't Nancy's distancing herself from any legal responsibility, if not from her moral responsibility, for Tessa, what let Nancy feel ready to see her? As well, couldn't there have been some concern or at least curiosity on Nancy's part about what had happened to Tessa over the preceding forty years that Nancy hoped would be resolved by conversing with her? And couldn't there have been something more specific that Nancy hoped would be answered, maybe something not directly involving Tessa at all, such as what had happened to Ollie?

To see Tessa, Nancy is directed to the bakery, where Tessa has been serving as the baker for years. There Nancy finds Tessa making blueberry pies, with the baking and the pies evoking (it would seem ironically) a world of fairy tales, and her helper, Elinor, making what are variously called "Little dough mice" (309), "'mousies'" (310), and finally "'Elinor's blind mice'" (312), evoking (it would seem ironically) a world of nursery rhymes. The seeming innocence sometimes assumed to be the essence of fairy tales or nursery rhymes appears in some ways appropriate to the character of Tessa and Elinor and other such inmates of hospitals in Michigan and elsewhere; hence, witnessing Tessa's smile, Nancy thinks of her as almost superhumanly possessing "Not exactly superiority, but

an extraordinary, unwarranted benevolence" (311) – the benevolence
we might associate with a compassionate God of The New Testament.
Yet the darker depths rightly identified by Bruno Bettelheim and Jack
Zipes and other modern readers of fairy tales and nursery rhymes offer
a truer insight into the suffering to which these people are subjected
and over which they sometimes heroically triumph.

Together, Nancy and Tessa discuss Wilf, Ollie, the awful history of
Tessa at the hospital, and then – Tessa having urged that they "'forget
all we were talking about'" (310) – turn to chatting about Nancy's children. Thereafter, at Nancy's insistence, they briefly discuss Tessa's psychic powers. Of these Tessa says, "'I just pretended'," to which Nancy
answers, "'You couldn't have'," at which point Tessa, wishing to end this
for her very painful part of the conversation, declares, in a comment that
reinforces the importance of the subtitle here, "'It bothers my head'" –
meaning both literally and metaphorically – "'to talk about it'" (311).
To this Nancy, perhaps merely politely but it would seem with genuine
empathy, replies, "'I'm sorry'" (311).

Tessa tells Nancy about a dream in which, seemingly as a result of
Tessa's apparently continuing psychic powers, she witnessed Ollie's
death: "'Oh, I saw him. He had his head wrapped up in a black coat.
Tied with a cord around the neck. Somebody did it to him. … Somebody
should have gone to the electric chair'" (309). Or perhaps this was a
wish-fulfilment dream of Tessa's symbolizing the fate she believed Ollie
deserved as a consequence of his uncaring treatment of her. Whatever
prompts Tessa's claim, it seems dubious literally, if not suspect symbolically, on account of Wilf and Nancy not having heard anything of
the sort. Reasonably, Nancy responds, "'Maybe that was a bad dream
you had. You might have got your dream mixed up with what really
happened'" (309).

Yet alternatively it is surely appropriate to regard Tessa's dream as
a dream-vision comprised of aspects that can best be experienced and
understood poetically in terms of the force and the significance of its
images, as John Metcalf argues so compellingly in his essays on Munro's
stories "Walker Brothers Cowboy" and "Images" contained in his critical
masterpiece, his anatomy of criticism, *The Canadian Short Story*. For elements of Tessa's dream do relate to other details in "Powers": the black
head-covering, which we subsequently learn was part of the apparatus

employed by Ollie with volunteers from the audience in the psychic shows, as well as likely symbolizing the punishment by death that Tessa presumably felt Ollie deserved, and the electric chair, which almost certainly represents an analogue for Tessa's electroshock treatments.

In any event, it's highly intriguing that Tessa can't seem to remember or else wishes to forget the name of someone – "'That man'" (308) – with whom she was so completely involved for years and who was responsible for arranging her incarceration in the hospital in Michigan and by extension responsible for all she has suffered there. Could Tessa's forgetting Ollie's name be a result of gaps in her memory produced by surgical experimentation on her head? For Tessa tells Nancy (and we have no reason to interpret this statement as being other than literally true), "'I had a hole in my head. I had it for a long time'" (309). Or does Tessa so intensely want to forget the horrors for her perpetrated by Ollie through his self-serving action of getting her institutionalized that she has repressed his very name?

What is most riveting about this dream is the possibility that understandable feelings deep in Tessa, repressed feelings of immense anger, might have led her to dream of Ollie suffering this fate. Contradicting what Tessa testifies both here and at the end of this scene – that Ollie must be dead – is the conclusion that readers may reach upon contemplating another interpretation of the surface remarks innocently made by Tessa when Nancy prepares to depart. For the novella's readers, if not for Tessa or for Nancy, there is clearly a double meaning, something "partly aboveground" (302) and something "lower" (303), like the hospital's two cellars, to the statement "'If he wasn't dead, ... why wouldn't he have come here and got me? He said he would'" (312). Affectionately disposed to Ollie as Nancy typically is except when she is angry at him, Nancy naively accepts the logic that if Tessa has remained in the hospital, then Ollie must be dead: "Of course she should have thought of Ollie's being dead if Tessa was here" (308). But an alternative interpretation surfaces as we keep thinking: an interpretation that takes Tessa's remarks as ironically hinting at something very different, something very unsettling. Namely, that Ollie might be alive and has chosen not to keep his promise to come for Tessa, or very possibly lied when he made that promise, leaving her confined, horribly, in this institution not for weeks or months or a year but for decades.

Nancy learns from Tessa that – aside from her electroshock treatments or "'shock *therapy*'" (305) as the Matron euphemistically says – "'They gave me the needles and the gas too. It was to cure my head. And to make me not remember. Certain things I do remember, but I have trouble with telling how long ago'" (309). Tessa finishes her description of this ordeal – no, that isn't strong enough; make that *this torture* – by adding another statement about just how far in that era and, it's terrifying to think, very possibly even now, "Scientific Curiosity" will go in the name of what Ollie has falsely described as "research of a legitimate nature" (299). "'There was that hole in my head for a very long time'" (309), Tessa reiterates convincingly. On first encountering the subtitle "A Hole in the Head" our response may well be to associate the phrase with its popular comic and metaphorical meaning designating something laughably unnecessary, such as when one says "You need that like you need a hole in the head." However, in this case the subtitle chosen also has a tragic and all too literal meaning that we realize upon recalling the research experiments on human subjects such as Tessa which left them literally with "A Hole in the Head." The treatment of Tessa makes a lasting statement about how far "Scientific Curiosity" will go not only in pursuing research but also in covering up any damage done by that research – covering this up in the manner of the heavy Joyce-like snowfall at the beginning of Munro's novella.

What I haven't told you yet is why Munro's account of the wholly unwarranted institutionalization and vicious medical treatment of Tessa exerts such a hold on me. But first, perhaps, I should request your indulgence for my writing here in a manner that I call "Making It Personal" – for writing in a way that, as John Metcalf says of Munro's story "Images," allows us access both as writers and as readers to "gifts from the dark" (Metcalf, "The Signs of Invasion" 598) – instead of choosing to set fierce boundaries in order to keep my writing style purely (dare I say "merely"?) academic. As I have come to see this endeavour both by myself and by others of all ages whom I take pride in encouraging, "Making It Personal" – whether it takes the form of personal testimony or a poem or a joke or a lament such as I will offer here – serves to expand, to deepen, to make more powerful any critical writing. And didn't Wallace Stevens remark in his "Adagia" that "One reads poetry with one's nerves" (162)?

I'm thinking at this moment of a near-devastating time in my own family history (I'm an only child) during my late adolescence. It's a story that until now I have had the courage to confide only to my bride of forty-five years, poet and short story writer and critic and now-retired English professor Marianne Micros, and our two daughters, Eleni and Joy. But after all, doesn't the act of reading Munro's stories require you to enter what, speaking in her brief essay "What Is Real?" of the sort of "house" (332) that each of her stories resembles, she calls "the black room at the centre of the house with all other rooms leading to and away from it" (334)? And doesn't the act of reading her stories require that you be truthful about all that you experience physically and emotionally and imaginatively there, that you be truthful about all that you go on feeling after being transported there?

A little over fifty years ago, during my late adolescence, my own mother found herself struggling not only with the immense grief she experienced following her mother's recent death but also with the effects of over-exerting herself for months prior to that while nursing my grandmother in our home in London, Ontario. As a result, my mother had been institutionalized, upon the recommendation of her doctor, and with the consent of my father, for several weeks at The London Psychiatric Hospital, where she was subjected to the same so-called "'shock *therapy*'" (305) as Tessa received. And when that didn't work for my mother (I say "didn't work" with the utmost irony, with the utmost contempt), it was thought that maybe something more radical might be the only possible "cure" (and again I use "cure" with the utmost irony, with the utmost contempt to describe this horrifying practice). Namely, the identical treatment – "'a hole in my head'" (309) – to which Tessa was subjected. The fate which Tennessee Williams' sister Rose suffered when she was incarcerated and which George Elliott Clarke in his essay on *Lives of Girls and Women* has suggested awaits the character Blanche DuBois in Williams' *A Streetcar Named Desire* when she is seized for institutionalization at that play's end.

And that is why the term "a lobotomy" – and Munro's account here in the third section of "Powers" – registers so forcefully for me. For without my fierce and decisive protest, that's very likely what would have been done to my gentle, lovely, caring mother in her mid-to-late-forties because of my father's desperation, his lack of knowledge, and his trust in medical opinion – thereby denying my dear mother, if that had happened, the full experience of all the soul-lifting moments of a life that would eventually extend, happily for all our family, for another forty years. "But you're only talking about a story," some might say of Munro's "Powers." Or, even, "But you're only talking about a lobotomy." Hence, if the point still needs emphasizing, the importance in an essay like this of a story like mine.

ACT FOUR: A Square, A Circle, A Star

The fourth part of the novella is told in third-person narrative point of view largely limited to Nancy and set a few years later in the early 1970s. Nancy, now age sixty-seven, upon returning from a cruise by way of Vancouver following the death about a year earlier of her husband, Wilf, experiences a series of three encounters or tests reminiscent of archetypal or allegorical patterns of three from ancient myth and fairy tales onwards. While the first encounter approaches, even enters, what Munro later in this part describes as "the realm of frivolity" (323), it also has a more serious function in reinforcing the idea and the device of prophecy carrying through the novella, including the "fortune-telling, or mind reading, or telepathy, or psychic entertainment" (324) provided by Tessa and Ollie during their years on the road and Munro's own use of details that can be seen, if only retrospectively, to anticipate others.

Initially, Nancy is confronted by a boy and a girl who solemnly invite her to purchase "a tiny scroll of paper"; when Nancy asks if it contains "her fortune," the girl replies "'Perhaps'" but the boy counters with "'It contains wisdom'" (313). On the surface, Munro presents the scene as if any wisdom that might be involved were no more than frivolity. In actuality, however, the seemingly silly reference to "'wisdom'" may be meant not so much to underline the "frivolity" and perhaps even the falseness of what is apparently unfolding realistically before us, but more to suggest something serious and true: a new level of knowledge that Nancy is striving to achieve. Seeing the scene and, more broadly, the entire novella in this way gives rise to an appreciation of "Powers" as an example of "wisdom literature" in the tradition of The Book of Job, which I consider to be the ur-form of the modern short story (Struthers, "In Search of the Perfect Metaphor" 191n2). For as ridiculous as it may seem, realistically, that the boy and the girl, when asked their names by

Nancy, would identify themselves as "'Adam and Eve'" (313), these names do serve a serious purpose: to remind us of the far greater mythic or allegorical or abstract dimension of what we are reading.

Nancy's second, darker encounter occurs without preparation when she peers through the window at "A hole-in-the-wall café" (313) – a phrase surely meant to recall the abhorrent surgical procedure identified by Tessa in "A Hole in the Head" – and sees "an angry-looking, wrinkled-up, almost teary creature with thin hair blowing back from her cheeks and forehead" (314). Shocked, Nancy recognizes the woman as herself. We are then told, in a line that reinforces the novella's dream motif: "It was as bad as those dreams in which she might find herself walking down the street in her nightgown, or nonchalantly wearing only the top of her pajamas" (314). The comparison brings to mind a powerful scene from a book that John Metcalf has reported Munro telling him greatly influenced her, Sherwood Anderson's *Winesburg, Ohio* (Metcalf, *What Is A Canadian Literature?* 86), the scene in which Alice Hindman runs naked down the sidewalk in front of her house in the rain.

In this second encounter, Nancy, thoroughly distressed at seeing the bedraggled image of herself in the mirror-like café window, reflects that "she had never had a jolt like this, a moment during which she saw not just some old and new trouble spots, or some decline that could not be ignored any longer, but a complete stranger" (314). And as noted emphatically in the single-sentence paragraph that follows: "Somebody she didn't know and wouldn't want to know" (314). In response to this revelation, Nancy self-consciously alters her expression and "promptly began to cast around for hope, as if there was not a minute to lose" (314). Thinking that she badly needs to buy some new cosmetics to improve her appearance, she turns around to head for the drugstore she has seen, crossing the street in order "not to have to pass by Adam-and-Eve again" (314) – the repetition of the names of that far-from-mythical pair at once extending the comic tone existing on the novella's surface and stressing the potential for reading "Powers" as allegory. And at this point, whether by chance or by fate, Nancy has her third and most consequential encounter.

Looking down the street, Nancy sees that "Another old person was coming along the sidewalk. A man.... // She knew almost right away. It was Ollie. But she stopped dead, having a considerable reason for believing that this could not be true. // *Ollie. Alive. Ollie*" (315). The encounter with Ollie is of course very much a surprise for Nancy because Tessa has convinced her that he is dead. Yet here the words chosen, and the emphasis afforded by italicizing them, reveals, on Nancy's part, astonishment, excitement, and hope. When Nancy sees Ollie walking towards her, Nancy's first reaction is, surprisingly, said to be "a moment of terror," though the expression exhibited on her face, as incomplete as it may be, is "pretty much the same as the expression on his. Incredulity, hilarity, apology" (315). A question is raised: "What was the apology about?" (315). And possible answers are suggested, though we may find these answers less than satisfactory: "The fact that they had not parted as friends, that they had never been in touch with each other in all these years? Or for the changes that had taken place in each of them, the way they had to present themselves now, no hope for it" (315).

Here we may suspect that we are being invited to add another statement beginning with "Or...," that we are being asked to provide a different answer not only to what an apology of one kind or another would be for but also to why an apology by one person or the other might be appropriate. At this point we may also find ourselves wondering – especially as we ponder the respective extents of Nancy's and Ollie's present feelings for one another – what exactly might be meant by the word "it" in the sentence-ending, paragraph-ending phrase "no hope for it" (315). Could this be a reference to the wholly relaxed intimacy that they once shared decades earlier – for example, in the scene where they sat together talking outside Tessa's house and refreshing themselves through their ritualistic drinking of the well water?

Speaking together again so many years later at a Japanese restaurant chosen by Ollie undoubtedly in the interest of secrecy, Nancy learns details about the earliest scientific experiments on Tessa using the "special ESP cards, with their own symbols" (322), which, we now realize, provided the basis for the subtitle, "A Square, A Circle, A Star," of this part of the novella. In addition, Ollie provides Nancy with details of the life on the road forced upon him and Tessa when the money from the research funding dried up with the Great Depression that followed the stock market crash of 1929. Thereafter, Ollie and Tessa performed their psychic act not in the "higher-class sort" of "Chautauqua-like shows made up of lectures and readings and scenes from Shakespeare and somebody singing opera and slides of travels (Education not Sensation)" but in the lower-class sort of "travelling shows" where "They shared the stage with the hypnotists and snake ladies and dirty monologuists and strippers in feathers" (324). By this point their act was now necessarily often faked, because "her powers, whatever they were, didn't prove so reliable" (325).

When Nancy turns the conversation to Tessa's subsequent fate, Ollie, evidently lying, claims, "'I must have written you'," and then, "'I must have written Wilf'" (326), both of which statements Nancy rejects. Then Ollie makes a probably dubious excuse for himself, "'Maybe I was at too low a point then'" (326), another comment aimed to elicit sympathy for himself and to direct attention away from the truth. But why would Ollie lie? What actions of his, what tracks, would he want the snow of his supposed explanations to cover up? And doesn't the by me unplanned juxtaposition of the word "Ollie" and the word "lie" when I asked "But why would Ollie lie?" prompt a new understanding of his name? "Ollie" – "all lies." To extend this interpretation to an allegorical level, wasn't Satan regarded as the father of lies? Further, looking ahead to the subtitle of the novella's next and final part, "Flies on the Windowsill," might it not be important again on an allegorical level to recall that one of the names for Satan is Beelzebub, meaning, literally, as William Golding well knew, "lord of the flies"? And might it not be important or at least interesting to note that the opening word of that final subtitle – if you drop the first letter, the f, from it – leaves, as Alice Munro's fellow writer and old friend Audrey Thomas would wryly observe, the word "lies"?

While we can fairly assume that certain of the details told by Ollie to Nancy are true, the story that Ollie then adds, as Nancy realizes, and as we comprehend having read the third part of the novella, is grotesquely and, we suspect, treacherously false. Ollie reports, to whatever degrees we can trust his accounts of both his feelings or actions and Tessa's worsening condition, that Tessa "grew weaker, and became covered with mysterious bruises" – ostensibly, he proposes, because "She had leukemia" (326), though we may instead suspect him of beating her. At this stage, Ollie explains, he felt obliged to take Tessa, although "He didn't want to have to take her" (327), to the local hospital in some "town in the mountains" (326) that was their most recent stop. And there, "in a matter of a couple of weeks, she died" (327), Ollie's version of events concludes, much to Nancy's astonishment and our own at the evidently self-serving motive for Ollie's desire to have Nancy believe his story. When Ollie is asked by Nancy if Tessa was buried in the little town where she supposedly died and why he had not asked Wilf and herself for money to permit a proper burial, Ollie, whose concerns never extend beyond his own self-interest, responds ambiguously, "'I felt that it was my responsibility'" (327) – meaning responsibility to himself, we recognize. He declares that "'I had her cremated'" (327), as he reports Tessa had said she wanted to be, then goes on to supply a presumably wholly concocted, merely sentiment-soliciting story about how in order to honour another of her last wishes, he had taken her ashes (a detail anticipating the final symbol in the novella) to the Coast. Tellingly and ironically, however, the phrase that he uses is "'I skipped town'" (327), like, we infer, somebody guilty of a crime.

Beyond the subject of Tessa's fate, specifically the greatly troubling discrepancy between the facts that Nancy knows about it as opposed to the fictions that Ollie fabricates about it, there is an important undercurrent carrying through this fourth part that involves something unfinished, something unfulfilled in the relationship between Nancy and Ollie. This undercurrent surfaces when Ollie drives Nancy back to her hotel and she thinks: "Her room had two beds in it. Twin beds. She might get a dirty look or two, trailing him in, but surely she could stand that. Since the truth would be a far cry from what anybody might be thinking" (328). Very interestingly, however, the statement "Since the truth would be a far cry from what anybody might be thinking" can be read in two ways. First: that the truth is *far more* mundane than the one-night stand that some might imagine it to be, namely, just to give Ollie a place to sleep since he had missed the series of ferries he needed to get back to his home on Texada Island. Second: that the truth is *far less* mundane than the one-night stand some might imagine it to be, namely, to permit Nancy to commence the romance with Ollie which, at an increasingly conscious level, she has long desired. For what held Nancy in its grip near the end of the first part of the novella when she was getting ready to marry Wilf was not as she thought "a whirlwind" (278) of wedding preparations, but rather "a whirlwind" of a much more troubling sort: her real feelings, which she sought to hide from herself, about probable difficulties posed by her agreeing to marry Wilf.

Readying herself at the hotel to invite Ollie to share her room and, we may perhaps infer, to share the rest of her life, Nancy "took a preparatory breath"; but Ollie, intuiting what she has yet to verbalize, replies "'No, Nancy'" (328). We are told: "All this time she had been waiting for him to say one true word. All this afternoon or maybe a good part of her life. She had been waiting, and now he had said it. // No" (328) – a comment anticipated by Ollie's use of the same word "No" many years earlier in response to a question posed by Nancy, while they walked back from visiting Tessa, about whether he would ask for Tessa's forgiveness if he were in Nancy's place. Intriguingly, Nancy regards Ollie's present reply as being "clear and tender and ... as full of understanding as any word that had ever been spoken to her. *No*" (329). And is it not at least possible to regard the combination of the first letter of the name Nancy with the first letter of the name Ollie as being designed to spell the word "NO" – as though the impossibility of their maintaining a profound romantic relationship is contained in, is foretold by, their very names? Nancy understands "The danger of her own desire, because she didn't really know what sort of desire it was, what it was for. They had shied away from whatever that was years ago, and they would surely have to do so now that they were old" (329). In turn, Ollie repeats "'No',", then asserts "'It wouldn't turn out well'" (329). The truth of this observation Nancy accepts for assorted reasons, including her sense that they were "not terribly old, but old enough to appear unsightly and absurd," that they had been "unfortunate enough to have spent their time together lying," and "that the first thing she was going to do when she got home was write to that place in Michigan and find out what had happened to Tessa, and bring her back to where she belonged" (329).

Nancy's letter to the hospital in Michigan was returned to her "unopened" (329), the hospital apparently having been closed; yet she resolves not to give up, decides to make other inquiries. Similarly, her letter to Ollie was returned to her "with one word written on the envelope. *Moved*" (330) – a message that we can't be certain, but are tempted to think, was written by Ollie in an attempt to prevent his being held responsible for the harm he had done not only to Tessa but also to Nancy. Interestingly, the fourth part of "Powers" closes with comments that invite us to imagine Nancy's innermost feelings when, in reference to her newest letter to Ollie, it is stated: "She could not bear to open it up and read what she had said.

Too much, she was sure" (330). A declaration of one kind, perhaps, in terms of Nancy's unending unforgiving anger towards Ollie for his treatment of Tessa? A declaration of another kind, perhaps, in terms of Nancy's unending unfulfilled love for Ollie? Or conceivably both? Munro's technique here – brilliantly – is to leave what Nancy "had said" (330) *unsaid* to us, that is, to leave it a mystery that we feel compelled to consider closely but that we may never, likely should never, be able to interpret wholly. We recall how Nancy at the end of the first part of "Powers" questioned in her diary if "something really unusual" (283) would eventually be revealed to her (or to us). We recall wondering if Nancy would record that – and, should this occur, if we would be *shown* it or, as we now see, be left to *imagine* it.

During the conversation between Ollie and Nancy at the Japanese restaurant we learned: "So Nancy had missed Ollie a lot without ever figuring out just what it was that she missed. Something troublesome burning in him like a low-grade fever, something she couldn't get the better of. The things that had got on her nerves during that short time she had known him turned out to be just the things, in retrospect, that shone" (320). And so we get a glimpse here and elsewhere of Nancy's feeling of connection with Ollie – and at some points, though not as deeply, his feeling of connection with her. As we learned in the second part of the novella when Ollie and Nancy sat together outside Tessa's house, completely relaxed in one another's company while waiting for her to be free to visit with them, "There were times when he did not need to ask why he was with her, when teasing her, being teased by her, made the time flow by with sparkling ease" (288). But as of now we imagine that, sadly for both of them but especially for Nancy, there would be "no hope for it" (315).

ACT FIVE: Flies on the Windowsill

The fifth and final and much the shortest part of the novella – and one in which the narrative point of view is again third person limited to Nancy – is set about a year later, on the day of the annual Canadian Football League championship game, Grey Cup Day, which, though Munro does not state this, occurs on a Sunday, "the Lord's Day" in Christianity and therefore significant in terms of comprehending "Powers" as a dream-vision allegory and itself a form of divination, presumably the highest form of seeing to which any of us, as readers, can aspire. Here Nancy declines to attend a potluck supper highlighted by watching the Grey Cup on TV, a game which, like other sports events involving trophies, needs to be considered, as Hugh Hood understood, a secular counterpart to the allegorical quest for the Holy Grail (Hood, *Strength Down Centre* 192). Instead, Nancy chooses to relax in the sunroom of her home, dozes, and has what in allegories such as William Langland's *Piers Plowman* and John Bunyan's *The Pilgrim's Progress* and Lewis Carroll's *Alice's Adventures in Wonderland* would be seen as a dream-vision. "The sunroom, the bright room behind her, has shrunk into a dark hall" (330) – most certainly a version of "the black room" (334) that Munro in her brief essay "What Is Real?" identifies as the disturbing presence at the heart of each house or story of hers.

At this time in her life Nancy's children are worried that she may be at risk of "Living in the Past" (330). However, in Nancy's own mind, "what she believes she is doing, what she wants to do if she can get the time to do it, is not so much to live in the past as to open it up and get one good look at it" (330) or, to echo the title of one of Ron Shuebrook's paintings, to get one good glimpse of it. Hence the importance of Nancy's own act of divination, her dream-vision, and the importance of its placement as the concluding part of the novella. In fact, Nancy's name is just one letter different from the suffix "mancy" – derived from the Greek word *manteia*, meaning "divination," and found in English in words such as "logomancy," meaning "divination by means of words," and "onomancy," meaning "divination by means of the letters in a name" – and thus Nancy's name might be considered to suggest her own potential powers of at least near-divination. To "get one good look at it" (330): equally an apt description of Munro's artistic purpose, of the personal challenge facing Nancy, and of our imaginative task as readers of "Powers."

In this dream-vision, Nancy sees Tessa and Ollie together in a hotel room at a point late in their time with the travelling shows. Ollie is so exhausted from driving that he collapses on the hotel bed, pretending to sleep but in fact peeking out to see Tessa "looking into the dresser mirror" (331), a classic symbol for self-examination, somewhat in the way that Nancy caught her own reflection in the café window. Tessa has chosen a new costume to wear, including a "black shawl patterned with roses" (details anticipated by the images of the shawl Tessa is wearing at the store and the walls of wild roses on the way to Tessa's house employed earlier in the novella) and appears with "Her hair ... pinned and sprayed, its rough curls flattened into a black helmet" (331). Her eyebrows are "lifted and blackened. Crow's wings" (331) – a description suggesting an association, mythically, with the ancient Celtic goddess Morrigan, described by Irish novelist Adrian McKinty as "Morrigan of the Black Eye. Morrigan of the sorrows, the great queen, the goddess of battle, fertility, and strife" (305) and by Classical and Celtic scholar Philip Freeman as "the fearsome goddess of battle and prophecy" (22). Tessa, it is emphasized, is wearing "a wig" (331), wording that I believe evokes – as I believe the title of the last story, "Wigtime," in Munro's collection *Friend of My Youth* (1990) evokes – wording from Old Norse, a language and a literature in which Munro's interest is made clear by the closing of the last story, "White Dump," in her preceding volume, *The Progress of Love* (1986). As I see it, the Old Norse words "*víg*," meaning "battle" (Arthur 11), and "*tími*," meaning "time" (Arthur 149), taken together, may be connected both to the name of Munro's story "Wigtime" and to the name of the plain "Vigrid" in Old Norse myth where the final battle of Ragnarok is fought (Jobes 1317-18), after which comes the twilight and perhaps the revival of the gods and their powers.

Accordingly, we may view Tessa here as attiring herself much in the ritualistic and symbolic way that the prophet-warrior of Blake's preface to his brief epic poem *Milton* prepares himself for the "Mental Fight" ahead by calling for "my Bow of burning gold," "my Arrows of desire," "my Spear," "my Chariot of fire!" Yet sadly in the case of Tessa, we see that her "eyelids pressed down heavily, like punishment, over her faded eyes. In fact her whole self seems to be weighted down by the clothes and the hair and the makeup" (331). Tessa "stands in front of the mirror looking at herself," feeling weighted down not only literally by "her heavy costume and hair" but also metaphorically by "her spirit" (331): "she walks around the room as if there are things to be done, but she cannot settle herself to do anything" (331-32). But as we already learned from the superhuman fortitude that Tessa maintains during the four decades of her incarceration, Tessa as prophet-warrior herself can, indeed will, as William Faulkner once wrote, "endure and prevail" (724).

In this for Nancy and for ourselves revelatory vision of the past, Nancy observes the sudden return in the hotel room of Tessa's powers. For before Tessa actually sees the small pile of dead "Flies on the Windowsill" identified in this fifth part's subtitle – with a nod, I strongly suspect, to the story "The Fly" by one of Munro's favourite short story writers, Katherine Mansfield, and probably also to the novel *Lord of the Flies* by William Golding, and, as Michael Trussler reminds us, to the lines beginning "As flies to wanton boys" in Shakespeare's *King Lear* (256) – Tessa sees the dead flies in her mind. Excited at the return of her powers, she hugs Ollie and, pressing her head against his chest, feels in an inside jacket pocket – and again likely identifies without direct examination, just as she once described the contents of his pants pocket – the "secret papers" (333) there. Ollie has obtained these, we learn, "from a man he met in one of these towns – a doctor who is known to look after touring people and to oblige them sometimes by performing services that are beyond the usual" (333-34).

For the moment we are assured about certain details which Ollie tells the doctor that "(this is all true)" (334). But then the account of Ollie's stated and unstated feelings about Tessa, his relationship with her, and his intentions for her continues more and more dubiously and disturbingly, with Ollie's account being filtered through Nancy in third-person-limited narration: "He has asked himself, then the doctor, if her extraordinary powers may not after all be related to a threatening imbalance in her mind and nature. Seizures have occurred in her past, and he wonders if something like that could be on the way again. She is not an ill-natured person or a person with any bad habits, but she is not a normal person, she is a unique person, and living with a unique person can be a strain, in fact perhaps more of a strain than a normal man can stand. The doctor understands this and has told him of a place that she might be taken to, for a rest" (334). Here we observe the dreadful harm awaiting Tessa that Ollie's rationalizing represents, beginning with his pretense of concern for her followed by the revelation of his true self-interestedness.

In Nancy's dream-vision, however, both Tessa and Ollie are seen as having second thoughts about their individual choices for their future actions. There must be a satisfying alternative, Tessa thinks, to the present situation in which "They have become a professional couple, they sleep and eat and travel together, close to the rhythms of each other's breathing," but can never, except when performing, "look into each other's faces, for fear that they will catch sight of something that is too frightful" (332). And what, we wonder, might that be? The entire tragic truth? The shallowness of Ollie's self-interest rather than love for Tessa that she could see in his eyes? The depth of Tessa's selflessness and love for Ollie that he could see in her eyes? But surely, Tessa thinks, "They could do something else, she believes, they could have another life" (334).

Tessa imagines herself – or, more precisely, Nancy envisions Tessa imagining herself – relinquishing her special powers contentedly, like Prospero at the close of *The Tempest*: "For if this is what it means to get back what she once had, the deep-seeing use of her eyes and the instant revelations of her tongue, might she not be better off without? And if it's a matter of her deserting those things, and not of them deserting her, couldn't she welcome the change?" (334). On Ollie's part, "He says to himself that he will get rid of the papers as soon as he can, he will forget the whole idea, he too is capable of hope and honor" (334). And, therefore, as the third-last section of this final part of the novella ends with Tessa's face pressed against the papers spelling her apparent doom, we experience with Tessa, if only temporarily, a feeling of reprieve: "Yes. Yes. Tessa feels all menace go out of the faint crackle under her cheek" (335). And in the second-last section of this final part, we experience the same feeling with Nancy: "The sense of being reprieved lights all the air. So clear, so powerful, that Nancy feels the known future wither under its attack, skitter away like dirty old leaves" (335).

Except that as we have already seen in the real world of the future beyond Nancy's dream-vision, Ollie isn't able to put goodness towards others ahead of his own self-interestedness, doesn't give up on his separate plans for Tessa and himself – and therefore she ends up incarcerated, experimented on, tortured in the private hospital in Michigan for a period lasting about forty years, only to be disposed of somewhere that remains unknown despite Nancy's ongoing efforts to find her. And thus as a result of Munro's and Nancy's and our own reflections, we bear witness to, we experience, an overwhelmingly sad feeling arising from the powerful juxtaposition of the *anagnorisis* or moment of self-discovery and the *peripeteia* or moment of reversal found in the greatest of Greek or Shakespearean or modern tragedy. But Munro's five-act drama doesn't end there.

EPILOGUE

I have long wondered if Alice Munro's stories, of which 148 have been collected in her fourteen luminous and numinous books of new work, might be appreciated equally for their theatricality, their narrativity, and their lyricism. Or more specifically in the present case, might we consider "Powers" equally as, first, drama, performance, theatre, then second, fictional autobiography in the third person, and third, a poetic allegory? As William Blake declared in a letter to Thomas Butts, "Allegory addressd to the Intellectual powers ... is My Definition of the Most Sublime Poetry" (730). Similarly here in the fifth and final part of "Powers," which Michael Trussler exuberantly describes as "a stylistic tour de force" (256), the allegorical nature of Munro's writing continues to be seen in, and is reinforced by, the poetically and emotionally concentrated qualities of her prose, which confirm her place amongst the very best writers – James Joyce, Katherine Mansfield, Sherwood Anderson, Eudora Welty – in the tradition that Eileen Baldeshwiler has named "The Lyric Short Story." Thus in reading the very last paragraph of "Powers" we marvel at the evocativeness of Munro's choices of language, the modulations in pacing, her style: "But deep in that moment some instability is waiting, that Nancy is determined to ignore. No use. She is aware already of being removed, drawn out of those two people and back into herself. It seems as if some calm and decisive person – could it be Wilf? – has taken on the task of leading her out of that room with its wire hangers and its flowered curtain. Gently, inexorably leading her away from what begins to crumble behind her, to crumble and darken tenderly into something like soot and soft ash" (335).

At the end of the novella, then, Nancy's dream-vision finishes with her leaving this "black room," led away from it by a mysterious figure whom she thinks may be her deceased husband, Wilf, led away, we find ourselves imagining, from the world of time towards the world of eternity. Now more at peace, Nancy returns from this "black room" of her dream-vision to the light of the sunroom of this fifth part's beginning. She comes full-circle; that is, as a result of the many changes in experience and knowledge she has undergone, as a result of having recently opened up her past and gotten "one good look at it" (330), Nancy is symbolically able to complete the circle of her life. The sunroom in which she reawakens is the one that Wilf had added to his house, as Munro slyly had Nancy state parenthetically in the first part of the novella as if this detail would be of no import later: "(I forgot to mention that Wilf has a sunroom built out from the opposite side of the house to his office and it makes a good balance.)" (273). Black room and sunroom: a good balance indeed, as Clark Blaise has remarked insightfully of the overall design, in particular the multiple closings, that he considers typical of Munro's stories. "That makes its own philosophical point," Blaise comments, "the one I think she's driving at in all her writing, a balance of equivalences" (Blaise in Struthers, "Learning To Read, Learning To Write" 344).

Of the ending of "Powers," Michael Trussler declares: "Munro's concluding paragraph is an astonishing rewriting of the final paragraph of Joyce's "The Dead"; instead of Gabriel Conroy perceiving imminent mortality in the whirling white snow, Nancy finds herself confronting something darker, 'something like soot and soft ash'.... Munro complicates this Joycean allusion by suggesting that Nancy is a version of Dante being guided by Virgil ... away from the Inferno. The purpose of the hero's journey into the underworld in classic epic poetry is to learn some necessary truths from the dead. What Munro does, unlike authors of the classic epic, is finish her collection with this journey, which is a way of making the reading experience part of the text itself. The reader is invited to be like Nancy, who tries to open up her life 'and get one good look at it'" (257). Now the light of the sunroom takes on even greater symbolic significance: to Munro in the act of completing the writing of this extraordinary novella, to Nancy in processing the intricate and often emotionally overwhelming complexities of life, and to ourselves, Munro's readers, in the sometimes disturbing but in the end unfailingly delighting act of reading. Nancy's name, it's important to note in the present context, is linked to the Hebrew word for "Grace" and, like Dante, Munro takes her protagonist and her readers from the Inferno through Purgatory to a vision of Paradise. Ultimately, then, allegorically, the light of the sunroom represents – or, we might well say, it prophesies – an entry into the transcendent, everlasting light of the closing of the Old Norse poem *Vǫluspá* and the closing of Dante's *The Divine Comedy*:

Do you still seek to know? And what?

A hall she sees standing,
brighter than the sun,
roofed with gold,
on Refuge from the Flames.
There shall the worthy
warrior bands dwell
and all their days of life
enjoy delight.
    — *Vǫluspá* 60-61, trans. Ursula Dronke

Oh grace abounding that had made me fit
  to fix my eyes on the eternal light
  until my vision was consumed in it!
    — Dante Alighieri, *The Paradiso*, Canto XXXIII, ll. 82-84,
      The Divine Comedy, trans. John Ciardi

Acknowledgements

I would like to thank the many supportive souls who offered me such vital encouragement and inspiration during the time I was writing and rewriting this essay, including its four dedicatees and the numerous other contributors to *Alice Munro Country* and *Alice Munro Everlasting*, my family and friends, and in particular, for their generous work with me on improving the phrasing throughout this essay, Elizabeth Standing and Kelsey McCallum and Marianne Micros.

Works Consulted

Anderson, Sherwood. *Winesburg, Ohio: Authoritative Text; Backgrounds and Contexts; Criticism*. Ed. Charles E. Modlin and Ray Lewis White. New York: W.W. Norton, 1996. A Norton Critical Edition.

Aristotle. "Poetics." *Classical Literary Criticism*. Trans. Penelope Murray and T.S. Dorsch. Introd. Penelope Murray. London: Penguin, 2000. 57-97.

Arthur, Ross G., comp. *English-Old Norse Dictionary*. Cambridge, ON: In Parentheses, 2002. Linguistics Ser. <www.yorku.ca/inpar/language/English-Old_Norse.pdf>.

Auerbach, Erich. *Dante: Poet of the Secular World*. Trans. Ralph Manheim. Chicago, IL: U of Chicago P, 1961.

Ayre, John. "Frye's Geometry of Thought: Building the Great Wheel." *The Visionary Tradition in Canadian Writing*. Ed. Russell Morton Brown and J.R. (Tim) Struthers. *University of Toronto Quarterly* 70 (2001): 825-38.

Baldeshwiler, Eileen. "The Lyric Short Story: The Sketch of a History." *Studies in Short Fiction* 6 (1969): 443-53. Rpt. in *Short Story Theories*. Ed. Charles E. May. Athens, OH: Ohio UP, 1976. 202-13. Rpt. in *The New Short Story Theories*. Ed. Charles E. May. Athens, OH: Ohio UP, 1994. 231-41.

Baring-Gould, William S., and Ceil Baring-Gould. *The Annotated Mother Goose: Nursery Rhymes Old and New, Arranged and Explained*. Illus. Walter Crane, Randolph Caldecott, Kate Greenaway, Arthur Rackham, Maxfield Parrish, and Early Historical Woodcuts. New York: Bramhall House, 1962.

Bettelheim, Bruno. *The Uses of Enchantment: The Meaning and Importance of Fairy Tales*. New York: Alfred A. Knopf, 1976.

Blaise, Clark. "How Stories Mean." *Selected Essays*. By Clark Blaise. Ed. John Metcalf and J.R. (Tim) Struthers. Windsor, ON: Biblioasis, 2008. 167-79.

Blake, William. *Milton. The Complete Poetry and Prose of William Blake*. Ed. David V. Erdman. Commentary by Harold Bloom. Rev. ed. Garden City, NY: Anchor, 1982. 95-144.

---. ["To Thomas Butts."] 6 July 1803. *The Complete Poetry and Prose of William Blake*. Ed. David V. Erdman. Commentary by Harold Bloom. Rev. ed. Garden City, NY: Anchor, 1982. 729-31.

Blodgett, E.D. "Forming Other Connections: Ethel Wilson's Novellas." *New Directions from Old*. Guelph, ON: Red Kite, 1991. 56-73. Canadian Storytellers 1.

Bloom, Harold. "Criticism, Canon-Formation, and Prophecy: The Sorrows of Facticity." *Poetics of Influence: New and Selected Criticism.* Ed. and introd. John Hollander. New Haven, CT: Henry R. Schwab, 1988. 405-24.

The Book of Job. *The Holy Bible.* Cambridge, Eng.: Cambridge UP, n.d. Authorized King James Vers.

Booth, Wayne C. *The Rhetoric of Fiction.* 2nd ed. Chicago, IL: U of Chicago P, 1983.

Boyanoski, Christine. *Sympathetic Realism: George A. Reid and the Academic Tradition.* Toronto: Art Gallery of Ontario, 1986.

Buchholtz, Mirosława. "Pseudo-Longinus and the Affective Theory in Alice Munro's Stories about Childhood." *Alice Munro: Writing Secrets.* Ed. Héliane Ventura and Mary Condé. *Open Letter* 11th ser., no. 9 - 12th ser., no. 1 (2003-04): 89-102.

Bunyan, John. *The Pilgrim's Progress: From This World to That Which Is To Come, Delivered Under the Similitude of a Dream.* London: Oxford UP, 1935. The World's Classics. Rpt. as *The Pilgrim's Progress.* Ed. and introd. W.R. Owens. Oxford, Eng.: Oxford UP, 2003. Oxford World's Classics.

Butt, William. "Killer OSPs and Style Munro in 'Open Secrets'." *Alice Munro: A Souwesto Celebration.* Ed. J.R. (Tim) Struthers and John B. Lee. *The Windsor Review* 47.2 (2014): 94-100. Rpt. (rev.) in *Alice Munro Country: Essays on Her Works I.* Ed. J.R. (Tim) Struthers. Toronto: Guernica Editions, 2020. Essential Writers Ser. 51.

---. "Southwestern Ontario, the Narrator, and 'Words with Power' in Alice Munro's 'Meneseteung'." *Alice Munro and the Souwesto Story.* Ed. J.R. (Tim) Struthers. *Short Story* ns 21.1 (2013 [2015]): 13-43.

Canitz, A.E. Christa, and Roger Seamon. "The Rhetoric of Fictional Realism in the Stories of Alice Munro." *Canadian Literature* 150 (1996): 67-80.

Carroll, Lewis. *Alice's Adventures in Wonderland. Alice in Wonderland: Authoritative Texts of Alice's Adventures in Wonderland, Through the Looking-Glass, The Hunting of the Snark; Backgrounds; Criticism.* Ed. Donald J. Gray. 3rd ed. New York: W.W. Norton, 2013. 1-97. A Norton Critical Edition.

Carscallen, James. *The Other Country: Patterns in the Writing of Alice Munro.* Toronto: ECW, 1993.

Clark, Miriam Marty. "Allegories of Reading in Alice Munro's 'Carried Away'." *Contemporary Literature* 37 (1996): 49-61.

Clarke, George Elliott. "Alice Munro's Black Bottom; or Black Tints and Euro Hints in *Lives of Girls and Women.*" *Alice Munro: Reminiscence, Interpretation, Adaptation and Comparison.* Ed. Mirosława Buchholtz and Eugenia Sojka. Frankfurt am Main, Ger.: Peter Lang, 2015. 147-71. Dis/Continuities: Toruń Studies in Language, Literature and Culture 8. Rpt. in *Alice Munro Country: Essays on Her Works I.* Ed. J.R. (Tim) Struthers. Toronto: Guernica Editions, 2020. Essential Writers Ser. 51.

Danby, Ken. *Sunbather, 1972. Ken Danby: Beyond the Crease; with Essays by Ihor Holubizky and Greg McKee.* Fredericton and Hamilton, ON: Goose Lane Editions and Art Gallery of Hamilton, 2016. 76-77.

Dante Alighieri. *The Divine Comedy.* Rendered into English Verse by John Ciardi. New York: W.W. Norton, 1970. Rpt. as *The Divine Comedy: The Inferno; The Purgatorio; The Paradiso.* Trans. John Ciardi. New York: New American Library-Penguin, 2003.

Dow, Helen J. *The Art of Alex Colville.* Toronto: McGraw-Hill Ryerson, 1972.

Dronke, Ursula, trans. *Vǫluspá. The Poetic Edda; Volume II: Mythological Poems.* Ed. with trans., introd., and commentary by Ursula Dronke. Oxford: Clarendon, 1997. 1-158.

Duffy, Dennis. "Alice Munro's Narrative Historicism: 'Too Much Happiness'." *The Genius of Alice Munro.* Ed. Robert Thacker. *American Review of Canadian Studies* 45 (2015): 196-207. Rpt. in *Alice Munro Everlasting: Essays on Her Works II.* Ed. J.R. (Tim) Struthers. Toronto: Guernica Editions, 2020. Essential Writers Ser. 52.

---. "Too Little Geography; Too Much History: Writing the Balance in 'Meneseteung'." *National Plots: Historical Fiction and Changing Ideas of Canada.* Ed. Andrea Cabajsky and Brett Josef Grubisic. Waterloo, ON: Wilfrid Laurier UP, 2010. 197-213, 215-36 passim. Rpt. as "Too Little Geography; Too Much History: Writing the Balance in Alice Munro" in *Alice Munro Country: Essays on Her Works I.* Ed. J.R. (Tim) Struthers. Toronto: Guernica Editions, 2020. Essential Writers Ser. 51.

Duval, Paul. *High Realism in Canada.* Toronto: Clarke, Irwin, 1974.

Falck, Colin. *Myth, Truth and Literature: Towards a True Post-Modernism.* 2nd ed. Cambridge, Eng.: Cambridge UP, 1994.

Faulkner, William. "Address upon Receiving the Nobel Prize for Literature." *The Portable Faulkner*. Ed. Malcolm Cowley. Rev. and expanded ed. New York: Viking, 1981. 723-24.

Frazer, Sir James G. *The Golden Bough: A Study in Magic and Religion*. Abridged ed. New York: Macmillan, 1951.

Freeman, Philip. *Celtic Mythology: Tales of Gods, Goddesses, and Heroes*. New York: Oxford UP, 2017.

Freud, Sigmund. *The Interpretation of Dreams*. Trans. James Strachey. Ed. James Strachey assisted by Alan Tyson. Ed. Angela Richards. London: Penguin, 1991. Vol. 4 of *The Penguin Freud Library*. 15 vols. 1990-93.

---. *Jokes and Their Relation to the Unconscious*. Trans. and ed. James Strachey. Ed. Angela Richards. London: Penguin, 1991. Vol. 6 of *The Penguin Freud Library*. 15 vols. 1990-93.

Frye, Northrop. *Anatomy of Criticism: Four Essays*. Princeton, NJ: Princeton UP, 1957.

---. "Blake's Reading of the Book of Job." *Spiritus Mundi: Essays on Literature, Myth, and Society*. Bloomington, IN: Indiana UP, 1976. 228-44. Rpt. as "Blake's Reading of the Book of Job (II)" in *Northrop Frye on Milton and Blake*. Ed. Angela Esterhammer. Toronto: U of Toronto P, 2005. 387-401. Vol. 16 of *Collected Works of Northrop Frye*. 30 vols. 1996-2012.

Frye, Northrop, and Jay Macpherson. *Biblical and Classical Myths: The Mythological Framework of Western Culture*. Toronto: U of Toronto P, 2004.

Genesis. *The Holy Bible*. Cambridge, Eng.: Cambridge UP, n.d. Authorized King James Vers.

Genette, Gérard. "Structure and Functions of the Title in Literature." Trans. Bernard Crampé. *Critical Inquiry* 14 (1987-88): 692-720. Rpt. (rev.) as "Titles" in *Paratexts: Thresholds of Interpretation*. By Gérard Genette. Trans. Jane E. Lewin. Fwd. Richard Macksey. Cambridge, Eng.: Cambridge UP, 1997. 55-103. Literature, Culture, Theory 20.

Gibson, Graeme. "Alice Munro." *Eleven Canadian Novelists*. Toronto: House of Anansi, 1973. 237-64.

Golding, William. *Lord of the Flies*. 1954. London: Faber and Faber, 2004.

Grafe, Adrian. "The Unreal Material." *"With a Roar from Underground": Alice Munro's* Dance of the Happy Shades. Ed. Corinne Bigot and Catherine Lanone. Paris: Presses Universitaires de Paris Ouest, 2015. 165-76.

Grieg, Edvard. "Morning Mood." *Peer Gynt, Op. 23.* 1875.

Hardy, Thomas. *Tess of the d'Urbervilles: An Authoritative Text; Backgrounds and Sources; Criticism.* Ed. Scott Elledge. 3rd ed. New York: W.W. Norton, 1991. A Norton Critical Edition.

Hollander, Lee M. General Introduction. *The Poetic Edda.* Trans. with an introd. and explanatory notes by Lee M. Hollander. 2nd ed., rev. Austin: U of Texas P, 1990. ix-xxix.

Hood, Hugh. "Sober Colouring: The Ontology of Super-Realism." *Canadian Literature* 49 (1971): 28-34. Rpt. (rev.) as "The Ontology of Super-Realism" in *The Governor's Bridge Is Closed: Twelve Essays on the Canadian Scene.* By Hugh Hood. Ottawa: Oberon, 1973. 126-35. Rpt. as "Sober Colouring: The Ontology of Super-Realism" in *How Stories Mean.* Ed. John Metcalf and J.R. (Tim) Struthers. Erin, ON: The Porcupine's Quill, 1993. 98-105. Critical Directions 3.

---. *Strength Down Centre: The Jean Béliveau Story.* Scarborough, ON: Prentice-Hall of Canada, 1970.

Hopper, Edward. *The Complete Oil Paintings by Edward Hopper.* Commentary by Gail Levin. New York: W.W. Norton, 2000.

Howells, Coral Ann. "Intimate Dislocations: Buried History and Geography in Alice Munro's So[u]westo Stories." *British Journal of Canadian Studies* 14.1 (1999): 7-16. Rpt. as "Intimate Dislocations: Buried History and Geography in Alice Munro's Souwesto Stories" in *Alice Munro Country: Essays on Her Works I.* Ed. J.R. (Tim) Struthers. Toronto: Guernica Editions, 2020. Essential Writers Ser. 51.

Ibsen, Henrik. *Peer Gynt: A Dramatic Poem.* Trans. William and Charles Archer. Introd. William Archer. New York: Charles Scribner's Sons, 1908. Vol. 4 of *The Collected Works of Henrik Ibsen.* 11 vols. 1906-08.

Jacob, Susannah. "Blow Out Your Candles: An Elegy for Rose Williams." *Arts & Culture. The Paris Review* 5 Dec. 2013. <https://www.theparisreview.org/blog/2013/12/05/blow-out-your-candles-an-elegy-for-rose-williams>.

Jobes, Gertrude. *Dictionary of Mythology Folklore and Symbols.* 2 vols. New York: Scarecrow, 1962.

Joyce, James. "The Dead." *Dubliners: Authoritative Text, Contexts, Criticism.* Ed. Margot Norris. Text ed. Hans Walter Gabler with Walter Hettche. New York: W.W. Norton, 2006. 151-94. A Norton Critical Edition.

---. "Grace." *Dubliners: Authoritative Text, Contexts, Criticism*. Ed. Margot Norris. Text ed. Hans Walter Gabler with Walter Hettche. New York: W.W. Norton, 2006. 128-51. A Norton Critical Edition.

---. "A Little Cloud." *Dubliners: Authoritative Text, Contexts, Criticism*. Ed. Margot Norris. Text ed. Hans Walter Gabler with Walter Hettche. New York: W.W. Norton, 2006. 57-70. A Norton Critical Edition.

---. "Realism and Idealism in English Literature (Daniel Defoe – William Blake)." *Occasional, Critical, and Political Writing*. Ed. and introd. Kevin Barry. Oxford, Eng.: Oxford UP, 2000. 163-82. Oxford World's Classics.

Keith, W.J. "Alice Munro." *A Sense of Style: Studies in the Art of Fiction in English-Speaking Canada*. Toronto: ECW, 1989. 155-74.

---. *Literary Images of Ontario*. Toronto: U of Toronto P, 1992. Ontario Historical Studies Ser.

Kenner, Hugh. "The Rose in the Steel Dust." *The Hudson Review* 3 (1950-51): 66-123.

Langland, William. *Piers Plowman: The C Version; Will's Visions of Piers Plowman, Do-Well, Do-Better, and Do-Best*. By George Russell and George Kane. London: Athlone, 1997.

LaPierre, Megan. "'The Music Itself': Musical Representation and Musicality in the Short Stories of Alice Munro." *Alice Munro Everlasting: Essays on Her Works II*. Ed. J.R. (Tim) Struthers. Toronto: Guernica Editions, 2020. Essential Writers Ser. 52.

Lee, Alvin A., gen. ed. *Collected Works of Northrop Frye*. 30 vols. Toronto: U of Toronto P, 1996-2012.

Loe, Thomas. "'The Dead' as Novella." *James Joyce Quarterly* 28 (1990-91): 485-97.

Lohafer, Susan. *Reading for Storyness: Preclosure Theory, Empirical Poetics, and Culture in the Short Story*. Baltimore: The Johns Hopkins UP, 2003.

Mansfield, Katherine. "The Fly." *Collected Stories of Katherine Mansfield*. London: Constable, 1945. 422-28.

Marlatt, Daphne. "'Perform[ing] on the Stage of Her Text'." *Readings from the Labyrinth*. Edmonton, AB: NeWest, 1998. 200-12. The Writer as Critic 6.

Martin, W.R. "Alice Munro and James Joyce." *Journal of Canadian Fiction* 24 (1979): 120-26. Rpt. in *Alice Munro Everlasting: Essays on Her Works II*. Ed. J.R. (Tim) Struthers. Toronto: Guernica Editions, 2020. Essential Writers Ser. 52.

Martin, W.R., and Warren U. Ober. "Alice Munro as Small-Town Historian: 'Spaceships Have Landed'." *Alice Munro Writing On....* Ed. Robert Thacker. *Essays on Canadian Writing* 66 (1998): 128-46. Rpt. in *The Rest of the Story: Critical Essays on Alice Munro.* Ed. Robert Thacker. Toronto: ECW, 1999. 128-46. Rpt. (abridged) in *Alice Munro Country: Essays on Her Works I.* Ed. J.R. (Tim) Struthers. Toronto: Guernica Editions, 2020. Essential Writers Ser. 51.

May, Charles E. "Living in the Story: Fictional Reality in the Stories of Alice Munro." *Alice Munro's Miraculous Art: Critical Essays.* Ed. Janice Fiamengo and Gerald Lynch. Ottawa: U of Ottawa P, 2017. 43-61. Reappraisals: Canadian Writers 38.

---. "The Nature of Knowledge in Short Fiction." *Studies in Short Fiction* 21 (1984): 327-38. Rpt. in *The New Short Story Theories.* Athens, OH: Ohio UP, 1994. 131-43.

McFarlane, James. Introduction. *Peer Gynt: A Dramatic Poem.* By Henrik Ibsen. Trans. Christopher Fry and Johan Fillinger. Oxford, Eng.: Oxford UP, 1988. vii-xiii. Oxford World's Classics.

McKinty, Adrian. *Gun Street Girl.* Amherst, NY: Seventh Street, 2015.

Metcalf, John. *The Canadian Short Story.* Windsor, ON: Biblioasis, 2018.

---. "Casting Sad Spells: Alice Munro's 'Walker Brothers Cowboy'." *Writers in Aspic.* Ed. John Metcalf. Montreal: Véhicule, 1988. 186-200. Rpt. in *Freedom from Culture: Selected Essays 1982-92.* By John Metcalf. Toronto: ECW, 1994. 173-87. Rpt. in *Shut Up He Explained: A Literary Memoir Vol. II.* By John Metcalf. Windsor, ON: Biblioasis, 2007. 85-99. Rpt. in *The Canadian Short Story.* By John Metcalf. Windsor, ON: Biblioasis, 2018. 506-22.

---. "A Conversation with Alice Munro." *Journal of Canadian Fiction* 1.4 (1972): 54-62.

---. "The Signs of Invasion: Alice Munro's 'Images'." *The Canadian Short Story.* Windsor, ON: Biblioasis, 2018. 488-506.

---. "Titles." *Shut Up He Explained: A Literary Memoir Vol. II.* Windsor, ON: Biblioasis, 2007. 9-21.

---. *What Is A Canadian Literature?* Guelph, ON: Red Kite, 1988.

Metcalf, John, and J.R. (Tim) Struthers, eds. *Canadian Classics: An Anthology of Stories.* Toronto: McGraw-Hill Ryerson, 1993.

Micros, Marianne. "'Girl in a Middy'." Message to the author. 5:20 p.m. 13 Jan. 2019. E-mail.

Mozart, Wolfgang Amadeus. *Eine kleine Nachtmusik.* 1787.

Munro, Alice. Afterword. *Emily of New Moon.* By L.M. Montgomery. Toronto: McClelland and Stewart, 1989. 357-61. The New Canadian Library.

---. Afterword. *The Equations of Love.* By Ethel Wilson. Toronto: McClelland & Stewart, 1990. 259-63. The New Canadian Library.

---. "Dance of the Happy Shades." *Dance of the Happy Shades.* Fwd. Hugh Garner. Toronto: Ryerson, 1968. 211-24.

---. "Dear Life." *Dear Life.* Toronto: McClelland & Stewart, 2012. 299-319.

---. "Differently." *Friend of My Youth.* Toronto: McClelland & Stewart, 1990. 216-43.

---. "Dimensions." *Too Much Happiness.* Toronto: McClelland & Stewart, 2009. 1-31.

---. "Golden Apples." *Eudora Welty at Ninety: A Tribute. The Georgia Review* 53 (1999): 22-24.

---. "Images." *Dance of the Happy Shades.* Fwd. Hugh Garner. Toronto: Ryerson, 1968. 30-43.

---. "My Mother's Dream." *The Love of a Good Woman.* Toronto: McClelland & Stewart, 1998. 293-340.

---. "Powers." *Runaway.* Toronto: McClelland & Stewart, 2004. 270-335.

---. "The Progress of Love." *The Progress of Love.* Toronto: McClelland and Stewart, 1986. 3-31.

---. "Spaceships Have Landed." *Open Secrets.* Toronto: McClelland & Stewart, 1994. 226-60.

---. "Spelling." *Who Do You Think You Are?* Toronto: Macmillan of Canada, 1978. 174-88.

---. "The Time of Death." *Dance of the Happy Shades.* Fwd. Hugh Garner. Toronto: Ryerson, 1968. 89-99.

---. "To Reach Japan." *Dear Life.* Toronto: McClelland & Stewart, 2012. 3-30.

---. "Too Much Happiness." *Too Much Happiness.* Toronto: McClelland & Stewart, 2009. 246-303.

---. "Vandals." *Open Secrets.* Toronto: McClelland & Stewart, 1994. 261-94.

---. "Walker Brothers Cowboy." *Dance of the Happy Shades.* Fwd. Hugh Garner. Toronto: Ryerson, 1968. 1-18.

---. "What Do You Want To Know For?" *The View from Castle Rock.* Toronto: McClelland & Stewart, 2006. 316-40.

---. "What Is Real?" *Making It New: Contemporary Canadian Stories.* Ed. John Metcalf. Toronto: Methuen, 1982. 223-26. Rpt. in *How Stories Mean.* Ed. John Metcalf and J.R. (Tim) Struthers. Erin, ON: The Porcupine's Quill, 1993. 331-34. Critical Directions 3.

---. "White Dump." *The Progress of Love.* Toronto: McClelland and Stewart, 1986. 275-309.

---. *Who Do You Think You Are?* Toronto: Macmillan of Canada, 1978.

---. "Wigtime." *Friend of My Youth.* Toronto: McClelland & Stewart, 1990. 244-73.

---. "Writing. Or, Giving Up Writing." *Writing Life: Celebrated Canadian and International Authors on Writing and Life.* Ed. Constance Rooke. Toronto: McClelland & Stewart, 2006. 297-300.

Munro, Sheila. *Lives of Mothers & Daughters: Growing Up with Alice Munro.* Toronto: McClelland & Stewart, 2001.

"Nancy." <http://www.biblical-baby-names.com/meaning-of-nancy.html>.

Nasgaard, Roald. *Abstract Painting in Canada.* Vancouver, BC: Douglas & McIntyre, 2007.

New, W.H. *Reading Mansfield and Metaphors of Form.* Montreal, QC and Kingston, ON: McGill-Queen's UP, 1999.

---. "Utrecht Allegory." *Alice Munro: Writing for Dear Life.* Ed. Corinne Bigot. *Commonwealth Essays and Studies* 37.2 (2015): 11-14.

Norris, Margot. *Suspicious Readings of Joyce's Dubliners.* Philadelphia: U of Pennsylvania P, 2003.

Ozick, Cynthia. "The Shawl." *The Shawl.* New York: Alfred A. Knopf, 1989. 1-10. Rpt. in *Elements of Fiction: Third Canadian Edition.* Ed. Robert Scholes and Rosemary Sullivan. Toronto: Oxford UP, 1994. 530-34.

Palusci, Oriana. "Breathing and the Power of Evil in 'Dimensions'." *Alice Munro and the Anatomy of the Short Story.* Ed. Oriana Palusci. Newcastle upon Tyne, Eng.: Cambridge Scholars, 2017. 111-25.

Perrault, Charles. "Little Red Riding Hood." *The Fairy Tales of Charles Perrault.* Trans. and with a fwd. by Angela Carter. Illus. with etchings by Martin Ware. London: Victor Gollancz, 1977. 23-28.

Poe, Edgar Allan. "Review of *Twice-Told Tales.*" 1842. Rpt. in *Short Story Theories.* Ed. Charles E. May. Athens, OH: Ohio UP, 1976. 45-51. Rpt. in *The New Short Story Theories.* Ed. Charles E. May. Athens, OH: Ohio UP, 1994. 59-64.

Prose, Francine. *Reading Like a Writer: A Guide for People Who Love Books and for Those Who Want To Write Them*. 2006. New York: Harper Perennial, 2007.

Rae, Ian. "Alice Munro and the Huron Tract as a Literary Project." *The Inside of a Shell: Alice Munro's* Dance of the Happy Shades. Ed. Vanessa Guignery. Newcastle upon Tyne, Eng.: Cambridge Scholars, 2015. 46-64. Rpt. (rev.) in *Alice Munro Country: Essays on Her Works I*. Ed. J.R. (Tim) Struthers. Toronto: Guernica Editions, 2020. Essential Writers Ser. 51.

Reaney, James. "Myths in Some Nineteenth-Century Ontario Newspapers." *Aspects of Nineteenth-Century Ontario: Essays Presented to James J. Talman*. Ed. F.H. Armstrong, H.A. Stevenson, and J.D. Wilson. Toronto: U of Toronto P, 1974. 253-66.

---. "Some Critics Are Music Teachers." *Centre and Labyrinth: Essays in Honour of Northrop Frye*. Ed. Eleanor Cook, Chaviva Hošek, Jay Macpherson, Patricia Parker, and Julian Patrick. Toronto: U of Toronto P, 1983. 298-308.

---. "Vision in Canada?" *The Visionary Tradition in Canadian Writing*. Ed. Russell Morton Brown and J.R. (Tim) Struthers. *University of Toronto Quarterly* 70 (2001): 937-46.

Reid, Dennis, ed. *Jack Chambers: Light, Spirit, Time, Place and Life*. Fredericton and Toronto: Goose Lane Editions and Art Gallery of Ontario, 2011.

The Revelation of St. John the Divine. *The Holy Bible*. Cambridge, Eng.: Cambridge UP, n.d. Authorized King James Vers.

Reynolds, Mary T. *Joyce and Dante: The Shaping Imagination*. Princeton, NJ: Princeton UP, 1981.

Reynolds, Stephen. "Autobiografiction." *The Speaker* new ser. 15, no. 366 (6 Oct. 1906): 28, 30.

Rohrberger, Mary. "Between Shadow and Act: Where Do We Go from Here?" *Short Story Theory at a Crossroads*. Ed. Susan Lohafer and Jo Ellyn Clarey. Baton Rouge: Louisiana State UP, 1989. 32-45.

---. *Hawthorne and the Modern Short Story: A Study in Genre*. The Hague, Neth.: Mouton, 1966.

---. "Origins, Development, Substance, and Design of the Short Story: How I Got Hooked on the Short Story and Where It Led Me." *The Art of Brevity: Excursions in Short Fiction Theory and Analysis*. Ed. Per

Winther, Jakob Lothe, and Hans H. Skei. Columbia, SC: U of South
    Carolina P, 2004. 1-13.

Rohrberger, Mary, and Dan E. Burns. "Short Fiction and the Numinous
    Realm: Another Attempt at Definition." *The Modern Short Story*. Pref.
    A. Walton Litz. *Modern Fiction Studies* 28 (1982): 5-12.

Ross, Catherine Sheldrick. *Alice Munro: A Double Life*. Toronto: ECW,
    1992. Canadian Biography Ser. 1.

---. "'At Least Part Legend': The Fiction of Alice Munro." *Probable Fictions:
    Alice Munro's Narrative Acts*. Ed. Louis K. MacKendrick. Downsview,
    ON: ECW, 1983. 112-26.

Rubio, Mary Henley. *Lucy Maud Montgomery: The Gift of Wings*. Toronto:
    Doubleday Canada, 2008.

---. "Re: <Montgomery-esque> ???." Message to the author. 6:55 p.m. 4
    Dec. 2018. E-mail.

Rubio, Mary, and Elizabeth Waterston, eds. *The Selected Journals of L.M.
    Montgomery; Volume III: 1921-1929*. Toronto: Oxford UP, 1992.

Shakespeare, William. *King Lear*. 8th ed. Ed. Kenneth Muir. London:
    Methuen, 1963. The Arden Edition of the Works of William Shakespeare.

---. *The Tempest*. 6th ed. Ed. Frank Kermode. London: Methuen, 1961. The
    Arden Edition of the Works of William Shakespeare.

Silcox, David P. *Painting Place: The Life and Work of David B. Milne*.
    Toronto: U of Toronto P, 1996.

Smart, Tom. *The Art of Mary Pratt: The Substance of Light*. Fredericton:
    Goose Lane Editions and The Beaverbrook Art Gallery, 1995.

Sophocles. *Oedipus the King*. Trans. David Grene. *The Complete Greek
    Tragedies; Volume II: Sophocles*. Ed. David Grene and Richmond
    Lattimore. Chicago, IL: U of Chicago P, 1959. 9-76.

Steinberg, Theodore L. Piers Plowman *and Prophecy: An Approach to
    the C-Text*. New York: Garland, 1991. Garland Studies in Medieval
    Literature 5.

Stevens, Wallace. "Adagia." *Opus Posthumous*. Ed. and introd. Samuel
    French Morse. New York: Alfred A. Knopf, 1957. 157-80.

---. "Notes Toward a Supreme Fiction." *The Collected Poems of Wallace
    Stevens*. New York: Alfred A. Knopf, 1954. 380-408.

Stich, Klaus P. "Munro's Grail Quest: The Progress of Logos." *Studies in
    Canadian Literature / Études en littérature canadienne* 32.1 (2007):
    120-40.

Strindberg, August. *A Dream Play*. *The Plays: Volume Two*. Trans. and
introd. Michael Meyer. London: Secker and Warburg, 1975. 555-632.

Struthers, J.R. (Tim). "In Search of the Perfect Metaphor: The Language of
the Short Story and Alice Munro's 'Meneseteung'." *Critical Insights: Alice
Munro*. Ed. Charles E. May. Ipswich, MA: Salem-EBSCO, 2013. 175-94.

---. "An Interview with Hugh Hood." *Hugh Hood's Work in Progress*. Ed. J.R.
(Tim) Struthers. *Essays on Canadian Writing* 13-14 (1978-79): 21-93.
Rpt. in *Before the Flood: Our Exagmination round His Factification for
Incamination of Hugh Hood's Work in Progress*. Downsview, ON: ECW,
1979. 21-93.

---. "Learning To Read, Learning To Write: An Interview with Clark Blaise
(2007)." *Clark Blaise: The Interviews*. Ed. J.R. (Tim) Struthers. Toronto:
Guernica Editions, 2016. 333-65. Essential Writers Ser. 45.

---. "Once More to the Lake: Towards a Poetics of Receptivity." *New Contexts of Canadian Criticism*. Ed. Ajay Heble, Donna Palmateer Pennee,
and J.R. (Tim) Struthers. Peterborough, ON: Broadview, 1997. 319-45.

---. "The Real Material: An Interview with Alice Munro." *Probable Fictions:
Alice Munro's Narrative Acts*. Ed. Louis K. MacKendrick. Downsview,
ON: ECW, 1983. 5-36.

---. "Remembrance Day 1988: An Interview with Alice Munro." *Alice
Munro Country: Essays on Her Works I*. Ed. J.R. (Tim) Struthers.
Toronto: Guernica Editions, 2020. Essential Writers Ser. 51.

---. "Song for Alice Munro." *Alice Munro and the Souwesto Story*. Ed. J.R.
(Tim) Struthers. *Short Story* ns 21.1 (2013 [2015]): 88-102.

---. "Story and Allegory, the Cast and the Mold: Reading Clark Blaise's
'The Birth of the Blues'." *Clark Blaise: Essays on His Works*. Ed. J.R.
(Tim) Struthers. Toronto: Guernica Editions, 2016. 205-34. Essential
Writers Ser. 44.

---. "Traveling with Munro: Reading 'To Reach Japan'." *Alice Munro:* Hateship, Friendship, Courtship, Loveship, Marriage; Runaway; Dear Life.
Ed. Robert Thacker. London: Bloomsbury, 2016. 163-83, 231-44 passim.

---. "Visionary Realism: Jack Hodgins, *Spit Delaney's Island*, and the
Redemptive Imagination." *On Coasts of Eternity: Jack Hodgins' Fictional
Universe*. Lantzville, BC: Oolichan, 1996. 66-86.

---. "A Visionary Tradition." *The Visionary Tradition in Canadian Writing*.
Ed. Russell Morton Brown and J.R. (Tim) Struthers. *University of
Toronto Quarterly* 70 (2001): 947-48.

Tabler, Dave. "Ollie Ollie In Come Free!" 21 June 2017. <http://www.appa-
    lachianhistory.net/2017/06/ollie-ollie-in-come-free.html>.
Tambling, Jeremy. *Allegory.* The New Critical Idiom. London: Routledge,
    2010.
Thacker, Robert. *Alice Munro: Writing Her Lives: A Biography.* 2005.
    Updated ed. Toronto: Emblem-McClelland & Stewart, 2011.
---. *Reading Alice Munro: 1973-2013.* Calgary: U of Calgary P, 2016.
Thomas, Audrey. "Basmati Rice: An Essay about Words." *How Stories Mean.*
    Ed. John Metcalf and J.R. (Tim) Struthers. Erin, ON: The Porcupine's
    Quill, 1993. 106-12. Critical Directions 3.
Thompson, Reg. "All Things Considered: Alice Munro First and Last."
    Alice Munro: A Souwesto Celebration. Ed. J.R. (Tim) Struthers and John
    B. Lee. *The Windsor Review* 47.2 (2014): 5-9. Rpt. in *Alice Munro Coun-
    try: Essays on Her Works I.* Ed. J.R. (Tim) Struthers. Toronto: Guernica
    Editions, 2020. Essential Writers Ser. 51.
---. "Re: A question that I hope to settle in the next couple of days...."
    Message to the author. 1:02 p.m. 30 Apr. 2019. E-mail.
Trussler, Michael. "Narrative, Memory, and Contingency in Alice Munro's
    Runaway." *Critical Insights: Alice Munro.* Ed. Charles E. May. Ipswich,
    MA: Salem-EBSCO, 2013. 242-58.
Ventura, Héliane. "The Female Bard: Retrieving Greek Myths, Celtic
    Ballads, Norse Sagas, and Popular Songs." *The Cambridge Companion
    to Alice Munro.* Ed. David Staines. Cambridge, Eng.: Cambridge UP,
    2016. 154-77.
---. "The Skald and the Goddess: Reading 'The Bear Came Over the Moun-
    tain' by Alice Munro." *The Short Stories of Alice Munro.* Ed. Héliane
    Ventura. *Journal of the Short Story in English / Les cahiers de la nouvelle*
    55 (2010): 173-85. Rpt. as "The Skald and the Goddess: A Reading of
    Alice Munro's 'The Bear Came Over the Mountain'" in *Alice Munro
    Everlasting: Essays on Her Works II.* Ed. J.R. (Tim) Struthers. Toronto:
    Guernica Editions, 2020. Essential Writers Ser. 52.
Welty, Eudora. *The Golden Apples.* 1949. New York: Harcourt, Brace &
    World, 1962. A Harvest Book.
Weston, Jessie L. *From Ritual to Romance.* 1920. Garden City, NY: Doubleday
    Anchor, 1957.
White, E.B. "Once More to the Lake." *Essays of E.B. White.* New York:
    Harper & Row, 1977. 197-202.

Williams, Tennessee. *A Streetcar Named Desire*. New York: New Directions, 1947.

Wilson, Ethel. *The Equations of Love*. Toronto: McClelland and Stewart. 1990. Afterword by Alice Munro. The New Canadian Library.

Woodcock, George. Introduction. *Canadian Writers and Their Works: Fiction Series · Volume Seven*. Ed. Robert Lecker, Jack David, Ellen Quigley. Toronto: ECW, 1987. 1-17. 12 vols. Rpt. as "One's Own Vision and Experience: Clark Blaise, Hugh Hood, John Metcalf, Alice Munro, Sheila Watson" in *George Woodcock's Introduction to Canadian Fiction*. Toronto: ECW, 1993. 100-16.

---. "The Plots of Life: The Realism of Alice Munro." *Queen's Quarterly* 93 (1986): 235-50. Rpt. in *Northern Spring: The Flowering of Canadian Literature*. Vancouver, BC: Douglas & McIntyre, 1987. 132-46.

Wordsworth, William. ["The World Is Too Much with Us."] *The Poetical Works of William Wordsworth*. Ed. Thomas Hutchinson. New ed. Rev. Ernest de Selincourt. London: Oxford UP, 1936. 206.

Yeats, W.B. "William Blake and His Illustrations to *The Divine Comedy*." *Ideas of Good and Evil*. London: A.H. Bullen, 1903. 176-225. Rpt. in *Essays and Introductions*. London: Macmillan, 1961. 116-45.

Zipes, Jack. *Why Fairy Tales Stick: The Evolution and Relevance of a Genre*. London: Routledge, 2006.

Messengers and Messaging in Alice Munro's *The View from Castle Rock*

William Butt

"I think I should understand that better," Alice said very politely,
"if I had it written down: but I can't quite follow it as you say it."
"That's nothing to what I could say if I chose," the Duchess
replied, in a pleased tone.
— Lewis Carroll, *Alice's Adventures in Wonderland* (122)

1. Rifling Around in the Past

As a species of memoir *The View from Castle Rock* is by definition about the past of the writer, or more accurately of the narrator (let's blatantly over-simplify and call her Alice), and the world she has lived in. It's "rifling around in the past" ("Messenger" 347). A kind of archaeology of time. From the book's first page we're in the Ettrick Valley, and referencing the far past and "the wall Hadrian built" ("No Advantages" 3). Alice Munro, says Catherine Sheldrick Ross, "has an archaeological sense of layers of human history" (26), including personal and family history. When Will Laidlaw leaves Ettrick's "poverty and ... ignorance," "He is a modern man" ("No Advantages" 26). Walter too on shipboard claims "'a modern turn of mind'" ("The View from Castle Rock" 62). But time is really times, and times change, like the floor in the house where Alice lived, "the linoleum ... repainted by my mother every spring" ("Home" 288). What once was modern, like the foundry where Alice's father

345

worked, "was soon to disappear" ("Working for a Living" 162). Change is personal; change also is geological, eons old: "The landscape here is a record of ancient events" ("What Do You Want To Know For?" 318). Every story in *The View from Castle Rock* – like most and perhaps all stories by Alice Munro – navigates differing layers of time, and voices from those times.

Over time, anything "can be dissolved" ("Home" 289). It may then become hard to locate, like the cemetery crypt in "What Do You Want To Know For?"; or the cemetery in Homer Township, Illinois – "It is useless.... I grope my way out" ("Messenger" 347); or most of what's abandoned in the dump in "Lying Under the Apple Tree" (208); or the text and image incised on beech bark in "Lying Under the Apple Tree," which has morphed and become obscure in the thirty-five years or so since its carving, "so that the outlines of the face had broadened at the sides to become blotches.... The rest of the date had been blotched out entirely" (212-13). It may be hard to read its message. But even dissolved, diffused, dissipated, as Coleridge has it in Chapter XIII of *Biographia Literaria* (1: 202), an object or substance chemically remains, suspended invisible in its medium, until precipitated through a subsequent reaction. Memory as chemistry. Often, once recovered from solution, the precipitate is purer somehow, easier to manage – or to re-create (Coleridge again, in the same passage) than when in its pre-dissolved state. "The past needs to be approached from a distance" ("What Do You Want To Know For?" 332).

To most people, like Alice's guide in the Lutheran church in "What Do You Want To Know For?," it seems as if you "take care of what's on the surface, and what is behind, so immense and disturbing, will take care of itself" (334). But Alice disagrees: What is buried or hidden underneath, in waste-dumps or under coats of paint or anywhere else in space or in time, by definition is obscure and dark, and our poor lights won't readily penetrate; "the ornate 'L' of Licht ... has faded or flaked off" ("What Do You Want To Know For?" 334). Underneath is the stricken heart of darkness, the writing on Belshazzar's wall in The Book of Daniel. The alien lump which medical explorers may scan down to could sit there in a breast inert and unobserved – "Oh, she says, they must not have seen it" ("What Do You Want To Know For?" 339). Or it may be cancer, malignant, and will metastasize and that's the end of you.

2. Prying Eyes

From first glance at its title we ought to know that this book is about –
presumably among much else – points of view. Rather unnerving eyes
peer throughout *The View from Castle Rock*. Alice's radiologist, who
makes her living with high-tech eye-extensions to scout out tumours and
such, has "almost colorless eyes enlarged, made owlish, by her glasses"
("What Do You Want To Know For?" 339). Alice's "grandmother's eyes
were a hazel color, but in one of them she had a large spot, taking up at
least a third of the iris, and the color of this spot was blue" ("Working for
a Living" 148). Eyes probe and intrude. From a hiding place, Alice and
Dahlia Newcombe secretly descry Dahlia's father. "'You want to come
with me?'" Dahlia asks Alice. "'You want to see how I do my spying?'"
("Fathers" 179). In "Hired Girl," late-teen Alice snoops on Mr. Foley in the
boathouse – "He never knew that I was there" (250). "I did not question
my right to pry" (252).

But eyes don't necessarily see very well. Mary Anne Montjoy "wore
heavy glasses even when sitting up in bed" ("Hired Girl" 231). And her
father – "When he took off his glasses you could see that one eye was
quick and squinty and the other boldly blue but helpless-looking, as if
caught in a trap" ("Hired Girl" 241). Alice's Uncle Cyril "wore glasses,
with one lens of dark amber glass, hiding the eye that had been injured
when he was a child. I don't know if this eye was entirely blind. I never
saw it, and it made me sick to think of it – I imagined a mound of dark
quivering jelly" ("The Ticket" 276). What one sees or seems to see with
one's flimsy visual apparatus is not all that meets the eye of another
observer or reader.

3. You Can Look It Up

More than Munro's other books which are expressly 'fiction,' *The View
from Castle Rock* regales us with documented and documentary fact.
We are favoured with almost exhibitionistic research, like the citations
from *Blackwood's* ("The View from Castle Rock" 82-83) and a *Statistical
Account of Scotland* ("No Advantages" 3). We see "the nineteenth-century
county atlases" ("What Do You Want To Know For?" 323), and a world

Historical Atlas ("Home" 291). Alice quotes – assures us that she quotes – from actual family memoirs. Of Walter Laidlaw in "The View from Castle Rock" (39-79, intermittently). Of Big Rob Laidlaw in "The Wilds of Morris Township" (111-17). Of her father, Robert Laidlaw, in "Working for a Living" (167-70). She quotes Andrew's shipboard letter, and Old James's letter to Robert his son back home, and another "addressed to the Editor of *The Colonial Advocate*" ("The View from Castle Rock" 79, 82-83, 83). We're told the name of a shipboard dance, "Strip the Willow" ("The View from Castle Rock" 71), and the details of an Illinois pioneer menu in spring: "There was pork to eat, with cabbage and boiled potatoes. The last of last year's potatoes, these were, and the meat had a good tough layer of fat. She filled up on fresh radishes and greens and new-baked bread" ("Illinois" 97). We get technical detail: Alice's trapper father "built up deadfalls, with a figure 4 trigger" ("Working for a Living" 137). Her mother makes fur clothing, and we're given almost a manual of how: "A fox scarf was one whole skin, a mink scarf was two or three skins. The head of the animal was left on and was given bright golden-brown glass eyes, also an artificial jaw. Fasteners were sewn on the paws" ("Working for a Living" 142). And in "What Do You Want To Know For?" we get catalogues: of ads on backroad signs – "Brown eggs, maple syrup, bagpipe lessons, unisex haircuts" – and of vegetation, "hawthorn trees, chokecherries, goldenrod, old-man's beard" (327). It hasn't always been like that – in "Walker Brothers Cowboy," the first story in Munro's first published book, *Dance of the Happy Shades*, a list trails off generically: "burdocks, plantains, humble nameless weeds all around" (2).

But can you trust even 'factual' objective accounts like this? Are not even these subjective? Journal writers both, Walter Laidlaw and Mr. Carbert aren't so certain:

> "I only write what happens," Walt says....
> ....
> "So you do not describe what you see? Only what – as you say – is happening?"
> Walter is about to say no, and then yes. ("The View from Castle Rock" 60)

4. Information Missing in Action

Despite the flaunted researchiness, information is made to seem casually, unsystematically distributed. Naming appears deliberately haphazard. In the book's title story Agnes, Walter's wife, gives birth (47); but we're not told her child's name till the story's last page, when we see it on the gravestone. Isabel. *"Born at Sea"* (87). Alice's grandmother isn't named till page 261: "my grandmother's name ... was Selina" ("The Ticket"). Her grandfather stays unidentified till page 278 – *"Will"* ("The Ticket") – though we've heard about him at least as early as page 126 ("The Wilds of Morris Township"). We don't hear Alice's father's name till pages 330-31, and then in a casual drop-in conversation. "'Bob Laidlaw. Bob Laidlaw was your dad. Well'" (What Do You Want To Know For?" 331). Or look at the place names. Reading "What Do You Want To Know For?" you could go to a map that will tell you there really is an actual Sullivan Township, Scone, and Williamsford (325, 329, 328). But in "Fathers," only a fictional map would show in Souwesto the Shelby Township that Bunt Newcomb's obit mentions (196). Truth or fiction? "There are always puzzles" ("What Do You Want To Know For?" 325), Alice muses, unrepentantly. And dates? Time after time we are left almost cavalierly to calculate dates on our own. When Alice visits the Lutheran church in Scone, Grey County, in "What Do You Want To Know For?," we are left to calculate for ourselves that the year is 1993: flipping amongst the pages in search, we find that Alice "had missed last year's" mammogram (317), and over twenty pages later that the most-recent preceding ones were "in 1990 and in 1991" (339).

5. Spinners of Tales

All through *The View from Castle Rock* people are talking; they're telling stories. Almost everyone is like Old James, "old tale-spinner spouting all over the boat" ("The View from Castle Rock" 64). Harry Crofton in "Home" "knows and always has known every story, rumor, disgrace, and possible paternity within many miles" (294). People are avid to tell and hear narrative. On the ship, Nettie "wants to know all about how Walter and his people live" ("The View from Castle Rock" 57). Alice hungers to hear from Mrs. Montjoy the story of her daughter Jane's death, though she has heard it already from Mary Anne. Huron County folk in this book see narrative as effectively a ceremonial practice, the way they see all of life: "I believe they saw [life] mostly as ritual" ("Working for a Living" 136). Stories "in the society I came from … were never buried for good, but ritualistically resurrected" ("Hired Girl" 252). Stories – gossip, rumour, suppositions, claims – become communal birthrights. The book is pointillist with such tales. "I heard reports" ("The Ticket" 274); "she is supposed to have said" ("No Advantages" 22); "The talk was" ("Working for a Living" 135). Magdalene Redekop compares this orality to eighteenth-century Ettrick: "a Scottish oral tradition informs Munro's craft at the deepest level, particularly as it has come to her through the writing of her ancestor James Hogg" (23).

6. To Be Trusted?

Old James Laidlaw from Castle Rock thinks he sees or claims he sees America, though we guess before his son Andrew figures it out that he was gazing north across the Firth of Forth – "he had been looking at Fife" ("The View from Castle Rock" 31). In her foreword Munro allows that the *Castle Rock* stories are not memoir "in an austere or rigorously factual way. … // … // You could say such stories pay more attention to the truth of a life than fiction usually does. But not enough to swear on" ([x]). As Magdalene Redekop deduces, Munro's ancestor James Hogg figures large behind this pronouncement: "it strikes me that her connection to Hogg, The Ettrick Shepherd, must be like having a trickster for an ancestor – a trickster who could not always control his shape-shifting" (31). Certainly Alice encourages us to see James Hogg this way. "Hogg poor man has spent most of his life in conning lies," Hogg's cousin James Laidlaw alleges ("No Advantages" 19). Alice herself writes of Hogg's "canny lying of the sort you can depend upon a writer to do," his "trimming and embroidering of material" ("No Advantages" 21). No wonder Alice is spellbound by the Dinesen *Tales*, with their air of the fantastic, the fabulous, a marvellously protean reality, legends, yarns, shifty fables.

Often the story-tellers are knowingly false. In "Illinois," the sawmill owner's daughter Susie and the teacher's daughter Meggie concoct a romantic narrative: to the stableboy they write "a love letter and sign it

Rose – the real name, as it happened, of the innkeeper's daughter" (102), and then they leave him a note on the baby – "*A PRESENT from one of your SWEETHEARTS*" (108). "Lying Under the Apple Tree" means more than a prone position – it also means telling falsehoods:

> "So. What were you doing there?"
> "Looking for something," I said.
> "Looking for something. Yeah. What?"
> "A bracelet."
> I had never owned a bracelet in my life. (201)

So. Young Alice lies too. "I am surely one of the liars," Alice cheerfully, off-handedly, has already admitted ("The View from Castle Rock" 84). Time and again in this book Munro is out to catch us up. It's almost capital-M "Mischief," the title of a story from *Who Do You Think You Are?*. In "Hired Girl," Mr. Montjoy on the story's last page turns without comment into "Mr. Mountjoy" (254), and if we're watchful we can see we're being played with: in this story shot through with late-teen sexual fantasy, a name to fit a character on some Bunyanesque ascent has segued into something like a lecher's name in a Restoration comic drama.

7. Varieties of Linguistic Experience

Humans tell tales primarily via language, and *The View from Castle Rock* is much about language *per se*; about words. Often, phrases come packaged in italics: to emphasize, make them 'stand out'; to call attention to their look and sound and spokenness, rather than only their 'meaning'. Phrases of Huron County folk get italicized:

> "*Calling attention to yourself*" ("No Advantages" 20);
> "*She's a wonder*" ("Home" 310);
> "*Sloppy,*" "*wishy-washy,*" "*unnecessary*" ("Hired Girl" 236);
> "*fond of each other*" ("The Ticket" 277);
> "*we seen you the other day*" ("The Ticket" 261);
> "*Get yo' hans outa my pocket*" ("Home" 307).

We even get dog-talk, Irlma's old mongrel's grunting as he tries to defecate: "*Hunh. Hunh.*" ("Home" 306).

Languages proliferate, each wondrous, exotic, idiosyncratic, but not easily comprehensible. On the boat we have Young James's aunt, Mary, garbling his idiosyncratic toddler-talk: "The boy on her hip makes his sound for bird. 'Sailor-peep, sailor-peep,' she says. She says the right word for *sailor* but his word for *bird.* She and he communicate in a half-and-half language – half her teaching and half his invention" ("The View from Castle Rock" 35); James's mother, Agnes, wonders if he's speaking "elfit" (35). Even Mary's way of speaking seems to most people only "a dribble of speech so faint and scrambled" (36). Nettie Carbert doesn't understand much of Walter's talk – "What do some of his words mean that she does not understand, and do all the people where he is talk like him?" ("The View from Castle Rock" 58). Then, there are the sailors: "'Some of them are English,' Nettie says, 'but from parts that sound foreign to us. Some are Portuguese. I cannot make them out either but I think that they are saying they see the rotches'" ("The View from Castle Rock" 63); the Portuguese word for 'rocks' is 'rochas'.

Incongruously we hear German – "*Gestorben*, here in Sullivan Township in Grey County in a colony of England, in the middle of the bush" ("What Do You Want To Know For?" 324). We hear Latin: "Nova Scotia. // 'It means New Scotland,' [Mary] says" ("The View from Castle Rock" 65). Alice's grandfather and his cousin "Sometimes ... talked in the broad Scots of the district from which they came," a tongue that "none of their descendants could understand" ("Working for a Living" 170). We hear yet another antic language, nonsense phonetically devolved from Longfellow's "A Psalm of Life": "*Liza Grayman Ollie Minus. / We can make Eliza blind*" ("Working for a Living" 127). Alice quotes a gleeful satirical piece by James Hogg, a specimen of Ettrick dialect: "*An if it be true* that the bairn born a fortnight past to -------- --------'s wife has an almighty look about it of --------, then wilt Thou Lord show mercy on all the participants ..." ("No Advantages" 25).

Voices and styles. Alice quotes gravestone epitaphs of her kinfolk in three countries, redolent of traditional local style, like "the far-famed Will o' Phaup, who for feats of frolic, agility and strength, had no equal in his day ..." ("No Advantages" 7). Still "another private passion I had ... was for lines of poetry," language dressed up ("Lying Under the Apple Tree"

198). The epigraph from Galsworthy's tale "The Apple Tree" "beguiled me. // *The apple tree, the singing and the gold ...*" (260), which comes from Gilbert Murray's ornate and scholarly translation of *Hippolytus* by Euripides, a typically elevated passage where the Chorus evokes an ideal world of Love from which the vicious, capricious goddess of Love will always bar us (Euripides 39).

Narrator Alice takes on these styles with gusto, the way an actor might take on a part. She renders Will O'Phaup's breezy folk-talk, "And what does he see down below but a whole company of creatures all about as high as a two-year-old child.... // ... // His own name is all the word in their mouths" ("No Advantages" 11). To continue Big Rob's story she puts on his simple, declarative style: "In the parcel was a new shirt of blue cotton, and half a loaf of bread and a fresh chunk of butter. All bread that the sisters made was excellent, and the butter tasty, being made from the milk of Jersey cows" ("The Wilds of Morris Township" 124). To tell the end of Bunt Newcombe, she imitates a small-town newspaper's obit ("Fathers" 196). And she mimics an adolescent's prose: "I swam that way, with the water sweetly dividing at my nipples ..." ("Hired Girl" 249). *Sweetly?*

8. Texts in Conversation

More than any other book by Alice Munro, *The View from Castle Rock* is explicitly intertextual, a gabble of authors and passages quoted from and referred to. The books and movies and other things we come upon when young may hold us more strongly, and for longer, because we read or watch with a greater capacity for amazement, and suspension of disbelief. There's a Peebles Subscription Library in Ettrick; a Public Library in Alice's town; a bookcase in her family's living room. Amidst the bibliophilic array we spot Homer's *Iliad* (348) and *Odyssey* (230), Dante's *Inferno* (5), *Wuthering Heights* (24, 226), James Hogg whose title *The Private Memoirs and Confessions of a Justified Sinner* (20) "could itself be a Munro title," as Margaret Atwood says (Introduction xii), and A.E. Coppard's "Dusky Ruth," of which the adult narrator Alice claims that except for the title she "can't remember anything else" ("The Ticket" 260), but which serves up lots of lines that her teenage self might have thought she would never forget:

In the close darkness he put his arms about her with no thought but to comfort her; one hand had plunged through the long harsh tresses and the other across her hips before he realized that she was ungowned.... // ... He felt for the bed with one hand, and turning back the quilt and sheets he lifted her in and, in his clothes, he lay stretched beside her comforting her. They lay so, innocent as children, for an hour.... (Coppard 94-95)

On the *Castle Rock* shelves with Coppard, we spot period titles from Alice's youth – Margaret Mitchell's *Gone with the Wind* from 1936 ("Lying Under the Apple Tree" 226), Thor Heyerdahl's 1950 *The Kon-Tiki Expedition* ("Hired Girl" 233), and Frederic Wakeman's now unreadably dated *The Hucksters* from 1946 ("Hired Girl" 245). These works interact with one another. The apple tree of Euripides calls us back to that title tree under which Alice experimentally reclines in "Lying Under the Apple Tree," and behind that we might hear allusion to the Andrews Sisters' hit song "Don't Sit Under the Apple Tree," which came out in 1942. Much 1930s and 40s popular culture keeps seeping in, the Craik family's hens "named after Mae West and Tugboat Annie and Daisy Mae and other personalities from the movies or comic strips or popular folklore" ("Lying Under the Apple Tree" 216); the magazines "*Life* and *Look* and *Time* and *Collier's*" ("Hired Girl" 237); and in Frances's living room – "a stack of movie magazines. I fell upon them at once" ("Fathers" 188). There we see the two rapt girls reading by a lamp whose "bulb shone through the pale-green glass of a lady's skirt. // 'That's Scarlett O'Hara,' Frances said" ("Fathers" 188).

So many writers, and they talk so often to Alice and she to them, and implicitly they talk to one another. In "Hired Girl" we get Isak Dinesen and her *Seven Gothic Tales*, a 1934 Book of the Month Club selection. At the end of "Hired Girl" Alice quotes from "The Supper at Elsinore," where "Neptune, with a trident, steered his team of horses through high waves" ("Hired Girl" 254; Dinesen 252): and the maritime mental traveller pictures the Homeric Mediterranean, and the trans-Atlantic voyage to Canada in "The View from Castle Rock," and Heyerdahl's Pacific Kon-Tiki raft contraption, and on to the unnamed sea of the shell on the book's last page. Included in what Alice quotes is Dinesen's description of the room where the lost dead brother appears to his sisters. "The walls of the room had once been painted crimson, but with time the

colour had faded into a richness of hues, like a glassful of dying roses"
("Hired Girl" 254; Dinesen 252). Through mischief or some Harold-Bloom
misprision or other intervention, Alice misquotes. She has left out one of
Dinesen's words – the original says "dying red roses" (Dinesen 252) – as
if to improve or even reprove, "red" being arguably redundant, the way
an unnamed reader spots redundancy in quaint early writing by Alice:
"*Softly, silently the yellow leaves fell – it was autumn. //* ... Except that
somebody pointed out that naturally it was autumn.... Why else would
the leaves be falling...?" ("The Ticket" 261).

9. What Do You Want To Go For?

J.R. (Tim) Struthers has mused on the vast amount of travelling in Alice
Munro stories, by car, bus, boat, plane, journeys "made by one or another
possible vehicle" ("Traveling with Munro" 164), and *The View from Castle
Rock* too is full of voyages. Always in *Castle Rock* these rampant dislocations lead to wider- and wider-spread uncertainty. They destabilize. Old
James and others trek up Castle Rock, and to him the view from there
is a summons to America. Will Laidlaw upped and moved to Illinois,
and "there was something about all this rushing away, loosing oneself
entirely from family and past ... that might not help a man" ("Illinois"
110). The rootless hapless Wainwrights in "Fathers" come from Chicago,
but soon leave Huron County in hope of greener pastures in Burlington,
Ontario. In "Home" Peggy and Joe have moved around, which is locally
taken as a sign of their being unseemly, unreliable. Likewise Uncle Leo:
he "took off ... he went places ... with a lumbering crew in Northern
Ontario ... with a harvesters' excursion ... out west" ("The Ticket" 271),
which to locals makes him seem shiftless, almost shifty.

Young Alice herself takes nonconformist bike rides into town, and
up and down concession roads, and later ventures off to university in
London, and then through marriage makes it all the way to Canada's
West Coast, and for her pains is "thought ... to some extent a traitor for
not staying where [she] belonged" ("The Ticket" 280). Alice's father reads
a world atlas and "knows about rivers in Asia and ancient boundaries
in the Middle East" ("Home" 299). Even the language can flare out unexpectedly to somewhere far away. A crypt in a cemetery south of Georgian

Bay is described as "like some giant wombat" ("What Do You Want To Know For?" 316), and suddenly we're in Australia. A Georgian Bay island is called Nausicaa, and we're transported to whatever Ionian-Sea island an original Nausicaa might have inhabited. On that same Georgian Bay island Mr. Hammond is "an amorous tame crocodile" ("Hired Girl" 249), and yet again we've been taken, to tropical eco-niches on any of four continents. Such imagery makes the local feel exotic, the near faraway, the familiar esoteric – and vice versa: "known and secret" ("Messenger" 344), the everyday "always springing some sort of surprise on us" ("What Do You Want To Know For?" 318).

10. God Knows?

God, it turns out, is all through *The View from Castle Rock*. "The society Munro writes about," says Margaret Atwood, introducing a selection of Munro's stories, "is a Christian one" (xvii). Munro writes of the early-eighteenth-century Presbyterian cleric Thomas Boston, preacher at her ancestor Will Laidlaw's Ettrick church. Boston's God is an angry, formidable God, stingy with His grace, unrelentingly demanding of piety, chastity, modesty, to a degree impossible to your average human. Vengeful, reproachful, inscrutable; a God who requires of believers in Him "wrestlings, self-castigation, and bouts of prayer" ("No Advantages" 15). A quarter of a millennium later, in "Home" in the 1970s, the evangelical Tabernacle's God hasn't changed much: "'I say to myself it's no wonder the Lord struck me blind. He struck me blind but I see his purpose in it. I see the Lord's purpose. We have not had a drop of liquor in the place since the first of July weekend'" (297). What kind of God strikes someone blind to get him to give up liquor? A ham-handed, inarticulate, gratuitously violent One.

In "Lying Under the Apple Tree," the God of Alice's 1944 Salvation Army boyfriend doesn't seem much different: He's God the Commander, "inflexible and impatient" (212). "'I'll have to do what God wants me to'" (212). The Army hymns to Him are exuberantly militant. "'There is Power, Power, Power, Power, Power in the Blood'" (205). This God calls for a sort of expressionist theatre. There are costumes, the blazoned Army uniforms. There are tambourines, "a fat boy on the drum. Also a tall boy to play the trombone, a girl playing the clarinet" (205). "Joy and lustiness infected the bystanders" (205). The Roman Catholic God shows a like taste for extravagant spectacle on the part of His humans, an almost Grand Guignol theatre of the kind Thomas Boston in "No Advantages" calls "Popish" (15), like self-scourging "with thorned whips" (15), a sort of contrived splendour that the early-1940s adolescent Alice "longed for" ("Lying Under the Apple Tree" 199). "It was almost like kneeling down in church, which in our church we didn't do. I had done it once, when I was friends with Delia Cavanaugh and her mother took us to the Catholic church on a Saturday to arrange the flowers. I crossed myself and knelt in a pew and Delia said – not even whispering – 'What are you doing that for? You're not supposed to do that. Just us'" ("Lying Under the Apple Tree" 199). To lower-church Protestants, the Anglicans "were sometimes thought of as next thing to Papists.... Their religion often seemed to out-siders to be all a matter of bows and responses, with ... much pomp and frivolity" ("Working for a Living" 133). In the case of Agnes, "Her under-standing of God is shallow and unstable.... She has always felt that God or even the idea of Him was more distant from her than from other people" ("The View from Castle Rock" 51). Probably she's not the only one. At Alice's house, God only shows up for meals and the rote "Bless-this-food-to-our-use-and-us-to-thy-service" ("Lying Under the Apple Tree" 217).

In this sort of spirit, Alice lies beneath a blossoming apple tree. A sort of proto-aesthetic experiment, it is also devotional:

> I was secretly devoted to Nature. The feeling came from books, at first. It came from the girls' stories by the writer L.M. Montgomery, who often inserted some sentences describing a snowy field in moonlight or a pine forest or a still pond mirroring the evening sky. ("Lying Under the Apple Tree" 198)

Montgomery's Anne of Green Gables, after an austerely doctrinal Pres-byterian "awfully long prayer" in church, reports back home that

> "I would have been dreadfully tired before he got through if I hadn't been sitting by that window. But it looked right out on the Lake of Shining Waters, so I just gazed at that and imagined all sorts of splendid things." (Montgomery 91)

All sorts of splendid things: this is how the adult Alice thinks of natural forms like kame moraines, "all wild and bumpy, unpredictable, with a look of chance and secrets" ("What Do You Want To Know For?" 321).

Fast-forward from Presbyterian PEI to a Lutheran church in Grey County, Ontario. To the words of two texts in German Gothic script from Psalms 121 and 119, uncovered on the church wall under paint, during cleaning and restoration after a fire. Alice renders them in unacknowl- edgedly (mischievously?) touched-up King James English:

> *I will lift up my eyes unto the hills, from whence cometh my help.*
> *Thy word is a lamp unto my feet and a light unto my path.*
> ("What Do You Want To Know For?" 333)

Alice ponders how "The words on the wall strike me to the heart, but I am not a believer and they do not make me a believer" (334). Mary Anne Montjoy in "Hired Girl" "did not believe in God or Heaven" (233), and eventually neither does narrator Alice – "I don't think about things like that. I did at one time, but not anymore" ("Home" 307). Stricken to the heart: this transports us to "The Flaming Heart" of Richard Crashaw's Saint Teresa, and the sword-stabbed heart of Mary the mother of Jesus (Luke 2.35). The words on the wall take us to God's prophetic message to Belshazzar (Dan. 5.25-28). Alice is not a 'believer' in the Old- or New-Testament God, not in Luther's Reformation God nor His late-twentieth-century Lutheran facsimile. Not from the Bible but from Chapman and Putnam's *The Physiography of Southern Ontario* cometh her help, its "special maps that we travel with" and "somewhat reveren- tially" consult ("What Do You Want To Know For?" 319). It's a lamp unto her feet; it lights and guides her path.

Alice's God, in some time when Alice might have been some sort of believer, might have been more a story-teller's God, marvellous and shifty, like the God envisaged by "the much-renowned story-teller Mira Jama himself" in Dinesen's "The Dreamers," "the inventions of whose mind have been loved by a hundred tribes" (Dinesen 272) and whom Alice quotes: "'To love [God] truly you must love change, and you must love a joke, these being the true inclinations of his own heart'" ("Hired Girl" 242; Dinesen 355).

11. What Do You Want To Narrate For?

Among other reasons far outside the scope of this essay, people tell stories to make connection. Old James Laidlaw at sea tells fairy tales from back in Ettrick, the neighbourhood he knows but has left for an unknown Canada West. Alice wrote a teenage letter of hers "to assure myself that I had some contact with the world" ("Hired Girl" 251). We need the flotsam of our environment "drawn ... into a pattern of things we know about" ("What Do You Want To Know For?" 336). Hence the pattern of bridges in these stories: from Ettrick Bridge ("No Advantages" 5) to the plank footbridge across the Maitland River, which Alice crosses with Dahlia, "heads soberly bowed" ("Fathers" 179), a bridge fragile enough that another time when Russell runs to meet her "The boards shuddered under my feet" ("Lying Under the Apple Tree" 206). Once stories are told about your world and the people in it, the world told about has momentarily been structured and humanised, made secure and familiar, a world you can count on and fit into. We're delighted at every new confirmation that the world is close, connected, familiar: "it is a small world. We say this, as people usually do, with a sense of wonder and refreshment" ("What Do You Want To Know For?" 331). The world beyond the small one is huge, unknown, complex, and even our own immediate personal futures, even something as conventionally forever as marriage, may be unpredictable. As Alice prepares to marry, her great-aunt Charlie hands her four fifty-dollar bills: "'If you change your mind,' she said" ("The Ticket" 283). Ultimately, Alice says, connectedness is at least one reason why people study and write up family history. Or any history, or any story:

> We can't resist this rifling around in the past, sifting the untrustworthy evidence, linking stray names and questionable dates and anecdotes together, hanging on to threads, insisting on being joined to dead people and therefore to life. ("Messenger" 347)

12. Hogg

On the first page of the foreword to *The View from Castle Rock* Munro mentions James Hogg, her ancestor whose "mother was a Laidlaw," and cites him as the first of a series of individuals in "every generation of our family ... who went in for writing" ([ix]). She mentions Hogg's best-known work, his novel *The Private Memoirs and Confessions of a Justified Sinner*, though only once ("No Advantages" 20), then zeroes in on Hogg's "knack for self-dramatization" (20). Alice goes on by recalling how "Self-dramatization got short shrift in our family" (20), but that is exactly the compulsion of Hogg's Sinner and Editor. The most encyclopaedically well-read devotee of postmodernist canons might be pressed to name a work more self-referential and indeterminate than James Hogg's *The Private Memoirs and Confessions of a Justified Sinner*. "What can this work be?" says the memoir's fictional Editor (whom Hogg-as-author seems cheerily to conflate with his own real-life editor) in the first line of his conclusion (240). Well, for one thing, it's "'traditionary history'" (241) – a term which is itself oxymoronic. What's true and what isn't? "I cannot tell," the Editor concludes (240). What we can tell is that the book is a hybrid early species or genetic sport of novel, a supposed memoir supposedly printed more than a century previous with handwritten addendum by the pathologically deluded eponymous Sinner. He's a murderer/libertine/Presbyterian solipsist fanatic, violently delusional and/or, if you prefer, grappling for souls with a demon. Compare the governess narrator in James's *The Turn of the Screw*. Imagine a character who seemingly might have been misbegotten by some haunted Byronic with some female equivalent of the Reverend Thomas Boston, presented through an Editor whose monomaniacal equal in literature didn't show up till Nabokov's *Pale Fire*.

Hogg's *Confessions* is a work by Alice's literary as well as genealogical progenitor. Call the *Confessions* the most important literary model for *Castle Rock*. Like Munro's book it's a memoir mélange of sometimes notionally, sometimes authentically (but not therefore necessarily accurate) documentary material, articles published by Hogg himself in *Blackwood's*, other published history, apparent folk-traditions of the Scottish seventeenth century, localist fantasy and superstition, diligently detailed archival researches, recollections, re-tellings that by point-of-view definition cannot be recollections and must be re-creations, religious embroideries, suppositions of varying validity, active lying – in short a blizzard of competing and mutually incompatible narratives. Both books end in a cemetery search. Hogg's fictional Editor accompanied by characters given real-life names opens the Sinner's grave where he has lain interred for well beyond a century. "To work we fell with two spades" (249), and they disinter beside the corpse "a leathern case ... wrapped round and round by some ribbon, or cord, that had been rotten from it," and inside that a "*printed pamphlet*" (252; emphasis in orig.) – "the very tract which I have here ventured to lay before the public, part of it in small bad print, and the remainder in manuscript" (253). Unlike Alice, who does not find that graveyard she seeks in Illinois but still comes away with her own book in hand or, rather, well in mind, Hogg's crew do indeed find not only the cemetery but also the very grave and corpse and supposed text – Hogg's book – which turns out no less impenetrably problematic than Alice's own *View*. J.R. (Tim) Struthers has shown that starting with stories in *Something I've Been Meaning To Tell You* (1974) Munro began to write "fiction that investigates itself, self-referring fiction, stories about storytelling" ("Alice Munro's Fictive Imagination" 103). Evolving from that earlier 'pure' fiction, this process comes to a concluding ripeness in the hybrid fiction of *The View from Castle Rock*.

13. Getting the Message

This is the final sentence of the epilogue, "Messenger," of *The View from Castle Rock* (349), the final and so most important sentence of the book:

> And in one of these houses – I can't remember whose – a magic door-stop, a big mother-of-pearl seashell that I recognized as a messenger from near and far, because I could hold it to my ear – when nobody was there to stop me – and discover the tremendous pounding of my own blood, and of the sea. (349)

Actually, lacking a main verb, this is not really a sentence, and therefore we are challenged to discern from the context of the rest of the book what this seashell *does*. The messenger seashell conveys its message, which only Alice with ears to hear can discern. It's a messenger from near *and* far – and that is also its message: near and far are united. In such shells you hear no verbal language, but a low sort of drone like a vowel in a religious chant, in and through which Alice can "discover the tremendous pounding of my own blood, and of the sea." In imagination in that tremendous moment, the blood in veins and the globe-girdling sea, the ocean that Alice's ancestors crossed to Canada West from Leith, are united.

In "What Do You Want To Know For?" Alice quotes an epitaph in German in a Grey County Lutheran cemetery, and ponders the trickery of language – "I always have the notion that I can read German, even though I can't" (324). In "Home," when Alice drives with her father through town, its "messages for me have drained away" (300). The light during some moment's glance at the Town Hall tower, a fragment of heard or overheard remark or suggestive snatch of anecdote, messages that for a moment poke the imagination and say – to the artist only (the messages are only "for me") – 'This may be an opening into some story.' We call this inspiration, whether Muse or God or Whatever composed and sent the message that calls out the making-power. But these messages pass, absorbed or not, acted on or not, what with tumours or inattention or other such failures, and always the Messenger is somewhere just offstage. "At the end of a Munro story," says Monika Lee, "through contemplation, we have a feeling of coming close to but never quite arriving at the ineffable truth" (120). In the shell's song, blood and sea, self and world are momentarily one, or One, like a Christian's Christ. Now *that's* ineffable. Maybe. For a moment.

As this essay's editor, J.R. (Tim) Struthers, reminded me, Wordsworth in the fifth book of the 1850 *Prelude* falls asleep reading *Don Quixote*, and in a dream is handed a shell by an Arab who seems also in dream-logic to be "the knight / Whose tale Cervantes tells" (V.122-23). Instructed by the Arab to put it to his ear he discerns "A loud prophetic blast of harmony" (V.95). The shell is

> ... a god, yea many gods,
> Had voices more than all the winds, with power
> To exhilarate the spirit, and to soothe,
> Through every clime, the heart of human kind. (V.106-09)

In his dream-logic Wordsworth knows clearly that the shell is also a book. The book/shell message is "ineffable" – but in a brief cryptic dream mediated and fragmentarily interpreted by a mysterious Arab who is himself within the dream within the poem. How far does Wordsworth, how far do we the readers, understand the shell's message and trust it? Wordsworth is a High Romantic and doesn't seem too doubtful. But Robertson Davies' savvy curmudgeon Samuel Marchbanks has a different take on seashell messaging:

> When I was a child I listened to this sea-noise eagerly, and believed in it. But now ... the Scientific Spirit has got hold of me and it gives me little peace. If I hold an empty beer bottle up to my ear I hear a noise, too; am I to believe that is the sound of a brewery? (Davies 352)

Or let us turn from this Marchbanks brewery to Elizabeth Brewster, writing in *Wheel of Change* of those 1940s years that *Castle Rock* is largely fermented in. One poem recalls the war across the Atlantic, and across the Pacific, "Bombs on a distant shore" that "shattered our hearts" (Brewster 70). Beachcombing on some fictive shore she discovers the same shell image to express but not resolve the inside/outside subject/object conflation that memoir is:

> What was that distant roar of waves receding,
> Like the hum of a seashell
> Echoing the thud of our own hearts? (Brewster 70)

Well, the seashell to Alice's ear at the end of "Messenger" is neither the elegantly unified Brewster variety nor the reductionist Marchbanks brand, nor that of the purely marvelling Wordsworth. It's somewhat of each. So much depends upon the messaging shell, and its provenance, and whose the listening ear. "Messengers," says Margaret Atwood in *Negotiating with the Dead*, "always exist in a triangular situation – the one who sends the message, the message-bearer, whether human or inorganic, and the one who receives the message" (125). Poet, Arab, sceptic grump, Souwesto Wonderlander? Who can best parse each writer's seashell, each reader's earful?

Works Cited

The Andrews Sisters. "Don't Sit Under the Apple Tree (with Anyone Else but Me)." Melody by Sam H. Stept. Lyrics by Lew Brown and Charles Tobias. Decca Records, 1942.

Atwood, Margaret. Introduction. *Alice Munro's Best: Selected Stories*. By Alice Munro. Toronto: McClelland & Stewart, 2006. vii-xviii.

---. *Negotiating with the Dead: A Writer on Writing*. Cambridge, Eng.: Cambridge UP, 2002.

Bloom, Harold. *The Anxiety of Influence: A Theory of Poetry*. 2nd ed. New York: Oxford UP, 1997.

Brewster, Elizabeth. "Poems for Seven Decades: 5. The Forties." *Wheel of Change*. Ottawa: Oberon, 1993. 70.

Brontë, Emily. *Wuthering Heights*. Ed. Hilda Marsden and Ian Jack. Oxford, Eng.: Clarendon, 1976.

Carroll, Lewis. *Alice's Adventures in Wonderland. The Annotated Alice:* Alice's Adventures in Wonderland *and* Through the Looking-Glass. Illus. John Tenniel. Introd. and notes by Martin Gardner. Rev. ed. Harmondsworth, Eng.: Penguin, 1970. 17-164.

Cervantes, Miguel de. *The Ingenious Gentleman Don Quixote de la Mancha*. Trans. and introd. Samuel Putnam. New York: The Modern Library, 1949.

Chapman, L.J., and D.F. Putnam. *The Physiography of Southern Ontario*. 2nd ed. Toronto: U of Toronto P, 1966.

Coleridge, S.T. *Biographia Literaria*. Ed. J. Shawcross. 2 vols. 1907. London: Oxford UP, 1962.

Conrad, Joseph. *Heart of Darkness*. Introd. Verlyn Klinkenborg. New York: Alfred A. Knopf, 1993. Everyman's Library 174.

Coppard, A.E. "Dusky Ruth." *The Collected Tales of A.E. Coppard*. New York: Alfred A. Knopf, 1948. 87-95.

Crashaw, Richard. "The Flaming Heart." *The Complete Poetry of Richard Crashaw*. Ed. and introd. George Walton Williams. New York: W.W. Norton, 1974. 62-65.

Dante Alighieri. *The Divine Comedy: The Inferno; The Purgatorio; The Paradiso*. Trans. John Ciardi. New York: New American Library-Penguin, 2003.

Davies, Robertson. *The Papers of Samuel Marchbanks*. Toronto: Irwin, 1985.

Dinesen, Isak [Karen Blixen]. *Seven Gothic Tales*. Introd. Dorothy Canfield. 1934. New York: Vintage, 1991.

Euripides. *The Hippolytus of Euripides*. Trans. Gilbert Murray. London: George Allen & Unwin, 1902.

Galsworthy, John. "The Apple Tree." *The Apple Tree & Other Tales*. New York: Charles Scribner's Sons, 1918. 199-278.

Heyerdahl, Thor. *The Kon-Tiki Expedition: By Raft Across the South Seas*. Trans. F.H. Lyon. London: George Allen & Unwin, 1950.

Hogg, James. *The Private Memoirs and Confessions of a Justified Sinner*. Ed. and introd. John Carey. 1969. Oxford, Eng.: Oxford UP, 1990. The World's Classics.

Homer. *The Iliad of Homer*. Trans. and introd. Richmond Lattimore. Chicago, IL: U of Chicago P, 1951.

---. *The Odyssey of Homer*. Trans. and introd. Richmond Lattimore. New York: Harper & Row, 1967.

James, Henry. *The Turn of the Screw: An Authoritative Text; Backgrounds and Sources; Essays in Criticism*. Ed. Robert Kimbrough. New York: W.W. Norton, 1966. A Norton Critical Edition.

Lee, Monika. "An Eerie and Numinous Place of Quiet Unknowing: Alice Munro's 'The Love of a Good Woman' in Context." *Alice Munro: A Souwesto Celebration*. Ed. J.R. (Tim) Struthers and John B. Lee. *The Windsor Review* 47.2 (2014): 102-23.

Longfellow, Henry Wadsworth. "A Psalm of Life." *The Complete Poetical Works of Longfellow*. Boston: Houghton, Mifflin, 1893. 2-3.

Mitchell, Margaret. *Gone with the Wind*. New York: Macmillan, 1936.

Montgomery, L.M. *Anne of Green Gables*. Illus. M.A. and W.A.J. Claus. Afterword by Margaret Atwood. Toronto: McClelland & Stewart, 1992. The New Canadian Library.

Munro, Alice. *Something I've Been Meaning To Tell You*. Toronto: McGraw-Hill Ryerson, 1974.

---. *The View from Castle Rock*. Toronto: McClelland & Stewart, 2006.

---. "Walker Brothers Cowboy." *Dance of the Happy Shades*. Fwd. Hugh Garner. Toronto: Ryerson, 1968. 1-18.

---. *Who Do You Think You Are?* Toronto: Macmillan of Canada, 1978.

Nabokov, Vladimir. *Pale Fire*. 1962. New York: Vintage, 1989.

Redekop, Magdalene. "Alice Munro and the Scottish Nostalgic Grotesque." *The Rest of the Story: Critical Essays on Alice Munro.* Ed. Robert Thacker. Toronto: ECW, 1999. 21-43.

Ross, Catherine Sheldrick. *Alice Munro: A Double Life.* Toronto: ECW, 1992. Canadian Biography Ser. 1.

Struthers, J.R. (Tim). "Alice Munro's Fictive Imagination." *The Art of Alice Munro: Saying the Unsayable.* Ed. Judith Miller. Waterloo, ON: U of Waterloo P, 1984. 103-12.

---. "Traveling with Munro: Reading 'To Reach Japan'." *Alice Munro: Hateship, Friendship, Courtship, Loveship, Marriage; Runaway; Dear Life.* Ed. Robert Thacker. London: Bloomsbury, 2016. 163-83, 231-44 passim.

Wakeman, Frederic. *The Hucksters.* New York: Rinehart, 1946.

Wordsworth, William. *The Prelude 1799, 1805, 1850: Authoritative Texts; Context and Reception; Recent Critical Essays.* Ed. Jonathan Wordsworth, M.H. Abrams, and Stephen Gill. New York: W.W. Norton, 1979. A Norton Critical Edition.

Alice Munro's Narrative Historicism: "Too Much Happiness"

Dennis Duffy

Alice Munro's "Too Much Happiness" relates the final years of its subject Sophia Kovalevsky, a nineteenth-century Russian mathematician, writer, and subsequent feminist icon.[1] Munro's narrative here, however, does not always fit with her previous fictional practice. Through an examination of earlier work, and a glance at a later sequence of narratives, my discussion attempts to outline the generic implications of "Too Much Happiness" as they apply to the remainder of Munro's fiction.

I begin with a brief notice of previous work throwing light on "Too Much Happiness." A funny thing happens in Alice Munro's "The Wilds of Morris Township." Appearing in her 2006 collection, *The View from Castle Rock*, this story contains a memoir which in turn lodges within it a portion of a 1994 narrative "A Wilderness Station." Examining these two pieces as well as a 1990 story "Meneseteung" helps us understand some of the ways in which "Too Much Happiness" arrests our attention through its differences from much of her earlier work. "Too Much Happiness" sticks very close to historical fact for its content, relying heavily upon biographical material that can be looked up. The narrative also includes a referential apparatus, an acknowledgments page accounting for the story's origins, the hold that the material exerted over Munro's imagination, and a key text that the author consulted in creating this account of her subject's life. Considering "Too Much Happiness" from the standpoint offered by the earlier work presents us with a focus for examining the story's generic aspects and their implications.

The fact that the lengthy tale – which first appeared in *Harper's* despite Munro's first-refusal contract with *The New Yorker* (Thacker 11)

– both concludes and furnishes the title for her 2009 collection indicates the author's regard for the story. Her showcasing of it extends even to the collection's dust jacket from McClelland & Stewart, which bears a miniature image which the back fold informs us is entitled "Snow Woman." (The Knopf dust jacket has that on the front and also includes a companion "Snow Man" on the back.) Its appearance is most easily attributed to "Too Much Happiness"'s reliance upon Russian characters and setting.[2] These underlinings plus the inclusion of an acknowledgments page (the text of which appeared as an endnote in the *Harper's* version [72]), assure a reader that "Too Much Happiness" merits critical discussion.

Arresting to a reader's gaze is the linkage between "A Wilderness Station" and "The Wilds of Morris Township." The latter appears in the first of the two sections that comprise the *Castle Rock* collection. Munro's foreword to that volume emphasizes the unique nature of these stories in her canon, based as they are on ancestral material, to be read neither as purely fictional nor as purely historical accounts. They are the result, she tells us, of "exploring a life, my own life, but not in an austere or rigorously factual way" (x). While the characters here may have been historical in origin, they took on a life of their own "and did things they had not done in reality" (x). That is – as a single-sentence paragraph admonishes – "These are *stories*" (x; emphasis in orig.). If the stories here indicate the author's conviction that "family history has expanded into fiction" (x), then we can retroject this process into the earlier publication of "A Wilderness Station."

"The Wilds of Morris Township" takes its title from a memoir appearing in a local antiquarian commemorative history (Robert B. Laidlaw 17). Munro's abridged and slightly altered version of "Big Rob's" memoir as she uses it in "Morris Township" covers his and his two cousins' – Thomas and John Laidlaw's – pioneering efforts in the early 1850s in the Huron County bush. The deadpan recital of the hardships accompanying that enterprise testifies to the memoirist's hardiness and resolve. A very brief portion of it – a three-sentence paragraph recounting the death of another cousin, James Laidlaw, as a result of a tree-felling accident (Robert B. Laidlaw 20) – furnishes the nucleus of Munro's earlier and explicitly fictional story "A Wilderness Station."

"A Wilderness Station" concerns the intentional killing (while logging) of one of the Herron brothers as a result of sexual and sibling rivalry. Told through a series of multiple accounts extending into a future beyond the life of the surviving Herron brother George, the tale leaves uncertain not only the facts of the killing, but even the exact role played by Annie McKillop Herron, who engineers the literal cover-up / home burial of the dead brother, her late husband. The story concludes with an account from the post-pioneer period, in which Annie has morphed into "Old Annie," a picturesque nanny whose bizarre presence embodies nostalgic reminders of the old days. The story's masterful complexity and stylistic vigour are not my focus here; I concern myself with the implicit views of time, history, and narrative encapsulated within the accounts that Munro relates within the two pieces.

The memoirist account of "Morris Township" rests within the conventions of historical discourse. It appears within a group of stories that Munro assures us "pay more attention to the truth of a life than fiction usually does. But not enough to swear on" (x). It passes easily as a relatively unsophisticated account of one man's past, an antiquarian document of the sort that might have nested among the records in Uncle Craig's jumbled miscellany in *Lives of Girls and Women*. That antiquarian obsession with a mummified past is exactly what Del Jordan later abjures (*Lives* 62-63). Robert B. Laidlaw's account of his past in "Morris Township" and its original appearance in the locally published document remind us that Munro's actual father, Robert E. Laidlaw, completed at the end of his life *The McGregors*, a fictionalized account of earlier times that his daughter saw through the final stages of publication. The Robert B. Laidlaw memoir as it appears in "Morris Township" follows the original, concluding with a conventional enough elegiac/nostalgic farewell to a now-distant past: "And the place that now knows us, will soon know us no more, for we are all old frail creatures" (117; Robert B. Laidlaw 21). Any irony found there is extra-textual. That is far from the case with the fictional "A Wilderness Station." The final segment tartly tempers the narrator's nostalgia with an authorial reminder of his flat pragmatic: "Except for woodlots, the bush is a thing of the past and I often think of the trees I have cut down and if I had them to cut down today I would be a wealthy man" (197).

"A Wilderness Station" is laden with such revelations about the hardscrabble conditions – environmental and moral – governing the protagonists' lives. How exactly did one brother die and what exactly had been going on between newly-minted widow and surviving brother remain matters of conjecture. The final section's narrator, Christena Mullen, a well-off, educated, independent, 'advanced' woman, a beneficiary of the comfortable, post-pioneering culture, has little grasp of "Old Annie's" past circumstances and of "'the terriblest dreams'" (225) that once haunted Annie's past. Her conventionalized position as an object of picturesque grotesquerie serves a cultural function similar to that of Hat Nettleton in Munro's 1978 story "Royal Beatings" (20-22). They exist as the scrubbed fossils found in a souvenir shop, polished tokens of a past no present-day observer cares to grasp in its embedded actuality.

Juxtaposing Munro's two accounts of the wilderness experience helps not only to lodge within the reader a sense of history's complexity and its dependence upon present-day observation and winnowing – what lies at the centre of one account lingers along the periphery of another – but also to convey historical memory's inherent weakness. "Their words and my words, a curious re-creation of lives, in a given setting that was as truthful as our notion of the past can ever be" (x).

Even in a story as purposive as an earlier 'historical' fiction that Munro produced, "Meneseteung" – a story (so the author tells us) offering homage to the author's literary ancestors – historical narrative displays its inherent weakness. "Meneseteung" originated, according to an authorial note appearing after its publication, in a wish to present at once the life of a woman writer in an uncouth land, as well to depict the drives – commercial, cultural, and sexual – that were resettling that territory ("Contributors' Notes" 322-23). Munro's commentary affirms her intent to acknowledge Clara Mountcastle of Clinton (1837-1908) and, presumably, Eloise Skimings of Goderich (1837?-1921; sources vary on her year of birth) and to convey the dedication to writing and versifying that such hinterland women writers of that time exhibited.[3] Munro's fiction here relies, however, upon an unreliable narrator who acknowledges her own fallibility in the final paragraph, excised from the *New Yorker* version.

Through such a narrative framework, Munro implicitly presents her own overarching narrative as a structure that is itself as provisional as the account provided by her fictional narrator. Rather than relating its story by means of a collection of purportedly positivist and actual documents that require assembly and conjectural evaluation (as would be the case with the "Wilderness Station" material), "Meneseteung" instead presents a single, univocal, redacted document. The matter of the document may be multivocal in nature – I am thinking of the heroine Almeda's verses, products of authorial fabrication – but it has been synthesized and harmonized by a narrator, herself not without flaws. The modern period's attempt at objective historiography, caught in "A Wilderness Station"'s mélange of documents, stutters to a halt in "Meneseteung," whose narrative structure remains itself as tentative and provisional as the account provided by the fictional narrator.

***

Similarly to "Meneseteung," "Too Much Happiness" employs as its subject an actual historical figure; it offers a very different reading experience, however. If the first story relies upon the author's imaginative grasp of the life and setting of its subject, the latter largely confines itself to historical fact, as the acknowledgments page makes evident. Munro had performed another version of this act of historical/fictional appropriation in "The Albanian Virgin," engaging a local librarian in a search for facts on one Minnie Rudd, a Clinton, Ontario resident who had been taken by Albanian bandits in 1900 or so. Munro locates her version of the Albanian virgin's story within as complex a narrative as any that she has written. My own commentary confines itself to the fact that – unlike Munro's usage of the Kovalevsky material – the author instead wove a framework about the historical story, offering a parallel, present-day narrative framing the tale of "Lottar" (Charlotte), her subject, a step reminiscent of Shakespeare's addition of the Gloucester subplot to his story of Lear. That, as Munro's biographer Robert Thacker tells us, the author drastically cut back on the present-day material along the way from manuscript to a final version leaves us with the impression that – since at least 1988, according to her correspondence – her imagination had been circling around actual, historical stories that could be transmuted into fiction (448).[4]

When Sophia Kovalevsky (1850-1891) sprang into Munro's consciousness, her earlier reliance upon a more overtly fictional framework disappeared. Her Russian heroine is no obscure figure. Kovalevsky and her career have generated a formidable body of biographical, critical, and celebratory literature; she appears on Russian postage stamps. As the concluding lines of the story assure us, she has had a crater on the moon named after her.[5] All this notice seems appropriate for a figure whom a Russian literary dictionary hails as "a source of inspiration for young women worldwide at the turn of the century" (Zirin 328).[6] "Too Much Happiness" follows the life of an actual person, in the manner of such present-day fictional works as Thomas Mallon's *Watergate: A Novel* (2012), Hilary Mantel's Thomas Cromwell novels, *Wolf Hall* (2009) and *Bring Up the Bodies* (2012), and Jerome Charyn's *I Am Abraham: A Novel of Lincoln and the Civil War* (2014).

In her brief span of forty-one years, Kovalevsky's achievements in mathematics helped to shatter the many barriers blocking any major female entry into scientific endeavour, both institutional and individual. She also wrote novels, a memoir, social and cultural commentary, all the while engaging in political and social activism that earned her a role in the attempts at the modernization of Russia that so engaged the intelligentsia of her day. Munro acknowledges that "The combination of novelist and mathematician immediately caught my interest" (305). The more we learn of Kovalevsky, the more struck we are by the opportunities for fictional exploitation that her life offered Munro. Yet we shall also learn that despite Munro's fidelity to her sources – after all, she owes the title of her story (and book) to the actual last words of Kovalevsky as reported by her biographers – Munro's very deployment of those sources makes clear the uniqueness of her story here.

A full exposition of the facts of Kovalevsky's life and the material that it furnishes for Munro's story is matter for another critical exploration. My effort here confines itself to exploring the implications of the story's reliance upon historicity for the vast majority of its content. Munro's acknowledgments page describes the force with which Kovalevsky pounced upon her imagination. It appears to have been a matter of serendipity, in which the author came across Kovalevsky's entry "while searching for something else in the Britannica one day," which in turn piqued her interest in Kovalevsky's "combination of novelist and mathematician" (305). Munro then "began to read everything about her [that she] could find," though she gives no sources beyond a biographical portrait of Kovalevsky by Don H. Kennedy and his wife, Nina (305). We have as yet no idea of what Munro encountered among the many works devoted to Kovalevsky and her achievements. We can conclude, however, that this initial discovery in fact led Munro further along a narrative path that she had been taking for some time.

Before exploring that pathway, let us consider briefly why such a figure exercised the hold that she did upon Munro's writerly imagination. Indeed, the facts of her life and its near-heroic record of struggle and achievement played their role in the capture of Munro, but Kovalevsky was also a memorialist of some complexity. Her fictionalized account of her early years, *A Russian Childhood*, concludes with an overwrought expression of nostalgia: "A feeling of inexplicable, boundless joy took hold of us both. God! How that life stretching out before us drew us to it and beckoned us on, and how boundless, mysterious and beautiful it appeared to us that night!" (199).

Yet a similarly warm memory – "Yes, that was a marvelous road! And it has remained perhaps the happiest memory of my childhood" (172) – is followed, in the draft manuscript of Kovalevsky's narrative, by an abrupt declaration of disillusionment: "But I am afraid to remember it. Once you start thinking back, you cannot go on" (208n11). So conflicted a figure naturally arrests a writer's gaze; Munro makes use, for example, of a real-life incident revealing her heroine's double-sidedness. Her husband's suicide as a result of a criminal investigation into his financial dealings propelled Kovalevsky into locking herself in her room and then refusing to eat. Five days later, however, revived from unconsciousness by a persistent friend, Kovalevsky quickly requested pencil and pad and began making math notes. Capable of tempestuous emotional moments, she does not appear to have been enslaved by them, able to cope with storm and calm alike.

Munro's retelling of Kovalevsky's life confines itself largely to her final years, limiting the account to five sections. The fifth is the lengthiest, occupying nearly a third of the text and including some matter commonly found in an epilogue. It is the most linear in shape, and concerns her final days. Earlier sections – with a single exception – mix present time with flashback, covering in detail the final three years of the heroine's life. Only the fourth section is set entirely in the past. Briefest of the story's divisions, it focusses largely on the death of the husband and Kovalevsky's at once tormented, theatrical, and idiosyncratic response to it. Thus the first three sections remain of approximately equal length and incorporate flashback.

In this way, the narrative's structure remains overall non-linear until its conclusion. That section opens in the final months of the heroine's life, expanding then into moments from past and present that build to an intense interlude set entirely in the past, then followed by a concluding sequence focussing chiefly on Kovalevsky's death, the circumstances bringing it about, and the fallout from that loss. It is a familiar enough mode of structuring episodic narrative, a staple of popular romantic print narrative, television, and film production. Experienced often cinematically, such a structure of exposition easily engages its audience as it shifts from immediate story, with its built-in progressive device featuring some past material, then consequently shifting to backstory, and then progressing toward a final revelation and conclusion. Such a structure, however familiar, nonetheless testifies to Munro's efforts to avoid producing another biographical tract on her subject's life, and instead to transform the stuff of history into the matter of fiction. Two incidents, one historical and the other imaginative, allow us to witness this process at work and to draw some conclusions from it.

The first item displays the author's determination to maintain her narrative's concentration. "Too Much Happiness" excludes a childhood incident falling outside the story's time frame, yet one that seems pregnant with fictional possibilities and well-nigh irresistible to a writer. Kovalevsky's *A Russian Childhood* relates how a household improvisation speeded up her own precocious adventures in mathematics (122-23). A miscalculation during a renovation of the Kovalevsky manor house (she came from a privileged, land-owning, and military background) threatened to stall the whole process. They had run out of new wallpaper. A search for a substitute turned up a set of examination notes on mathematics, printed in broadside form, that her father – an artillery officer and therefore engaged in such training – had relied upon in his student days at the military academy. The sheets of calculus problems and their solutions were slathered on the nursery wall and exposed to Sophia's scrutiny, inspiring her later mathematical mastery. Munro ignores such compelling material in order to maintain the tightness of her narrative focus.

The second incident actually occurs in the story, as an imaginative interpolation by the author that recalls to the reader one of the narrative drivers of Thomas Mann's "Death in Venice." Kovalevsky's premature death may well have been triggered by the exhaustion and soaking that she experienced in changing trains from an express to a meandering slow train during her return to Stockholm where her life concluded. The historical record tells us only that Kovalevsky – exhausted by a series of lecture dates following her departure from the company of her on-again, off-again lover – was sufficiently impressed by rumours of a devastating smallpox plague in Copenhagen to switch trains in order to avoid the stricken city. Munro personifies that rumour in the figure of a mysterious physician from Bornholm sharing a train compartment with Kovalevsky. He warns her of the smallpox epidemic – a special horror to a woman aware of her own beauty and charm – and in his concern for her passes to her an unidentified drug in powder form that "had brought ... solace, ... when necessary, to him" (302). Was the powder cocaine, which we know alike from the career of Freud and the fiction of Conan Doyle enjoyed widespread legitimacy at the time (Dalby, Markel)? Could that powder have stimulated her into overtaxing her already debilitated self upon her return to Stockholm? This is a matter of imaginative speculation alone, the forcing of a minor narrative detail. Its appearance concerns me because – outside of her a-chronological retelling of events – the doctor from Bornholm represents what seems to me Munro's sole imaginative intervention into the life-story that she tells with a strict fidelity to the historical record.

Certainly the historical record needed no reinforcement. After all, it tells us of Kovalevsky's resistance-lowering lengthy trek with her bags in a downpour, itself occasioned by her roundabout route taken on the strength of a rumour. Why bother to personify a social process as thoroughly credible and appropriate as this one appears to be? Why go to the trouble to give that intrusive doctor a few sentences in the story's epilogue mentioning his regret at Kovalevsky's death and noting the usefulness to him of the drug he so casually passed along to her? What formal and imaginative gains result from this personification? Furthermore, what conclusions can we draw from the contrast between the imaginative material's inclusion and the historical material's exclusion? We could, of course, shortcut the whole discussion by noting merely that imaginative writers pick and choose between whatever is there and whatever they wish to be there. To venture beyond truism compels turning our attention to the particular nature of the narrative that Munro has put before us and to the response that it demands from the reader.

The earlier stories that I mentioned indicate an authorial oscillation between modernist 'objective' epistemology and postmodernist mythic reconstruction in Munro's usage of history. What do I mean? The narrative structure of "A Wilderness Station" concerns itself with the use of sources, in the manner of scientific historiography. The narrative carefully denotes the material out of which it has been constructed, presenting admittedly fictitious material in the manner of a scrupulously positivist account of an event, with the implicit admission that each source is unique and not necessarily objective, but rather one account among many other possibilities as the nucleus of "A Wilderness Station"'s appearing in "The Wilds of Morris Township" attests. We are examining a set of historical documents; such an exercise demands a careful attempt to evaluate the actuality of events and above all the reliability of the narration of them. "A Wilderness Station" confines us within a historical archive, where the meaning of no single document exists autonomously. Rather, each item rearranges the context in which we set the narrative, whose meaning we in turn derive from our stay within it.

If we shift our gaze from "A Wilderness Station" and "Meneseteung" to a later set of narratives, then Munro seems at play in the opening five historical stories in *The View from Castle Rock*. After masking herself as the familiar omniscient narrator for fifty-seven of the title story's sixty-one pages, she insouciantly breaks character with the announcement that she "can look it up" (83) in a letter that she has in her possession today. I find this interjection more significant formally than, say, Jane Eyre's statement that begins the concluding chapter of Charlotte Brontë's novel, "Reader, I married him" (676).[7] The Victorian reader would not have taken that speaker to have been Currer Bell; she would have assumed that the speaker was in fact the novel's fictional heroine and no one of any greater existential weight. The reader of *The View from Castle Rock* instead is faced with a collection of family lore, of recollected and transmitted experience, subject to all the alterations that time, distance, and shifts in narrators compel. We are reading what we might call a background to objective autobiography, "something closer to what a memoir does" (x), according to the author.

The opening five *Castle Rock* stories may be presented as historical in nature in their origin, but they appear before us as the first of two sections in a volume of Munro narratives that seem typically representational in form and realistic in tone, subject, and setting: stories of the sort that a reader familiar with Munro will recognize. Again, the author's placement and inclusion of the works gathered in this collection, and the burden of her foreword, ultimately implies Munro's refusal to make any hard and fast distinction between discursive and imaginative narrative; it also implies that such shifts between modes of narration can happen within individual stories and within collections. This, to leap forward for a moment, accounts for the fact that in *Dear Life* the final group of four narratives labelled *"autobiographical"* (255) fragments, whatever their origin, exhibit no essential difference in tone or content from the assuredly fictional narratives found elsewhere in the collection.

Viewed from the position that I have assumed, Munro emerges as a producer of multivalent narrative, in which the factual and the imaginative exist within an equivalency. This practice, to return to the question I asked a few paragraphs ago, accounts for Munro's invention of the monitory physician in "Too Much Happiness." That is, she emphasizes that as a writer she produces narrative, period; questions of factuality and historical reliability are not central in the stories' presentation to the reader. Any questions raised by generic differences between narratives are sidelights, avenues to be explored once a reader has absorbed the initial impact of the story at hand.

My argument must now return to "Too Much Happiness." Blending historical fact and narrative with imaginative reconstruction, the story adds another interpretation to the many focussing on the life of its subject. As I have mentioned, Munro picked Kovalevsky's last days for her time frame, with flashbacks to previous periods. Her narrative refuses to break its concentration; it excludes the engaging childhood material already mentioned. Yet it includes Sophia's sister Anna's revolutionary activity, thereby underlining the importance of women's political struggle.[8] Munro obviously has a particular story to tell about women savants and the obstacles they encounter, a pointed, even didactic tale of the trials endured by women. Thematically, she has paralleled the fictional setbacks experienced by Almeda Joynt Roth in "Meneseteung" with the historical ones visited upon Sophia Kovalevsky. In blending the actual with the symbolic and imaginative, Munro has swung her style of narrative far enough forward to have it whip back far into the past, into the conditions of the exemplary narrative, a staple of earlier narrative modes, of edifying lives of the saints and legendary heroes. "Too Much Happiness" proffers the pointed exposition of an exemplary life whose ultimate meaning lies beyond that of the particular moment in material history caught in the story.

This practice of employing varying narrative modes bears a number of generic implications. It should now seem obvious that "Too Much Happiness" to some extent stands apart generically from the remainder of Munro's fictional work. As we know, and as Biblical scholars can outline in detail, generic conventions "create a set of unstated expectations between the writer and the reader" (Pennington 20). Their presence is central to the meaning we derive from the narrative and the respect we bestow upon it. At the same time, we recall that "attribution of membership in a generic class is conjectural, not prescriptive" (Corman 187). One of fiction's greatest theorists, M.M. Bakhtin, observed that the novel by its very nature is marked by heteroglossia, by a multiplicity of discourses rendering generic neatness problematic (320-24). That same characteristic can be true for short fiction as well. It is also true that generic designation only partially explains a narrative's impact. Sometimes a generic designation can be a simple labelling, almost a marque or logo: for example, the radio station that is playing while I write this classifies itself as "classical." Another on my listening list may call itself "classic rock." The difference between the two is as great as that between a horse chestnut and a chestnut horse, but the label reveals little as to format and specificity of the fare to be found there.

Assigning a work to a particular genre can be an exacting and overly-detailed task, one that fits the material in question only in an inexact and Procrustean fashion, standing like a scrim between the narrative and our experience of it. Yet my attempt to explain the uniqueness of "Too Much Happiness" relies upon a consideration of genre. If we examine what I have termed the epilogue (the heroine's after-life), the material found there reveals much of the story's nature. The story proper's final sentence – "Sophia's name has been given to a crater on the moon" (303) – in eleven words presents us with an instance of what classical scholars know well as "catasterisation," the elevation of an earthly figure of myth to a position in the starry sky as an indication of his or her significance and immortality. For a modern secular scientific age, that cosmically monumentalizing process takes place in the meritocratic assignment of a slot in some sort of material or materially-based phenomenon. Based upon renown rather than an aspect of 'naming rights' for donors, such labels as the kilopascal, the joule, and the Van Allen belts share with the Kovalevskaya lunar crater the fact that they are all examples of this process of apotheosizing; they are our contemporary version of catasterisation.

Munro, who knows better, nonetheless describes her heroine's elevation in the passive voice, delivering the sense of a generalized and worshipful process rather than a historical process involving the politics of culture and science.[9] She wants to call our attention to the quasi-mythical exercise that she has undertaken as a narrator. This concluding and momentary de-historicizing of Kovalevsky conveys Munro's generic play. Not only does this story present another example of the equation of historical narrative with other more orthodox 'fictional' narratives. This step registers "Too Much Happiness" as an exemplary tale, a gauge of the importance that Munro assigns to her subject. She has proven herself willing to step aside from her usual generic mould to deliver a tale that – told through such fictional devices as a non-chronological and non-linear temporal structure and the depiction of a character's inner life – belongs to an older and very heterogeneous form of narration.

I am thinking here of an outstanding instance of the exemplary genre, the Gospel narrative, with its mixture of the historical, the mythical, and the devotional. Not that "Too Much Happiness" functions as a full-blown example of Gospel narrative. It is not wholly "exemplary, didactic, polemic, and mnemonic," as one New Testament scholar labels such narratives (Pennington 24).[10] Yet it does share enough of these characteristics to announce that the writer has gone beyond her usual narrative limits. Beneath the skin of "Too Much Happiness" – its fictional representation – lies the skeleton of a far older creature, the tale told to inform, hearten and inspire, didactic in nature, at odds with other forms of modern fictional narrative. Writers, as everyone knows, do not always confine themselves to familiar practices, especially as they proceed toward the ends of their careers.

***

I want to conclude my discussion of "Too Much Happiness" with some speculation about what the story reveals about a writing career that Munro herself has recently announced has reached its conclusion (McGrath). Can we now consider the serendipity at work in Munro's discovery of Kovalevsky's story? Let me offer an analogy to this process of discovery: a recovering alcoholic may drift past a dozen bars on his way across town, but it is surely no improbable coincidence when and if he marches into one of those bars. That is, you do not have to be consciously alert in order to be alert, as Munro's discovery of Kovalevsky suggests to me. This discovery indicates the major role that a writer like Munro has played in the cause of feminism (by which I mean the recognition and reformation of the role played by women in our culture, rather than a specific theoretical position). Anyone attempting to determine Munro's role in the larger culture of her time, extending that role beyond the purely literary, understands that Munro's default subject has been the role played by women in the settings that she treats.

Her discussion has extended well beyond the lives of girls and women (whether considered as demographic or as subjects for her second book) and treated women both as producers and as objects of desire. Women exploited, women exploiters, woman-as-object of male aggression, woman-as-subverter of male aggression: all these roles and dozens more have been captured within the specificity of particular Munrovian narratives and their action. It should come as no surprise that, amid all these myriad ways of constructing women's stories, Munro should arrive at a way of recounting a particular woman's story in a way that epitomizes the heroic image of a woman who in some ways was done to death by her culture's restrictions and who in other ways strengthened the chains of her bondage through her own recklessness.

A brief sentence from "Royal Beatings" displays Munro's masterful exploitation of experience's ambiguity; it occurs within a description of what we would now term child abuse: "He is acting, and he means it" (16). Stepmother Flo and Rose's father may conduct the royal beatings, but the story also conveys the degree to which Rose herself helps to instigate the repetition of this sick family ritual, this cycle of provocation, retaliation, and post-orgasmic apology. If we reduce Munro's fiction to the level of social commentary alone, then its chief value resides in the complexity of what she depicts. For it is her uncomfortably honest treatment of the role played by victims in the cruelties visited upon them that renders her commentary so valuable and so enduring.

Leaving aside the social role that I have touched upon so briefly, I would emphasize instead that Munro's *oeuvre* 'covers' the exploitation and the resistance of women through a generic continuum of narrative devices and hybridization ranging from the quotidian realistic to the historical to the exemplary. A reader need not esteem equally every genre that Munro adopts in practice. The point is to acknowledge that behind the serendipity of Munro's discovery of Kovalevsky's story lies a career-length preoccupation with the feminine questions and dilemmas that "Too Much Happiness" treats.

As Erich Auerbach wrote three quarters of a century ago,

> The historical event which we witness, or learn from the testimony of those who witnessed it, runs much more variously, contradictorily, and confusedly; not until it has produced results in a definite domain are we able, with their help, to classify it to a certain extent; and how often the order to which we think we have attained becomes doubtful again, how often we ask ourselves if the data before us have not led us to a far too simple classification of the original events! (19)

In line with Auerbach's "preoccupation with the problematic" (23), we must reflect that we will never know exactly what Sophia Kovalevsky meant by her dying words; nor can we at present tell anyone exactly what meaning Munro assigned to that phrase.

What all of us readers can agree upon is that beneath the irony lurking in those words – can one really be afflicted by too much happiness? – lies the profound sadness of human experience and its roots in the inescapably mixed nature of our motivations and responses. This central fact Munro has once again brilliantly treated.

Notes

1. I am indebted to comments on a draft of this essay provided by an anonymous referee for the *American Review of Canadian Studies*, where this essay was first published.

2. For remarks on the artist and the image see Volk: "Wearing a coat, boots, and scarf, and with her hands clasped behind her back, the woman stands alone in the center of the page. She's a forthright presence, but she also seems engulfed by the white expanse, which makes her seem frail and lost" (15).

3. For Mountcastle see Godard. For Skimings see "Skimings, Eloise A." Munro reaffirmed her involvement in local history as a means of developing her composite fictional character (and acknowledged the aid of a local librarian) in her 1994 *Paris Review* interview (McCulloch and Simpson 245).

4. Robert Thacker's illuminating exposition and clarification of the complex set of research and publishing circumstances around "The Albanian Virgin" also recalls to me the great debt that I owe him for his insight and encouragement during the preparation of this essay.

5. For biographical information see Zirin; Kennedy; Koblitz; Kochina. Even a profusely illustrated, coffee-table treatment is available: see Audin.

6. For Kovalevsky's place in Russian literature and science see Cooke; Engel; Koblitz; Marcus; McReynolds and Popkin; Naginski; Paperno; Pozefsky; Stites.

7. Another interesting Brontë echo can be heard in the name of the heroine of "Meneseteung." As J.R. (Tim) Struthers has pointed out, "Almeda" was the name that Emily Brontë gave to herself in the fantasy world that she and her siblings created: see Wiseman; Struthers 185.

8. Kovalevsky treated this topic at length in her narrative of her political development, *Nihilist Girl*.

9. Just how politicized and perhaps even monetized that process may be can be determined by reading between the lines of a website devoted to the society responsible for mapping and naming those lunar memorializations: <http://www.lunasociety.org/>.

10. See also Burridge 26-54.

Works Cited

Audin, Michèle. *Souvenirs sur Sofia Kovalevskaya*. Paris: Calvage & Mounet, 2008. Orizzonti 101.

Auerbach, Erich. *Mimesis: The Representation of Reality in Western Literature.* 1953. Trans. Willard R. Trask. Princeton, NJ: Princeton UP, 1968.

Bakhtin, M.M. *The Dialogic Imagination: Four Essays.* Ed. Michael Holquist. Trans. Caryl Emerson and Michael Holquist. Austin: U of Texas P, 1981. U of Texas P Slavic Ser. 1.

Brontë, Charlotte. *Jane Eyre.* Introd. Diane Johnson. Notes by James Danly. New York: The Modern Library, 1997.

Burridge, Richard A. *What Are the Gospels?: A Comparison with Graeco-Roman Biography.* Cambridge, Eng.: Cambridge UP, 1992. 2nd ed. Grand Rapids, MI: William B. Eerdmans, 2004. The Biblical Resource Ser.

Charyn, Jerome. *I Am Abraham: A Novel of Lincoln and the Civil War.* New York: Liveright-W.W. Norton, 2014.

Cooke, Roger. "Sonya Kovalevskaya's Place in Nineteenth-Century Mathematics." *The Legacy of Sonya Kovalevskaya.* Ed. Linda Keen. *Contemporary Mathematics* 64 (1987): 17-51.

Corman, Brian. "Chicago Critics." *The Johns Hopkins Guide to Literary Theory & Criticism.* Ed. Michael Groden, Martin Kreiswirth, and Imre Szeman. 2nd ed. Baltimore: Johns Hopkins UP, 2005. 185-88.

Costlow, Jane. "Love, Work, and the Woman Question in Mid Nineteenth-Century Women's Writing." *Women Writers in Russian Literature.* Ed. Toby W. Clyman and Diana Greene. Westport, CT: Greenwood, 1994. 61-75.

Dalby, J. Thomas. "Sherlock Holmes's Cocaine Habit." *Irish Journal of Psychological Medicine* 8.1 (1991) 73-74.

Engel, Barbara Alpern. *Mothers and Daughters: Women of the Intelligentsia in Nineteenth-Century Russia.* Cambridge, Eng.: Cambridge UP, 1983.

Godard, Barbara. "Mountcastle, Clara H." *Dictionary of Canadian Biography.* Vol. 13. <http://www.biographi.ca/en/bio/mountcastle_clara_h_13E.html>.

Kennedy, Don H. *Little Sparrow: A Portrait of Sophia Kovalevsky.* Athens, OH: Ohio UP, 1983.

Koblitz, Ann Hibner. "Career and Home Life in the 1880s: The Choices of Mathematician Sofia Kovalevskaia." *Uneasy Careers and Intimate Lives: Women in Science 1789-1979.* Ed. Pnina G. Abir-Am and Dorinda Outram. New Brunswick, NJ: Rutgers UP, 1987. 172-90.

---. *A Convergence of Lives: Sofia Kovalevskaia: Scientist, Writer, Revolutionary.* Boston: Birkhäuser, 1983.

---. *Science, Women and Revolution in Russia.* Amsterdam: Harwood Academic, 2000.

---. "Sofia Kovalevskaia – A Biographical Sketch." *The Legacy of Sonya Kovalevskaya.* Ed. Linda Keen. *Contemporary Mathematics* 64 (1987): 3-16.

Kochina, Pelageya. *Love and Mathematics: Sofya Kovalevskaya.* Ed. A. Yu. Ishlinsky. Trans. Michael Burov. Moscow: Mir, 1985.

Kovalevsky, Sophia. *Nihilist Girl.* Trans. Natasha Kolchevska with Mary Zirin. Introd. Natasha Kolchevska. New York: The Modern Language Association of America, 2001. Texts and Translations 8.

---. *A Russian Childhood.* Trans., ed., and introd. Beatrice Stillman. New York: Springer-Verlag, 1978.

Laidlaw, Robert. *The McGregors: A Novel of an Ontario Pioneer Family.* Toronto: Macmillan of Canada, 1979.

Laidlaw, Robert B. "Diary of Robert B. Laidlaw." *Blyth: A Village Portrait.* Gen. ed. Susan Street. Blyth, ON: n.p., [1977]. 17-21.

Luna Society International: Official Website of the Moon. <http://www.lunasociety.org/>.

Mallon, Thomas. *Watergate: A Novel.* New York: Pantheon, 2012.

Mann, Thomas. "Death in Venice." *Death in Venice and Seven Other Stories.* Trans. H.T. Lowe-Porter. 1936. New York: Vintage, 1963. 3-75.

Mantel, Hilary. *Bring Up the Bodies.* Toronto: HarperCollins, 2012.

---. *Wolf Hall.* Toronto: HarperCollins, 2009.

Marcus, Jane. "Invincible Mediocrity: The Private Selves of Public Women." *The Private Self: Theory and Practice of Women's Autobiographical Writings.* Ed. Shari Benstock. Chapel Hill, NC: U of North Carolina P, 1988. 114-46.

Markel, Howard. *An Anatomy of Addiction: Sigmund Freud, William Halsted, and the Miracle Drug Cocaine.* New York: Pantheon, 2011.

McCulloch, Jeanne, and Mona Simpson. "Alice Munro: The Art of Fiction CXXXVII." *The Paris Review* 131 (1994): 226-64.

McGrath, Charles. "Alice Munro Puts Down Her Pen To Let the World In." *The New York Times* 1 July 2013. <http://www.nytimes.com/2013/07/02/books/alice-munro-puts-down-her-pen-to-let-the-world-in.html?pagewanted=all&_r=0>.

McReynolds, Louise, and Cathy Popkin. "The Objective Eye and the Common Good." *Constructing Russian Culture in the Age of Revolution: 1881-1940*. Ed. Catriona Kelly and David Shepherd. New York: Oxford UP, 1998. 57-105.

Munro, Alice. "The Albanian Virgin." *Open Secrets*. Toronto: McClelland & Stewart, 1994. 81-128.

---. "Contributors' Notes." *The Best American Short Stories 1989*. Ed. Margaret Atwood with Shannon Ravenel. Introd. Margaret Atwood. Boston: Houghton Mifflin, 1989. 322-23.

---. *Dear Life*. Toronto: McClelland & Stewart, 2012.

---. *Lives of Girls and Women*. Toronto: McGraw-Hill Ryerson, 1971.

---. "Meneseteung." *Friend of My Youth*. Toronto: McClelland & Stewart, 1990. 50-73.

---. "Meneseteung." *The New Yorker* 11 Jan. 1988: 28-38.

---. "Royal Beatings." *Who Do You Think You Are?* Toronto: Macmillan of Canada, 1978. 1-22.

---. "Too Much Happiness." *Harper's* Aug. 2009: 53-72.

---. "Too Much Happiness." *Too Much Happiness*. Toronto: McClelland & Stewart, 2009. 246-303.

---. *Too Much Happiness*. Toronto: McClelland & Stewart, 2009.

---. "A Wilderness Station." *Open Secrets*. Toronto: McClelland & Stewart, 1994. 190-225.

---. "The Wilds of Morris Township." *The View from Castle Rock*. Toronto: McClelland & Stewart, 2006. 111-26.

Naginski, Isabelle. "A *Nigilistka* and a *Communarde*: Two Voices of the Nineteenth-Century Russian *Intelligentka*." *Woman as Mediatrix: Essays on Nineteenth-Century European Women Writers*. Ed. Avriel H. Goldberg. Westport, CT: Greenwood, 1987. 145-58. Contributions in Women's Studies 73.

Paperno, Irina. *Chernyshevsky and the Age of Realism: A Study in the Semiotics of Behavior*. Stanford, CA: Stanford UP, 1988.

Pennington, Jonathan T. *Reading the Gospels Wisely: A Narrative and Theological Introduction*. Grand Rapids, MI: Baker Academic, 2012.

Pozefsky, Peter C. "Love, Science, and Politics in the Fiction of *Shesti-desiatnitsy*: N.P. Suslova and S.V. Kovalevskaia." *The Russian Review* 58 (1999): 361-79.

"Skimings, Eloise A." *Canada's Early Women Writers.* <https://digital.lib. sfu.ca/ceww-735/skimings-eloise>.

Stites, Richard. *The Women's Liberation Movement in Russia: Feminism, Nihilism, and Bolshevism 1860-1930.* Princeton, NJ: Princeton UP, 1978.

Struthers, J.R. (Tim). "In Search of the Perfect Metaphor: The Language of the Short Story and Alice Munro's 'Meneseteung'." *Critical Insights: Alice Munro.* Ed. Charles E. May. Ipswich, MA: Salem-EBSCO, 2013. 175-94.

Thacker, Robert. *Alice Munro: Writing Her Lives: A Biography.* 2005. Updated ed. Toronto: Emblem-McClelland & Stewart, 2011.

Volk, Gregory. "Slant Truth: Five Sections for Peggy Preheim." *Peggy Preheim.* New York: The Aldrich Contemporary Art Museum / Gregory R. Miller, [2008]. 8-19.

Wiseman, Sharon. "Emily Brontë's Muse and Symbolism." *The Victorian Web: Literature, History, & Culture in the Age of Victoria.* <http://www. victorianweb.org/authors/bronte/ebronte/wiseman1.html>.

Zirin, Mary. "Kovalévskaia, Sóf'ia Vasíl'evna." *Dictionary of Russian Women Writers.* Ed. Marina Ledovsky, Charlotte Rosenthal, and Mary Zirin. Westport, CT: Greenwood, 1994. 328-29.

Fractal Fiction in Alice Munro's "Too Much Happiness"

Monika Lee

"Too Much Happiness," the novella that concludes the 2009 volume of the same title, is an anomaly in Munro's literary *oeuvre*: described by Robert Thacker as "unlike anything Munro had ever done" (*Reading Alice Munro* 198), the narrative unfolds during the nineteenth century, it reproduces a biography, and it transpires in continental Europe. Although, as Dennis Duffy has observed, Munro treats historical and biographical material in "Meneseteung" (1990), "A Wilderness Station" (1994), "The Wilds of Morris Township" (2006), and the "Finale" to *Dear Life* (2012), "'Too Much Happiness' sticks very close to historical fact for its content" (Duffy 196). As the conclusion of one of Munro's most darkly gothic books (*Too Much Happiness* opens with "Dimensions," a shocking story about the aftermath of a man's brutal murder of his three young children), the novella reads initially as a rambling and elliptical addendum chronicling incidents from the life of Sofia Kovalevskaya (1850-1891), or in English Sophia Kovalevsky, a famous Russian mathematician and the first woman in Northern Europe to be granted a full professorship. The story is told out of sequence and in a fragmentary, disordered fashion, yet this apparent tumult obscures remarkably tight patterns of signification in what may well be Munro's most intensive and complex exploration of the idea of alternate realities, a prototypical Munrovian concept.[1] Concurrent narratives exist simultaneously in alternate realities and on multiple levels, including historical, fictional, intertextual, mathematical, and political. We are left with a sense that this story, all stories, and indeed all human thought, action, and

387

imagination convey only part of a hidden reality, a multiverse or mega-verse beyond our immediate, conscious comprehension.

Sophia Kovalevsky's memoir, "Recollections of Childhood" (1895), begins with musings about the unreliability of memory and the conse-quent uncertainty of her ensuing autobiographical narration: "I cannot myself in the least determine which of these impressions I really remem-ber; that is to say, I cannot decide which of them I really lived through, and which of them I only heard about later on, – in my childhood, – and imagine that I recall, when, in reality, I only remember the accounts of them. Worse still, I can never succeed in evoking a single one of these original recollections in all its purity; I involuntarily add to it something foreign during the very process of recalling it" (1). Later, Anna Carlotta Leffler's biography, an attempt to complete Kovalevsky's "Recollections,"[2] challenges notions of objectivity and truth-telling in her preface: "From an objective point of view the life-history I have sought to depict of my friend may perhaps be considered not real. But is the objective stand-point necessarily the true one when we deal with the interpretation of character?" (157). It is small wonder that Alice Munro became absorbed by these accounts, both Kovalevsky's and Leffler's, since she has long been attracted to the combined treachery and potentiality of memory as creative space, and her characters frequently express a confusion similar to Kovalevsky's in recalling the past, hearing or telling accounts of it, retracing their memories, what may or may not have happened, and whether or not facts are either stable or knowable.

Leffler rejects *mimesis* in favour of *diegesis*, an approach to charac-ter later dramatized in Munro's "Too Much Happiness" when Sophia Kovalevsky, changing trains alone in Paris, witnesses a man who resem-bles her lover Maxsim Maxsimovich Kovalevsky: "As she hurried toward her train she saw a man wearing a fur hat like Maxsim's. A big man, in a dark overcoat. She could not see his face. He was moving away from her. But his wide shoulders, his courteous but determined manner of making way for himself, strongly reminded her of Maxsim" (265). Subsequent to this observation, Sophia thinks of reasons why "Of course it could not be Maxsim" (265). The questions about why and what he would be doing in Paris are settled with "And when she thought she saw him she had just wakened out of an unnatural unhealthy sleep. She had been hallucinating" (266). But this emotionally satisfying explanation does not last. After enduring the treacherous detour of Copenhagen because of an ostensible smallpox epidemic, and herself now quite ill, she recalls the "marvellous assurance he has" (294) and "Now she had an image of him – Maxsim, not sheltering her at all but striding through the station in Paris as befitted a man who had a private life. // His commanding headgear, his courtly assurance. // That had not happened. It was not Maxsim. Assuredly it was not" (294-95).

What interests us about this incident, and Sophia's weighing of the possibilities, is that for the readers, and arguably for Sophia herself, both interpretations, both realities exist – that Maxsim was in Paris on some private, possibly amorous business but that Sophia is rationalizing away the fact and that Maxsim was not in Paris but only imagined by a slightly groggy, infatuated, and paranoid Sophia. The ensuing smallpox outbreak is a similar fissure in the text, because, though Sophia has no reason to doubt the authority of the doctor from Bornholm, other characters know nothing of the outbreak of the disease. Here the reader is not so much denied access to the facts as given simultaneous, contradictory, and equally valid alternate realities. Munro does not refuse an explanation but rather provides us with multiple explanations, each of which has as much textual reality and empirical probability as the other. As an example of the calculated randomness that Munro wishes to emphasize here, the doctor from Bornholm, as Dennis Duffy has noted, is the one facet of Munro's version of events not found in her historical sources (201). That Maxsim is in Paris and that he is not, that there is a smallpox outbreak in Copenhagen and that there is not – without preference, these contradictory narrative details co-habit the same story, just as sub-atomic particles can be in different places at the same time, a fact proven by Nobel Laureates from 2012, physicists Serge Haroche and David J. Wineland (Kaku).

Munro's sense of fiction-writing as an exploration of multiple versions in a search for something real or true draws symbolically from the parallel between mathematics and literature which she discovered in Sophia Kovalevsky's life; for, as Munro imagines Sophia's mentor Karl Weierstrass thinking, "there must be something like intuition in a first-rate mathematician's mind, some lightning flare to uncover what has been there all along" (270). What Munro has achieved in fiction, and particularly in the precise but non-linear novella "Too Much Happiness,"

Kovalevsky too accomplished in her "Theory of Partial Differential Equations": "Instead of using linear time as the only independent variable of an equation ..., Sophia's theory envisages other independent variables and thus paves the way to non-linear mathematics, dynamic phenomena and theories of chaos" (Boucherie 148).

The word "equations" has significance for the structure of the novella, in that the doublings, parallels, and layerings of situations and characters are like partial differential equations. When Sophia dreams of her sister, for instance, Aniuta is a doubled person, fictional and historical, partially differentiated the one from the other. Aniuta's husband, Victor Jaclard, "a genuine hero" (256), is set up in a parallel or an equation with, though partially differentiated from, both Harold of Hastings – the hero for whom the heroine dies in Aniuta's short story published by Fyodor Dostoyevsky – and Dostoyevsky himself.

In "A Defence of Poetry" (1818), P.B. Shelley wrote that "Reason is the enumeration of quantities already known; Imagination the perception of the value of those quantities, both separately and as a whole. Reason respects the differences, and Imagination the similitudes of things" (510). Munro's reason respects the differences and her imagination respects the similitudes of things. Sophia's mind – in her dreams, her fiction, and her mathematical discoveries – finely balances the two, and "Too Much Happiness" as a whole performs much as a variable in a larger equation with Don and Nina Kennedy's biography of Kovalevsky,[3] her memoir, "Recollections of Childhood," her novel, *Nihilist Girl* (1892), and Munro's own life and literary works. These stories all interact as part of an ever-expanding universe of stories about and around Kovalevsky, Munro, and us – a macrocosmic complex differential equation.

Éva Zsizsmann observes that Munro "plays the game of the realist while using metafictionalist techniques" (209), perhaps because there is a shared sense in Munro and Kovalevsky that the real is something that can be imagined or intuited, that the line between historical record and fictional re-enactment is anything but clearly demarcated. In Kovalevsky's words, "'Many persons that have not studied mathematics confuse it with arithmetic and consider it a dry and arid science. Actually, however, this science requires great fantasy, and one of the first mathematicians of our century very correctly said that it is not possible to be a mathematician without having the soul of a poet. Of course it must be understood that one must abandon the old supposition that a poet must compose something non-existent, that fantasy and invention are one and the same'" (Kovalevsky in Kennedy 264). This final point, that fantasy and invention are not the same thing, is critical to our understanding of Munro, whose epigraph to her tale is from this Kovalevsky quotation and whose realism is remarkably inventive though not at all fantastical. Intensifying the multivalence of Munrovian fiction, "Too Much Happiness" explores mathematics as metaphor and history as fiction.

   Little Sparrow: A Portrait of Sophia Kovalevsky, the book by Don and Nina Kennedy that inspired Alice Munro's "Too Much Happiness," ends with a chapter whose title is also "Too Much Happiness" – Sophia's last words, spoken to her friends Teresa Gulden and Ellen Key and Sophia's daughter, Fufu (Kennedy 313). Munro's story, focussing as it does on the end of Kovalesky's life, proposes an alternative version of this final chapter, a story parallel to the one told in *Little Sparrow*, the biography itself being a reflection of various stories from Sophia, her friends, and her family members. At the time she published *Too Much Happiness*, Munro did say that it would be her last book, and one way of reading the concluding novella would be to see it as a possible coda or literary epitaph to her writing career, with the prodigiously talented and heartbroken Sophia Kovalevsky as a stand-in of sorts for the talented but misunderstood Munro. Certainly, there are parallels between these two women – both rebellious for their time and era, both quietly feminist, both having a sister, both having a marriage followed by another relationship, both mothers whose professions made them feel guilty, each living for a long time in self-imposed exile from her place of origin but, as Thacker observes, drawn back to it (*Alice Munro* 3), both celebrated and bedecked with prizes traditionally accorded to men. Some of Kovalevsky's themes, heartbreak and unrequited love, or the failure of the mother to provide sufficient emotional nurture, would strike Munro as familiar territory. "Too Much Happiness," consistent with the source material in the biographical and autobiographical works, presents Kovalevsky's successes as both integral to Sophia's personality and compensatory for her profound sense of emotional estrangement.

   Paradoxically, then, the last words attributed to Kovalevsky are the first words of Alice Munro's novella, "Too Much Happiness." The phrase, though apparently exuberant, resonates with irony, but, as usual with Munro's titles, the ironies tend in multiple directions. Sophia Kovalevsky certainly had more than the usual allotment of success in life, and in the nineteenth century the word "happiness" still carried its primary meaning of good fortune or good luck (Little 1: 924). In that sense, Kovalevsky may be understood to have had "Too much happiness," or a surfeit of good fortune. However, the more obvious and modern tendency of this title is the suggestion that her life was somehow lacking in happiness or joy, and that her last words then represent either a passing illusion, a brief experience, and/or ironical bitterness. Because Sophia writes to her friend, Julia, about her engagement to Maxsim, "it is to be happiness after all. Happiness after all. Happiness" (253), the fact that she does not marry him and claim a fulfilled life as both mathematician and wife implies that such an outcome would have been "Too much happiness," a delight denied to Kovalevsky, though she would have been unrealistically optimistic if she assumed a marriage to an emotionally withdrawn man would permit happiness. The Kennedys explain the phrase in this way: "When at the end she exclaimed, 'Too much happiness,' seemingly she meant that the happiness she believed she had found at last was being snatched away, as though she did not really deserve it" (318). It is in this appraisal that we find a suggestion of much of Munro's meaning in adapting the words to her fictionalization, but Munro's novella raises the multivalence of the phrase as it applies retrospectively to Kovalevsky and as it comments on human life in a collection of some of her least "happy" stories.

   Anna Carlotta Leffler's "Sónya Kovalévsky: A Biography" explores the meaning of "happiness," a word which recurs throughout its pages. Leffler is notably preoccupied by Sophia's lack of happiness, her hopes for it, and her eventual renunciation of it: "She no longer yearned for that complete happiness the ideal of which had ever consumed her soul with its burning flame. But she now longed, with ardent, clinging love, for the broken gleams of the happiness which had of late cast a light upon her path" (Leffler 291). Moreover, Kovalevsky and Leffler, in the first-ever successful literary collaboration of two women, co-wrote two parallel plays with the same title, *The Struggle for Happiness*, to be staged on two consecutive nights (Kennedy 267). As Sophia explained, while the characters and the situation remain the same in both plays, the first shows "'that which really happened'" or struggle (Kovalevsky's version) and the second dramatizes "'that which might have happened'" or happiness (Leffler's version) (Kovalevsky in Kennedy 267, 294). In later years, Sophia's thwarted hopes, her struggles with Maxsim, so painfully rendered in Munro's story, contrast starkly with Anna Carlotta's professed happiness: Leffler "had attained a height of human felicity which almost made her tremble. And indeed the last years of her life were a luminous progress to ever intenser joys" (Wolffsohn 313). About her friend Anna Carlotta's engagement, Sophia wrote, "'That is really a fate worthy of such a lucky soul as yours. But it has always been so. You were *happiness*, and I am, and most likely shall always be, *struggle*'" (Kovalevsky in Kennedy 294). Hence, the two versions of the same play, like the two lives which they symbolize or prefigure, represent alternative realities or stories, analogous to those suggested mathematically by Abelian functions and to those represented metaphorically as an equation through the structure of Munro's narrative style. In other words, the multi-directional irony of Munro's title, like an elliptic function, also hypothesizes parallel worlds of meaning.

On one level "Too Much Happiness" appears as an oblique gloss on a biography – a novella which Éva Zsizsmann describes as one of various stories by Munro that "provide fully sourced and yet elliptical historical fiction" (201) – and yet it is one of Munro's most complex stories because of its grappling with large political, social, and historical movements, and its evocation of philosophical, artistic, and mathematical contexts. One way to conceive of the layers of reality and fiction which provide the mosaic of Munro's novella is to understand them intertextually as a complex web of interrelationships. The text of Sophia's life acts as a metonym for the larger intertext formed by European political, historical, mathematical, and literary texts, all of which converge and diverge throughout Munro's narrative. Critics such as Marijke Boucherie and Éva Zsizsmann are quick to notice the parallels between Munro and Kovalevsky, but Munro's mapping of Sophia onto the history of the advent of socialism, the rise of the turn-of-the-century women's movement, and as a character in the writings of people other than Kovalevsky and Munro – the writings, among others, of Fyodor Dostoyevsky, George Eliot, Karl Weierstrass, Anna Carlotta Leffler, and Henrik Ibsen – indicates how richly one life can affect another through the written transmission of language and thought. The fact that Munro does not construct any simple one-to-one allegories while treating this complexity is a testimony to the maturity of her literary vision. The overall narrative (full of gaps and interstices) and even the textual histories underlying it are not sufficient to express the truths toward which Munro lures us, as though these texts, like the languages of Western Europe, are "paltry substitutes for true human speech" (248).

Sophia Kovalevsky made many mathematical advances, but the one of most enduring significance is probably her work on elliptic functions. An elliptic function "is periodic in two directions" and "is determined by its values on a fundamental parallelogram, which then repeat in a lattice" ("Elliptic function"). Given the preoccupation with parallel realities in this novella and elsewhere in Munro, the mathematical discoveries serve as metaphors for story elements, those of biography, politics, and literature. Munro acknowledges that it was this "combination of novelist and mathematician" which immediately interested her when she stumbled on an entry for Sophia Kovalevsky in the *Encyclopedia Britannica* (Acknowledgments [305]).

As Boucherie notes, "It is very interesting that the non-linear and non-static picture of Sophia's life created by Munro is analogous to the new conception that Sophia helped to introduce in mathematics. Sophia Kovalevsky's 'Theory of *Partial* Differential Equations' brings movement and dynamics into mathematics and breaks with the paradigm of static and exact analytical solutions" (148). The substance of Sophia's mathematical work is addressed within "Too Much Happiness" as a counterbalance or alternate reality to her obsession with Maxsim: the mathematical principles to which she turns her attention from thinking of Maxsim and daydreaming prove symbolic of Munro's partial differential narrative technique.

The train ride which forms the linear structure of the narrative is often evoked as a metaphor in discussions of the laws of physics because Albert Einstein employed it to explain the relativity of simultaneity (Einstein 10-12); Sophia's final train ride, "the long and troublesome route across the Danish islands" (Leffler 289), implies the elements of non-linearity, chaos, and randomness associated with "[t]he never-ending change of trains in bad weather" (Leffler 289). In other words, this train journey introduces independent variables into a linear equation in such a way as to suggest randomness or chaos. The human tragedy is that such chaos, mapped out as a train ride across disparate islands, ends in Sophia's premature death at the age of only forty-one.

Sophia Kovalevsky is famous in mathematics for solving what was referred to as "the mathematical mermaid": a problem so named because of its attractive, elusive, and perplexing properties. The mathematical problem, like the legendary mermaid, is beguiling but impenetrable, which traits create a problem for any man who falls in love with or is sexually captivated by her. Mathematically, "The Mermaid Problem," so-called by male mathematicians, was the problem of determining the formulae for the rotations of solid bodies about fixed points: "By putting restrictions on the characteristics of rotating objects (shape, center of gravity), mathematicians came up with three classes of objects for which this type of motion was defined by means of partial differential equations" (Saberhagen). The first two classes of objects had been solved before Kovalevsky, but it was she who solved this mathematical problem for the third class of objects, by introducing time as a complex variable.

"The Mermaid Problem" is foregrounded in "Too Much Happiness" in a juxtaposition of the mathematical mermaid with Sophia's love affair: "She tore herself from thoughts of him, from daydreams, back to the movement of rigid bodies and the solution of the so-called mermaid problem by the use of theta functions with two independent variables" (249). The solving of this longstanding problem wins Kovalevsky the prestigious Bordin Prize in mathematics in 1888, but at the same time her achievement causes her to lose, at least temporarily, the affection of Maxsim (Leffler 266-69). The irony that it was a woman who penetrated the mermaid and, in doing so, foregoes the love of a man, would not have been lost on Munro.

As a result, the mathematical triumph connects Munro's story with a different mermaid problem, one in which Munro admits to holding a particular interest, the problem of Hans Christian Andersen's *The Little Mermaid*, about which she, in 2013 upon being awarded the Nobel Prize in Literature, said the following:

> I got interested in reading very early, because a story was read to me, by Hans Christian Andersen, which was *The Little Mermaid*, and I don't know if you remember *The Little Mermaid*, but it's dreadfully sad. The

little mermaid falls in love with this prince, but she cannot marry him, because she is a mermaid. And it's so sad I can't tell you the details. But anyway, as soon as I had finished this story I got outside and walked around and around the house where we lived, at the brick house, and I made up a story with a happy ending, because I thought that was due to the little mermaid, and it sort of slipped my mind that it was only made up to be a different story for me, it wasn't going to go all around the world, but I felt I had done my best, and from now on the little mermaid would marry the prince and live happily ever after, which was certainly her desert, because she had done awful things to win the prince's power, his ease. She had had to change her limbs. She had had to get limbs that ordinary people have and walk, but every step she took, agonizing pain! This is what she was willing to go through, to get the prince. So I thought she deserved more than death on the water. And I didn't worry about the fact that maybe the rest of the world wouldn't know the new story, because I felt it had been published once I thought about it. So, there you are. That was an early start, on writing. (Munro in Åsberg)

The mathematical mermaid problem was the impetus for a brilliant mathematical triumph for Kovalevsky, and the literary mermaid problem was, according to Munro's own account, the seminal text, the originary motive launching a future literary career for Alice Munro.[4]

Instead of adopting a male perspective that sees the problem with mermaids as their combination of attractiveness and impenetrability, Munro positions her female perspective through the lens of Hans Christian Andersen's heartbreaking story. For her the bigger mermaid problem is the utter injustice for the little mermaid, the feminine predicament of compulsory self-sacrifice, and the tragedy that the sacrifices for the beloved turn out to be unrequited, futile, and even self-destructive, as indeed they turn out to be for Sophia, her sister Aniuta, and a wide variety of other characters in Munro's *oeuvre* from Del Jordan in *Lives of Girls and Women* to Vivien Hyde in "Amundsen."

Sophia's marriage to Vladimir Kovalevsky, not consummated during the first seven years they were married (Leffler 192), presents the more traditional androcentric mermaid problem, since the conundrum of the sexual attractiveness of mermaids to men is the celibacy enforced by the scaly fishtail on the lower portions of a female body. Of note is the fact that Sophia's mathematical abilities, an impediment to love, are framed in bestial images: for the Parisians she is "a learned chimpanzee" (266), for the Swedes "a multilingual parrot" (267), for her friends "the little sparrow" (Leffler 171). Also, as in the fairy tale, in "Too Much Happiness" the sisters, Sophia and Aniuta, are parted because of idealistic and self-sacrificial understandings of romantic love, which they privilege over their much stronger sisterly love, and which are crucial to Munro's reworking of the literary mermaid problem. A theme with variations (life-threatening sacrifices for love) plays out differently for each sister. Like Andersen's mermaid – small, petite, and gifted – Munro's Sophia repeatedly chooses between mathematics or literature (her voice) and love (marriage). In the end, she does not marry the man she loves, Maxsim, and she also foregoes her mathematical and literary voice, just as Andersen's little mermaid loses all. Her faith that her sacrifice will be rewarded by the man for whom she makes it is unfounded, and her love is unrequited – "'If I loved you I would have written differently',' Maxsim ends a letter to Sophia (250).

The dissatisfaction the reader feels at the thwarted desire for "happiness," a happiness toward which all Sophia's decisions have directed her, may be similar to what Munro felt as a young girl in the face of *The Little Mermaid*. On one level, the solid body, or "rigid bodies" (249), of the math problem is the mermaid or the female body, and the fixed point is either love itself or the object of one's love, the prince or Maxsim. If the solution to the mathematical mermaid is to introduce time as a variable, it is noteworthy that "Too Much Happiness" also presents time as a variable to solve the quintessential problem of feminine sacrifice for love, or the other mermaid problem. In an interview with Thomas E. Tausky, Munro says that she set about "[t]rying to make a story like 'The Little Mermaid' [by Hans Christian Andersen] and then later on trying to make a story like *Wuthering Heights*: those were not daydream stories – there was some apprehension there of what fiction is" (Munro qtd. in Tausky x). In "Too Much Happiness," Munro succeeds in re-envisioning *The Little Mermaid*, and, in solving this mermaid problem, the variable which Munro introduces is time; the story takes us through a process of time travel back into the nineteenth century to explain a phenomenon, puzzling and baffling on mathematical, literary, and human levels. As Héliane Ventura astutely observes, Munro "puts the existential reality of the given facts on the same syntagmatic axis as the imaginary existence of the fantasy" (106).

At the outset of Munro's story, an act of reading is foregrounded through the activity of Maxsim, Sophia's distant and alienating lover, who serves as a stand-in for the reader and readerly activity. Like Munro in compiling the research for "Too Much Happiness," and like us in our reading, Maxsim is engaged from the outset in acts of reading and interpretation, "crouching over tombstones and writing in his notebook, collecting inscriptions and puzzling over abbreviations not immediately clear to him" (246). His role is Munro's and ours, metafictionally presented as an obsession with the dead, while only being half-aware of – "Only half listening" to (247) – the living, breathing person beside him, Sophia, who will also be dead before the year is over and the story is completed.

Maxsim's nonchalance on the threshold of life and death is similar to ours, as we peruse a story about a story with little initial authentic investment. This introduction to the characters is significant, because we do not yet know who they are or what world we are entering. Yet a comparison between his body and his body of knowledge – "His knowledge is as expansive as his physique" (246) – renders us predisposed to like this witty, popular, knowledgeable Maxsim Maxsimovich Kovalevsky, a master of several languages, who scoffs slightly at his companion's superstitiousness that "'One of us will die this year,'" "'Because we have gone walking in a graveyard on the first day of the New Year'" (247).

The narrator introduces Maxsim by his full name, and introduces his female companion in a satellite role, noting merely that "The woman with him is also a Kovalevsky" (247). Maxsim is "Only half listening" (247) as the reader too is only half reading, not aware of the prescience of this woman's intuition or Munro's foreshadowing: "They leave melted, black footprints where they've walked" (247). Hence the beginning of the story creates in us a double consciousness, part identification and part detachment on the threshold of death, but mostly viewing death more as a text than as a reality. From Munro's opening, we would never guess that the female Kovalevsky is not only the main character in the story, but also by far the more important of the two Kovalevskys depicted in its early pages, since the language focusses on Maxsim, his significance, his bulk, his name, his profession, and tells us little about his small, birdlike, and superstitious female companion. Irony emerges from this gap between narrative perspective and historical consequence.

Another kind of doubling occurs in the realm of secondary characters, almost all of whom are based on famous and/or influential personages from European history, though their fame is not at all overt in Munro's representations of them; rather, they appear as merely small players in the life of a seemingly ordinary woman. If we think a little about the people and their achievements, however, we quickly realize how immeasurable their impact is. Karl Weierstrass and Henri Poincaré, for example, like Kovalevsky herself, are enormously significant figures in the development of science and mathematical theory; through their work, they paved the way for special relativity, chaos theory, and a host of modern inventions reaching all the way to quantum mechanics and the subsequent digital revolution. Moreover, the fact that Sophia's life should have intersected so meaningfully with the lives of some of the most influential writers of the past two hundred years – Fyodor Dostoyevsky, George Eliot, Ivan Turgenev, Leo Tolstoy, Karl Marx, Friedrich Engels, and Henrik Ibsen – is remarkable.

"Too Much Happiness" obscures the influential reach of Kovalevsky's circle by ignoring and downplaying celebrity, except as it acts as a stressor in Kovalevsky's personal life, causing her lover to abandon her when she is too much fêted after she wins the prestigious Bordin Prize in mathematics. The people she knew changed the world politically, socially, culturally, scientifically, economically, and artistically in profound ways. Communist and quantum revolutions, major developments in literature, and even the modern women's movement arose from their life's work. Yet these historical and intellectual breakthroughs and transformations form merely the faintest of allusions in this fractal fictionalization.

Of all the many literary and cultural influences on Munro's writing, the Russian one may be the most infrequently studied. Though Munro is often called "the Canadian Chekhov," most influence studies focus on her literary forebears in American, Canadian, or occasionally British literature. "Too Much Happiness" may be a corrective insofar as it signals the presence of Kovalevsky, Tolstoy, Dostoyevsky, and Chekhov in Munro's literary approach, a deeply psychological and character-based one as rooted in time and place and as richly realistic as the Russian storytellers' productions. Alice Munro acknowledges Tolstoy and Chekhov as early influences (Simpson)[5], and states that Chekhov "was terribly important to me" (Feinberg). Moreover, in "A Conversation with Alice Munro," published just after the release of *Too Much Happiness* but recorded a decade earlier, Munro is quoted as saying: "I have recently re-read much of Chekhov and it's a humbling experience. I don't even claim Chekhov as an influence because he influenced all of us. Like Shakespeare his writing shed the most perfect light – there's no striving in it, no personality. Well, of course, wouldn't I love to do that!" While it is impossible to locate all the threads of this rich intertextual tapestry, it is clear that Munro has read widely in the nineteenth-century European classics, and she does more than nod to the Russian literary influences which permeate "Too Much Happiness."

The interpretive energy in Munro's "Too Much Happiness" intensifies during the dream sequence on the arduous train ride from Nice to Stockholm. Sophia's dreams are interpretations of memory and, like narrative itself, provide alternate realities, parallel to the actual, subjective re-working of events, which possess hermeneutic potential. Munro has observed that

> Memory is the way we keep telling ourselves our stories – and telling other people a somewhat different version of our stories. We can hardly manage our lives without a powerful ongoing narrative. And underneath all these edited, inspired, self-serving or entertaining stories there is, we suppose, some big bulging awful mysterious entity called THE TRUTH, which our fictional stories are supposed to be poking at and grabbing pieces of. What could be more interesting as a life's occupation? One of the ways we do this, I think, is by trying to look at what memory does (different tricks at different stages of our lives) and at the way people's different memories deal with the same (shared) experience. The more disconcerting the differences are, the more the writer in me feels an odd exhilaration. ("A Conversation with Alice Munro")

Sophia's dreams explore these disconcerting differences in memories, their narratives, and their interpretations.

The first dream focusses on Aniuta, Sophia's sister, in her tower room in the home, where she is reading *Harold: The Last of the Saxon Kings* (1848) by Edward Bulwer-Lytton and impersonating "Edith Swan-neck, the mistress of Harold of Hastings" (255). In the dream Aniuta plans to write her own novel about Edith, and she "has already written a few pages describing the scene where the heroine must identify her butchered lover's body by certain marks known only to herself" (255). This dream signals layered readings as a fundamental ground for self-understanding: we read Munro, a writer, writing about a writer, Sophia Kovalevsky, dreaming about a writer, Aniuta, acting out the passage from a book by yet another writer, Bulwer-Lytton, which is, like Munro's novella about Kovalevsky, a fictional reconstruction of the writings of historians.

In the dream, "Having somehow arrived on this train [Aniuta] reads these pages to Sophia who cannot bring herself to explain to [Aniuta] how things have changed and what has come about since those days in the tower room" (255). So the dream not only highlights a complex and receding intertext and an allegory of writing as remembering, but it figures the act of reading (Aniuta here as the symbolic implied reader) and interpretation (Sophia's, which is separate and alien from Aniuta's understanding). In this way, Munro signals the alienation of her story from the biographical material it pretends to treat, even as she proposes intersections and mirroring between them; through the dream text as narrative, she dramatizes conflicting readerly responses any text is bound to elicit. Our meta-awareness of the shortcomings of our subjective response represents a kind of exhilaration.

The dream concludes therefore with Sophia's alter ego, her sister Aniuta, reading her re-written account of her own alter ego, Edith Swan-neck, in a complex layering of many themes and characters. There is a prefigurative element to Aniuta's identification with Edith Swan-neck (whose fictionalization not coincidentally occurred in 1848, known as "the year of revolutions" because of populist and democratic revolutions which broke out across Europe), since in later life Aniuta suffers for her own husband, Victor Jaclard, a military and revolutionary hero of the Paris Commune. The theme of a woman sacrificing herself in marriage to a greater cause is found in Kovalevsky's novel, *Nihilist Girl*: "in some sense she had written that story in tribute to Aniuta. It was the story of a young woman who gives up the prospect of any normal life in order to marry a political prisoner exiled to Siberia" (281).

The dream also refers to Sophia's own life in that she married Vladimir for science and women's rights rather than for love. Finally, at the end of her life, Sophia undertakes another impersonation of the martyred female lover in her new engagement to the remote and distant Maxsim Kovalevsky, and she also intuits her imminent death. Through this perception of multiple planes, dimensions, and representations, Munro does not trade in certainties, only in versions, one death being merely the refracted mirror of others, whether fictional, dreamed, or lived. The distinctions among fictional, dreamed, and lived are not only blurred, but almost metaphysical – they explore and reach for understandings of truth, each as valid as another.

Hence this first dream sets up a number of parallel lives and realities, including a dream reality with which the awakened Sophia compares what happened in "real" life: "When she wakes Sophia thinks how all that was true – Aniuta's obsession with medieval and particularly English history – and how one day that vanished, veils and all, as if none of it had ever been, and instead a serious and contemporary Aniuta was writing about a young girl who at her parents' urging and for conventional reasons rejects a young scholar who dies. After his death she realizes that she loves him, so has no choice but to follow him in death" (255). That the everyday "reality" parallel to the dream "reality" vanishes just as surely as if it had been a dream itself is an idea that Munro picks up a few pages later in her novella, when Sophia remembers thinking, in relation to aspirations to posthumous fame, that "Every one of us will be forgotten" (259). The salient point here is that reality, such as it is, vanishes from human memory. The finality of such a disappearance reveals Munro's ultimate concern with the ironic truth of those last words, "Too much happiness," our mortality, and the inescapability of death.

Munro's "Too Much Happiness," like Hans Christian Andersen's *The Little Mermaid*, is predominantly tragic, yet a proviso, in the form of the non-linearity of time, affords some consolation, since in the post-Einsteinian world, realism becomes far more multivalent and bizarre than the Victorians, Tolstoy, or Dostoyevsky could have anticipated. University of Columbia physicist Brian Greene sums up the contemporary problem of the boundaries of knowledge with articulate deftness: "what we've long thought to be *the* universe is only one component of a far grander, perhaps far stranger, and mostly hidden reality" (4). Munro's elliptical and fractal fiction "Too Much Happiness" bewilders us with the complexity of its diegetical patterns and presents in earnest the possibility of parallel realities. This multiverse is both fictional and real, the linguistic embodiment of a far stranger reality than the one constrained by our preconceptions and our physical senses, a vision of reality intuited by that writer and early pioneer of pre-quantum mathematical thought, Sophia Kovalevsky.

Notes

1. In *Alice Munro's Narrative Art*, Isla Duncan writes that "There has always been an awareness of alternative worlds in Munro's fiction, notably in work published after 1990" (160).
2. The opening words of Anna Carlotta Leffler's "Sónya Kovalévsky: A Biography" read, "Immediately, on receiving the news of Sónya Kovalévsky's unexpected and sudden death, I felt that it was a duty incumbent upon me to continue, in one form or another, the reminiscences of her early life which had been published in Swedish under the title of 'The Sisters Raevsky'" (155).
3. Although Don H. Kennedy is credited as the sole author of the biography, nevertheless, because of the considerable extent of Nina Kennedy's contributions to her husband's work, I prefer to think of Nina as joint author together with her husband of *Little Sparrows*, exactly as Munro does in her Acknowledgments included at the end of *Too Much Happiness*. John Stuart Mill attributed most of the ideas and much of the writing of *The Subjection of Women* to his wife, Harriet Taylor, but they both agreed apparently that the work should be published under his name. Munro clearly thinks, as do I, that Nina Kennedy did enough work on the volume – most notably in translating all the relevant Russian texts needed to be rendered in English – to be included in at least an informal citation of her efforts.
4. In her article "Things You May Not Know about Alice Munro," Andrea Walker notes that "As a child, Munro was constantly telling herself stories. One of the first was 'The Little Mermaid,' by Hans Christian Andersen, whose ending she couldn't bear. The mermaid has to make a choice between killing the prince and going back to join her mermaid sisters, a decision that Munro thought was horribly unfair. So she made up a new, happier ending."

5.   In her article "A Quiet Genius," Mona Simpson remarks of Munro
that "Among the writers she considered early influences Munro
included Tolstoy, Chekhov, Proust, and James, but also Erica Jong."

Works Consulted

Amutha, Maria Mercy. "The Cultural Significance of Women: A Repre-
sentation Through a Historical Short Story – *Too Much Happiness*."
Journal of Literature, Culture and Media Studies 2.4 (2010): 319-29.
<https://papers.ssrn.com/so13/papers.cfm?abstract_id=2984031>.
Andersen, Hans Christian. *The Little Mermaid*. Trans. Eva Le Gallienne.
Illus. Edward Frascino. New York: Harper & Row, 1971.
Åsberg, Stefan. "Alice Munro: In Her Own Words." 2013. <https://www.
nobelprize.org/prizes/literature/2013/munro/lecture/>.
Bigot, Corinne. *Alice Munro: Les silences de la nouvelle*. Rennes, Fr.:
Presses Universitaires de Rennes, 2014. Collection ‹‹Interférences››.
Boucherie, Marijke. "'Disturbing to Others': The Too Great Happiness
of Alice Munro and Sophia Kovalevsky." *Reviones: Revista de critica
cultural* 6 (2010): 145-55. <https://dadun.unav.edu/bitstream
/10171/19601/1/13.%20Marijke%20Boucherie%20REV%2006.pdf>.
Cox, Ailsa. "'Age Could Be Her Ally': Late Style in Alice Munro's *Too Much
Happiness*." *Critical Insights: Alice Munro*. Ed. Charles E. May. Ipswich,
MA: Salem-EBSCO, 2013. 276-90.
Dostoyevsky, Fyodor. *The Idiot*. Trans. and introd. David Magarshack.
Harmondsworth, Eng.: Penguin, 1956.
Duffy, Dennis. "Alice Munro's Narrative Historicism: 'Too Much Happi-
ness'." *The Genius of Alice Munro*. Ed. Robert Thacker. *American Review
of Canadian Studies* 45 (2015): 196-207.
Duncan, Isla. *Alice Munro's Narrative Art*. New York: Palgrave Macmillan,
2011.
Einstein, Albert. *Relativity: The Special and the General Theory*. Trans.
Robert W. Lawson. New York: Three Rivers, 1961.
"Elliptic function." *Wikipedia, The Free Encyclopedia*. 22 Jan. 2017.
<https://en/.wikipedia.org/wiki/Elliptic_function>.

Feinberg, Cara. "Bringing Life to Life." *The Atlantic* Dec. 2001. <https://www.theatlantic.com/magazine/archive/2001/12/bringing-life-to-life/303056/>.

Greene, Brian. *The Hidden Reality: Parallel Universes and the Deep Laws of the Cosmos.* New York: Alfred A. Knopf, 2011.

Kaku, Michio. "Nobel Prize Awarded to Two Quantum Physicists." <https://bigthink.com/dr-kakus-universe/nobel-prize-awarded-to-two-quantum-physicists>.

Kennedy, Don H. *Little Sparrow: A Portrait of Sophia Kovalevsky.* Athens, OH: Ohio UP, 1983.

Kovalevsky, Sophia. *Nihilist Girl.* 1892. Trans. Natasha Kolchevska with Mary Zarin. Introd. Natasha Kolchevska. New York: The Modern Language Association of America, 2001. Texts and Translations 8.

---. "Recollections of Childhood." *Sónya Kovalévsky: Her Recollections from Childhood.* By Sophia Kovalevsky. Trans. Isabel F. Hapgood. Biography by Anna Carlotta Leffler, Duchess of Cajanello. Trans. A.M. Clive Bayley. Biographical Note by Lily Wolffsohn. New York: Century, 1895. 1-151. <https://archive.org/stream/sonyakovalevsky00kovaiala/sonyakovalevsky00kovaiala_djvu.txt>.

Leffler, Anna Carlotta. "Sónya Kovalévsky: A Biography." Trans. A.M. Clive Bayley. *Sónya Kovalévsky: Her Recollections from Childhood.* By Sophia Kovalevsky. Trans. Isabel F. Hapgood. Biography by Anna Carlotta Leffler, Duchess of Cajanello. Trans. A.M. Clive Bayley. Biographical Note by Lily Wolffsohn. New York: Century, 1895. 153-297. <https://archive.org/stream/sonyakovalevsky00kovaiala/sonyakovalevsky00kovaiala_djvu.txt>.

Little, William, H.W. Fowler, and Jessie Coulson. *The Shorter Oxford English Dictionary on Historical Principles.* Rev. and ed. C.T. Onions. 3rd ed. 1944. With Etymologies rev. G.W.S. Friedrichsen. Vol. 1. Oxford, Eng.: Clarendon, 1973. 2 vols.

Munro, Alice. Acknowledgments. *Too Much Happiness.* Toronto: McClelland & Stewart, 2009. [305].

---. "Amundsen." *Dear Life.* Toronto: McClelland & Stewart, 2012. 31-66.

---. "A Conversation with Alice Munro." Reading Group Center, Knopf Doubleday Publishing Group. 8 Jan. 2010. <knopfdoubleday.com/2010/01/08/alice-munro-interview/>.

---. "Dimensions." *Too Much Happiness*. Toronto: McClelland & Stewart, 2009. 1-31.

---. "Finale." *Dear Life*. Toronto: McClelland & Stewart, 2012. 255-319.

---. *Lives of Girls and Women*. Toronto: McGraw-Hill Ryerson, 1971.

---. "Meneseteung." *Friend of My Youth*. Toronto: McClelland & Stewart, 1990. 50-73.

---. "Too Much Happiness." *Too Much Happiness*. Toronto: McClelland & Stewart, 2009. 246-303.

---. "A Wilderness Station." *Open Secrets*. Toronto: McClelland & Stewart, 1994. 190-225.

---. "The Wilds of Morris Township." *The View from Castle Rock*. Toronto: McClelland & Stewart, 2006. 111-26.

Painter, Rebecca M. "Too Much Happiness, Too Much Suffering ... Never Enough Reality Through Narrative." *Destiny, the Inward Quest, Temporality and Life*. Ed. Anna-Teresa Tymieniecka. *Analecta Husserliana: The Yearbook of Phenomenological Research*. Vol. 109. New York: Springer, 2011. 283-97. <https://link.springer.com/chapter/10.1007/978-94-007-0773-3_21>.

Saberhagen, Joan Spicci. "Sofya Kovalevskaya's Mathematical Work." [1998.] <www.joanspicci.com/kovalevskaia/svk_mathwork.htm>.

Shelley, Percy Bysshe. "A Defence of Poetry." *Shelley's Poetry and Prose: Authoritative Text; Criticism*. 2nd ed. Ed. Donald H. Reiman and Neil Fraistat. New York: W.W. Norton, 2002. 509-35. A Norton Critical Edition.

Simpson, Mona. "A Quiet Genius." *The Atlantic* Dec. 2001. <https://www.the-atlantic.com/magazine/archive/2001/12/a-quiet-genius/302366/>.

Spicci, Joan. *Beyond the Limit: The Dream of Sofya Kovalevskaya*. New York: Forge, 2002.

Tausky, Thomas E. "Biocritical Essay." *The Alice Munro Papers First Accession: An Inventory of the Archive at The University of Calgary Libraries*. Comp. Jean M. Moore and Jean F. Tener. Ed. Apollonia Steele and Jean F. Tener. Biocritical Essay by Thomas E. Tausky. Calgary: U of Calgary P, 1986. ix-xxiv. Rpt. as "Alice Munro: Biocritical Essay." <https://dspace.ucalgary.ca/bitstream/handle/1880/43983/Biocrit%20-;jsessionid=2E3E4EDC72904EB8CF4FA8281778E803?sequence=1>.

Thacker, Robert. *Alice Munro: Writing Her Lives: A Biography*. 2005. Updated ed. Toronto: Emblem-McClelland & Stewart, 2011.

---. "No Problem Here: A Review of *Too Much Happiness* (2009)." *Reading Alice Munro: 1973-2013.* Calgary: U of Calgary P, 2016. 227-30.

Ventura, Héliane. "The Setting Up of Unsettlement in Alice Munro's 'Tell Me Yes or No'." *Postmodern Fiction in Canada.* Ed. Theo D'haen and Hans Bertens. Amsterdam: Rodopi, 1992. 105-23. Postmodern Studies 6.

Walker, Andrea. "Things You May Not Know about Alice Munro." *The New Yorker* 4 Oct. 2008. <https://www.newyorker.com/culture/new-yorker-festival/things-you-may-not-know-about-alice-munro>.

Wolffsohn, Lily. "Biographical Note." *Sónya Kovalévsky: Her Recollections from Childhood.* By Sophia Kovalevsky. Trans. Isabel F. Hapgood. Biography by Anna Carlotta Leffler, Duchess of Cajanello. Trans. A.M. Clive Bayley. Biographical Note by Lily Wolffsohn. New York: Century, 1895. 304-14. <https://archive.org/stream/sonyakovalevsky00kovaiala/sonyakovalevsky00kovaiala_djvu.txt>.

Zsizsmann, Éva. "Escaping Flimsy Formal Cages: Alice Munro's *Too Much Happiness* as Fictionalised Biography." *Brno Studies in English* 37.2 (2011): 201-10. <https://digilib.phil.muni.cz/bitstream/handle/11222.digilib/118150/1_BrnoStudiesEnglish_37-2011-2_17.pdf?sequence=1>.

"Stabbed to the Heart ... By the Beauty of Our Lives Streaming By": Munro's Finale

Robert Thacker

Each of us is moving, changing, with respect to others.
As we discover, we remember; remembering, we discover;
and most intensely do we experience this
when our separate journeys converge.
— Eudora Welty, *One Writer's Beginnings* (112)

In 1999 Alice Munro published an essay, "Golden Apples," in *The Georgia Review*'s tribute issue on the occasion of Eudora Welty's ninetieth birthday. She begins by invoking the image of her own copies of Welty's books on her shelf; leaving them there but thinking about what they contain, Munro then "sat down to discover what bits of the stories would surface in my mind from all those pages I had read and reread. And so many things came crowding in ... that I had to settle on one book, which happened to be the first book of hers that I ever read and the one that has turned out, finally, to be my favorite – *The Golden Apples*" (22). Munro then offers a succession of paraphrased incidents from Welty's book, one made up of interconnected stories and first published in 1949, but then says "I have to stop" (23) recalling what is there. Continuing, she writes: "I stop not just because there's so much coming back to me, but because I am overwhelmed with a terrible longing. Stabbed to the heart, as Miss Kate Rainey or perhaps Miss Perdita Mayo would say, by the changes, the losses in our lives. By the beauty of our lives streaming by, in Morgana and elsewhere" (23). Rainey and Mayo are characters in *The Golden Apples*; Morgana, Mississippi is the mythic town where it is set.

Munro discovered and first read *The Golden Apples* during the very late 1950s in Vancouver, a difficult time for her as a writer: her daughters were young (about six and two) so finding time to write was a problem; at the behest of Robert Weaver at the CBC – then her sole literary connection – she had been trying to write a novel but the results were always unsatisfactory; she did not much like Vancouver or the neighbourhood where she lived (see Thacker *Alice* 141-43). As she explains in the Welty essay, she discovered *The Golden Apples* in the West Vancouver library and remembered "the quote on the cover, though I don't remember who had provided it: 'She writes exquisitely, she creates a world'" (23).[1] Munro demurs over the first part of this assertion, "But 'creates a world' – that was more like it" (23). Welty's stories are not just mimetic, offering more than just accurate detail, she says; rather, in them there is something much more, for "she 'creates a world'." Recalling her discovery of the book within the memories of what she found there as a reader, Munro in her "Golden Apples" acknowledges knowing then that what she found Welty doing in *The Golden Apples* was exactly what she wanted to do in her own stories with her own material: "The story must be imagined so deeply and devoutly that everything in it seems to bloom of its own accord and to be connected, then, to our own lives which suddenly, as we read, take on a hard beauty, a familiar strangeness, the importance of a dream which can't be disputed or explained. Everything is telling you: Stop. Hold on. Here it is. Here too. Remember" (24).

Remember. When she found Welty's book and, reading it, discovered its stories to be talismanic, Munro had already been remembering as the basis of her own work. She had written and published stories in which she may be seen creating a world herself ("The Time of Death" [1956], "Thanks for the Ride" [1957]) yet, after her discovery of *The Golden Apples*, there seems to have been a shift toward more autobiographical remembrance as the basis of her stories. What is more, Munro found a ready outlet for these stories in *The Montrealer* where, between 1961 and 1965, she published five stories and a nonfiction essay – the stories all later included in *Dance of the Happy Shades* (1968), her first book.[2] By the time she was doing this, also, Munro had published "The Peace of Utrecht" (1960), an elegiac story based on the circumstances surrounding the death in February 1959 of her mother, Anne Chamney Laidlaw, after years of struggle with Parkinson's Disease (see Thacker *Alice* 150-54,

Thacker "This" 17). This story is one Munro has often mentioned in interviews, acknowledging that it "was the story where I first tackled personal
material. It was the first story I absolutely had to write" (Struthers interview 21). As well, it was "the first time I wrote a story that tore me up"
(Metcalf interview 58). But more than a single story, "Peace" proved to be
the first of a succession in Munro's stories where Anne Chamney Laidlaw
figures centrally: "The Ottawa Valley" (1974), "Chaddeleys and Flemings:
1. Connection" (1978), "Friend of My Youth" (1990), "Soon" (2004), and
most of the "Finale" to *Dear Life* (2012). "Everything is telling you: Stop.
Hold on. Here it is. Here too. Remember" (24). Just as Munro wrote in
the late 1990s about Welty, just as she wrote then too about her own
ongoing practice and accomplishment. Remember.

All of this is context here: this essay examines Munro's "Finale" in
Dear Life, and in particular the final story, "Dear Life," through two
prisms: through Munro's own trajectory as a writer and, concomitantly,
through some of Welty's account of her own trajectory as a writer in
One Writer's Beginnings (1984). Munro's later collections, most especially
The View from Castle Rock (2006), reveal her recalling and revisiting earlier stories, refashioning them to serve the imaginative and aesthetic
needs of that later time in her life and career, complementing them with
new stories, newly written and often newly researched. Thus Munro's
"Finale" is the culmination of a finale she had been heading toward for
some time. That this was so is wholly consistent with Munro's practice.
As I have long argued on the basis of the archival evidence, Munro may
always be seen working on the endings of stories to get them just right –
perpetually. Sometimes in concert with an editor, sometimes in defiance
of that editor asking for final approval of a perfectly fine existing ending,
sometimes alone: the endings of Munro's stories always matter most to
her, they get her most frequent attention, the most frequent changes.
The idea of the last four stories in *Dear Life* as a named "Finale" was
Munro's alone, as it should have been, for it is both a finale to what will
likely be her last book and a finale to her entire career. And following
Welty, that career has been all about remembering.[3]

One Writer's Beginnings is made up of revised versions of three lectures
Welty presented in April 1983 to inaugurate The William E. Massey Sr.
Lectures in the History of American Civilization at Harvard University.

Accordingly, Welty divides the book into three sections, "I. Listening," "II. Learning To See," and "III. Finding a Voice." She dedicates the book *"To the memory of my parents,"* "Christian Webb Welty (1879-1931)" and "Chestina Andrews Welty (1883-1966)" ([v]), two northerners – the one from Ohio, the other West Virginia, "Yankees" – who moved south to make a home and life together in Jackson, Mississippi. They had three children, Eudora and her younger brothers Edward and Walter. The father died young while the mother lived on into her eighties.

"Learning To See" recounts the vacation the family took in 1917 or '18 – when Eudora was eight or nine – "in our five-passenger Oakland touring car on our summer trip to Ohio and West Virginia to visit the two families ..." (47). "[M]y mother was the navigator. She sat at the alert all the way at Daddy's side as he drove, correlating the AAA Blue Book and the speedometer, often with the baby on her lap" (47). Remembering, recreating the trip in vivid detail, most especially with regard to each of her parents' personalities, Welty continues:

> I rode as a hypnotic, with my set gaze on the landscape that vibrated past at twenty-five miles an hour. We were all wrapped by the long ride into some cocoon of our own.
>
> The journey took about a week each way, and each day had my parents both in its grip. Riding behind my father I could see that the road had him by the shoulders, by the hair under his driving cap. It took my mother to make him stop. I inherited his nervous energy in the way I can't stop writing on a story. It makes me understand how Ohio had him around the heart, as West Virginia had my mother. Writers and travelers are mesmerized alike by knowing of their destinations. (48)

This passage is reminiscent of Munro's "Miles City, Montana" (1985), a story first appearing just after *One Writer's Beginnings*, though unlikely one connected in any way to the influence of Welty's book. Yet even so it makes clear that these two writers are engaged in similar projects and that they are both using similar methods.

As she is about to conclude "Finding a Voice," Welty offers two salient passages, the first of which I use as an epigraph here: "As we discover, we remember; remembering, we discover; and most intensely do we experience this when our separate journeys converge" (112). She then quotes a long passage from her novel, *The Optimist's Daughter* (1972) – as *One Writer's Beginnings* makes clear, she is herself through her father "the optimist's daughter" – which centres on a character's memory, a remembrance of realizing while looking out the window of a train while heading south to be married, that she is seeing for the first time the confluence of the Ohio and the Mississippi rivers at Cairo, Illinois a literal great confluence which becomes a metaphorical one. After ending the quotation, Welty steps back and elaborates her meaning:

> Of course the greatest confluence of all is that which makes up the human memory – the individual human memory. My own is the treasure most dearly regarded by me, in my life and in my work as a writer. Here time, also, is subject to confluence. The memory is a living thing – it too is in transit. But during its moment, all that is remembered joins, and lives – the old and the young, the past and the present, the living and the dead. (113-14)

Welty is here referring to her own work and accounting for herself but, even so, what she says points readily to Munro, and to her work from the late 1970s on.

After the full force of her return to Huron County to live in late 1975 had begun to display itself in her work, Munro was enormously productive during the late 1970s and early 80s: the confluence of the past with the present had taken hold of her imagination as she lived again in her home place, Huron County (see Thacker "This" 20-24). Examples of this abound: for instance, in 1981 Munro published a memoir, "Working for a Living" (1981); it began as a fiction, was rejected in that form by *The New Yorker*, was revised into a memoir, and was rejected by the magazine in that form. It first appeared in the inaugural issue of *Grand Street* (see Thacker *Alice* 367-70). About that time, too, as she was assessing the stories she had on hand in October 1980, looking to the next book, Munro commented on "Working" to her editor, Douglas Gibson: "There is also a long Memoir I wrote about my father, which I think is pretty good, but I think it should be kept out for a kind of family book I want to do someday – maybe about the Laidlaws in Huron County and in Ettrick & James Hogg whose mother was a Laidlaw."

In this letter, Munro then offers Gibson a comment that, seen now in the fullness of her accomplishment from *The Moons of Jupiter* through *Dear Life*, is certainly prescient, if not prophetic: "I know people going on about their families can be very tiresome but *maybe* I can do something unexpected with it" (Munro to Gibson). Munro here is of course envisioning the book which over twenty-five years later became *The View from Castle Rock* (2006), but she is also foreseeing much of her career to come. Writing this in 1980, having been back in Huron County then for five years, Munro had been, as she once commented, "sociologically" "picking up the details" of her own life (Thacker interview with Munro, 23 Apr. 2004) and of her own legacies, "the Laidlaws in Huron County" (Munro to Gibson).[4] And she did draw upon her own life and legacies as a central element in many of her most accomplished stories – autobiographical remembrance may be seen as key in "Chaddeleys and Flemings" (1978, 1979), "The Moons of Jupiter" (1978), "The Progress of Love" (1985), "Friend of My Youth" (1990), "Cortes Island" (1998), "Jakarta" (1998), "Family Furnishings" (2001), and even "Wenlock Edge" (2005). But beyond the identifiably autobiographical, Munro draws upon her rootedness in Huron County to create stories with hardly even a glimmer of the autobiographical. Such stories as "Meneseteung" (1988), "Carried Away" (1991), "The Albanian Virgin" (1994), and especially "The Love of a Good Woman" (1996). She carried this approach on throughout her later collections.

Munro's 1980 comment to Gibson, with its "*maybe* I can do something unexpected with it," is indicative of both intention and, looking back now after *The View from Castle Rock*, accomplishment. There, Munro created a synthesis: she wrote researched (but also imagined) historical narrative about her Laidlaw ancestors' emigration to Canada in the early nineteenth century and melded it, within the structure she defined, with autobiographically inflected fictions about her own life, most long published. In two cases, "Home" (1974) and "Working for a Living" she includes straight memoir in this mix.[5]

While a detailed analysis of *Castle Rock* is not possible here, I would nevertheless point to "The Ticket" to make a point relevant to the "Finale" in *Dear Life*. Munro wrote that story specifically for *Castle Rock*; focussed as it is on the time just before Alice Laidlaw married James Munro – late fall and early winter 1951 – she needed to fill the chronology between "Hired Girl" (1994), a reminiscent story in which the narrator is in high school, and "Home," a memoir in which Munro is in her early forties, divorced, and returned to Ontario. "The Ticket" focusses on her relations with her grandmother and her great aunt Charley, the grandmother's sister, as the two widows help bride-to-be Alice prepare for her wedding. These two women are also central in "The Peace of Utrecht" while the aunt and her husband figure in "Heirs of the Living Body" in *Lives of Girls and Women* (1971).

In the midst of shaping *Castle Rock*, a book which melds newly written and researched family narrative with what Munro in her foreword to the book calls "a special set of stories," which "were not memoirs but they were closer to my own life than the other stories I had written, even in the first person" ([x]). These were stories she had held back from her collections over the years. "In the stories I hadn't collected ... I was doing something closer to what a memoir does – exploring a life, my own life, but not in an austere or rigorously factual way. I put myself in the center and wrote about that self, as searchingly as I could. But the figures around this self took on their own life and color and did things they had not done in reality" ([x]).[6] "The Ticket," while not previously published, adheres to the method Munro describes here – she very clearly puts her late-1951, about-to-be-married self in the centre of the story and remembers her widowed grandmother and aunt, their expectations and fears for her, and her own feelings and desires then.

Thus Munro writes, remembering further:

And yet the town was enticing to me, it was dreamy in these autumn days. It was spellbound, with a melancholy light on the gray or yellow brick walls, and a peculiar stillness, now that the birds had flown south and the reaping machines in the country round about were silent. One day as I walked up the hill on Christena Street, towards my grandmother's house, I heard some lines in my head, the beginning of a story.

All over the town the leaves fell. Softly, silently the yellow leaves fell – it was autumn.

And I actually did write a story, then or sometime later, beginning with these sentences – I can't even remember what it was about. (261; emphasis in orig.)

Munro did. The story was called "The Yellow Afternoon." The beginning is not exactly what Munro remembers here, but it is quite close. She probably wrote it during the fall of 1951. It was never published, although it was broadcast on the CBC's *Anthology* program in 1955.[7]

This brief invocation of "The Yellow Afternoon" is indicative of just where Munro was going after *Runaway* (2004). That collection is made of stories which are primarily imaginative – stories of the sort Munro describes in her foreword to *Castle Rock* where "the chief thing I was doing was making a story" ([x]). "Soon," as I have already said, features the death of Anne Chamney Laidlaw, but its details are imagined and at some distance. With the assembling of *Castle Rock*, the "family book" she had been imagining since the late 1970s, Munro literally returned to her younger self, both as a person and as a writer, as she constructed the collection in its artful and assertive ways – with researched family history, imagined situations, and remembered presences from her own experience.

The glimpse of "The Yellow Afternoon," something of a random allusion known to only a few readers, is the key; it subtly asserts a shift in Munro's focus to a critical moment in her past – again, as a person and an artist. As she walked through the town toward her grandmother's house, Munro was drawn to (and then remembering in the early 2000s, drawn back to) the stories she would eventually write. This happened just as she was about to take what was arguably the critical act of her young life: marrying James Munro (see "The Ticket": "He deserved better than me, Michael did. He deserved a whole heart" [281]), leaving the town that she would write so much about, and above all leaving Anne Chamney Laidlaw, her mother, to the throes of Parkinson's and to the care of others. She had to become the artist she became.

"Wenlock Edge" was held out of *The View from Castle Rock* and was included in Munro's next collection, *Too Much Happiness* (2009). There, its ending was changed from that found in the *New Yorker* version (5 Dec. 2005) which reads "I kept on learning things. I learned that Uricon, the Roman camp, is now Wroxeter, a town on the Severn River" (91).[8] The reference here is to A.E. Housman's poem XXXI in *A Shropshire Lad* (1896) beginning "On Wenlock Edge the wood's in trouble" (42), a poem which figures centrally in Munro's story and from which she took her title. This crux is notable because it is indicative of Munro's later work:

by telescoping here back to Roman times, by invoking poetry she knows well (Munro once told me that that she could recite a considerable portion of *A Shropshire Lad* from memory), she lends her story an historic depth, a wisdom, which resonates.

Life is life, people are people, human issues are the same. Examples of this resonate: In "Hateship, Friendship, Courtship, Loveship, Marriage" (2001), Munro ends the story with a direct quotation from Horace's famed "seize the day" ode; in "Face" (2008), the story's revelatory moment depends on a dream-like reading of an elegiac poem by Walter de la Mare; "Deep-Holes" (2008) and "Axis" (2011) – Munro's sole uncollected later story – display what should be called a deep geological awareness (see Thacker "Introduction" 8-20, 217-18). And then there is the title story of *Too Much Happiness*: an extended historical fiction focussed on the life and death of a nineteenth-century Russian mathematician, Sophia Kovalevsky; like nothing else Munro had ever done, certainly, but also a story which occasions a long perspective.

Beyond these considerations there are in *Too Much Happiness* two more stories which reveal Munro looking back at her former selves and, implicitly, looking forward to the finale that she ultimately makes. The first of these is an anomalous story, "Wood," first published in *The New Yorker* in 1980 during the fecund period when she was writing to Gibson about her projected "family book." It was considered for but held out of each of the eight collections Munro assembled from *The Moons of Jupiter* (1982) on. And even when it was being considered for *Too Much Happiness*, it almost did not make the cut (Thacker interview with Close). The much-revised version in *Too Much Happiness* is more complex and improved over its first appearance, and its placement in the collection is aesthetically powerful in that "Wood" represents Munro's traditional home place – the protagonist is an upholsterer whose real passion is going to the bush and cutting hardwood – and it is followed by "Too Much Happiness," another world altogether. Moving from one to another, the reader experiences a pleasing jarring.

Equally subtly, Munro in *Too Much Happiness* also offers a story called "Fiction" (2007). There the protagonist, Joyce, rediscovers a former student, the daughter of a woman who years before had supplanted her with her longtime lover; Joyce sees her at a party and is told she writes and has just published a book. Discovering the woman's book in a store, she buys a copy and, looking at it, thinks, "*How Are We to Live* is the book's title. A collection of short stories, not a novel. This in itself is a disappointment. It seems to diminish the book's authority, making the author seem like somebody who is just hanging on to the gates of Literature, rather than safely settled inside" (49-50). Here Munro is harkening back to herself in the late 1950s, struggling to write a novel, managing only stories. By the time she wrote "Fiction" in the 2000s, such a comment is both self-revelatory and also a wry joke.

Beginning to read the book that night in bed with her husband, not yet having discovered that she herself appears as a central figure in a story *How Are We to Live* contains, Joyce looks at and evaluates the author photo and, while her husband talks of something else,

... Joyce shifts her knees so that she can position the book against them and read the few sentences of the cover biography.

Christie O'Dell grew up in Rough River, a small town on the coast of British Columbia. She is a graduate of the UBC Creative Writing Program. She lives in Vancouver, British Columbia, with her husband, Justin, and her cat, Tiberius. (50; emphasis in orig.)

As with the wry joke about the expectation that she produce a novel, an expectation which vexed her throughout her early career, Munro is looking back here to another story about writers and their ways: "Material." Narrated by a writer's former wife who discovers and reads a story by her former husband, Hugo, one also based on a real person they then knew, Munro has that narrator contemplate the author biography she finds in the book. There, however, and with considerable venom, the narrator dissects the biography, sneering at its pretensions: "But listen to the lies, the half-lies, the absurdities" (29). After over a page of such dissection, the narrator concludes: "Look at you, Hugo, your image is not only fake but out-of-date. You should have said you'd meditated for a year in the mountains of Uttar Pradesh; you should have said you'd taught Creative Drama to autistic children; you should have shaved your head, shaved your beard, put on a monk's cowl; you should have shut up, Hugo" (31). This narrator goes on to read the story she found, one based on a woman they both knew early in their marriage, when Hugo was a graduate student and the narrator was pregnant, and finds it to be quite good. But though she tries, she cannot bring herself to write and tell him so, for like her husband and so like men generally, Hugo is "not *at the mercy*" (44). "I do blame them. I envy and despise" such men, she says (44).[9]

Revisiting "Material" over thirty years later in "Fiction," Munro offers quite a different perspective. The narrator at the end of "Material" is roiled, but not so Joyce in "Fiction." She has taken her copy of *How Are We to Live* to a book signing at the store where she purchased it and, commenting to O'Dell on the story drawn from their shared experience and offering the author a present, she realizes that "There is not a scrap of recognition in the girl's face. She doesn't know Joyce from years ago in Rough River or two weeks ago at the party. You couldn't even be sure that she had recognized the title of her own story. You would think she had nothing to do with it. As if it was just something she wriggled out of and left on the grass. And as for whatever was true, that the story came from – why, she acted as if that was disposed of long ago" (60-61). As in "Material," Munro undercuts the writer here – in both stories she acknowledges her own implications in these equations – yet Joyce is not roiled, only affected by the sharp realization she has had; after a break in the text, though, this is how "Fiction" ends: "Walking up Lonsdale Avenue, walking uphill, she gradually regains her composure. This might even turn into a funny story that she would tell some day. She wouldn't be surprised" (61).[10] The matter-of-fact tone, the ending without emphatic insight, typifies late Munro: this incident has happened; it holds Joyce's attention briefly. Life goes on. These contexts, aesthetic and biographical, lead finally to Munro's "Finale" in *Dear Life*, her own finale.

Wendell Berry once wrote that "We think of a poem and in the same thought think of what it is about, if it is about anything. Literature involves more than literature, or we would not be grateful for it" (87). This seems particularly true for Munro, whose work has from at least the publication of *Dance of the Happy Shades* evoked gratitude along with deep admiration. More than this – even though there have been critics who have decried the "ordinariness" of Munro's characters and situations – much of this gratitude stems from the ubiquity of the human situations she probes: individual understanding, relationships, cultural history in the home place, families. And most especially to the perspective she brings to her task, to her art.

Thus turning finally to Munro's "Finale" in *Dear Life* as her finale, it seems fair first to ask following Berry just what the balance of *Dear Life* involves and just how, once that question has been asked and answered, it sets up the "Finale" within the collection. Given Munro's lengthy histories with the endings of her stories – other examples just invoked through my discussions of the endings of "Wenlock Edge" and "Fiction" – the construction of an avowed and self-conscious finale to end what she saw as her final collection was one gone about methodically as she moved through the collection toward the "Finale" and toward that finale's finale: "Dear Life," the story. It also, like "Wenlock Edge" and "Fiction," had a significantly changed ending between its first publication in *The New Yorker* and its final appearance in a book.

While not avowedly autobiographical in any clear way, the ten stories that precede the "Finale" in *Dear Life* are reminiscent of the whole of Munro's *oeuvre* (see Thacker "This" 30-35, 37n11). Echoes of previous stories and other connections abound. The party the narrator attends in Vancouver in "To Reach Japan" and the man she meets there and later reconnects with in Toronto owe to actual connections Munro had in Vancouver herself. "Leaving Maverley" (2011), "Haven" (2012), "Pride" (2011), and "Corrie" (2010) with their small-town Ontario settings, their placement in time and recognitions of its passage, and the sorts of characters they treat all echo past stories, but they do so in ways that any reader familiar with what has often been called "Alice Munro Country" recognizes. "Pride" seems to bear some direct connection to "Face" and, in a *New Yorker* interview published on-line just as *Dear Life* was being published, Munro commented that her "favorite scene" is that story's ending "where the little baby skunks walk across the grass" (Treisman interview). As he and a friend watch this, Munro's narrator ends the story by saying, again evenly but not emphatically or with any type of insight, "We were as glad as we could be" (153).

So these stories bear the weight of those that have preceded them, and readers feel that weight. It is less a matter of the detailing of specific actions as it is a matter of how characters understand their circumstances, how they understand what happens in their lives. In that same interview, Munro comments that of the stories in the collection she is "partial to 'Amundsen' – it gave me so much trouble" (Treisman interview) in its revision.[11] "The girl has her first experience with a helplessly selfish man – that's the type that interests her. A prize worth getting, always, though she ends up more realistic, stores him away in fantasy" (Treisman interview). That story ends with the briefest of reunions as, years later, the two principals spot each other crossing a crowded Toronto street, speak without stopping, and move on. Seeing this "helplessly selfish man" again, the man who sent her away years before, the narrator reacts to the way, here again, "one of his eyes opened wider": "And it always looked so strange, alert and wondering, as if some whole impossibility had occurred to him, one that almost made him laugh. // For me, it was the same as when I left Amundsen, the train dragging me still dazed and full of disbelief. // Nothing changes really about love" (66).

Other comments might be made over these stories, but two in particular need to be set apart for my purposes here: "Train" (2012) and "Dolly" (2012), the first for its relevance to Munro's methods, her remembrance, and her history; the second for its contextual effect in the structure of *Dear Life*. Among the novels Munro worked on from the later 1950s into the 1960s was one called "The Boy Murderer." It features a character named Franklin coming home from the Second World War who jumps off the train before it gets to his hometown, Goldenrod. The *Alice Munro Fonds* at the University of Calgary reveal that Franklin and his circumstances became something of a continuing presence as Munro grew as a writer. No such novel ever emerged, but there is evidence that Franklin was a presence in some of the 1960s stories which appeared in *Dance*, in *Lives of Girls and Women*, in *Who Do You Think You Are?* (1978) (37.10.42, 37.14.23.5, 37.14.24.1, 37.16.28, 37.13.29). There is also a scene involving this Franklin which anticipates the opening of "Miles City, Montana" (1985), and he figures as well in draft versions of "The Progress of Love" (1985) (see Thacker *Reading* 154-59).

Suffice to say, when Munro came to write "Train," she had been thinking about Franklin jumping off that train during the mid-1940s for some considerable time. When that story was included in *The Best American Short Stories 2013* Munro commented that it "examines a man's desire to avoid his past mistakes by essentially becoming someone new, someone in whom others can place trust and belief and even memories of loved ones now gone" ("Contributors' Notes"). In it Jackson – not Franklin – jumps off the train coming home from the war before he gets to his town and, ascertaining his new surroundings, wonders "What are you doing here? Where are you going? A sense of being watched by things you didn't know about. Of being a disturbance. Life around coming to some conclusions about you from vantage points you couldn't see" (177).

Just after this, as Jackson starts to comprehend his new circumstances and his new life, he hears an unidentifiable sound:

> The road rose up a hill … and from over that hill came a clip-clop, clip-clop. Along with the clip-clop some little tinkle or whistling.
>
> Now then. Over the hill came a box on wheels, being pulled by two quite small horses. Smaller than the one in the field but no end livelier. And in the box sat a half dozen or so little men. All dressed in black, with proper black hats on their heads.
>
> The sound was coming from them. It was singing. Discreet high-pitched little voices, as sweet as could be. They never looked at him as they went by.
>
> That chilled him. (180)

Munro offers this image within Jackson's life as another talismanic epiphany – and here Welty's example in *The Golden Apples* is likely relevant – akin to the baby skunks at the end of "Pride."

Here Jackson begins the new life Munro describes and, years later, begins another; when the person from his past whom he had jumped off the train in the first instance to avoid appears and impinges, he sets off to begin yet again, taking yet a different train north to Kapuskasing. On that train, "He slept off and on during the night and in one of those snatches he saw the little Mennonite boys go by in their cart. He heard their small voices singing" (216).

When "Dolly" first appeared in *Tin House* in 2012 it had a very different ending than it has in the book version – the narrator describes herself as "a perfectly ordinary and savage woman," a phrase Munro subsequently dropped, and the final paragraph reads: "That made me think about the conversation we'd had earlier in the fall and our notion of being beyond all savagery and elation" (80). That ending is more abrupt than that found in *Dear Life*, itself more equivocal and in keeping with other and more balanced endings in late Munro. In the *Tin House* version too, the protagonist's name is Jackson, though the two Jacksons do not seem to be the same man. This duplication pointed out, Munro changed the name of the man in "Dolly" to Franklin.

"Dolly" owes to Munro's life with Gerald Fremlin in Clinton between 1975 and 2013, when he died. "That fall there had been some discussion of death" (233), the book version begins. "Our deaths. Franklin being eighty-three years old and myself seventy-one at the time, we had naturally made plans for our funerals (none) and for the burials (immediate) in a plot already purchased. We had decided against cremation, which was popular with our friends. It was just the actual dying that had been left out or up to chance" (233). While biographical specifics are a bit off here, the general outline is one consistent with Fremlin and Munro's circumstances as the 2010s began; Fremlin was older, had served overseas during the war, and once he returned and went to university he published some poetry – all details consistent with the narrator and Franklin. Also, they had been living together for some time and, given age and infirmity, were certainly aware of their mortality. They also had purchased a cemetery plot.[12]

Yet what "Dolly" is about is life having been lived, life still being lived. The "discussion of death," Munro makes clear, seems to foreshorten the realities of ongoing life – what in the *Tin House* version she calls "our notion of being beyond all savagery and elation" (80). Whatever the personal experiences which led to the story's imagined situations, Munro in publishing "Dolly" at age eighty-one offers an assertion that life, with its variety and vicissitude, is the same, it continues on, until it does not. Munro thus ends the story placed just before the "Finale" of *Dear Life* with a sharp, even caustic, image of herself as she was entering her ninth decade.

***

With that "Finale," Munro sharply juxtaposes her 2010-12 present with four relatively brief stories – "*not quite stories*" (255; emphasis in orig.) she calls them in the headnote to the section – which revisit her most cherished material: she returns to herself as young girl living in the house in Lower Town Wingham, living within her family. These four pieces are, she believes, *"the first and last – and the closest – things I have to say about my own life"* (255; emphasis in orig.). With them, Munro leaves herself as she was as she wrote and returns through memory to the place she started out from, to the place and time that has been so central to her art (echoes of other stories abound, especially in "Dear Life").[13] Munro focusses on four episodes – except for "Dear Life," these stories are noticeably shorter than most of hers; they reveal the individual situations of each of her parents during her childhood, most especially her mother before the onset of Parkinson's Disease about 1942, although its ultimate arrival and her struggle with it are acknowledged presences throughout. Throughout them too, Munro abandons any real pretense of fiction; she has said that they happened as she wrote them, although in her headnote to the section she keeps the fictional door ajar: the four "form a separate unit, one that is autobiographical in feeling, though not, sometimes, entirely so in fact" (255; Thacker interview with Munro, 6 Sept. 2013).

Opening "The Eye," Munro takes the reader back to when she was five years old, when her time as celebrated only child came to an end with the arrivals, in a brief span, of her brother and then, about a year later, her sister. "Up until the time of the first baby I had not been aware of ever feeling different from the way my mother said I felt. And up until that time the whole house was full of my mother, of her footsteps her voice her powdery yet ominous smell that inhabited all the rooms even when she wasn't in them" (257). Having offered this image, Munro steps back and asks, "Why do I say ominous? I didn't feel frightened. It wasn't that my mother actually told me what I was to feel about things" (257-58). Munro meditates on this time and on her sense of her mother's directives. As she recalls her own uncertainties then, her wonderings are genuine. Still, she concludes that "It was with my brother's coming, though, and the endless carryings-on about how he was some sort of present for me, that I began to accept how largely my mother's notions about me might differ from my own" (258).

With this "Finale," the gathering of four stories she designed as the ending to what she expected to be her last book, Munro returns again and finally to the ending of "The Ottawa Valley" (1974). There she famously asserted that "The problem, the only problem, is my mother. And she is the one of course that I am trying to get; it is to reach her that this whole journey has been undertaken. With what purpose? To mark her off, to describe, to illumine, to celebrate, to *get rid* of, her; and it did not work, for she looms too close, just as she always did" (246). These words, this meditation, still apply as Munro composed her "Finale" to *Dear Life*: "Why do I say ominous?" Munro asks. She wonders yet and still wants to know, to understand, and is still "trying to get" as she heads toward the end of her own "dear life." That this is so is evident throughout the "Finale" and becomes especially so in the changed ending to "Dear Life," as will be shown presently. There, just before she ends "Dear Life," the "Finale," and (probably) her career as a writer, Munro recalls a moment occasioned by something she saw in the Wingham paper while she was living in Vancouver and comments matter-of-factly in the face of more wonderment, "But the person I would really have liked to talk to then was my mother, who was no longer available" (318).

Returning to "The Eye," its focus is on Sadie, a hired girl the Laidlaws employed to help when Munro's siblings were babies; Munro accounts for Sadie's presence in the house and her activities in the town – working at the radio station and going to dances at the Royal-T – before accounting for her death in an accident walking home alone from the Royal-T. While Munro knows that "My mother wanted something very badly" and suggests possibilities, she also asks if one of the possibilities was "me as I used to be, with my sausage curls that I didn't mind standing still for, and my expert Sunday School recitations" (263). With the babies, her mother has no time, but even so "something in me was turning traitorous, though she didn't know why, and I didn't know why either. I hadn't made any town friends at Sunday School. Instead, I worshipped Sadie. I heard my mother say that to my father. 'She worships Sadie'" (263).

Munro establishes all this and then, shifting the narrative in time, takes the reader to the viewing after Sadie's death – Munro and her mother went. Upon their arrival her mother speaks to the host, saying that "She hopes it was all right to bring me," "that I was especially fond of Sadie" (205). As they arrive too, Munro notices an older boy from school – she was then in the first grade – "making a disgusted face" (265).

She comments that "Then I became aware of my mother's especially gentle and sympathetic voice, more ladylike even than the voice of the spokeswoman she was talking to, and I thought maybe the face was meant for her. Sometimes people imitated her voice when she called for me at school" (265). As this suggests, Munro is probing the position of her mother within the society in which they lived – she does so again in "Voices" here – but while those wonderings complement the overall trajectory of the "Finale," the balance of "The Eye" combines remembrance of her mother's behaviour as she orchestrated Munro's first sight of a dead body. At the time, an old woman who turns out to be Sadie's mother "let out a howl. She did not look at any of us and the sound she made seemed like a sound you might make if some animal was biting or gnawing at you" (266).

After accounting for Sadie's death – she was hit by a car from behind while walking home alone, "'A girl without a boyfriend going to dances on foot'" (267), one woman judges – Munro returns to her own situation:

> Now after the old woman's outburst it seemed to me we might turn around and go home. I would never have to admit the truth, which was that I was in fact desperately scared of any dead body.
>
> Just as I thought this might be possible, I heard my mother and the woman she seemed now to be conniving with speak of what was worse than anything.
>
> Seeing Sadie.
>
> Yes, my mother was saying. Of course, we must see Sadie.
>
> Dead Sadie. (267-68)

Munro details their approach to the coffin, and as she does so her concern is more with her mother's behaviour than with her own apprehensions. "'Come now,' she said to me. Her gentleness sounded hateful to me, triumphant. // She bent to look into my face, and this, I was sure, was to prevent me from doing what had just occurred to me – keeping my eyes squeezed shut" (268). Munro is tracing her mother's efforts to behave appropriately herself and, the more significantly, to force her into the same conventional forms.

As she recalls the scene, Munro has them in a confrontation, one that is followed by the revelation of Sadie laid out:

Then I heard my mother sniffling and felt her pulling away. There was a click of her purse being opened. She had to get her hand in there, so her hold on me weakened and I was able to get myself free of her. She was weeping. It was attention to her tears and sniffles that had set me loose.

I looked straight into the coffin and saw Sadie.

... The trick was in seeing a bit of her quickly, then going back to the cushion, and the next time managing a little bit more that you were not afraid of. And then it was Sadie, all of her or at least all I could reasonably see on the side that was available.

Something moved. I saw it, her eyelid on my side moved. (268-69)

This movement of the eyelid was just enough "to be able to see out through the lashes. Just to distinguish maybe what was light outside and what was dark" (269). Following this, Munro addresses two changes that, recalled now, point to both maturation and change. Focussed on the putative movement of Sadie's eyelash, Munro writes: "I was not surprised then and not in the least scared" (269). Then after she and her mother go outside, they "got into the car and began to drive home. I had an idea that she would like me to say something, or maybe even tell her something, but I didn't do it" (269-70).

Munro's refusal here toward the end of the first of the "*not quite stories*" (255; emphasis in orig.) of her "Finale," appropriately enough, echoes and reverses another one which appeared toward the ending of "The Ottawa Valley." There her mother refused to answer her daughter's "recklessly, stubbornly" pursued question, "'Is your arm going to stop shaking?'" (244) – a question asked when Munro was eleven years old during their 1942 visit to her mother's relatives still living near Carleton Place, Ontario, where Anne Chamney Laidlaw had grown up.[14] Following this exchange, Munro relates:

I demanded of her now, that she turn and promise me what I needed.

But she did not do it. For the first time she held out altogether against me. She went on as if she had not heard, her familiar bulk ahead of me turning strange, indifferent. She withdrew, she darkened in front of me, though all she did in fact was keep on walking along the path that she and Aunt Dodie had made when they were girls running back and forth to see each other; it was still there. (244)

Thus in a very real sense Munro in "The Eye" is still probing, wondering over, the mutual refusals which characterized her relationship with her mother. She takes an actual incident – her visit with her mother to view Sadie laid out – and again probes her recollections of what she saw, her responses, her mother's intentions and behaviours, and most especially the changes in her understandings over some seventy-five years that have now passed. Long after Sadie's death, long after the onset of her mother's disease, long after she married and went away to leave her mother to the care of others. Speaking of the supposed movement of Sadie's eyelid that day, Munro writes as the final, matter-of-fact sentence ending "The Eye": "Until one day, one day when I may even have been in my teens, I knew with a dim sort of hole in my insides that now I didn't believe it anymore" (270).

In "Night," the next story in the "Finale," Munro moves on to her teen years, when she had to have her appendix removed and when, afterwards, she learned that the doctor had also removed "A growth, my mother said, the size of a turkey's egg. // But don't worry, she said, it's all over now" (272). Looking back and comparing that time (the 1940s) to this, Munro writes that "The thought of cancer never entered my head and she never mentioned it. I don't think there could be such a revelation today without some kind of question, some probing about whether it was or it wasn't" (273). Owing to her operation and the inactivity it enforced, Munro had trouble sleeping and was also plagued with terrible thoughts – of strangling her sister in the bunkbed below – so she takes to walking about outside during the night of the early late-spring and early-summer mornings. "One night – I can't say whether it could be the twentieth or the twelfth or only the eighth or the ninth that I had got up and walked – I got a sense, too late for me to change my pace, that there was somebody around the corner" (280). "Who was it? Nobody but my father. He too sitting on the stoop looking towards town and that improbable faint light" (281). Munro also comments, "Now that I come to think of it, why wasn't my father in his overalls? He was dressed as if he had to go into town for something, first thing in the morning" (281).

The two greet each other, he asks about and she explains her trouble sleeping and her bad dreams, and eventually she tells him that she is walking about because she fears she would hurt her little sister.

"'Strangle her,' I said then. I could not stop myself, after all. // Now I could not unsay it, I could not go back to the person I had been before" (283). Her father, for his part, is probably surprised by this, but

> Then he said not to worry. He said, "People have those kinds of thoughts sometimes."
> He said this quite seriously and without any sort of alarm or jumpy surprise. People have these kinds of thoughts or fears if you like, but there's no real worry about it, no more than a dream, you could say.
> ....
> He did not blame me, though, for thinking of it. Did not wonder at me, was what he said. (283)

As she has done throughout her "Finale," Munro considers what might have happened today:

> he might have made an appointment for me to see a psychiatrist. (I think that is what I might have done for a child, a generation and an income further on.)
> The fact is, what he did worked as well. It set me down, but without either mockery or alarm, in the world we were living in.
> People have thoughts they'd sooner not have. It happens in life.
> If you live long enough as a parent nowadays, you discover that you have made mistakes you didn't bother to know about along with the ones you do know about all too well. You are somewhat humbled at heart, sometimes disgusted with yourself. I don't think my father felt anything like this. I do know that if I had ever taxed him, with his use on me of the razor strap or his belt, he might have said something about liking or lumping it. Those strappings, then, would have stayed in his mind, if they stayed at all, as no more than the necessary and adequate curbing of a mouthy child's imagining that she could rule the roost. (283-84)

Just as at the end of "Dear Life" Munro gives her readers a summary assessment of her mother – two, in fact, given the two published endings involved – here she offers a final image of her father: "on that breaking morning he gave me just what I needed to hear and what I was even to forget about soon enough" (284). And given her contemplations of her own parenting, something she quite knows about herself, she does so with real appreciation. But because this is a finale, her finale, that is not quite enough for Robert E. Laidlaw. Wondering still why he was not dressed in his accustomed overalls that morning, she thinks "that he was maybe in his better work clothes because he had a morning appointment to go to the bank, to learn, not to his surprise, that there was no extension to his loan. He had worked as hard as he could but the market was not going to turn around and he had to find a new way of supporting us and paying off what we owed at the same time. Or he may have found out that there was a name for my mother's shakiness and that it was not going to stop. Or that he was in love with an impossible woman" (284-85).

Before briefly taking up "Voices" – another story of Munro's mother before Parkinson's, one that like "The Eye" connects to Munro's incipient maturation and, as well, her awareness of sexuality – and moving finally to "Dear Life," I want to return briefly to Welty's *One Writer's Beginnings*. Again in the third section, "Finding a Voice," Welty writes:

> It seems to me, writing of my parents now in my seventies, that I see continuities in their lives that weren't visible to me when they were living. Even at the times that have left me my most vivid memories of them, there were connections between them that escaped me. Could it be because I can better see their lives – or any lives I know – today because I'm a fiction writer? See them not as fiction, certainly – see them, perhaps, as even greater mysteries than I knew. Writing fiction has developed in me an abiding respect for the unknown in a human lifetime and a sense of where to look for the threads, how to follow, how to connect, find in the thick of the tangle what clear line persists. The strands are all there: to the memory nothing is ever really lost. (98)

As is evident, the understanding Welty offers here is just what Munro had done before in her stories and is doing again in her "Finale" but with sharp focus on herself – and she did so at much the same time in her life as Welty had.

In "Voices" Munro offers an account of a home dance which she and her mother – her father was not a dancer – attend very briefly; they leave almost at once because Mrs. Laidlaw discovers that a local madam and one of her girls is there. Munro is again remembering each of her parents, making connections, finding the continuities Welty notes. Thus toward the beginning of "Voices" Munro writes that "My father, who was much better liked than my mother, was a man who believed in taking whatever you were dealt. Not so my mother. She had risen from her farm girl's life to become a schoolteacher, but this was not enough, it had not given her the position she would have liked, or the friends she would have liked to have in town" (287). Her father "slipped into whatever exchange was going on – he understood that the thing to do was never to say anything special. My mother was just the opposite. With her everything was clear and ringing and served to call attention" (290). As she and her mother arrived at the home dance, Munro knew "that was happening and I heard her laugh, delightedly, as if to make up for nobody's talking to her. She was inquiring where we might put our coats" (290).

For Munro, the whole scene is a wonder – the people, their behaviours, the dancing. The madam – whose identity was then unknown to Munro – nevertheless makes a striking impression on her as she dances "wearing a dress of golden-orange taffeta, cut with a rather low square neck and a skirt that just covered her knees. Her short sleeves held her arms tightly and the flesh on them was heavy and smooth and white, like lard. // This was a startling sight. I would not have thought it possible that somebody could look both old and polished, both heavy and graceful, bold as brass and yet mightily dignified. You could have called her brazen, and perhaps my mother later did – that was her sort of word. Someone better disposed might have said, stately" (292). Remembering, Munro recreates her own mystification at the scene along with her long perspective – on both what occurred and how her mother reacted to it. Looking at her description of this notorious woman, Munro also offers a salient comment as something of an aside: "I think that if I was writing fiction instead of remembering something that happened, I would never have given her that dress. A kind of advertisement she didn't need" (292).

"Dear Life" – which was first submitted to *The New Yorker* as "Visit" before becoming "A Visitation" before acquiring its title and being first published there as "Personal History" in September 2011 – has a similar passage in its midst. Throughout this memoir Munro emphasizes the geography of her childhood – her walks back and forth along the Lower Town Road to and from school – and especially the situation of the Laidlaws' house: "It turned its back on the village; it faced west across slightly downsloping fields to the hidden curve where the river made what was called the Big Bend. Beyond the river was a patch of dark evergreen trees, probably cedar but too far away to tell. And even farther away, on another hillside, was another house, quite small at that distance, facing ours, that we would never visit or know and that was to me like a dwarf's house in a story. But we knew the name of the man who lived there, or had lived there at one time, for he might have died by now. Roly Grain, his name was, and he does not have any further part in what I'm writing now, in spite of his troll's name, because *this is not a story, only life*" (306-07; emphasis added).

Munro had mentioned Roly Grain previously in just this way in "Working for a Living" (*View* 147), but here she asserts the accuracy of the man's name, just as in "Voices" she does with the woman's dress. And the road Munro walks along is "The Flats Road" from *Lives of Girls and Women*; the people who live along it – some of whom, we see again here, are connected to prostitutes – we have seen before as living in Lower Hanratty in *Who Do You Think You Are? / The Beggar Maid* (1978, 1979). There are echoes too in "Dear Life" of other Munro stories, fictional but drawn from life: "The Peace of Utrecht," "Boys and Girls," "Red Dress – 1946," and, repeatedly as she writes of the interior of that house facing west with "its back on the village" to the room in which the "Royal Beatings" (1977) were administered. Beyond these, there are other echoes too, both in "Dear Life" and throughout the "Finale."

"[T]his is not a story, only life." "Dear Life" begins: "I lived when I was young at the end of a long road, or a road that seemed long to me. Back behind me, as I walked home from primary school, and then from high school, was the real town with its activity and its sidewalks and its streetlights for after dark" (299). Here again is the place Munro started out from where, as Willa Cather wrote to Alexander Woollcott in 1942 about her last novel, *Sapphira and the Slave Girl* (1940), "my end was my beginning." Thus in "Dear Life" we get the walk to and from school, we get the Lower Town school Munro attended for two unhappy years, and we get the oddball inhabitants along the Lower Town road – here is "Waitey Streets, a one-armed veteran of the First World War" (302-03) who "kept some sheep and had a wife I saw only once in all those years.... Waitey liked to joke about the long time I had been at school and how it was a pity that I could never pass my exams and be done with it" (303). Her parents, their personalities and ambitions, the fox farm, her mother's illness, Munro's increased duties running the household as her mother's health declined. All of this is here, but at the centre of "Dear Life" is the visit which gave the memoir its first title.

That visit, a story told to Alice by her mother, who called it a "visita-tion" (315), was paid by Mrs. Netterfield, one of the oddballs living on the road, known as "the crazy woman [who] had pursued the delivery boy with a hatchet" (312) because she said he forgot the butter she had ordered. Mr. Laidlaw was gone and Mrs. Laidlaw had left Alice outside in her baby carriage when she saw Mrs. Netterfield "walking down our lane" (313) and, reacting, she ran outside through "the kitchen door to grab me out of my baby carriage. She left the carriage and the covers where they were and ran back into the house, attempting to lock the kitchen door behind her. The front door she did not need to worry about – it was always locked" (313). Anne Chamney Laidlaw was grabbing her daughter Alice, she always said afterwards as she recounted its events, and as the expression goes, "for dear life" (318). She could only try to lock that door for, as we saw in "Night" and Munro tells us again here, the Laidlaws "locked" that door by leaning a chair under its doorknob from the inside. Her mother hiding by the dumbwaiter, hoping in the quiet that Mrs. Netterfield had gone home. "Not so" (314), Munro continues.

> She was walking around the house, taking her time, and stopping at every downstairs window. The storm windows, of course, were not on now, in summer. She could press her face against every pane of glass. The blinds were all up as high as they could go, because of the fine day. The woman was not very tall, but she did not have to stretch to see inside.
> ....
> I don't know when my mother first told me this story, but it seems to me that that was where the earlier versions stopped – with Mrs. Net-terfield pressing her face and hands against the glass while my mother hid. But in later versions there was an end to just looking. Impatience or anger took hold and then the rattling and the banging came. No mention

of yelling. The old woman may not have had the breath to do it. Or perhaps she forgot what it was she'd come for, once her strength ran out.
 Anyway, she gave up; that was all she did. After she had made her tour
of all the windows and doors, she went away. (314-15)

As ever, in what has been called "the miraculous art" of Alice Munro,
"Dear Life" and "Finale" come down to their ending. After she tells the
story, Munro writes that "I don't mean to imply that my mother spoke
of this often. It was not part of the repertoire that I got to know and, for
the most part, found interesting. Her struggle to get to high school" (315)
and to become a teacher, her experiences there. "The visitation of old
Mrs. Netterfield, as she called it, was not something I was ever required
to talk about. But I must have known about it for a long time" (315-16).
At one point Munro asked what happened to Mrs. Netterfield and her
mother replied that "'They took her away.... Oh, I think so. She wasn't
left to die alone'" (316).
 But Anne Chamney Laidlaw was, or at least that is how her oldest
daughter still feels, judging by "Dear Life," and by going briefly back
to "The Peace of Utrecht," Munro's first rendering of her mother's sick-
ness and death. As she talks about her mother's repertoire of stories,
Munro offers this paragraph that takes us back to the 1940s and her
high-school years:

I could always make out what she was saying, though often, after her
voice got thick, other people couldn't. I was her interpreter, and sometimes I was full of misery when I had to repeat elaborate phrases or what
she thought were jokes, and I could see that the nice people who stopped
to talk were dying to get away. (315)

"The Peace of Utrecht" offers a more elaborated fictional account of the
circumstances of Anne Chamney Laidlaw's illness and death, but the
narrator Helen and her sister Maddy are interpreters for their mother,
who "kept herself as much in the world as she could, not troubling about
her welcome; restlessly she wandered through the house and into the
streets of Jubilee" (*Dance* 199). Townspeople ask the visiting Helen "why
I did not come home for the funeral" (*Dance* 195) and, later, one of her
aunts – the same figures who feature in "The Ticket" – tells her that her

mother escaped from the hospital into the January snow. "'Oh, Helen, when they came after her she tried to run. She tried to *run*.' // The flight that concerns everybody" (*Dance* 208; see Thacker *Alice* 147-54).

When *The New Yorker* first considered "Dear Life," then entitled "Visit," the next episode in the published version – Mrs. Netterfield's daughter sending a letter including a poem from Oregon and having it published in her hometown paper (which we imagine to be, though it is unnamed, the Wingham *Advance-Times*) – was placed about midway in the narrative. The ending, with some small changes in diction, is as now published although Munro also writes just before what is now the last paragraph, "Old Mrs. Nethery who had it in her to become a witch" (Edited Munro Typescript, 4 Feb. 2011). Accepted, set in type, and edited by Deborah Treisman – now titled "Visitation" – the letter to the editor and poem have been moved to its published penultimate position in the text, the previous ending deleted, and this one offered instead: "When my mother herself was dying she got out of the hospital somehow, at night, and wandered around until someone who was not at all connected spotted her and took her in. If this were fiction it would be too much, but it is true" (Edited Proof, 19 July 2011: 16). Although Munro changed the ending between the typescript and the typeset version, Treisman suggests in her edited proof that Munro bring back the first ending and combine it with this new one – she attaches a typed sheet with both to the end of the proof. The next proof – now entitled "Dear Life" – indicates that Munro accepted the suggestion and it ran in *The New Yorker* with both endings (again, but for slight changes in diction) (Undated Proof, [26 Aug. 2011], author's possession). When "Dear Life" was published in *Dear Life* as the finale to its "Finale," the second ending – the paragraph about Anne Chamney Laidlaw's escape – had been dropped. As both Munro and Close have told me, they agreed that it was too late to introduce anything so harrowing (Thacker interview with Munro, 6 Sept. 2013 and Close e-mail to Thacker, 3 May 2016).

After Munro recounts her discussion of Mrs. Netterfield, she shifts to her memory of seeing a letter in the hometown paper from her daughter, Emma Netterfield Cooper, which included a poem about the Maitland River seen from the Laidlaw farm. Munro quotes three stanzas from the poem (and improves their punctuation), summarizes and comments upon what Cooper says about her relation to her hometown, and writes just before she moves to her ending: "This woman said that she was born in 1876. She had spent her youth, until she was married, in her father's house. It was where the town ended and the open land began, and it had a sunset view. // Our house" (318).[15] Breaking the narrative, Munro then asks: "Is it possible that my mother never knew this, never knew that our house was where the Netterfield family had lived and that the old woman was looking in the windows of what had been her own home? // It is possible." Munro then meditates – as she has continually throughout her own life, and with some specificity – on the possibilities of Mrs. Netterfield's situation:

> Had she been left a widow, short of money? Who knows? And who was it who came and took her away, as my mother said? Perhaps it was her daughter, the same woman who wrote poems and lived in Oregon. Perhaps that daughter, grown and distant, was the one she was looking for in the baby carriage. Just after my mother had grabbed me up, as she said, for dear life.
>
> The daughter lived not so far away from me for a while in my adult life. I could have written to her, maybe visited. If I had not been so busy with my own young family and my own invariably unsatisfactory writing. But the person I would really have liked to talk to then was my mother, who was no longer available. (318)[16]

Here we are back, and with an emphatic quality borne of the fact that Munro is about to reach the finale she has been planning for a very long time, to that most essential assertion at the end of "The Ottawa Valley": "The problem, the only problem, is my mother" (246). That story, its own finale to the collection in which it first appeared, picks up from "The Peace of Utrecht" and heads through the intervening stories to the finale Munro was about to accomplish in "Dear Life."

Just after she quotes and comments on Emma Netterfield Cooper's poem, Munro writes "In fact, I had once made up some poems myself, of a very similar nature, though they were lost now, and maybe had never been written down. Verses that commended Nature, then were a bit hard to wind up. I would have composed them right around the time that I was being so intolerant of my mother, and my father was whaling the unkindness out of me. Or beating the tar out of me, as people would cheerfully say back then" (317). "Stabbed to the heart ... by the changes, the losses in our lives. By the beauty of our lives streaming by, in Morgana and elsewhere" ("Golden Apples" 23). So Alice Munro, the long-contemplated finale achieved, the problem still her mother, her own dear life now a text. "If this were fiction, as I said, it would be too much, but it is true" ("Dear Life," *The New Yorker* 47). "But in this book my end was my beginning: the place I started out from" (Cather to Woollcott).

Notes

1. This quotation is by Lewis Gannett of the *New York Herald Tribune*. It is on the back cover of the Harvest Book edition of *The Golden Apples*.
2. The stories that were first published in *The Montrealer* were "Dance of the Happy Shades" (Feb. 1961), "An Ounce of Cure" (May 1961), "The Office" (Sept. 1962), "Boys and Girls" (Dec. 1964), and "Red Dress – 1946" (May 1965). The nonfiction essay is "Remember Roger Mortimer: Dickens' 'Child's History of England' Remembered" (Feb. 1962).
3. Regarding the archival evidence of Munro's perpetual work on the endings of her stories, I make the same point – using some of the same language – in *Alice Munro: Writing Her Lives* (563). Both Ann Close and Douglas Gibson, Munro's editors, have told me that the idea for the finale grouping was Munro's alone, although Gibson suggested the need for and placement of the headnote in his editorial suggestions dated 22 Mar. 2012.
4. Recalling herself writing about Huron County, Ontario from the West Coast between 1952 and 1973, Munro told me in 2004 that "When I was in British Columbia, writing about home, it was just an enchanted land of your childhood. It was very odd to say that Lower Town was the enchanted land, but it was. It was sort of out of time and place." In the same interview, she commented that when she returned to Huron Country in 1975 and wrote about it, she was seeing it more "sociologically" (Thacker interview with Munro, 23 Apr. 2004).
5. This combination of materials was wholly Munro's doing, her editors and agent have assured me (see Thacker *Alice* 535-44). To take but a single instance: because she was engaged in the shaping of *Castle Rock* at the same time I was finishing *Alice Munro: Writing Her Lives*,

and her book contained both autobiographical and biographical material, Munro generously allowed me to see her manuscript as it was in the summer of 2005. At that time, "Wenlock Edge" was included in the manuscript and "What Do You Want To Know For?" was not. Both Ann Close, Munro's editor at Knopf, and Virginia Barber, her longtime agent, argued against the inclusion of "Wenlock Edge" since some readers would see its central incident as autobiographical. They went back and forth with Munro but ultimately prevailed. See, for example, Munro's letter to Virginia Barber dated 2 Aug. 2005. Here Munro sends a revised "Wenlock Edge" and comments "though I still think it probably should not be included." She also includes a revised "What Do You Want To Know For?" and writes "*I* think it could replace 'Wenlock'."

6.   While Munro emphasizes the compulsion of narrative here – "These are *stories*," she asserts toward the end of the foreword ([x]) – both "Home" and "Working for a Living," and perhaps "What Do You Want To Know For?," are arguably memoirs.

7.   There is a notation on the manuscript in the archives indicating that Munro dated it as having been written during the summer of 1951.

8.   In the final version of "Wenlock Edge," the narrator slips her revealing letter into the mail slot and then looks about at the other students around her, seeing them in the final sentence as "On their way to deeds they didn't yet know they had in them" (92). That is, the reference to Housman at the end of the *New Yorker* version was dropped. Munro added this sentence – a typeset proof of the book version ends "… a game of bridge in the Common Room" – to the proof (Proof, 14 May 2009: 94). The typed setting copy of *Too Much Happiness* had these paragraphs after a space. Typed but scratched out, probably by Munro:

> That was all.
>
> # [Add space here]
>
> Uricon is now the village of Wroxeter, on the Severn River. Wroxeter is also a village in Ontario, on another river.
>
> Names are sturdy and persistent. Like our wickedness.
>
> To learn the ways of our own wickedness[.] (MsC 343 – Typed Setting Copy 1.3-1.4)

9. Probably more than any single early Munro story, "Material" has been the site of considerable disagreement as to the veracity and motivation of the narrator. See McGill.

10. The ending of "Fiction" when it was originally published in *Harper's* – the story's presence there a confirmation that *The New Yorker*, with which Munro has had a right-of-first-refusal contract since the late 1970s, passed on the story – had a different final paragraph: "This could turn into a fairly funny story someday. Joyce would not be surprised. That's what she often does with her life" (80). By the time that ending got to the typed setting copy of *Too Much Happiness*, that paragraph became three:

    > Walking up Lonsdale Avenue, walking uphill, she feels flattened, but gradually regains her composure. This might even turn into a funny story that she would tell some day. She wouldn't be surprised.
    >
    > She muses a bit on stories. How they spring up fresh and distracting, then toughen into familiarity, work their way into you so you're never likely to get rid of them.
    >
    > Writers are the lucky ones, tossing them out.

    Munro crossed these last two paragraphs out, and then wrote in holograph:

    > She muses a bit on stories. How they spring up fresh and distracting, then toughen into familiarity, into jokes.
    >
    > Such a lot left out. (MsC 343 – Typed Setting Copy 1.3-1.4)

    When the text is set, the ending is as published but Munro tries her hand with two more paragraphs after the published one, elaborating on "funny stories." It is crossed out (Proof, 14 May 2009: 63).

11. "Amundsen" took an inordinate amount of rewriting with her editors. Close has explained that this story was not included in the first draft of *Dear Life* which Close received from Munro (E-mail to Thacker).

12. Either because she did not wish Fremlin to see it, or because he objected to it after reading it, Munro kept her story "Axis" out of *Dear Life* (see Thacker "Introduction" 12-20, 217-18).

13. Given my own ways of seeing, knowing, and remembering, as well as Munro's own acknowledgement of Willa Cather's presence and influence, too, I want to mention her last novel, *Sapphira and the Slave Girl* (1940). It is from Cather that I got my phrasing here and, as well,

there seem to be parallels with Cather's epilogue to that novel – she announces that the scene of Nancy's return to Virginia is one she herself witnessed as a child (272-79). Thus she makes herself a character in the fiction she is just ending. And she appends a note on names to the epilogue's end that makes "Willa Cather" the last words in the novel (288). In 1942, writing to the critic and editor Alexander Woollcott, Cather comments that she is glad he likes the last chapter – the epilogue – saying "Many people didn't. But in this book my end was my beginning: the place I started out from." She then offers an account of the memory of "the thrill that went through me" whenever she recalled the scene of Nancy's return. While there is neither space nor time for such a comparison here, Cather's ending and Munro's "Finale" seem to emerge from the same methods and to do similar things.

14. In *Alice Munro: Writing Her Lives* I stated that this trip took place during the summer of 1943 (72). Since then, I have learned that the visit took place in 1942. There is a notice in the Almonte [Ontario] *Gazette* stating that "Mrs. Robert Laidlaw and her two daughters, of Wingham, visited old friends in this section recently. Mrs. Laidlaw is the former Annie Chamney and she taught school here some 16 years ago" (3 Sept. 1942: 8). I thank Reg Thompson for locating and providing this information to me.

15. The letter Munro refers to was dated 31 Jan. 1955, and it was also republished locally in a volume devoted to Huron County with the notation, "This poem is describing the Laidlaw farm." I have a copy of the letter from this source but no record of its publication. Munro renders the letter's information accurately, although Emma Netterfield Cooper says she was born in Wingham in 1875, not 1876. In the poem, Munro drops some commas and adds two dashes.

16. In the *New Yorker* version of "Dear Life," her phrasing here is "my own invariably torn-up writing" (47).

Works Cited

Berry, Wendell. "Sweetness Preserved." *Imagination in Place*. Berkeley, CA: Counterpoint, 2010. 87-101.

Cather, Willa. Letter to Alexander Woollcott. 5 Dec. 1942. Pierpont Morgan Library, New York, NY.

---. *Sapphira and the Slave Girl*. 1940. Historical Essay and Explanatory Notes by Ann Romines. Ed. Charles W. Mignow, Kari A. Ronning, and Frederick M. Link. Lincoln: U of Nebraska P, 2009. Willa Cather Scholarly Edition.

Close, Ann. E-mail to Robert Thacker. 3 May 2016.

Gibson, Douglas. "Alice Munro: *Dear Life*." E-mail to Ann Close. 22 Mar. 2012. *Alice Munro Fonds*. University of Calgary Archives, Calgary, AB. 2017.103.1.06.

Housman, A.E. *A Shropshire Lad*. 1896. Fwd. Tom Paulin. London: Hesperus, 2008.

Laidlaw, Alice. "The Time of Death." *The Canadian Forum* June 1956: 63-66.

McGill, Robert. "'Daringly Out in the Public Eye': Alice Munro and the Ethics of Writing Back." *University of Toronto Quarterly* 76 (2007): 874-89.

Metcalf, John. "A Conversation with Alice Munro." *Journal of Canadian Fiction* 1.4 (1972): 54-62.

Munro, Alice. *Alice Munro Fonds*. University of Calgary Archives, Calgary, AB.

---. "Axis." *The New Yorker* 31 Jan. 2011: 62-69.

---. "Contributors' Notes." *The Best American Short Stories 2013*. Ed. Elizabeth Strout with Heidi Pitlor. Introd. Elizabeth Strout. New York: Houghton Mifflin Harcourt, 2013. 333.

---. *Dance of the Happy Shades*. Fwd. Hugh Garner. Toronto: Ryerson, 1968.

---. *Dear Life*. Toronto: McClelland & Stewart, 2012.

---. "Dear Life: A Childhood Visitation." *The New Yorker* 19 Sept. 2011: 40-42, 44-47.

---. "Dolly." *Tin House* 13.4 [front cover] / 52 [contents page] (2012): 65-80.

---. "Fiction." *Harper's* Aug. 2007: 71-80.

---. "Golden Apples." *Eudora Welty at Ninety: A Tribute. The Georgia Review* 53 (1999): 22-24.

---. Letter to Douglas Gibson. 13 Oct. 1980. *Macmillan Company of Canada Fonds*. McMaster University Library, Hamilton, ON. 429.3.

---. Letter to Virginia Barber. 2 Aug. 2005. *Alice Munro Fonds*. University of Calgary Archives, Calgary, AB. 947/14.12.

---. "Material." *Something I've Been Meaning To Tell You*. Toronto: McGraw-Hill Ryerson, 1974. 24-44.

---. *New Yorker* Papers. 1 World Trade Center, New York, NY 10007.

---. "Night." *Granta* 120 (2012): 59-71.

---. "The Ottawa Valley." *Something I've Been Meaning To Tell You*. Toronto: McGraw-Hill Ryerson, 1974. 227-46.

---. "The Peace of Utrecht." *The Tamarack Review* 15 (1960): 5-21.

---. "Remember Roger Mortimer: Dickens' 'Child's History of England' Remembered." *The Montrealer* Feb. 1962: 34-37.

---. "Thanks for the Ride." *The Tamarack Review* 2 (1957): 25-37.

---. *Too Much Happiness*. Toronto: McClelland & Stewart, 2009.

---. *The View from Castle Rock*. Toronto: McClelland & Stewart, 2006.

---. "Wenlock Edge." *The New Yorker* 5 Dec. 2005: 80-91.

---. "Wood." *The New Yorker* 24 Nov. 1980: 46-54.

---. "The Yellow Afternoon." *Alice Munro Fonds*. University of Calgary Archives, Calgary, AB. 37.16.34.f1-11.

Struthers, J.R. (Tim). "The Real Material: An Interview with Alice Munro." *Probable Fictions: Alice Munro's Narrative Acts*. Ed. Louis K. MacKendrick. Downsview, ON: ECW, 1983. 5-36.

Thacker, Robert. *Alice Munro: Writing Her Lives: A Biography*. 2005. Updated ed. Toronto: Emblem-McClelland & Stewart, 2011.

---. Interview with Alice Munro. Comox, BC. 23 Apr. 2004.

---. Interview with Alice Munro. Bayfield, ON. 6 Sept. 2013.

---. Interview with Ann Close. New York, NY. 21 July 2010.

---. "Introduction: 'Durable and Freestanding': The Late Art of Munro." *Alice Munro:* Hateship, Friendship, Courtship, Loveship, Marriage; Runaway; Dear Life. Ed. Robert Thacker. London: Bloomsbury, 2016. 1-20, 217-18, 231-44 passim.

---. *Reading Alice Munro 1973-2013*. Calgary: U of Calgary P, 2016.

---. "'This Is Not a Story, Only Life': Wondering with Alice Munro." *Alice Munro's Miraculous Art: Critical Essays*. Ed. Janice Fiamengo and Gerald Lynch. Ottawa: U of Ottawa P, 2017. 15-40. Reappraisals: Canadian Writers 38.

Treisman, Deborah. "On 'Dear Life': An Interview with Alice Munro." 20 Nov. 2012. <https://www.newyorker.com/books/page-turner/on-dear-life-an-interview-with-alice-munro>.

Welty, Eudora. *The Golden Apples*. 1949. New York: Harvest-Harcourt, Brace & World, 1962.

---. *One Writer's Beginnings*. 1984. New York: Warner, 1985.

---. *The Optimist's Daughter*. 1972. New York: Vintage, 1978.

About the Writer

What could I say about ALICE MUNRO, the first Canadian writer, the first short story writer, and only the thirteenth woman to win the Nobel Prize in Literature? Perhaps that this very morning, the 455th anniversary of the birth of William Shakespeare, I awoke joyfully from a dream of meeting her for the first time in many years – Alice now in old age yet continuing to look so radiant. I had been wondering what I could possibly write about her and thinking that I would like to adapt a line deeply entrenched in my mind but remaining just out of reach: a line beginning with a question something like "What could I say about...?" From Shakespeare, perhaps? – I considered. Then, just as I arrived downstairs to prepare breakfast, I remembered the source. Alice Munro, of course. It's the thought that goes through the mind of the actress Rose in the last sentence of the final, title story of *Who Do You Think You Are?* – a book to which, long ago, I had devoted a chapter of my Ph.D. dissertation on the Canadian story cycle. Rose has seen a story in her hometown newspaper reporting the death in middle age of a childhood schoolmate, a mimic, and responds, "What could she say about herself and Ralph Gillespie, except that she felt his life, close, closer than the lives of men she'd loved, one slot over from her own?" I cannot think of a declaration more fitting to describe the feelings of so many remarkable readers about the ever-mesmerizing work of Alice Munro.

About the Artist

RON SHUEBROOK is a Canadian artist who is Professor Emeritus at OCAD University in Toronto where he served as President from 2000 to 2005 and as Vice-President, Academic from 1998 to 2002. He has taught and been an administrator at six other Canadian universities and art schools and is a former President of the Royal Canadian Academy of Arts and a former President of the Universities Art Association of Canada. He received an Honorary Doctorate from OCAD in 2005 as well as a Queen Elizabeth II Diamond Jubilee Medal in 2012. He is currently Senior Artist in Residence at Boarding House Arts in Guelph, Ontario. Shuebrook exhibits nationally and internationally and is represented by Olga Korper Gallery as well as other galleries. His work is in more than sixty public and corporate collections, including the National Gallery of Canada and the Art Gallery of Ontario, and in numerous private collections. An image of an untitled painting of his from 1989 (in the Art Gallery of Guelph collection) is reproduced in *Abstract Painting in Canada* by Roald Nasgaard. And a pair of drawings of his from 2013 were used as the cover art for Guernica Editions' companion volumes *Clark Blaise: Essays on His Works* and *Clark Blaise: The Interviews*. He lives in Guelph, Ontario and Blandford, Nova Scotia.

About the Editor

Highly respected nationally and internationally by scholars and creative writers for his work as a bibliographer, an interviewer, a literary critic, an editor, and the publisher of Red Kite Press, J.R. (TIM) STRUTHERS has edited some thirty volumes of theory, criticism, autobiography, fiction, and poetry – including works in honour of, or by, such important writers as Clark Blaise, George Elliott, Jack Hodgins, Hugh Hood, John Metcalf, and Alice Munro. Among these titles are his earlier pair of Guernica Editions collections, *Clark Blaise: Essays on His Works* and *Clark Blaise: The Interviews*, published in 2016. For more than forty-five years Tim has been writing about Canadian literature, particularly the short story, including, in 1975, the first two scholarly articles published world-wide on Alice Munro. He has conducted some forty interviews with Canadian writers and has been described by W.J. Keith, FRSC, as "probably the best literary interviewer in Canada." An enthusiastic teacher, he has taught English full-time at the University of Guelph for thirty-five years. Tim lives in Guelph with his bride of now forty-five years, poet and short story writer and scholar Marianne Micros, inspired and delighted by the company of their two daughters, Eleni and Joy, and their four grandchildren, Matteo, Rowan, Asher, and Reed.

Contributor Biographies

Born in Montreal, NEIL K. BESNER grew up in Brazil, where he continues to travel and teach widely. He taught Canadian literature at the University of Winnipeg from 1987 to his retirement in 2017. He held various senior administrative posts there; in 2012 he became Provost and Vice-President, Academic. He writes mainly on Canadian literature, with a book on Mavis Gallant (1988), a monograph on Alice Munro (1990), and an edited collection on Carol Shields (1995; 2003), as well as co-edited books on the short story (1991) and on poetry (1997). His prize-winning translation into English of a Brazilian biography of the poet Elizabeth Bishop (2002) was the major source for the 2013 feature film *Reaching for the Moon*. In 2001-02 he was the Seagram's Chair at the McGill Institute for the Study of Canada, and from 2002 to 2004 he served as President of ACCUTE (the Association of Canadian College and University Teachers of English). Since 2004 he has been the general editor of the Laurier Poetry Series (LPS), a contemporary Canadian poetry series published by Wilfrid Laurier University Press, with some thirty volumes issued to date. He continues to teach and to speak about Canadian literature in a variety of countries.

WILLIAM BUTT has worked in seventeen different countries, and has published articles in Canada, the U.S.A., Europe, Africa, and Asia. He has written drama scripts produced for and broadcast on CBC television and other networks, and has had seven of his theatre scripts produced, all based on subjects from local histories. He was co-founder and for eight years artistic director of a music and video production studio in Quelimane, Mozambique, where he was based as communications consultant for the United Church of Canada. He has published criticism on individual Canadian writers including Margaret Avison, Clark Blaise, George Elliott, Robert Gourlay, Jack Hodgins, Eli Mandel, and Alice

Munro, as well as *Behind Our Doors: A Memoir of Esther Warmerdam as Told to William Butt* (2011), reminiscences of World War Two in Holland by a woman who was then a teenage girl. He has a Ph.D. in English from The University of Western Ontario, where he wrote his dissertation on the social conflicts that resulted in the Donnelly mass murders and on the ensuing cultural legacy in legend, literature, and other popular art forms. He is based now in Southwestern Ontario.

DENNIS DUFFY, now Professor Emeritus at the University of Toronto and formerly Principal of Innis College there, is the author of the monograph *Marshall McLuhan* (1969), the studies *Gardens, Covenants, Exiles: Loyalism in the Literature of Upper Canada/Ontario* (1982) and *Sounding the Iceberg: An Essay on Canadian Historical Novels* (1986), and three volumes focussing on nineteenth-century Southwestern Ontario writer Major John Richardson, including *A World Under Sentence: John Richardson and the Interior* (1996). He is the author, as well, of essays on numerous modern Canadian writers including Hugh Hood, Al Purdy, George Elliott, Timothy Findley, Robertson Davies, Rudy Wiebe (aka Ruby Weed, according to very young Jonathan Redekop, Dennis's beloved stepson), Michael Ondaatje, and, more recently, Alice Munro, along with articles on popular American writers such as L. Frank Baum and Annie Fellows Johnston and Edward Stratemeyer. He has also produced historical and cultural studies on topics ranging from the origins of Algonquin Park to the impact of the Vimy memorial to the preoccupations of William Lyon Mackenzie King. His reviews and commentaries have been appearing in various Toronto and national outlets over the last 50+ years. Dennis continues to live and write in Toronto.

JANICE FIAMENGO is a writer, recently-retired Professor of English, and advocate for men's issues and free speech. She taught literature at the University of Ottawa from 2003 to 2019 and is the author of a study of early Canadian female journalists, *The Woman's Page: Journalism and Rhetoric in Early Canada* (2008), and of numerous periodical essays. She edited the collection *Other Selves: Animals in the Canadian Literary Imagination* (2007), edited the collection *Home Ground and Foreign Territory: Essays on Early Canadian Literature* (2014), and, with Gerald Lynch, co-edited *Alice Munro's Miraculous Art: Critical Essays* (2017).

She has published on-line articles criticizing feminism and political correctness in magazines such as *PJ Media*, *FrontPage*, and *American Thinker* and is the creator of The Fiamengo File YouTube series. Her most recent book is *Sons of Feminism: Men Have Their Say* (2018). She lives in the Thousand Islands region of Ontario with her husband, poet and songwriter David Solway.

GWENDOLYN GUTH has published criticism on Marian Engel, D.C. Scott and A.J.M. Smith, E.J. Pratt, Archibald Lampman, James De Mille, Margaret Murray Robertson, and public poetics in Canada. She holds a Ph.D. from the University of Ottawa (Governor General's gold medal in 1999) as well as a B.Ed. She has published poetry in a number of chapbooks and in collections such as *The Ivory Thought: Essays on Al Purdy* (2008), *Rogue Stimulus: The Stephen Harper Holiday Anthology for a Prorogued Parliament* (2010), and *Motherhood in Precarious Times* (2018). She has taught since 2005 in the English Department at Cégep Heritage College in Gatineau, Québec, serving five years as Department Chair. She lives in Ottawa with her husband and three sons.

KAREN HOULE is a Professor of Philosophy at the University of Guelph. Houle is the author of more than forty refereed articles published in international scholarly journals and anthologies and of the book *Responsibility, Complexity, and Abortion: Toward a New Image of Ethical Thought* (2014). She is also the co-editor of two collections, *Hegel and Deleuze: Together Again for the First Time* (2013, with Jim Vernon) and a groundbreaking anthology on classical ethics and reanimating ethical thinking and teaching, *Minor Ethics: Deleuzian Variations* (forthcoming, with Casey Ford and Suzanne McCullagh). Houle has translated the writings of French percussionist and cultural theorist Lê Quan Ninh, *Improvising Freely: The ABCs of an Experience* (2014) and is the author of three books of poetry, *Ballast* (2000), *during* (2005), and, most recently, *The Grand River Watershed: A Folk Ecology* (2019), one of five finalists that year for the Governor General's Literary Award for Poetry.

MEGAN LaPIERRE was awarded both the first annual Kaya Firth Undergraduate Scholarship in English and the Essay Prize in Music while pursuing her B.A. (Hon.) at the University of Guelph, reflecting her passion for music, literature, and their convergence in musico-literary studies. Upon enrolling as a Cultural Studies Master's student at Queen's University, LaPierre found her multidisciplinary background lending itself fluidly to the program's interdisciplinarity. She is eager to continue these investigations, support for finishing her M.A. having been provided by the Social Sciences and Humanities Research Council of Canada, with a view to carrying out further study of the intertextuality of word-music relationships and the psychosocial influences that underpin them. LaPierre's current research investigates the efficacy, across academic disciplines and artistic practices, of different methods for rendering musical experience resonantly in text.

MONIKA LEE is a Canadian writer and literary scholar. She is a Professor in the English Department at Brescia University College at Western University in London, Ontario, where she has served as Chair of the School of Humanities. Her publications include two poetry books, *gravity loves the body* (2008) and *If water breathes* (2019), two poetry chapbooks, *slender threads* (2004) and *skin to skin* (2016, co-authored with Shelly Harder), and numerous poems in literary journals and anthologies, including *The Antigonish Review, Ariel, Ascent, Atlantis, Canadian Literature, Dalhousie Review, Event, The Fiddlehead, Harpweaver, The Nashwaak Review, A Room of One's Own, Quills, Qwerty, Scrivener Creative Review, vallum: contemporary poetry*, and *The Windsor Review*. Her play, *The Petting Zoo*, was performed in 2012 as part of the 10th-anniversary PlayWrights Cabaret at the McManus Theatre in London, Ontario. She also published the critical study *Rousseau's Impact on Shelley: Figuring the Written Self* (1999), in addition to many scholarly articles on the poetry and poetics of P.B. Shelley, nineteenth-century literature, and contemporary Canadian literature, including one on Munro's novella "The Love of a Good Woman" in *Alice Munro: A Souwesto Celebration* (2014), a special issue of *The Windsor Review*.

LOUIS K. MacKENDRICK, now Professor Emeritus at the University of Windsor, edited the very first volume of criticism about Munro, *Probable Fictions: Alice Munro's Narrative Acts* (1983); he has also written a monograph on Munro, *Some Other Reality: Alice Munro's* Something I've Been Meaning To Tell You (1993), in addition to a monograph on

poet Al Purdy, *Al Purdy and His Works* (1990). A critic or, rather, a writer
who not only has contributed to the understanding of many aspects of
Canadian (and American) literature but also has elevated readers' sense
of the possibilities of language and style in the art – criticism – that he
practises, Kim continues to live and laugh in Windsor, Ontario, where at
one point in time he earned the nickname "Hole-in-One MacKendrick."

W.R. MARTIN, before his death in 2015, one day short of his ninety-fifth
birthday, was Distinguished Professor Emeritus in the University of
Waterloo Department of English, where he also received the coveted
Distinguished Teacher Award. Born in South Africa, he received his doctorate from Natal University and taught at Stellenbosch University before
coming to Canada with his family in 1961. After a year at the Agricultural
College in Guelph, he came to the fledgling English Department at the
University of Waterloo where he taught until his retirement. He was also
very involved with starting the University of Waterloo Drama Department.

While writing *Alice Munro: Paradox and Parallel*, Walter and his wife
Patricia, on a drive through "Alice Munro Country," decided to drop in on
Munro's father, still living in Wingham. Robert Laidlaw was surprised but
also very welcoming when they explained their mission. It seems that
nobody had ever come to see him about his famous daughter. Walter
wrote to Alice Munro about the visit and she responded saying her father
had mentioned it and had been very pleased. When Walter's book on
Munro was published, he sent her a copy, not really expecting to hear
anything about it. Months later, Munro sent a postcard (of Clinton)
saying that although she felt uncomfortable being written about, she
thought he had done "a fine job."

W.R. Martin's *Alice Munro: Paradox and Parallel* was published in 1987
– the first full-length study of her stories by an individual hand – and was
followed by articles and notes on Munro mostly co-written with Warren
U. Ober. The two were co-authors of *Henry James's Apprenticeship: The
Tales: 1864-1882* (1994), co-editors of a facsimile reproduction of James's
1910 short story collection *The Finer Grain* (1986), and co-editors of
Trees: A Browser's Anthology (1998). They also collaborated on a total of
eighteen articles on Henry James.

LAWRENCE MATHEWS is Professor Emeritus at Memorial University of Newfoundland, where he taught in the English Department from 1984 to 2015. He founded Memorial's Creative Writing Program and served as its coordinator from 2006 to 2015. His academic publications include over twenty articles on a variety of Canadian authors, such as (among others) Margaret Avison, Mavis Gallant, Hugh Hood, Norman Levine, Alice Munro, David Adams Richards, Leon Rooke, Keath Fraser, and Douglas Glover. As a fiction writer, Larry has published over two dozen stories in various journals and anthologies. He has also edited *The Breakwater Book of Contemporary Newfoundland Short Fiction* (2015) and authored three books himself: *The Sandblasting Hall of Fame* (stories, 2003), *The Artificial Newfoundlander* (novel, 2010), and *An Exile's Perfect Letter* (novel, 2018). He lives in St. John's with his wife, the editor and novelist Claire Wilkshire.

CHARLES E. MAY is Professor Emeritus at California State University, Long Beach, where he taught the short story for forty years. He is the author/editor of nine books on the short story, including *Short Story Theories* (1976), *Edgar Allan Poe: A Study of the Short Fiction* (1991), *The New Short Story Theories* (1994), *The Short Story: The Reality of Artifice* (1995), *Critical Insights: Flannery O'Connor* (2012), *Critical Insights: Alice Munro* (2013), and *"I Am Your Brother": Short Story Studies* (2013). He has published over three hundred articles, essays, and reviews on the form and has presented academic papers on the short story in the United States, Canada, Norway, Ireland, France, Italy, Portugal, and Spain. He was a Senior Fulbright Scholar on the Short Story in 1996-97 at University College, Dublin and Trinity College, Dublin. For ten years, he has maintained a blog on Reading the Short Story at may-on-the-short-story.blogspot.com.

TIMOTHY McINTYRE holds a Ph.D. from Queen's University, where he wrote a dissertation entitled "Ethics and Love in the Aesthetics of Alice Munro." His critical writing includes essays published in *Stirrings Still: The International Journal of Existential Literature*, *J.M. Coetzee: Critical Perspectives*, and *Historical Perspectives on Canadian Publishing*. He has published three essays on Alice Munro: "'The Way the Stars Really Do Come Out at Night': The Trick of Representation in Alice Munro's 'The Moons of Jupiter'" in *Canadian Literature* (2009) and reproduced in *Alice*

Munro Everlasting (2020) edited by J.R. (Tim) Struthers; "Doing Her Duty and Writing Her Life: Alice Munro's Cultural and Historical Context" in *Critical Insights: Alice Munro* (2013) edited by Charles E. May; and "'This Is Not Enough': Gesturing Beyond the Aesthetics of Failure in Alice Munro's 'Material'" in *The Genius of Alice Munro* (2015), a special section of the *American Review of Canadian Studies* edited by Robert Thacker.

CATHERINE SHELDRICK ROSS, FRSC, is Professor Emerita at Western University in London, Ontario, where she taught in the Faculty of Information and Media Studies (FIMS) and also served in various administrative roles including Acting Dean of Graduate Studies and founding Dean of FIMS. Interested in texts, authorship, readers, and the reading experience, she has published numerous articles on Canadian literature, librarianship, and reading as well as interviews that she conducted with Canadian writers including Margaret Atwood, Clark Blaise, Dennis Lee, Jean Little, Alice Munro, and James Reaney. Her published books include four children's books – among them, *Triangles: Shapes in Math, Science and Nature*, short-listed for the 1994 Science Writers of Canada Award, and *Squares: Shapes in Math, Science and Nature*, winner of the 1996 Science Writers of Canada Award; two co-authored books on communication and interviewing written for practising librarians, each in its third edition; a biography, *Alice Munro: A Double Life* (1992); and three books on the experience of reading for pleasure: *The Pleasures of Reading: A Booklover's Alphabet* (2014), the co-authored *Reading Matters* (2006), and the co-authored *Reading Still Matters* (2018). In 2013, she was awarded the American Library Association's Margaret E. Monroe Award for "significant contributions to library adult services."

SANDRA SABATINI is the author of a scholarly book, *Making Babies: Infants in Canadian Fiction* (2003), two collections of short stories, *The One with the News* (2000) and *The Dolphins at Sainte-Marie* (2006), and one novel, *Dante's War* (2009). Her writing has twice been a finalist for the Journey Prize. She is the Manager of Research and Communications in the College of Arts at the University of Guelph and also serves as associated graduate faculty for Guelph's MFA in Creative Writing. She is working on a new novel about a middle-aged woman who is forced by circumstance to reconsider what it means to have a happy family.

J.R. (TIM) STRUTHERS has been publishing on Alice Munro and the short story for over forty-five years. His recent critical work on Munro includes several seminal essays – among them, a greatly expanded version published in *Short Story Criticism*, Vol. 208 (2015) of his pioneering 1975 essay "Alice Munro and the American South"; two essays on "Meneseteung," one published in *Critical Insights: Alice Munro* (2013) edited by Charles E. May and one published in *Alice Munro: A Souwesto Celebration* (2014), a special issue that Tim and John B. Lee edited for *The Windsor Review*; an essay on "To Reach Japan" in *Alice Munro* (2016) edited by Robert Thacker; and a new essay on Munro's novella "Powers" in *Alice Munro Everlasting* (2020).

Other recent critical writing includes an essay on Clark Blaise's story "A Fish Like A Buzzard" featured in 2011 as the lead article in the inaugural issue of the British journal *Short Fiction in Theory and Practice* and an essay on Clark Blaise's story "The Birth of the Blues" in *Clark Blaise: Essays on His Works* (2016). He has in addition carried out some forty interviews with Canadian writers, including two with Alice Munro. An initial interview, conducted in 1981, was published in *Probable Fictions: Alice Munro's Narrative Acts* (1983), the very first volume of criticism about Munro, edited by Louis K. MacKendrick; the second, conducted in 1988, appears for the first time in *Alice Munro Country* (2020).

His extensive research has resulted in foundational bibliographical works by him on Clark Blaise, Jack Hodgins, Hugh Hood, John Metcalf, Alice Munro, and Leon Rooke, including two recent studies surveying critical, cultural, and theoretical readings he considers important to understanding Munro's world and style: the creative/critical essay "Song for Alice Munro" published in *Alice Munro and the Souwesto Story* (2013 [2015]), a special issue that Tim edited for the American journal *Short Story*, and his 401-item "A Bibliographical Tour of Alice Munro Country" published in *Alice Munro Country* (2020).

He views the companion volumes *Alice Munro Country* and *Alice Munro Everlasting* not as an end but as a beginning.

ROBERT THACKER is Charles A. Dana Professor of Canadian Studies and English Emeritus at St. Lawrence University in Canton, New York. The author of over seventy academic articles on Alice Munro, Willa Cather, the North American West, and Canadian Literature in English, his books include *The Great Prairie Fact and Literary Imagination* (1989), *Alice Munro: Writing Her Lives: A Biography* (2005; updated ed., 2011), and *Reading Alice Munro, 1973-2013* (2016). His Munro biography was completed with Ms. Munro's cooperation and, at her request, he wrote the Munro biography now available on the Nobel Foundation website.

Beyond his own writing, Thacker has been widely active. He was the Editor of the *American Review of Canadian Studies* (1994-2002), edited two volumes of critical essays on Munro (*The Rest of the Story* [1999], *Alice Munro* [2016]), co-edited two volumes comparing the Canadian and the U.S. West (*One West, Two Myths* [2004, 2006]), and co-edited three volumes of *Cather Studies* (*Canadian and Old World Connections* [1999], *A Writer's Worlds* [2010], and *Willa Cather at the Modernist Crux* [2017]). He edited a volume of Cather's poems in the Alfred A. Knopf Everyman series (2013) and is historical editor of Cather's *Collected Poems*, forthcoming in the Willa Cather Scholarly Edition from the University of Nebraska Press.

Thacker is now one of three editors of the *Willa Cather Review*. He organized and co-directed three International Willa Cather Seminars (Quebec City and Grand Manan [1995], Paris and Abbey St-Michel de Frigolet [2007], and Arizona [2013]) and has been President (1997-98) and Executive Secretary (1999-2009) of the Western Literature Association. He now lives in Fort Collins, Colorado.

MICHAEL TRUSSLER has published literary criticism, poetry, short stories, and creative nonfiction. His literary criticism has examined the work of Alice Munro, Mavis Gallant, Barry Callaghan, Gloria Sawai, Raymond Carver, Richard Ford, George Saunders, Rick Moody, Salman Rushdie, John Edgar Wideman, and Deborah Eisenberg. He has also written on film and photography. His short story collection, *Encounters*, won the Book of the Year Award from the Saskatchewan Book Awards in 2006. His collection of poetry, *Accidental Animals*, was short-listed for the same awards in 2007. JackPine Press published *A Homemade Life*, an experimental chapbook blending photographs and text, in 2009. The Alfred Gustav Press published the poetry chapbook, *Light's Alibi*, in 2018. He teaches English at the University of Regina, where he was the Editor of *Wascana Review* from 2002 to 2008.

HÉLIANE VENTURA is a professor of contemporary and Canadian literatures at the University of Toulouse-Jean Jaurès. Her area of special-ization is the contemporary short story in the anglophone world with special emphasis on the rewriting of the canon, intermedial relation-ships, and the emergence of transatlantic literatures. She has written two monographs on Margaret Atwood (1998) and Alice Munro (2015) respectively, edited or co-edited five volumes of essays and over fifteen special issues of academic journals including three on Munro, and written more than ninety articles published in Canada, France, Great Britain, Italy, and The Netherlands principally on Alice Munro and women short story writers from Britain, Canada, and New Zealand as well as on Aboriginal writers.

TRACY WARE did his M.A. and Ph.D. at The University of Western Ontario. After teaching American Literature, Romanticism, and Post-colonial literature at Western, Dalhousie, and, for seven years, Bishop's, he taught Canadian literature at Queen's from 1994 to 2017 and is now Professor Emeritus there. He has published some thirty articles and chapters on Wordsworth, Byron, Percy Shelley, Poe, Lionel Trilling, V.S. Naipaul, Thomas Keneally, and various aspects of Canadian literature. He edited two Canadian Critical Editions for Tecumseh Press: Susan Frances Harrison's *Crowded Out! and Other Sketches* and *A Northern Romanticism: Poets of the Confederation.* He edited five texts for the Cana-dian Poetry Press: Bliss Carman's *Low Tide on Grand Pré*, Charles G.D. Roberts' *Songs of the Common Day* and *In Divers Tones, The Uncollected Stories of Duncan Campbell Scott*, and Levi Adams' *Jean Baptiste.* He has been on the Editorial Board of *Canadian Poetry: Studies, Documents, Reviews* since 1993, and Reviews Editor since 2010. From 2008 to 2013, he was (with Allan Hepburn) co-editor of the Hugh MacLennan Poetry Series of McGill-Queen's University Press. He has written the following articles on Munro: "Tricks with 'a Sad Ring': The Endings of 'The Ottawa Valley'" in *Studies in Canadian Literature* 31.2 (2006); "'And They May Get It Wrong, After All': Reading Alice Munro's 'Meneseteung'" in *National Plots: Historical Fiction and Changing Ideas of Canada* (2010) edited by Andrea Cabajsky and Brett Josef Grubisic; "Teaching and Conflict in Munro from 'The Day of the Butterfly' to 'Comfort'" in *Alice Munro* (2016) edited by Robert Thacker; "Momentous Shifts and Unimagined Changes in 'Jakarta'" in *Alice Munro's Miraculous Art: Critical Essays* (2017) edited by Janice Fiamengo and Gerald Lynch; and "A Comic Streak: The Two 'Fairly Happy' Heroines of Alice Munro's 'Wigtime'" in *Alice Munro Everlasting* (2020) edited by J.R. (Tim) Struthers.

Acknowledgements

Neil K. Besner's "Remembering 'Every Last Thing': Alice Munro's Epilogue to *Lives of Girls and Women*" is adapted from his *Introducing Alice Munro's* Lives of Girls and Women: *A Reader's Guide.*

Dennis Duffy's "Alice Munro's Narrative Historicism: 'Too Much Happiness'" was first published in *The Genius of Alice Munro*, a special section of the *American Review of Canadian Studies* edited by Robert Thacker.

Louis K. MacKendrick's "A Series of Metaphorical Epitaphs: Alice Munro's 'The Ottawa Valley'" is adapted from his *Some Other Reality: Alice Munro's* Something I've Been Meaning To Tell You.

W.R. Martin's "Alice Munro and James Joyce" was first published in *Journal of Canadian Fiction.*

Lawrence Mathews' "*Who Do You Think You Are?*: Alice Munro's Art of Disarrangement" was first published in *Probable Fictions: Alice Munro's Narrative Acts* edited by Louis K. MacKendrick.

Timothy McIntyre's "'The Way the Stars Really Do Come Out at Night': The Trick of Representation in Alice Munro's 'The Moons of Jupiter'" was first published in *Canadian Literature.*

Héliane Ventura's "The Skald and the Goddess: A Reading of Alice Munro's 'The Bear Came Over the Mountain'" was first published in *The Short Stories of Alice Munro*, a special issue of *Journal of the Short Story in English / Les cahiers de la nouvelle* edited by Ventura.

J.R. (Tim) Struthers wishes to offer his heart-felt appreciation to Alec Follett, Eleni Kapetanios, Kelsey McCallum, Marianne Micros, Joy Struthers, and in particular Elizabeth Standing for their generous, perceptive, and good-humoured editorial assistance and support while he prepared the companion volumes *Alice Munro Country: Essays on Her Works I* and *Alice Munro Everlasting: Essays on Her Works II*. He would also like to thank the many other kind souls who offered him such vital encouragement and inspiration during the four years he spent on these two volumes, including the very special dedicatees of his essay on Munro's novella "Powers," William Butt and Marianne Micros and Catherine Sheldrick Ross and Ron Shuebrook, including good friend and researcher *extraordinaire* of local history Reg Thompson, along with all the other distinguished contributors to these two volumes, most notably the twenty individuals who enthusiastically agreed to produce such bold new work in honour of Alice Munro. Finally, at the University of Guelph, Tim wishes to thank the ever-helpful InterLibrary Loan staff and the ever-courteous Circulation staff at the McLaughlin Library, the benevolent and personable Manager of Information Technology Systems for the College of Arts, Chris Lee, and Tim's constantly encouraging Director in the School of English and Theatre Studies, Ann Wilson.

 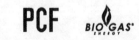